A POCKET LEXICON

TO THE

GREEK NEW TESTAMENT

BY

ALEXANDER SOUTER, M.A.

(MAGDALEN COLLEGE)

SOMETIME YATES PROFESSOR OF NEW TESTAMENT GREEK
AND EXEGESIS IN MANSFIELD COLLEGE

OXFORD
AT THE CLARENDON PRESS

OXFORD UNIVERSITY PRESS
AMEN HOUSE, E.C. 4
LONDON EDINBURGH GLASGOW
LEIPZIG NEW YORK TORONTO
MELBOURNE CAPETOWN BOMBAY
CALCUTTA MADRAS SHANGHAI
HUMPHREY MILFORD
PUBLISHER TO THE
UNIVERSITY

Impression of 1929
First edition, 1916

Printed in Great Britain

PREFACE

THE present work is the third and last volume of the tiny trilogy which I have been permitted to contribute for the use of students of the New Testament.[1]

In my Oxford days I was particularly struck by the fact that many theological works, which in their German form cost a small sum, were only to be obtained at a greatly increased price, when they appeared in an English dress. It seemed to me that there was at least as large a public for such productions in Britain and America as in Germany, and I could never see that the usual improvement in form justified the higher cost. The supineness of the clergy and others interested has been and is to me a subject of wonder, especially as few of them are men of means. I have long held the view that the most necessary knowledge in all departments should be available to the English reading public at a moderate price, and in this view I have been heartily encouraged by the Delegates of the Clarendon Press.

The last quarter of a century or so has, as is well known, seen a vast accession to the material of value for the textual interpretation of the Greek New Testament, particularly in Greek papyri discovered in Egypt. These documents are for the most part written in the non-literary Greek, the κοινή (διάλεκτος), 'the common dialect' or *lingua franca*, spoken and written through-

---

[1] The others are *Novum Testamentum Graece, Textui a Retractatoribus Anglis adhibito brevem Adnotationem Criticam subiecit A. S.* (Oxford, Clarendon Press, 1910, 1911, reprinted 1913); *The Text and Canon of the New Testament* (London, Duckworth & Co., 1913).

out almost the whole Graeco-Roman world. Of this Greek an excellent account will be found in A. Meillet's *Aperçu de la langue grecque* (Paris, 1913), a delightful volume which all interested in Greek ought to read. A number of years ago I formed the plan of a small pocket dictionary, in which as much of this new knowledge as possible should be incorporated in an unobtrusive way. This plan had been quite given up before the end of 1911, but in 1912 such pressure was applied by the Delegates of the Clarendon Press that I felt compelled to take it up again and do what I could with it.

The aim I have set before me is to give the forms of Greek words in the New Testament and their meanings as exactly as possible, according to the best knowledge available at the present time. I have studied brevity throughout, omitting matters connected with declension, conjugation, gender, &c., and even references to passages in the New Testament itself, except in cases where the reader might be left in doubt which of two or more senses to choose. I have thus been able to secure space for extended explanation, where the simplicity of the language is merely specious. I have endeavoured also to assign all borrowings of words or idioms from other languages (Latin, Aramaic, Hebrew) as accurately as possible. It may be assumed, where no such borrowing is indicated, that the evidence now favours the vernacular origin of word or idiom. Occasionally I have added the Latin word expressing the meaning of the Greek.

As readers, I hope to have all who are interested in

the Greek New Testament, from the working man, who with Moulton's smaller grammar [1] and the present work struggles to understand the meaning of the New Testament as exactly as possible, to the experienced scholar, who sometimes forgets the meaning of a word, and may be grateful for some of the information culled from the Latin Fathers and not readily accessible. Most readers, however, will belong to the class of theological students or ministers, who, whether at home or in the train, may be glad to have a handy volume to turn to in a difficulty. Unless I am mistaken, the newer knowledge sheds a flood of light on passages hitherto misunderstood or regarded as unprofitable (e. g. 1 Cor. x. 11, James i. 3, 1 Pet. ii. 2), and sweeps into the dustbin a deal of the well-meant but hair-splitting theology of the past (cf. εἰς), quite unsuited as it was to the comprehension of plain first-century Christians.

Naturally a work like the present is deeply indebted to many former publications. It is based not on any preceding dictionary of New Testament Greek—to them I am under almost no direct obligation at all— but on the Concordance of Moulton and Geden. The best available modern commentaries on the New Testament are my main source. I should like to express my deep indebtedness to the posthumous commentaries of Hort in particular, for the precise definitions of words, unsurpassed anywhere, which they contain. His method, working as he did with material less abundant and of far inferior usefulness,

[1] *Introduction to New Testament Greek* (London, Kelly, 3rd edition).

PREFACE

has led him again and again by a divination, which belongs only to the finest scholarship, to conclusions made certain by the newer knowledge. Next, I am under the profoundest obligation to the *Vocabulary* of Moulton and Milligan, which gives one in an extremely attractive form, gracefully concealing a severe philological discipline unequalled in the world, all the important lexical knowledge accruing from the recent finds. My book also bears traces of the closest study of the invaluable *Prolegomena* of Moulton. For the proper names I am indebted above all to the *Kurzes Bibelwörterbuch*, edited by H. Guthe (Tübingen and Leipzig, 1903). In addition to these works I have made use of many others, and I trust that their authors will regard this acknowledgement as sufficient.

Of personal, apart from literary, obligations, I ought to mention my indebtedness to the true friend of many years, Dr. Sanday, for constant counsel and interest; to Dr. Milligan, for so kindly lending me the first part of the *Vocabulary* in proof, while it was still unpublished; and, finally, to two former pupils, Mr. John Fraser, M.A., Lecturer in Latin and Lecturer in Comparative Philology in the University of Aberdeen, from whose scholarly revision the book has greatly benefited, and Rev. C. H. Dodd, M.A., now Lecturer, Mansfield College, Oxford, whose critical faculty I have often had occasion to appreciate. For the defects that remain—and even in a small work like this, where thousands of statements are made, they are inevitable—I am entirely responsible.

University of Aberdeen, 1915.

BRIEF BIBLIOGRAPHY

A. Deissmann, *The Philology of the Greek Bible, its Present and Future* (London, 1908).

A. LEXICAL.

J. H. Moulton and G. Milligan, *The Vocabulary of the Greek Testament*. Parts I and II (containing A–Δ) (London, 1914–15), the rest meantime in *The Expositor*, 1908 II, p. 567, and later vols. to 1912 II.

G. A. Deissmann, *Bible Studies, Contributions chiefly from Papyri and Inscriptions to the History of the Language, the Literature, and the Religion of Hellenistic Judaism and Primitive Christianity*. Translated by A. Grieve. 2nd ed. (Edinburgh, 1903).

—— *Light from the Ancient East, the New Testament illustrated by recently discovered Texts of the Graeco-Roman World*. Translated by L. R. M. Strachan. 2nd ed. (London, 1911).

H. Ebeling, *Griechisch-deutsches Wörterbuch zum Neuen Testamente mit Nachweis der Abweichungen des neutestamentlichen Sprachgebrauchs vom Attischen und mit Hinweis auf seine Übereinstimmung mit dem hellenistischen Griechisch* (Hannover u. Leipzig, 1913).

Pioneer work of great value in

E. L. Hicks, *On Some Political Terms employed in the New Testament* (Classical Review, vol. i [1887], pp. 4 ff., 42 ff.).

W. M. Ramsay, *The Greek of the Early Church and the Pagan Ritual* in the *Expository Times*, vol. x (1898–1899), pp. 9 ff., 54 ff., 107 ff., 157 ff., 208 ff.

B. GRAMMATICAL.

J. H. Moulton, *A Grammar of New Testament Greek*, vol. i, Prolegomena. 3rd ed. (Edinburgh, 1908). Better still, *Einleitung in die Sprache des Neuen Testaments* (Heidelberg, 1911).

BRIEF BIBLIOGRAPHY

A. T. Robertson, *A Grammar of the Greek New Testament in the Light of Historical Research* (New York, and London, 1914). The most comprehensive ever published.

L. Radermacher, *Neutestamentliche Grammatik: das Griechisch des Neuen Testaments im Zusammenhang mit der Volkssprache* (Tübingen, 1911). A delightful sketch.

Only less valuable is H. St. J. Thackeray, *A Grammar of the Old Testament in Greek according to the Septuagint*, vol. i, Introduction, Orthography, and Accidence (Cambridge, 1909).

C. COLLECTIONS OF DOCUMENTS.

H. Lietzmann, *Griechische Papyri ausgewählt und erklärt* (2. Aufl.) (Bonn, 1910). 8*d.*

G. Milligan, *Selections from the Greek Papyri*, edited with translations and notes (Cambridge, 1910). 5*s.*

L. Mitteis u. U. Wilcken, *Grundzüge und Chrestomathie der Papyruskunde* (2 vols., 4 parts) (Leipzig, 1912). £2.

D. TRANSLATIONS.

J. Moffatt, *The New Testament: a New Translation.* 3rd ed. (London, 1914).

A. Menzies, *The Epistle to the Galatians*, in the *Expositor* (December, 1913).

A. Souter, *The Pastoral Epistles*, in the *Expositor* (November, 1913; January, 1914).

E. COMMENTARIES.

Handbuch zum Neuen Testament . . . herausg. v. Hans Lietzmann (Tübingen, 1906 ff.). (Lk. and Rev. still unpublished: the Gospel parts of particular excellence.)

Allen's Commentary on Mt. (Edinburgh, 1907), Zahn's on Lk. (Leipzig, 1912–1913), J. Weiss's on 1 Cor. (Göttingen, 1910), J. Armitage Robinson's on Eph., 2nd ed. (London, 1904), G. Milligan's on 1 and 2 Thess. (London, 1908), E. Riggenbach's on Hebr. (Leipzig, 1913).

A

A, the first letter of the Greek alphabet, see ἄλφα.

Ἀαρών (Hebr.), *Aaron*, son of Amram and Jochebed, younger brother of Moses.

Ἀβαδδών (Hebr.), *Destroyer* (i. e. *Destroying Angel*) or '*place of destruction*' (personified).

ἀβαρής, *unburdensome, bringing no weight or oppression upon.*

ἀββά (ἀββᾶ) (Aramaic) (voc.), *Father!*

Ἀβειληνή (sc. χώρα), *the Abilenian territory, the territory of Abila* (in Syria), a small principality in the mountains WNW. of Damascus.

Ἄβελ (Hebr.), *Abel*, second son of Adam and Eve, brother of Cain.

Ἀβιά (Hebr.), *Abijah*, founder of the eighth class of priests (1 Chron. xxiv 10).

Ἀβιάθαρ (Hebr.), *Abiathar*, a priest in King David's time.

Ἀβιληνή, see Ἀβειληνή.

Ἀβιούδ (Hebr.), *Abiud*, son of Zorobabel and father of Eliakim.

Ἀβραάμ (Hebr.), *Abraham*, progenitor of the Hebrew race; hence the phrase θυγατέρα Ἀβραάμ (Lk. xiii 16) means simply *a woman of Hebrew race.*

ἄβυσσος (ἡ), *the abyss, the unfathomable depth*, an especially Jewish conception, the home of the dead and of evil spirits.

Ἄγαβος, *Agabus*, a Christian prophet (Ac. xi 28, xxi 10).

ἀγαθοεργέω (ἀγαθουργέω), *I work that which is good, I perform good deeds.*

ἀγαθοποιέω

ἀγαθοποιέω, *I do that which is good* (ἀγαθοποιῶν nom. sing. masc. pres. pcpl.) (opp. κακοποιέω).

ἀγαθοποιΐα, *the doing of that which is good.*

ἀγαθοποιός (adj. as noun), *a doer of that which is good* (ἀγαθοποιῶν gen. pl. masc., 1 Pet. ii 14) (opp. κακοποιός).

ἀγαθός, (intrinsically) *good, good* (in nature), *good* (whether it be seen to be so or not), the widest and most colourless of all words with this meaning (opp. πονηρός, κακός): τὰ ἀγαθά (bona), *the goods,* Lk. xii 18.

ἀγαθουργέω (contracted form of ἀγαθοεργέω, which see).

ἀγαθωσύνη, (intrinsic) *goodness* (especially as a personal quality), with stress on the kindly (rather than the righteous) side of goodness.

ἀγαλλίασις, *wild joy, ecstatic delight, exultation, exhilaration.*

ἀγαλλιάω, *I exult, I am full of joy.*

ἄγαμος, *unmarried, not married,* of a person not in a state of wedlock, whether he or she has formerly been married or not.

ἀγανακτέω, *I am angry, I am incensed.*

ἀγανάκτησις, *feeling of anger, vexation.*

ἀγαπάω, *I love* (never of love between the sexes, but nearly always of the love of (the) God or (the) Christ to us, and of our love to Him and to our fellow creatures, as inspired by His love for us).

ἀγάπη (a word exclusively Biblical, curtailed from ἀγάπησις [from ἀγαπάω]: in LXX generally of sexual love; first in higher sense not before about 100 B.C.), *love* [this was the sense of the word *charity* in the time of the A.V.], as that of (the) God or (the) Christ to us, and our love to Him and to our fellow creatures thus inspired: ἀγάπη τοῦ θεοῦ, τοῦ χριστοῦ are sometimes ambiguous, when it is doubtful whether (the) God's, (the) Christ's love for us, or our love for (the) God, (the) Christ, is intended; in most cases the former is probably the primary thought: ἀγάπαι plur. (Jude, verse 12) concr., of the *love-feasts* of

2

the Christians, evening meals partaken of by Christians in the early Church, either accompanied or followed by the Eucharist. Such common meals were sacred, and intended to be expressive of the union of Christians in their Head.

ἀγαπητός, *loved, beloved,* with two special applications, (a) ὁ ἀγαπητός, *the Beloved,* a title of the Messiah (Christ), as beloved beyond all others by the God who sent Him ; (b) of Christians, as beloved by God, Christ, and one another.

Ἄγαρ (Hebr.), *Hagar,* the servant of Sarah, wife of Abraham, and interpreted by Rabbinic lore, countenanced by Paul, as a type of Mt. Sinai, where the Mosaic Law was given (Gal. iv 24–5).

ἀγγαρεύω (from a Persian word, meaning *to impress for the postal service*), *I impress* (into my service), *I send* (on an errand).

ἀγγεῖον, *a vessel, flask, can.*

ἀγγελία, *a message.*

ἀγγέλλω, *I report, I announce* (as messenger).

ἄγγελος, *a messenger,* generally : *a* (supernatural) *messenger from God, an angel,* conveying news or behests from (the) God to men : almost *an intermediary,* Gal. iii 19.

ἄγγος, *a vessel.*

ἄγε (properly imperative of ἄγω), an interjection, *come now! ho now!*

ἀγέλη, *a herd.*

ἀγενεαλόγητος, *unprovided with a genealogy, whose descent cannot be traced.*

ἀγενής, literally, *without γένος (family)* ; hence *ignoble.*

ἁγιάζω (apparently exclusively Biblical), *I make ἅγιος, treat as ἅγιος* (set apart, holy), *sanctify, hallow* (see ἅγιος).

ἁγιασμός, *the process of making* or *becoming ἅγιος (set apart, holy).*

ἅγιος, *set apart* by (or for) the God, *holy, sacred,* e. g. ἁγία πόλις (of Jerusalem) Mt. iv 5 ; τὸ ἅγιον πνεῦμα,

ἁγιότης

practically synonymous with τὸ πνεῦμα τοῦ θεοῦ; ὁ ἅγιος τοῦ θεοῦ (Mk. i 24) of the Messiah; οἱ ἅγιοι, of the Christians as the new people of God, taking the place of the Hebrews: τὸ ἅγιον, τὰ ἅγια, *the temple*; τὰ ἅγια τῶν ἁγίων, *the inmost part of the temple, the inner shrine.*

ἁγιότης, *holiness* (see **ἅγιος**), as an abstract quality.

ἁγιωσύνη, the resulting state of the ἅγιος, *holy* or *sanctified state.*

ἀγκάλη, *an arm,* especially as bent to receive a burden.

ἄγκιστρον, *a fish-hook.*

ἄγκυρα, *an anchor.*

ἄγναφος, (of cloth) *unfulled, unmilled, not yet dressed* (by the fuller).

ἁγνεία, *purity, chastity.*

ἁγνίζω, *I make pure,* either (a) ceremonially (e.g. Ac. xxi 24), or (b) actually (e. g. 1 Pet. i 22).

ἁγνισμός, (ceremonial) *purification.*

ἀγνοέω, *I do not know, I am ignorant of* (a person, thing, or fact), sometimes with the idea of wilful ignorance.

ἀγνόημα, *an offence committed through ignorance, an error due to* (wilful or culpable) *ignorance.*

ἄγνοια, *ignorance, inadvertence*; sometimes with the idea of *wilful blindness* (Eph. iv 18).

ἁγνός (originally, *in a condition prepared for worship*), *pure* (either ethically, or ritually, ceremonially); *chaste.*

ἁγνότης, *purity, chastity.*

ἁγνῶς, *purely, with pure motives, honestly.*

ἀγνωσία, disgraceful *ignorance.*

ἄγνωστος, *unknown, unknowable.*

ἀγορά, *market-place, market.*

ἀγοράζω, *I buy.*

ἀγοραῖος, (a) *a lounger in the market-place,* perhaps with the idea of *agitator,* Ac. xvii 5; (b) ἀγοραῖοι (understand ἡμέραι), *market days*; or (understand σύνοδοι, conuentus) *assizes.*

ἄγρα, *catching, a catch.*

4

ἀδάπανος

ἀγράμματος, *unlettered, illiterate, uneducated*, perhaps with the narrower idea, *unacquainted with Rabbinic teaching.*

ἀγραυλέω, *I spend the night in the open, bivouac.*

ἀγρεύω, *I catch, capture.*

ἀγριέλαιος, *a wild olive.*

ἄγριος, *wild.*

Ἀγρίππας, *Agrippa*, i. e. Herod Agrippa II (M. Iulius Agrippa) (A. D. 28—about 93), son of Agrippa I (the Herod of Ac. xii), king of Chalcis (A. D. 50), and afterwards of the old tetrarchies of Philip and Lysanias also.

ἀγρός (a word rare in papyrus documents, and now obsolete), *a field*, especially as bearing a crop; *the country*, Mk. xv 21, xvi 12 : plur. ἀγροί, *lands, property in land, a country estate.*

ἀγρυπνέω, *I am not asleep, I am awake*; especially *I am watchful, careful.*

ἀγρυπνία, *the state of being awake* (at night).

ἄγω, (a) *I lead, I lead away, I bring* (a person, or animal); thus *I bring* before a court of justice; (b) especially in 1st pers. plur. subjunct. ἄγωμεν, intr. *let us depart* (e. g. Mk. i 38); (c) *I hold, keep, celebrate* : ἀγοραῖοι ἄγονται (Ac. xix 38), *assizes are held.*

ἀγωγή, *leading*; hence, *mode of life, conduct.*

ἀγών, *an* (athletic) *contest*; hence, *a struggle* (in the soul).

ἀγωνία (properly the feeling of the athlete before a contest), *great fear, terror*, of death ; *anxiety.*

ἀγωνίζομαι, *I am struggling* (as in an athletic contest or warfare); sometimes with the object ἀγῶνα expressed.

Ἀδάμ (Hebr.), *Adam*, the first man, the first parent of the human race : ὁ ἔσχατος Ἀδάμ, its latest ideal representative, who inaugurates the new age, Jesus the Messiah (1 Cor. xv 45).

ἀδάπανος, *without expense, for which nothing has to be paid.*

5

’Αδδεί (Hebr.), *Addei*, son of Cosam, and father of
Melchei, one of the ancestors of Jesus (Lk. iii 28).

ἀδελφή, (a) *a sister*; (b) *a woman (fellow-)member of
a church, a Christian woman* (Rom. xvi 1; 1 Cor. vii
15, &c.).

ἀδελφός, (a) *a brother* (so probably even in Rom. xvi 23,
2 Cor. xii 18); (b) (a use characteristic of Jewish
literature but not confined to it) *a member of the
same religious community*, especially *a fellow-Christian*
(particularly in the plural).

ἀδελφότης, *brotherhood* (in the collective sense), *the
members of the Christian Church, Christendom*.

ἄδηλος, *unseen, inconspicuous, indistinct* (also of sound).

ἀδηλότης, *the quality of being unseen (of disappearing),
indefiniteness, uncertainty*.

ἀδήλως, *out of sight, obscurely, inconspicuously*; in 1 Cor.
ix 26 perhaps=*uncertainly, without certain aim*.

ἀδημονέω (originally, *I am bewildered*, from δήμων, *knowing, prudent*), *I feel fear, I lack courage*; *I am dis-
tressed*.

ᾅδης (in LXX=Sheol), *Hades, the unseen world*, into
which the spirits of all persons pass at death.

ἀδιάκριτος, *without dividings of mind, undivided, whole-
hearted*.

ἀδιάλειπτος, *unceasing, unremitting*.

ἀδιαλείπτως, *unceasingly, without remission*.

ἀδικέω, *I act unjustly towards, I injure, I harm* (animate
or inanimate).

ἀδίκημα, (a) *a legal wrong, a crime* (with which one is
charged), *a misdeed*; (b) *a crime against God, a sin*
(Rev. xviii 5).

ἀδικία, *injustice, unrighteousness, hurt*; sometimes in
a Hebraistic genitive, equivalent to the adjective
ἄδικος (e. g. Lk. xvi 8, xviii 6).

ἄδικος, *unjust, unrighteous* (opp. δίκαιος).

ἀδίκως, *unjustly*.

’Αδμείν (Hebr.), *Admein*, son of Arnei, father of Naasson,
one of the ancestors of Jesus.

ἀδόκιμος, *failing to pass the test, unapproved, counterfeit.*

ἄδολος, *unadulterated, pure.*

Ἀδραμυντηνός (Ἀδραμυττηνός), *belonging to Adramyttium,* a port in Mysia, NW. Asia Minor.

Ἀδρίας, *the Hadria,* a name given by sailors not merely to the Adriatic Sea, to which it properly belonged, but also to the open Mediterranean to the south-east of Italy, to the sea that lay between Malta, Italy, Greece, and Crete.

ἀδρότης, *lavishness, lavish generosity.*

ἀδυνατέω, of things, *to be impossible.*

ἀδύνατος, (a) of persons, *incapable* (Ac. xiv 8, Rom. xv 1); (b) of things, *impossible*; τὸ ἀδύνατον, either *the inability,* or *that which is impossible* (Rom. viii 3).

ᾄδω, *I sing.*

ἀεί (rare in colloquial Greek), *always.*

ἀετός, *an eagle.*

ἄζυμος, *unleavened,* especially in the neut. plur. τὰ ἄζυμα, *the unleavened bread,* a festival of the Hebrews, held from 15 to 21 Nisan, in commemoration of their deliverance from Egypt: in a moral sense, 1 Cor. v 7–8.

Ἀζώρ (Hebr.), *Azor,* son of Eliakim and father of Zadok, an ancestor of Jesus.

Ἄζωτος, *Azotus, Ashdod,* a coast town of Palestine belonging to the ancient Philistia, and part of Herod's kingdom.

ἀήρ, *air,* the lower air we breathe.

ἀθανασία, *immortality, imperishability, freedom from death.*

ἀθέμιτος, *illegal, unlawful*; thus (nefastus) *abominable.*

ἄθεος, *without god, without (the only true) god, godless.*

ἄθεσμος, *lawless, ignoring the (divine) ordinances.*

ἀθετέω, *I annul, make of no effect, set aside, ignore, slight; I break faith with,* Mk. vi 26.

ἀθέτησις, *annulment.*

Ἀθῆναι, *Athens,* the intellectual capital of Greece.

7

Ἀθηναῖος, *Athenian, belonging to Athens.*
ἀθλέω, *I engage, compete, in an* (athletic) *contest.*
ἄθλησις, *a struggling* (as in an athletic contest).
ἀθροίζω, *I gather together, collect.*
ἀθυμέω, *I lose heart, am despondent.*
ἀθῷος (sometimes, *unpunished*), *guiltless, innocent.*
αἴγειος, *of a goat.*
αἰγιαλός, *sea-coast,* (sandy) *beach*; *shore* (of sea or lake), *land.*
Αἰγύπτιος, *Egyptian.*
Αἴγυπτος, *Egypt.*
ἀΐδιος, *lasting for ever.*
αἰδώς (apparently absent from papyri), *shame, modesty.*
Αἰθίοψ, *Ethiopian, Abyssinian.*
αἷμα, *blood* (especially as shed): σὰρξ καὶ αἷμα (αἷμα καὶ σὰρξ), a Hebraistic expression for *a human being, human beings, human nature.*
αἱματεκχυσία, *a shedding* or *pouring forth of blood* (in sacrifice).
αἱμορροέω, *I suffer from a continual flow* (*oozing*) *of blood.*
Αἰνέας, *Aeneas,* a citizen of Lydda.
αἴνεσις, *praise, commendation.*
αἰνέω, *I praise.*
αἴνιγμα, *a riddle.*
αἶνος, *praise.*
Αἰνών, *Aenon.* Eusebius and Jerome place this site 8 (Roman) miles south of Scythopolis near the Jordan.
αἱρέομαι, *I choose.*
αἵρεσις (originally, *choosing, choice*), *a self-chosen opinion*: a religious or philosophical *sect.*
αἱρετίζω, *I choose.*
αἱρετικός, *disposed to form sects, sectarian, factious.*
αἴρω, (a) *I raise, lift up*; (b) *I take away, remove.*
αἰσθάνομαι, *I perceive.*
αἴσθησις, *perception.*
αἰσθητήριον, *perceptive faculty.*

αἰσχροκερδής, *fond of base gain.*
αἰσχροκερδῶς, *in a spirit of eagerness for base gain.*
αἰσχρολογία, *filthy speech, foulmouthedness.*
αἰσχρός, *base, disgraceful.*
αἰσχρότης, *baseness.*
αἰσχύνη, *shame*; *shamefacedness.*
αἰσχύνομαι, *I am ashamed.*
αἰτέω, *I ask, request, beg, petition* : middle voice αἰτέομαι, *I ask for myself* (perhaps with entreaty).
αἴτημα, *a request.*
αἰτία, (a) *a cause, reason*; *excuse*; (b) *a charge, accusation*; (c) *guilt*; (d) *relationship, matter, circumstances, case* (= causa), Mt. xix 10.
αἴτιον (neut. of adj. αἴτιος), *cause* shading into *crime*; *guilt, criminality.*
αἴτιος (adj.), *the cause of, the originator of*; *responsible for.*
αἰτίωμα, *a charge, accusation.*
αἰφνίδιος, *sudden.*
αἰχμαλωσία, *captivity*: Hebraistically = *captives*, Eph. iv 8.
αἰχμαλωτεύω, *I take captive* (in war).
αἰχμαλωτίζω, *I take captive* (in war), *I subdue, I ensnare.*
αἰχμάλωτος, *a captive* (in war), hence generally.
αἰών (from a root meaning *life*, especially *long life, old age*), *an age, a cycle* (of time), especially of the present age as contrasted with the future age, and of one of a series of ages stretching to infinity: ἀπʼ αἰῶνος, *from the beginning of the present age, from the beginning of time*, Lk. i 70, &c. : εἰς αἰῶνα (in saeculum, in aeternum, Ambros. *expos. ps.* cxviii 12 7 § 1) : αἰῶνες αἰώνων, a Hebraistic expression, moreʼemphatic than the simple αἰῶνες Gal. i 5, &c.
αἰώνιος, (a) *age-long*, and, therefore, practically *eternal, unending*; (b) partaking of the character of that which lasts for an age, as contrasted with that which is brief and fleeting.

ἀκαθαρσία, *uncleanness, impurity.*

ἀκάθαρτος, *unclean, impure* : in reference to demons, spirits, Mt. x 1, &c.

ἀκαιρέομαι, *I am without a suitable opportunity* (to effect something).

ἀκαίρως, *unseasonably, out of due season, inopportunely.*

ἄκακος, *innocent, guileless* ; *simple,* Rom. xvi 18.

ἄκανθα, *a thorn-bush.*

ἀκάνθινος, *made of thorns.*

ἄκαρπος, *fruitless, profitless.*

ἀκατάγνωστος, *uncondemned, unimpeachable.*

ἀκατακάλυπτος, *not veiled, unveiled.*

ἀκατάκριτος, *uncondemned* (probably an attempt to translate the Latin *re incognita* or *causā indictā,* '(our, one's) case not having been tried ').

ἀκατάλυτος, *indissoluble, that cannot be broken up.*

ἀκατάπαστος, a colloquial spelling of ἀκατάπαυστος, q. v.

ἀκατάπαυστος, *not ceasing from, not abandoning* (*giving up*), c. gen.

ἀκαταστασία, *disturbance, upheaval, revolution,* almost *anarchy,* first in the political, and thence in the moral sphere.

ἀκατάστατος (in LXX *staggering, reeling*), *unsettled, unstable* (though these are hardly strong enough equivalents), almost *anarchic.*

Ἀκελδαμάχ, see Ἀχελδαμάχ.

ἀκέραιος, (lit. *unmixed*) *simple, unsophisticated.*

ἀκλινής, *unbent, unyielding, resolute.*

ἀκμάζω, *I reach maturity, become ripe* : *I am in full vigour.*

ἀκμήν, (properly adverbial acc. of ἀκμή [full time, maturity], and meaning *just now*) *thus,* Mt. xv 16 (where parallel in Mk. vii 18 has οὕτως).

ἀκοή, (a) *hearing, faculty of hearing* ; *ear* : in ἀκοῇ ἀκούειν (Mt. xiii 14, &c.), a Hebraistic (?) expression, the ἀκοῇ is emphatic ; (b) *report, rumour.*

ἀκολουθέω (takes the place of the old ἕπομαι), *I accompany, attend.*

ἀκούω, *I hear, listen*; in the passive, *is heard, is reported*: ἀκοῇ ἀκούειν, see **ἀκοή**.

ἀκρασία (= ἀκράτεια), *incontinence, intemperance* (in wide sense).

ἀκρατής, (*impotent*, hence) *lacking self-control, inclined to excess*.

ἄκρᾱτος (from κεράννυμι), *unmixed, undiluted*.

ἀκρίβεια (diligentia), *accuracy, exactness, attention to detail, scrupulousness*.

ἀκριβής (diligens), *careful, accurate, exact, strict, scrupulous, precise*.

ἀκριβόω, *I examine carefully, inquire strictly*.

ἀκριβῶς (diligenter), *carefully, exactly, strictly*.

ἀκρίς, *a locust*.

ἀκροατήριον, *auditorium, recitation hall*; *court room* (for hearing cases).

ἀκροατής, *a hearer of, a listener to*.

ἀκροβυστία (a technical word of Jewish use, adapted from ἀκροποσθία[?]), *foreskin, prepuce*: used sometimes as a slang term by Jews, of Gentiles (Eph. ii 11).

ἀκρογωνιαῖος (= Attic γωνιαῖος) (adj.), *in the corner* (of a building), *corner*-(stone).

ἀκροθίνιον (lit. *top of a heap*), *spoil, treasure* (taken in war).

ἄκρον (neut. of adj. ἄκρος), *edge, tip*.

Ἀκύλας, the Greek way of writing the Latin *Aquila*, a male proper name; the husband of Priscilla (Prisca), and a Jew, of a family belonging to (Sinope in?) Pontus.

ἀκυρόω, *I annul, make of no effect, cancel*.

ἀκωλύτως (characteristic of legal documents), *without let or hindrance*.

ἄκων, *unwilling*, generally used where English would express by an adverb, *unwillingly* (cf. inuitus).

ἀλάβαστρος, *an alabaster phial* or *bottle*.

ἀλαζονεία, *arrogant display, ostentation*; plur. = *occasions of ostentation*.

ἀλαζών (gloriosus), *boastful*, giving one's self airs in a loud and flaunting way.

ἀλαλάζω

ἀλαλάζω (onomatopoeic, cf. Hebrew), *I cry aloud*, generally of persons (in Mk. v 38 from sorrow): κύμβαλον -άζον; a *clanging* or *clashing* cymbal (1 Cor. xiii 1).

ἀλάλητος, *unutterable, that baffles words.*

ἄλαλος, *dumb.*

ἄλας (neut.), *salt.*

ἀλεεύς (a modification of the earlier ἁλιεύς), *a fisherman.*

ἀλείφω, *I anoint.*

ἀλεκτοροφωνία (galli cantus, gallicinium), *cockcrow*, as a period of time, between midnight and 3 a.m.

ἀλέκτωρ, *a cock.*

Ἀλεξανδρεύς, *an Alexandrian*, a native (or resident) of Alexandria in Egypt.

Ἀλεξανδρινός (or -ῖνος), *belonging to Alexandria* in Egypt.

Ἀλέξανδρος, *Alexander*, a proper name of Greek origin, borne by four, possibly five, persons in the N.T., (a) an early Christian, son of Simon of Cyrene, who carried the Cross, Mk. xv 21; (b) a leading non-Christian Jew in Jerusalem, Ac. iv 6; (c) an Ephesian Jew, Ac. xix 33; (d) a renegade Christian at Rome (1 Tim. i 20), probably to be identified with Alexander the coppersmith (2 Tim. iv 14).

ἄλευρον, *meal.*

ἀλήθεια, *truth*, but not merely truth as spoken; truth of idea, reality, sincerity, truth in the moral sphere, straightforwardness: ἐπ' ἀληθείας, *really, truly.*

ἀληθεύω, *I say (speak) truth*, Gal. iv 16; *I do truth, I maintain truth (the truth)* (see ἀλήθεια for the sense of ' truth ').

ἀληθής, *true* in fact; hence more widely (see ἀλήθεια).

ἀληθινός (less common than ἀληθής), *true* (lit. *made of truth*), *real, genuine.*

ἀλήθω, *I grind.*

ἀληθῶς, *truly, verily.*

ἁλιεύς, see ἀλεεύς.

ἁλιεύω, *I fish.*

ἁλίζω, *I salt, salten, sprinkle with salt* (of sacrifices or of those who offer sacrifice), *keep fresh and sound,* and so acceptable to God.

ἁλίσγημα (from ἁλισγέω, read in Freer MS. at Mk. ix 49), *pollution,* perhaps *a polluted thing* (specially of food).

ἀλλά (used very like πλήν), *but; except,* Mk. iv 22, Mt. xx 23 ; ἀλλ' ἤ, *except,* 2 Cor. i 13 ; in Mk. vi 9 ἀλλά is probably a misrendering of an Aramaic word meaning *and not.*

ἀλλάσσω (transitive), *I change, alter.*

ἀλλαχόθεν, *from another quarter,* practically *by another way.*

ἀλλαχοῦ (= ἄλλοσε, ἀλλαχόσε, *elsewhither*), *elsewhere.*

ἀλληγορέω, *I allegorize, I interpret as an allegory.*

ἀλληλουιά (Hebr.), *Hallelujah, Praise the Lord.*

ἀλλήλων &c. (a reciprocal word = inter se, in uicem), *one another.*

ἀλλογενής, *a man of another race, a foreigner.*

ἄλλομαι, *I leap, leap up.*

ἄλλος (alius), *other, another* (of more than two), *different;* see under ἕτερος ; ὁ ἄλλος, *the other* (of two only), Mt. v 39, &c. ; ἄλλοι ἄλλο τι . . . *some—one thing, some —another thing.*

ἀλλοτριοεπίσκοπος (a word of uncertain application, perhaps) *a pryer into other men's affairs,* by means of soothsayers, astrologers, &c.

ἀλλότριος (alienus), *belonging to another person, belonging to others.*

ἀλλόφυλος, *a foreigner.*

ἄλλως, *otherwise:* τὰ ἄλλως ἔχοντα, *things that are otherwise.*

ἀλοάω, *I thresh* (corn).

ἄλογος, *without (devoid of) human reason ; unreasonable, senseless.*

ἀλόη, *aloes,* the powdered fragrant aloe wood.

ἅλς, *salt.*

ἁλυκός, *salty, saline.*

13

ἄλυπος, *free from pain* (*grief, trouble*).

ἄλυσις, *a* (light) *chain*.

ἀλυσιτελής, *profitless, unprofitable*.

ἄλφα, *alpha*, the first letter of the Greek alphabet, cf. **A**.

'Αλφαῖος, *Alphaeus*, apparently two persons, (a) father of Levi (Mk. ii 14); and (b) father of James (Mk. iii 18, &c.). (Some say = Aramaic Chalphai, and identify with Clopas, John xix 25.)

ἄλων (= ἅλως), *a threshing-floor*.

ἀλώπηξ, *a fox*.

ἅλωσις, *capture, capturing*.

ἅμα, (a) adv. *at the same time, therewith*; (b) prep. *along with, together with*.

ἀμαθής (very rare in Hellenistic period), *unlearned*.

ἀμαράντινος, *unfading, fadeless*.

ἀμάραντος, *unfading*.

ἁμαρτάνω, originally, *I miss the mark*; hence, (a) *I make a mistake*; (b) *I sin, I commit a sin* (against God); sometimes (Lk. xvii 4, Ac. xxv 8, &c.) the idea of sinning against a fellow-creature is present.

ἁμάρτημα (erratum), *a fault, a sin*.

ἁμαρτία (error, *a wrong state of mind* or *soul*), *a sin*.

ἀμάρτυρος, *unwitnessed, untestified to*.

ἁμαρτωλός, (a) *sinning, sinful*; (b) frequent as a translation of a contemptuous Aramaic word, with reference to particular classes despised by strict Jews, *a sinner*.

ἄμαχος (originally a military word), *not quarrelsome, peaceable*.

ἀμάω, *I mow, reap*.

ἀμέθυστος, *amethyst* (a kind of rock crystal: the best specimens are the colour of unmixed wine, whence perhaps the name).

ἀμελέω, *I neglect*.

ἄμεμπτος, *blameless*.

ἀμέμπτως, *blamelessly*.

ἀμέριμνος, *free from anxiety* (though 'anxiety' is rather too strong a word).

14

ἀνακλίνω, (a) *I make to recline* (especially at a dinner-table); (b) mid. and pass. *I recline at a table.*

ἀνακράζω (colloquial), *I shout* (aloud).

ἀνακρίνω, *I examine, inquire into* (judicially : see **ἀνάκρισις**); of the preliminary examination, preceding the trial proper : hence with derived applications.

ἀνάκρισις, *judicial examination, preliminary inquiry.*

ἀνακυλίω, *I roll back.*

ἀνακύπτω, *I raise myself, become erect* (Lk. xiii 11); *I look up* (Lk. xxi 28).

ἀναλαμβάνω, (a) *I take up, raise*; (b) *I pick up*, 2 Tim. iv 11, or *take on board*, Ac. xx 13, 14; (c) *I carry off, lead away*, Ac. xxiii 31.

ἀνάλημψις, *a taking up, lifting up* (of the Ascension; lit. *Assumption*).

ἀναλίσκω, *I destroy, annihilate* (in 2 Thess. ii 8 text is doubtful).

ἀναλογία, *proportion, measure.*

ἀναλογίζομαι (from λόγος = *account*), *I reckon up, count over.*

ἄναλος, *saltless, tasteless, flat.*

ἀνάλυσις, *departing, departure* (from this life). (Probably a metaphor from the yoking and unyoking of transport animals.)

ἀναλύω (see **ἀνάλυσις**), *I depart*, Phil. i 23; perhaps, *I return*, Lk. xii 36 (Jerome demands this sense also in Phil. i 23).

ἀναμάρτητος, *sinless.*

ἀναμένω, *I await* (one whose coming is expected).

ἀναμιμνήσκω, (a) act. *I remind*; (b) mid. or pass. *I am reminded, remind myself, remember, recall.*

ἀνάμνησις, *a recalling, remembrance, memory.*

ἀνανεόομαι (regularly a legal word), *I am renewed.*

ἀνανήφω, *I become sober again, I recover sound sense.*

'Ανανίας, *Ananias*, (a) husband of Sapphira, a member of the early church at Jerusalem, Ac. v; (b) a member of the church at Damascus, Ac. ix 10, &c.; (c) the high priest at Jerusalem, Ac. xxiii 2, xxiv 1.

ἀναντίρητος

ἀναντίρητος (ἀναντίρρητος), *that cannot be gainsaid, undeniable.*

ἀναντιρήτως (ἀναντιρρήτως), *without saying anything against* (the request), *unquestioningly.*

ἀνάξιος, *unworthy.*

ἀναξίως, *unworthily, in an unworthy manner.*

ἀνάπαυσις, *a resting, rest,* especially *a respite* or *temporary rest* as a preparation for future toil.

ἀναπαύω, (a) act. *I make to rest, I give rest to*; (b) mid. and pass. *I rest, take my ease* (see ἀνάπαυσις).

ἀναπείθω, *I urge by* (evil) *persuasion, I tempt.*

ἀνάπειρος, see ἀνάπηρος.

ἀναπέμπω, (a) *I send up* (to a higher tribunal), Lk. xxiii 7, Ac. xxv 21, &c.; (b) *I send back,* Philem. 12, &c.

ἀναπηδάω, *I leap up.*

ἀνάπηρος (debilis), *maimed.*

ἀναπίπτω, *I lie down, recline* (at a dinner-table), *I fall back upon* (the breast of another person reclining at dinner).

ἀναπληρόω, (a) *I fill up, make up, complete the measure of,* Phil. ii 30; (b) *I fulfil, I carry out the commands* (*provisions,* &c.) *of,* Mt. xiii 14, Gal. vi 2, &c.

ἀναπολόγητος, *without* (ground of) *defence, indefensible, inexcusable.*

ἀναπτύσσω (euoluo), *I unroll* (reading uncertain).

ἀνάπτω, *I kindle.*

ἀναρίθμητος, *uncountable, innumerable, that cannot be numbered.*

ἀνασείω, *I shake up, stir up, excite.*

ἀνασκευάζω, *I pack up*; hence, *I carry away,* or *dismantle*; hence, *I upset, destroy, overthrow, subvert* (lit. and metaph.).

ἀνασπάω, *I drag up, pull up.*

ἀνάστασις, *a rising again, resurrection.*

ἀναστατόω (perhaps a political metaphor), *I turn upside down, upset, unsettle.*

ἀνασταυρόω, *I crucify again* (so the sense seems to require, but elsewhere simply = σταυρόω, *I crucify*).

ἀναστενάζω, *I groan.*

ἀναστρέφω, (a) *I overturn, turn upside down,* John ii 15 (text doubtful); (b) *I return,* Ac. v 22, xv 16 (in a Hebraistic idiom, where the verb means little more than the adverb *again*); (c) mid. and pass. (conuersari) *I conduct (behave) myself, live* (with reference to the manner of life, especially in a moral and religious aspect), Mt. xvii 22 (text doubtful), &c., often with *ἐν* and a noun indicating condition or circumstances.

ἀναστροφή (conuersatio) (not in papyri, common in inscriptions), *dealing with* other men, *going up and down* among men, *life, manner of life.*

ἀνατάσσομαι, *I arrange, draw up,* but perhaps, as Blass thought, *I set down from memory, I restore from memory,* Lk. i 1.

ἀνατέλλω, (a) *I make to rise,* Mt. v 45; (b) *I rise, shine* (generally of the sun, and hence metaphorically).

ἀνατίθεμαι, *I lay* (a case) *before, I impart, I communicate, I relate* (with a view to consulting).

ἀνατολή, (a) *rising* of the sun; hence, (b) (sing. and plur.) the quarter whence the sun rises, *the East.*

ἀνατρέπω, *I overturn* (lit. or metaph.) (in John ii 15 text is doubtful).

ἀνατρέφω, *I rear, bring up* (in Lk. iv 16 text is doubtful).

ἀναφαίνω, (a) a nautical term, *I sight* (a place); (b) mid. *I appear* (as it were, out of the unseen).

ἀναφέρω, (a) *I carry up, lead up*; (b) *I offer up* (on a high altar) as a sacrifice, *I offer up* to God on high.

ἀναφωνέω, *I call out, shout.*

ἀνάχυσις (probably literary), *outpouring, excess.*

ἀναχωρέω, (a) *I return,* Mt. ii 12; (b) *I retire, depart* (underlying idea perhaps of taking refuge from danger or of going into retirement).

ἀνάψυξις (refrigerium), *refreshing, refreshment.*

ἀναψύχω, *I refresh, revive, comfort.*

ἀνδραποδιστής, *an enslaver,* one who forcibly enslaves, *a kidnapper.*

21

Ἀνδρέας (a Greek name), *Andrew*, brother of Simon Peter, and one of the disciples of Jesus, belonging to Bethsaida (John i 44).

ἀνδρίζομαι, *I act in manly fashion, I play the man, I display manly qualities.*

Ἀνδρόνικος, *Andronicus*, a member of the Roman church, probably husband of Junia, and a kinsman or fellow-tribesman of St. Paul.

ἀνδροφόνος, *a murderer.*

ἀνέγκλητος, *irreproachable* (especially in private life), *blameless.*

ἀνεκδιήγητος, *indescribable, that cannot be thoroughly related.*

ἀνεκλάλητος, *incapable of expression in speech.*

ἀνέκλειπτος (ἀνέγλειπτος), *unfailing.*

ἀνεκτός, *endurable, tolerable.*

ἀνελεήμων, *unpitying, unmerciful.*

ἀνέλεος, *unmerciful.*

ἀνεμίζομαι, *I am blown with the wind* (referring to the gentler motions of the air).

ἄνεμος, *wind* (literally, and in Eph. iv 14 metaph.): in the sense *quarter of the heaven, cardinal point*, as both Greeks and Romans habitually defined the quarters of the heaven by the winds which came from those quarters, Mt. xxiv 31 (Mk. xiii 27).

ἀνένδεκτος, *impossible.*

ἀνεξεραύνητος, *that cannot be searched into, inscrutable.*

ἀνεξίκακος, *enduring evil, patient of evil.*

ἀνεξιχνίαστος (perhaps from Job LXX), *that cannot be tracked out, inexplorable, unsearchable.*

ἀνεπαίσχυντος, *not ashamed* (of his work).

ἀνεπίλημπτος, *giving no cause for accusation.*

ἀνέρχομαι, *I go up* (to the capital).

ἄνεσις (opposite of θλῖψις, lit. *loosening, relaxing*), (a) *relief, remission, indulgence, freedom*, Ac. xxiv 23; (b) *rest.*

ἀνετάζω, *I examine* (a person on trial, a witness) *judicially* (frequently by the aid of torture).

ἄνευ, *without, without the co-operation* (or *knowledge*) *of* (Mt. x 29).

ἀνεύθετος, *unfitted, unsuitable.*

ἀνευρίσκω, *I find by seeking out.*

ἀνέχομαι, *I endure* (in 2 Thess. i 4, and Mt. vi 24 = Lk. xvi 13, text doubtful).

ἀνεψιός, (male) *cousin,* whether on the father's or on the mother's side.

ἄνηθον, *dill* (anethum graveolens).

ἀνήκω, in third person, especially of imperfect (cf. Eng. *ought = owed*), *is due, becoming, suitable, proper.*

ἀνήμερος, *ungentle; untamed.*

ἀνήρ (uir), *a male human being, a man* (contrast ἄνθρωπος); often in addresses, at the beginning of speeches = *Gentlemen; a husband.*

ἀνθίστημι, only in intransitive tenses of active, and in all tenses of the middle or passive, *I take a stand against, oppose, resist.*

ἀνθομολογέομαι, *I confess* (so e.g. the Latin and Sahidic versions), *acknowledge, formally admit: I give thanks* (so e.g. the Peshitta Syriac and the Bohairic versions, and moderns generally). (The senses *I agree, I answer to* (*come up to*), *I come to an understanding with,* appear in papyri.)

ἄνθος, *bloom,* possibly a reference to the bright flowers, such as poppies (among the grass).

ἀνθρακιά, *a coal-fire.*

ἄνθραξ, *a coal.*

ἀνθρωπάρεσκος, *a men-pleaser, a renderer of service to human beings* (as opposed to God).

ἀνθρώπινος, *belonging to human beings* (especially as contrasted with God), *human* (as contrasted with divine): perhaps *moderate,* Rom. vi 19, 1 Cor. x 13.

ἀνθρωποκτόνος (homicida) (borrowed from poetry), *a murderer.*

ἄνθρωπος, *a human being:* υἱὸς ἀνθρώπου, notable because of the singular (rather than the plural ἀνθρώπων), a Hebraistic expression of a somewhat frequent type (see under υἱός), indicating *a human being with all the characteristics of a human being* (ὁ υἱὸς τοῦ ἀνθρώπου, a Messianic title especially favoured by our Lord for this very reason).

ἀνθύπατος (pro consule, proconsul), a *proconsul*, a title applied to the governor of a senatorial province under the Empire, such as Cyprus (Ac. xiii 7, 8, 12), Achaia (Ac. xviii 12), and Asia (Ac. xix 38, where the plural is general and does not mean that there were more than one at a time). The word means originally *one with the rank and insignia of a consul* (i. e. the chief Roman magistrate), but was later applied to those who had not yet held the office of consul as well as to those who had.

ἀνίημι, *I let go, loosen, release, give up.*

ἄνιπτος, *unwashed.*

ἀνίστημι, *I raise up, set up* : only the fut. ἀναστήσω and the 1 aor. ἀνέστησα are used in this transitive sense in the N.T. ; much more frequent are the middle voice and the 2 aor. of the active in the intr. sense *I rise*, especially ἐκ νεκρῶν, *from among (the) dead bodies, dead persons, the dead.*

Ἄννα (the aspirated form Ἅννα, favoured by W-H, is contradicted by the evidence of the versions), *Anna*, a prophetess, who visited the infant Jesus.

Ἄννας, *Annas*, high priest at Jerusalem.

ἀνόητος, *senseless* (in Gal. iii 1 pathos is behind the use of the word, according to Ramsay, *Historical Commentary*, pp. 308 ff., and it describes a state of culture unworthy of the Romanized Galatians).

ἄνοια, *senselessness.*

ἀνοίγω, *I open.*

ἀνοικοδομέω, *I rebuild, build up* (what has fallen or been razed to the ground): sometimes merely *I build.*

ἄνοιξις, *opening* (abstr.).

ἀνομία, *lawlessness* ; especially *disobedience to the* divine *law, sin.*

24

ἄντικρυς

ἄνομος, *lawless, disobedient to the law* of God, *sinful*; *illegal*: ἄνομος θεοῦ=ἄνευ νόμου θεοῦ, 1 Cor. ix 21.

ἀνόμως, *without law.*

ἀνορθόω, *I make upright (straight) again, I rear again, restore.*

ἀνόσιος, *regarding nothing as holy.*

ἀνοχή, *forbearance; suspense* or *delay* (of punishment).

ἀνταγωνίζομαι, *I struggle against.*

ἀντάλλαγμα, *an exchange, purchasing price.*

ἀνταναπληρόω, *I fill up in place of some one else.*

ἀνταποδίδωμι, *I give in return.*

ἀνταπόδομα, *a gift in return* (for another), *a return, a recompense.*

ἀνταπόδοσις, orig. abstr., *giving in return*, but in Col. iii 24 practically = ἀνταπόδομα.

ἀνταποκρίνομαι, *I give a hostile answer.*

ἀντεῖπον, *I said in reply* (with idea of hostility, contradiction).

ἀντέχομαι, *I hold fast (firmly) to.*

ἀντί (originally local, *in front of, opposite*), (a) *instead of, in return for, in exchange for, as a substitute for*; λύτρον ἀντὶ πολλῶν Mk. x 45 (=Mt. xx 28), *a ransom to buy the many, for the many*; cf. Heb. xii 16 and ἀντίλυτρον; (b) ἀντὶ ἐμοῦ, *on my behalf*, Mt. xvii 27; (c) ἀνθ᾽ ὧν (literally, *in return for which things*) has become a conjunction, *wherefore, because.*

ἀντιβάλλω, *I throw at in opposition* (or quasi-opposition), *I exchange* (words) *with*; perhaps, *I compare.*

ἀντιδιατίθεμαι, *I am adversely affected against, I oppose.*

ἀντίδικος (aduersarius), *an opponent* (in a lawsuit): probably so even in 1 Pet. v 8.

ἀντίθεσις, *a proposition, tenet, opinion* advanced by one party *against* another.

ἀντικαθίστημι: 2 aor. *I stoutly resisted.*

ἀντικαλέω, *I invite in return.*

ἀντίκειμαι (used as a passive for ἀντιτίθημι, just as κεῖμαι is a passive for τίθημι), *I resist, oppose.*

ἄντικρυς, *right opposite, off* (nautical sense).

ἀντιλαμβάνομαι

ἀντιλαμβάνομαι, *I lay hold of* (in order to help), *I aid* (*succour*); *I take in hand* (lit. and met.), *I undertake*; *I partake of, enjoy*, 1 Tim. vi 2.

ἀντιλέγω, *I speak* or *say in opposition, I contradict* (*oppose, resist*): σημεῖον ἀντιλεγόμενον, *a disputed sign, a sign that is debated about.*

ἀντίλημψις, *a lending a hand to, a helping* (cf. ἀντιλαμβάνομαι, both being often used in petitions).

ἀντιλογία, *contradiction, dispute.*

ἀντιλοιδορέω, *I abuse in return, I give abuse for abuse.*

ἀντίλυτρον, a stronger form of λύτρον, *a ransom.*

ἀντιμετρέω, *I measure in return, I give equivalent measure,* Lk. vi 38 (text doubtful).

ἀντιμισθία, *a reward, recompense* (a more emphatic expression than the simple μισθός).

Ἀντιόχεια, *Antioch* (derived from Antiochus, a king of the Seleucid dynasty), (a) *Antioch* on the river Orontes, capital of the Province Syria ; (b) ʻ Pisidian ʼ *Antioch*, not in Pisidia, but near Pisidia, in the Roman Province Galatia, where was a Roman colony founded by Augustus, Ac. xiii 14, xiv 19, 21, 2 Tim. iii 11.

Ἀντιοχεύς, *an Antiochian, an inhabitant of* (Syrian) *Antioch.*

ἀντιπαρέρχομαι, *I pass opposite,* on the *opposite* side of the road.

Ἀντίπας (Ἀντείπας, Ἀντίφας, a pet form of Ἀντίπατρος), *Antipas,* a Christian martyr of Pergamum.

Ἀντιπατρίς, *Antipatris,* a town, where was a Roman colony, on the road between Caesarea and Jerusalem.

ἀντίπερα, *opposite.*

ἀντιπίπτω, *I fall foul of* ; *I resist, oppose.*

ἀντιστρατεύομαι, *I campaign against, war against.*

ἀντιτάσσομαι, *I range myself against, resist* (the attack of).

ἀντίτυπος (from τύπος, *impress, impression left by a die*), *typical of, representing by type* (or *pattern*), *corresponding to*: neut., as noun, *an image.*

ἀντίχριστος, *antichrist,* either *one who puts himself in the*

26

place of or *the enemy* (*opponent*) *of the Messiah*, a figure first appearing in the N.T., identified with various historical persons: the plur., of many such, in 1 John ii 18.

ἀντλέω, *I draw* (generally water from a deep well in the ground); perhaps, *I draw out*, John ii 9.

ἄντλημα, *a pail* attached to a rope, by which it is let down into a well.

ἀντοφθαλμέω, *I face* (lit. 'I present my eye to'); *I resist*.

ἄνυδρος, *waterless*.

ἀνυπόκριτος (literary), *unfeigned, unassumed*.

ἀνυπότακτος, *unsubjected, unruly*.

ἄνω (adv.), *up, above*; ἕως ἄνω, *up to the top, up to the brim*, John ii 7; τὰ ἄνω, *things above, heaven, the heavenly region*: see ἀνώτερον.

ἄνωθεν, (a) *from above*, sometimes strengthened by ἀπό, *from heaven* (locally and spiritually); (b) *from the beginning, from their origin* (*source*), *from of old*, Lk. i 3, Ac. xxvi 5, Gal. iv 9, James i 17; (c) *again* (the meaning taken out of Jesus' words by Nicodemus, John iii 4, where δεύτερον is his paraphrase of ἄνωθεν (iii 3)).

ἀνωτερικός, *upper, higher-lying* (the high central plateau of Asia Minor in contrast to the road through the valley).

ἀνώτερον (compar. of ἄνω, q. v.), (a) *higher, to a more honourable place* (at the dinner-table), Lk. xiv 10; (b) (superius) *previously, in an earlier passage* (of the book), *above*.

ἀνωφελής, *useless, unprofitable* (perhaps also with the further idea, *harmful*, as in Plato).

ἀξίνη, *axe*.

ἄξιος, *worthy*; *worthy of, deserving*.

ἀξιόω, *I account* or *treat as worthy*.

ἀξίως, *worthily*; *in a manner worthy of* ....

ἀόρατος, *unseen, invisible*.

ἀπαγγέλλω, *I report* (from one place to another), *I bring a report, I announce*.

27

άπάγχομαι

άπάγχομαι, *I choke, strangle, hang myself.*

άπάγω, *I lead away,* [for example (=duco) *I lead away* to execution, Ac. xii 19]; hence, in the moral sphere, 1 Cor. xii 2 ; also, of a road *leading* to a place.

άπαίδευτος, *untrained, uneducated, showing a want of training or education.*

άπαίρω, *I take away, remove.*

άπαιτέω (requiro), *I ask back,* or *I ask what is my due.*

άπαλγέω (lit. *I cease to feel* [*my*] *pain*), *I am past feeling, cease to care* (suggesting sometimes despair, sometimes recklessness), *I become callous.*

άπαλλάσσω, *I free* (a person) *from* (anything); oftener in the middle voice, *I am released from, I am rid of* (a person or thing).

άπαλλοτριόομαι, lit. *I am being alienated from* : the perf. pcpl. pass. is practically a noun=*aliens.*

άπαλός, *tender.*

άπαντάω, *I meet.*

άπάντησις, the act of *meeting*; εἰς άπάντησιν, *to meet* (a phrase seemingly almost technical for the reception of a newly arrived official).

ἅπαξ, *once* ; *once for all.*

άπαράβατος, *inviolate, inviolable.*

άπαρασκεύαστος, *unprepared.*

άπαρνέομαι, *I deny, disown, repudiate* (either another person or myself).

άπάρτι (properly άπ᾽ ἄρτι, lit. *from now*), *henceforth* ; *even now.*

άπαρτισμός, *setting up, erection* ; hence *completion.*

άπαρχή, *first-fruits, the earliest crop* of the year ; hence also metaph., for example, of the earliest converts in a district. There is evidence in favour of rendering in some passages merely by *sacrifice, gift.*

ἅπας, *all, whole* (cf. πᾶς). It is rather a literary word and is used by preference after consonants.

άπασπάζομαι, *I greet at parting, I give parting greetings to.*

28

ἀπατάω (becoming obsolete in most countries), *I deceive, cheat.*

ἀπάτη (*deceit, deception*, or more probably, according to a Hellenistic sense), *pleasure* in Mk. iv 19 (= Mt. xiii 22, cf. Lk. viii 14), 2 Pet. ii 13.

ἀπάτωρ, *without* (recorded) *father, of unknown father.*

ἀπαύγασμα, *a light flashing forth* (from), *radiation, gleam.*

ἀπείθεια, *disobedience, rebellion, contumacy* : for υἱοὶ τῆς ἀπειθείας, see υἱός.

ἀπειθέω, *I disobey, I rebel, I am disloyal.*

ἀπειθής, *disobedient.*

ἀπειλέω (apparently going out of popular speech), *I threaten.*

ἀπειλή, *threatening, a threat.*

ἄπειμι (A), *I am absent.*

ἄπειμι (B), *I shall go away, I go away* (only Ac. xvii 10).

ἀπεῖπον : in middle, ἀπειπάμην, *I have renounced.*

ἀπείραστος, *untried, inexperienced* (c. gen. = *in*); or *untempted* (c. gen. = *to*).

ἄπειρος (from πεῖρα), *inexperienced* (in), *without experience* (of), *unacquainted* (with).

ἀπεκδέχομαι (rare), *I expect eagerly, I wait for eagerly.*

ἀπεκδύομαι (probably coined by Paul), *I put off* (as a garment) *from myself, I throw off.*

ἀπέκδυσις (probably coined by Paul), *a putting off* (as of a garment), *a casting off.*

ἀπελαύνω, *I drive away.*

ἀπελεγμός, *refutation, rejection* ; hence *disrepute.*

ἀπελεύθερος, *a freedman*, one who has been a slave but has been manumitted by his master.

Ἀπελλῆς, *Apelles*, a Christian (man) in Rome.

ἀπελπίζω (ἀφελπίζω), *I despair* : in Lk. vi 35, if μηδέν be the correct reading, μηδὲν ἀφελπίζοντες must be translated, *despairing not at all*, if μηδένα ἀφ., *despairing of no one.*

ἀπέναντι, *over against, opposite* ; *in view of, in presence of.*

ἀπέραντος, *unaccomplished, unending, endless.*

ἀπερισπάστως, *without distraction, without being dis-tracted.*

ἀπερίτμητος, *uncircumcised*; hence practically *unclean*; met. used of rankness, want of restraint.

ἀπέρχομαι, *I go away from* (a place).

ἀπέχω, (trans.) *I have received* (payment), a formula of receipts: so prob. also in Mk. xiv 41, ὁ 'Ιούδας being understood as subject (there is hardly any other example in Greek of the meaning *it is sufficient*, but see Field ad loc.); (intrans.) *I am away* (*distant*) (from), of places and objects; (middle voice) *I keep myself away* (from), *I refrain* (from), *I abstain* (from).

ἀπιστέω, (a) *I am unfaithful*; (b) *I disbelieve.*

ἀπιστία, *unbelief.*

ἄπιστος, *unbelieving, incredulous*; *unchristian*: some-times substantivally, *unbeliever.*

ἁπλότης (simplicitas, sinceritas), *singleness of mind, sincerity.*

ἁπλοῦς (simplex), *single*: of the eye, *directed towards one object.*

ἁπλῶς, *singly, simply*: in James i 5 either *graciously* or *unreservedly, without reserve.*

ἀπό, with nouns or adverbs, *from*, (as distinguished from ἐκ) = *from the outside of, away from*: ἀπ' ἀγορᾶς, *fresh from market*, Mk. vii 4, ἀπ' ἀγροῦ, *fresh from the country*, Mk. xv 21: Rev. i 4, construction is peculiar: οἱ ἀπὸ τῆς 'Ιταλίας, *those who are in* (?) *Italy*, Heb. xiii 24: φοβεῖσθαι ἀπό, see φοβέομαι: *by* (expressing agent), e. g. Lk. viii 43: = gen. of material, Mt. iii 4, xxvii 21.

ἀποβαίνω (*I go away*), (a) *I disembark*; (b) ἀποβαίνειν εἰς, *to result in, to end in.*

ἀποβάλλω, *I cast away, I cast off*: *I lose*, Heb. x 35.

ἀποβλέπω, *I look away from* one thing to another, *I turn my attention* to.

ἀπόβλητος, *worthy to be cast away, worthless.*

ἀποβολή, *a casting away, a loss.*

ἀπογίνομαι (denascor) (opposite of γίνομαι : therefore, *I go out of being, I cease to be*), with the dat., *I die away from.*

ἀπογραφή, *an enrolment, a census-taking,* in which particulars not only of the persons but also of their property were generally given on the census-papers. The system began 10-9 B.C., and such an enrolment took place every fourteen years.

ἀπογράφομαι, *I enrol myself* (for the census); hence Heb. xii 23, in another connexion.

ἀποδείκνυμι, (a) *I show off, display, exhibit,* 1 Cor. iv 9 ; (b) *I make good, demonstrate,* Ac. xxv 7 ; (c) *I make out* (to be so and so), *proclaim* (to be), 2 Thess. ii 4 ; (d) *I designate, nominate, appoint,* Ac. ii 22.

ἀπόδειξις, *display, exhibition* (abstr.) ; the ordinary sense is *proof.*

ἀποδεκατεύω, *I take off* (*deduct*) *a tenth part* (of my property) (and give it away), *I pay tithe.*

ἀποδεκατόω, (a) as ἀποδεκατεύω ; (b) c. acc. pers. *I take a tenth part from.*

ἀπόδεκτος, *worthy to be received* (*welcomed*), *acceptable, welcome.*

ἀποδέχομαι, *I receive, welcome, entertain* (with hospitality); hence metaph. Ac. ii 41, xxiv 3.

ἀποδημέω (ἀπό *from*, δῆμος *parish*), *I am away from my parish, I am away from home, I am absent.*

ἀπόδημος (see ἀποδημέω), *away from home.*

ἀποδίδωμι (reddo), (a) *I give back, return, restore ;* (b) *I give, render,* as due ; (c) middle, *I sell,* Ac. v 8, &c.

ἀποδιορίζω (*I make a* [*logical*] *distinction*), *I make an* (invidious) *distinction.*

ἀποδοκιμάζω, *I reject after testing* (*examination*), *I disqualify.*

ἀποδοχή (properly *reception, welcome,* of guests), *acceptance, appreciation, approbation.*

ἀπόθεσις, *a putting off, a laying down.*

ἀποθήκη, *a store-house, store-room* for food-stuffs, *a barn*.

ἀποθησαυρίζω, *I store up, treasure up*.

ἀποθλίβω (lit. *I rub*), *I jostle*.

ἀποθνῄσκω, *I am dying* (= obsolete θνῄσκω), Lk. viii 42, 2 Cor. vi 9, Heb. xi 21 : aor. **ἀποθανεῖν**, *to die* : the present is frequentative in 1 Cor. xv 22, Heb. vii 8, x 28, Rev. xiv 13 (different individuals), iterative in 1 Cor. xv 31 (same person), equivalent to the future, John xxi 23, 1 Cor. xv 32.

ἀποκαθιστάνω, ἀποκαθίστημι, *I set up again, I restore to its original position* or *condition*; hence, *I restore, give back*.

ἀποκαλύπτω, *I unveil, reveal* (correlative to μυστήριον, *secret*).

ἀποκάλυψις, *an unveiling, uncovering, revealing*.

ἀποκαραδοκία (perhaps coined by Paul), *eager expectation*.

ἀποκαταλλάσσω, *I reconcile*.

ἀποκατάστασις, *re-establishment, restoration*.

ἀπόκειμαι, *I have been put away, I am stored*.

ἀποκεφαλίζω, *I behead*.

ἀποκλείω, *I shut*.

ἀποκόπτω, (a) *I cut off, I cut loose*; (b) *I emasculate, castrate* (Gal. v 12, where middle = passive, probably).

ἀπόκριμα (rescriptum), *an answer* (of God to the apostle's appeal, preserved in his heart).

ἀποκρίνομαι, *I answer* (either a spoken or an unspoken question): **ἀπεκρίθην**, &c. (absent from papyri after second cent. B.C.), are borrowed by N.T. from LXX : **ἀπεκρινάμην**, *I uttered solemnly*, Lk. iii 16, John v 17, 19, Ac. iii 12 ; *I replied* in a court of law, Mt. xxvii 12, Mk. xiv 61, Lk. xxiii 9 (cf. John v 11 v. l.).

ἀπόκρισις (rare in N.T. times), *answering, answer*.

ἀποκρύπτω, *I hide away, conceal*.

ἀπόκρυφος, *hidden away, secret*.

ἀποκτείνω, ἀποκτέννω, ἀποκτεννύω (absent from papyri of N.T. times), *I kill*.

ἀποκυέω, *I bring forth, give birth to* (a child), a medical or physical word, marking the close of pregnancy.

ἀποκυλίω, *I roll* (trans.) *away from.*

ἀπολαμβάνω, (a) *I get back, I receive back*; (b) *I get* (*receive*) *as due* (*deserved*); (c) middle, *I draw aside, separate*, Mk. vii 33.

ἀπόλαυσις, *the faculty* or *experience of enjoyment.*

ἀπολείπω, *I leave behind*: in Heb. iv 6 ἀπολείπεται is impers. (= restat), *it remains.*

ἀπόλλυμι, (a) *I destroy*; (b) *I lose*: (mid.) *I am perishing* (the resultant death being viewed as certain).

Ἀπολλύων (properly pres. pcpl. of ἀπολλύω, cf. ἀπόλλυμι), *The Destroying One*, a Greek translation of the Hebr. *Abaddon.*

Ἀπολλωνία, *Apollonia*, a city of Macedonia.

Ἀπολλώς (Ἀπολλῶς) (a pet, familiar form of Ἀπολλώνιος), *Apollos*, a Jew of Alexandria.

ἀπολογέομαι, *I give a defence, I defend myself* (especially in a law court): it can take an obj. of what is said in defence.

ἀπολογία, *a defence* (particularly in a law court).

ἀπολούω, *I wash off*; mid. *I wash away* (my sins, in baptism).

ἀπολύτρωσις, *ransoming, deliverance, liberation* (from captivity), *ransoming away, emancipation, manumission* (of a slave by his master) (the idea of payment, though originally present, seems wholly to have disappeared in N.T.).

ἀπολύω (dimitto), *I let loose, set free, release, permit to depart*: middle, *I withdraw myself, depart*, Ac. xxviii 25.

ἀμομάσσομαι, *I wipe off myself* (on to another).

ἀπονέμω, *I apportion, render* (as due).

ἀπονίπτω, *I wash dirt off.*

ἀποπίπτω, *I fall away* (from), *I fall off.*

ἀποπλανάω, *I cause to wander astray*: 1 Tim. vi 10 (aor. pass.), *I have wandered away.*

ἀποπλέω, *I sail away.*

ἀποπνίγω, (a) *I choke, drown*; (b) *I stop the growth of.*

ἀπορέω

ἀπορέω (lit. *I lose the way*), esp. in mid., *I am in difficulties, I am at my wits' end.*

ἀπορία, *state of difficulty, distress.*

ἀπορίπτω, *I throw away* from, *I throw overboard.*

ἀπορφανίζω, *I separate from* some one.

ἀποσκίασμα, either *a shadow cast* by an object, or *a faint image* or *copy* of an object.

ἀποσπάω, lit. *I wrench away from, I drag away*; but perhaps sometimes in the well-attested weakened sense, *I withdraw.*

ἀποστασία, *a revolting, revolt,* especially religious *apostasy.*

ἀποστάσιον, *divorce.*

ἀποστεγάζω, *I unroof, take the roof off.*

ἀποστέλλω, *I send away, commission*; *I put forth*, Mk. iv 29.

ἀποστερέω, *I deprive* one *of* something, *I rob*; absol. in Mk. x 19 (1 Cor. vii 5).

ἀποστολή, *commission, duty of* ἀπόστολος (*apostle*), *apostle-ship.*

ἀπόστολος, *a messenger, an envoy, a delegate,* one commissioned by another to represent him in some way, especially a man sent out by Jesus Christ Himself to preach the Gospel, *an apostle.*

ἀποστοματίζω (literary, from ἀπὸ στόματος), *I draw out* by questioning.

ἀποστρέφω (seems mostly literary) (trans.), (a) *I turn away* (*from*); (b) (mid.) *I turn myself away from*; (c) (metaph.) *I pervert*, Lk. xxiii 14.

ἀποστυγέω, *I shrink from* (with horror).

ἀποσυνάγωγος, *away from the synagogue, expelled the synagogue, excommunicated.*

ἀποτάσσομαι, *I give parting instructions; I say farewell* (*good-bye*), *I take leave.*

ἀποτελέω, *I complete, accomplish*, Lk. xiii 32; *I form fully*, James i 15.

ἀποτίθεμαι, *I put off* (*away*), *cast off* (*away*) *from myself*; hence, *I put, store* (in).

ἀποτινάσσω, *I shake off.*

34

ἀποτίνω, *I repay, pay what is due* (by way of punishment or fine).

ἀποτολμάω (literary), *I break out boldly.*

ἀποτομία (lit. *sheerness*, of a rock), *peremptoriness, inexorableness, harshness, severity.*

ἀποτόμως, *sharply, severely.*

ἀποτρέπομαι, *I turn myself away from.*

ἀπουσία, *absence.*

ἀποφέρω, *I carry, bear away* (sometimes with violence, as Mk. xv 1).

ἀποφεύγω, *I flee from.*

ἀποφθέγγομαι, *I utter forth, speak out.*

ἀποφορτίζομαι, *I discharge my cargo.*

ἀπόχρησις, *using up.*

ἀποχωρέω, *I go away, depart.*

ἀποχωρίζομαι, *I separate myself from.*

ἀποψύχω, *I faint* or *I die.*

Ἄππιος, *Appius* (censor 312 B. C.), after whom the township *Appi Forum* on the Appian Way, 43 Roman miles from Rome, was named.

ἀπρόσιτος, *unapproachable.*

ἀπρόσκοπος, (*free from hurt* or *harm*, hence) *not offending, not causing offence, blameless.*

ἀπροσωπολήμπτως (literary and Jewish), *without any preference* (*undue favour, partiality*) *for a person.*

ἄπταιστος (literary and rare), *not stumbling.*

ἄπτω, (a) act. *I light, kindle* ; (b) mid. c. gen. *I lay hold of, I cling to* (eagerly).

Ἀπφία, Ἀφφία, *Apphia*, a Christian lady of Colossae, either wife or sister of Philemon.

ἀπωθέομαι, *I push* (*thrust*) *away from myself.*

ἀπώλεια, *destruction, ruin, loss.*

Ἀρ (rather Ἁρ), *Ar, Har*, only in the combined expression Ἁρ Μαγεδών, Hebr. *har mᵉgiddōn*, 'the hill of Megiddo.' In the neighbourhood of Megiddo the sovereignty of Palestine was often decided by battle. Hence name transferred to the place of the decisive battle on the Day of Judgement.

ἄρα, an inferential particle, *then, therefore* : found also in combination with other particles, such as γε and οὖν, &c. ; εἰ ἄρα (si forte), *if perchance*, Mk. xi 13, &c.

ἆρα (num, numquid, numquidnam), a particle asking a question, to which a negative answer is expected.

ἀρά, *cursing, a curse.*

Ἀραβία, *Arabia*, the district south of Palestine.

Ἀράμ (Hebr.), *Aram*, son of Esrom and father of Aminadab.

ἄραφος, *without seam.*

Ἄραψ, *an Arabian.*

ἀργέω, *I am idle* (*unemployed, without occupation*) (generally, outside N.T., of necessity, and not blame-worthily).

ἀργός, (a) *idle, lazy* ; (b) *thoughtless*, Mt. xii 36.

ἀργύρεος (contracted ἀργυροῦς), *made of silver, silvern.*

ἀργύριον, *a piece of silver-money* (except 1 Cor. iii 12, where *silver*).

ἀργυροκόπος (*silver-cutter*, literally), *a silversmith.*

ἄργυρος (rare in papyri), *silver* as a metal (except Mt. x 9, where *silver used as money*).

Ἄρειος Πάγος (lit. *Hill of Ares* [the Athenian war-god, corresponding to Mars]), *the Areopagus*, a hill in Athens. As on this hill the Council of the Areo-pagus (ἡ ἐξ Ἀρείου Πάγου βουλή), the supreme court of Athens, had met in early times, the expression ὁ Ἄρειος Πάγος came to be used (as in Ac. xvii 19, 22) for the *Council of the Areopagus*, wheresoever it met.

Ἀρεοπαγίτης, *member of the Council of the Areopagus, an Areopagite.*

ἀρέσκεια, *pleasing, willing service.*

ἀρέσκω, *I please*, with the idea of willing service rendered to others ; hence almost *I serve.*

ἀρεστός, *pleasing, satisfactory, acceptable.*

Ἀρέτας (Ἀρέτας, for Ἀρέθας, Arabic Ḥārilā), *Aretas*, Aretas IV, King of the Nabataeans.

ἀρετή (uirtus, a word of wide significance in non-

Christian ethics), *excellence*, particularly *moral excellence*; *manifestation of power*, 2 Pet. i 3.

(ἀρήν), *a lamb*: acc. pl. ἄρνας (Lk. x 3); the nom. (= ϝαρήν) is found only in early times, and its place is taken by ἀρνίον.

ἀριθμέω, *I number, count.*

ἀριθμός, *a number, total.*

Ἀριμαθαία, *Arimathaea*, a place in Palestine, identical with Ramathaim, the birthplace of Samuel. Originally part of Samaria, it with its surrounding district was united to Judaea under the Maccabees.

Ἀρίσταρχος, *Aristarchus*, a Christian, belonging to Thessalonica in Macedonia.

ἀριστάω, *I breakfast.*

ἀριστερός, *on the left hand*: ἡ ἀριστερά (understand χείρ), Mt. vi 3; ἐξ ἀριστερῶν, *on the left hand.*

Ἀριστόβουλος, *Aristobulus*, a Christian in Rome.

ἄριστον, *breakfast.*

ἀρκετός (rare), *sufficient.*

ἀρκέω, (a) act. *I am sufficient, I suffice*; impers. John xiv 8; (b) mid. c. dat. *I am content, satisfied (with).*

ἄρκος (a later form of ἄρκτος), *a bear.*

ἅρμα, *a chariot.*

Ἀρμαγεδών, see Ἁρ.

ἁρμόζομαι, *I fit, join* (the middle indicating deep personal interest).

ἁρμός, *a joint* of the body.

Ἀρνεί (Hebr.), *Arnei*, son of Esrom, and father of Admein.

ἀρνέομαι, (a) *I deny* (a statement); (b) *I repudiate* (a person, or belief).

ἀρνίον (originally, *a little lamb*, but diminutive force was lost), *a lamb*: see ἀρήν.

ἄρνας, see ἀρήν.

ἀροτριάω, *I plough.*

ἄροτρον, *a plough.*

ἁρπαγή, *robbery, robbing.*

ἁρπαγμός, either (a) *snatching, robbery, the action of*

37

αρπάζω

plundering, rapacity, self-aggrandizement, or (b) *a thing to be snatched, plunder, prey, booty, a prize, spoil.*

ἁρπάζω, *I seize, snatch, obtain by robbery.*

ἅρπαξ, *snatching, robbing, greedy*: subst. *swindler, extortioner,* 1 Cor. v 10.

ἀρραβών (ἀραβών, a word of Semitic origin) (arra), *an earnest, earnest-money,* a large part of the payment, given in advance as a security that the whole will be paid afterwards.

ἄρραφος, see ἄραφος.

ἄρρην, see ἄρσην.

ἄρρητος, *not to be uttered* (because too sacred), *secret.*

ἄρρωστος, *infirm* ; *sick, ill.*

ἀρσενοκοίτης, *a paederast.*

ἄρσην (ἄρρην), *male.*

Ἀρτεμᾶς (a pet form of Ἀρτεμίδωρος), *Artemas,* a Christian in Rome.

Ἄρτεμις, *Artemis,* a goddess, worshipped principally at Ephesus, typifying fertility (she had no relation with the other Artemis, the maiden huntress, to whom corresponded the Latin Diana).

ἀρτέμων, *a foresail,* set on the bow.

ἄρτι (of present time). *now, just now.*

ἀρτιγέννητος, *newly begotten, newly born.*

ἄρτιος, *perfect.*

ἄρτος, *bread, a loaf.*

ἀρτύω, *I season.*

Ἀρφαξάδ (Hebr.), *Arphaxad,* son of Shem, and father of Cainam.

ἀρχάγγελος, *a ruler of angels, a superior angel, an archangel.*

ἀρχαῖος, *original, primitive*; *ancient,* Mt. v 21, &c.

Ἀρχέλαος, *Archelaus,* Herod Archelaus, son and successor of Herod I, reigned over Judaea from 4 B.C. to A.D. 6 and died before A.D. 18.

ἀρχή, (a) *rule* (kingly or magisterial); (b) plur., in a quasi-personal sense, almost *rulers, magistrates,* Tit.

ἀσέλγεια

iii 1 ; (c) *beginning* : in the very difficult John viii 25 τὴν ἀρχήν would naturally mean *originally*, but the passage is not yet explained.

ἀρχηγός (auctor), *originator, author, founder.*

ἀρχιερατικός, *high priestly, to which the chief priest belongs.*

ἀρχιερεύς, *high priest, chief priest.*

ἀρχιποίμην, *chief shepherd.*

Ἄρχιππος, *Archippus*, a Christian of Colossae.

ἀρχισυνάγωγος, *a leader of the synagogue,* a leading man (or woman) connected with the synagogue : sometimes there was only one, and the name was in some cases merely honorary.

ἀρχιτέκτων, *master-builder.*

ἀρχιτελώνης, *head of a custom-house, chief tax gatherer.*

ἀρχιτρίκλινος (arbiter bibendi), *master of ceremonies* at a dinner, *master of the feast.*

ἄρχω, (1) act. c. gen. *I rule* ; (2) mid. *I begin* ; sometimes in this sense the word is otiose, being merely an imitation of O.T. language or a literal translation of Hebrew or Aramaic, e. g. repeatedly in the Synoptic Gospels, and particularly in Mk., Lk. iii 8, &c.

ἄρχων, *a ruler, governor, leader, leading man* ; with the Jews, *an official member* (*a member of the executive*) of the γερουσία.

ἄρωμα, *spice.*

ἀσάλευτος, *unshaken, immovable.*

Ἀσάφ (Hebr.), *Asaph, Asa,* son of Abijah and father of Jehoshaphat, king of Judah about 900 B.C. for 41 years.

ἄσβεστος, *inextinguishable, unquenchable.*

ἀσέβεια, *impiety, irreverence.*

ἀσεβέω, (a) intr. *I am impious, irreverent* ; (b) tr. *I do impiously.*

ἀσεβής, *impious, irreverent, irreligious.*

ἀσέλγεια (*outrageous conduct* ; *conduct shocking to public decency* ; *a wanton violence*), *wantonness, lewdness.*

39

ἄσημος

ἄσημος (lit. *unmarked, unstamped*), *undistinguished, obscure.*

Ἀσήρ (Hebr.), *Asher,* one of the sons of Jacob, and founder of one of the Twelve Tribes.

ἀσθένεια, *want of strength, weakness, illness.*

ἀσθενέω, *I am weak* (physically : then morally), *I am sick.*

ἀσθένημα, *weakness.*

ἀσθενής (lit. *not strong*), (a) *weak* (physically, or morally); (b) *ill.*

Ἀσία (prouincia Asia), *the Roman province Asia,* roughly the western third of Asia Minor.

Ἀσιανός, *belonging to the Roman province Asia.*

Ἀσιάρχης, *Asiarch,* an official connected with the worship of Rome and the Emperor in the Roman province Asia.

ἀσιτία, either *lack of corn, lack of food* (the lit. meaning), or *abstinence from food, loss of appetite, sea-sickness* (the extended meaning).

ἄσιτος, either *without corn, without food,* or *sea-sick.*

ἀσκέω, *I train, practise, exercise.*

ἀσκός, *a wine-skin.*

ἀσμένως, *joyfully, with delight.*

ἄσοφος, *unskilled, unwise, foolish.*

ἀσπάζομαι (saluto, a term regularly used at the end of a letter), *I greet, salute; I pay my respects to,* Ac. xxv 13.

ἀσπασμός (very rare in papyri), *a greeting, salutation.*

ἄσπιλος, *unstained, undefiled.*

ἀσπίς, *an asp* (*hooded-snake, cobra da capello*).

ἄσπονδος, *untrue to one's promise.*

ἀσσάριον (assarius, dimin. of as), *a penny* ($\frac{1}{16}$ of a δηνάριον and the tenth part of a drachma or franc).

ἆσσον (compar. of ἄγχι adv.), *nearer.*

Ἄσσος, *Assos,* a port of Mysia, in the Roman province Asia.

ἀστατέω, *I am unsettled, have no place of abode, lead a vagabond life.*

ἀστεῖος (lit. *belonging to the city* : then *witty, clever*), *elegant, pretty, fair, fine.*

ἀστήρ, *a star.*

ἀστήρικτος (rather literary) (lit. *unpropped*), *unsteady, unstable.*

ἄστοργος, *unloving, devoid of affection.*

ἀστοχέω, *I miss the mark, miss my aim, make a false aim.*

ἀστραπή, *a flash of lightning.*

ἀστράπτω, *I flash,* (with, then like, lightning).

ἄστρον, *a star.*

ἀσύμφωνος, *inharmonious, disagreeing.*

ἀσύνετος (insipiens, non intellegens, Ambros. *expos. in ps. cxviii* **20** 55 § 2), *unintelligent, without wisdom, unwise, undiscerning* (implying probably moral defect, like ἀμαθής sometimes in classical Greek).

ἀσύνθετος, *not covenanting, untrue to an agreement, treacherous.*

Ἀσύνκριτος, *Asyncritus,* a Christian in Rome.

ἀσφάλεια, *safety* ; *security, reliability,* Lk. i 4.

ἀσφαλής (lit. *unfailing*), *safe, reliable, trustworthy.*

ἀσφαλίζω, *I make safe* (*secure, fast*).

ἀσφαλῶς, *securely.*

ἀσχημονέω, *I am unseemly, I behave unbecomingly* (or even *dishonourably*); perhaps, *I consider* (something) *unseemly.*

ἀσχημοσύνη, *unseemly behaviour, indecency,* or concrete, *an indecent* (*lewd*) *act.*

ἀσχήμων, *unseemly, indecent.*

ἀσωτία, *wantonness, profligacy.*

ἀσώτως, *prodigally* : ζῶν ἀσώτως, *with prodigal living* (Field).

ἀτακτέω (lit. *I march out of order* ; then *I riot, I rebel*), *I am disorderly, I neglect my duty, I am careless* (or *idle*) *in habits.*

ἄτακτος (lit. *out of order*), *disorderly, slack* (in performance of duty).

ἀτάκτως, *in a disorderly manner* (see ἄτακτος, ἀτακτέω).

ἄτεκνος, *childless.*

41

あてにいぞ

ἀτενίζω

ἀτενίζω, *I direct my gaze, I look steadily.*
ἄτερ (originally poetical), *apart from, without.*
ἀτιμάζω, *I disgrace, treat disgracefully, dishonour, insult; I despise.*
ἀτιμία, *disgrace, dishonour.*
ἄτιμος, *unhonoured, without honour, unesteemed.*
ἀτμίς, (a) *breath*; (b) *steam, vapour.*
ἄτομος (lit. *that cannot be cut*), an indivisible part of time, *a second.*
ἄτοπος (lit. *out of place, unusual, unbecoming*), *improper, unrighteous, perverse, froward:* almost = *evil,* Ac. xxviii 6.
Ἀττάλεια, *Attalia,* the port of Perga in Pamphylia.
αὐγάζω, *I flash, gleam, appear white, bright* (as in LXX), but perhaps, *I see, I see clearly* (as in classical poetry).
αὐγή, *light (of day).*
Αὔγουστος, *Augustus,* a title conferred on the first Roman Emperor, C. Iulius Octauianus, denoting sanctity (almost divinity); grecized as **Σεβαστός** (q. v.).
αὐθάδης, *self-satisfied*; hence *arrogant.*
αὐθαίρετος, *of one's own accord.*
αὐθεντέω (a colloquial word, from **αὐθέντης**, ʻ master ʼ, ʻ autocrat ʼ [= αὐτός + root *sen*, ʻ accomplish ʼ, in ἀνύω]), *I domineer over.*
αὐλέω, *I play the flute.*
αὐλή, *court-yard, fore-court*; but it may be understood as *palace, house,* e. g. Mt. xxvi 3.
αὐλητής, *a flute-player.*
αὐλίζομαι, *I bivouac, I pass the night.*
αὐλός, *a flute.*
αὐξάνω (**αὔξω**), (a) tr. (augeo) *I cause to increase*; (b) intr. (cresco) *I increase, grow*; with cogn. acc. Col. ii 19.
αὔξησις, *increasing, increase, growth.*
αὔξω, see **αὐξάνω**.
αὔριον, *to-morrow.*
αὐστηρός (tristis), *grim, severe; strict, exacting.*

42

αφεσις

αὐτάρκεια, *self-sufficiency, independence.*

αὐτάρκης, *self-sufficient, independent, contented* (a literary use).

αὐτοκατάκριτος (perhaps a new coinage), *self-condemned.*

αὐτόματος, *of its own accord.*

αὐτόπτης, *eye-witness.*

αὐτός (fem. αὐτή, neut. αὐτό), (a) *he*, &c. ; (b) *self*; e. g. αὐτός ὁ, &c. (ipse ille), *the very*, but often weakened to mean simply *that*; αὐτός = αὐτόματος, *of his own accord*, John xvi 27 ; (c) ὁ αὐτὸς (idem), &c., *the same.* Parts of αὐτός are sometimes added pleonastically to the relative pronoun (colloquial) (where the usage is not due to inferior culture, it is due to translation-Greek), cf. Mk. vii 25 ; αὐτοῦ, adv., *there* ; ἐπὶ τὸ αὐτό, κατὰ τὸ αὐτό, *together.*

αὐτοῦ = ἑαυτοῦ, of altogether uncertain existence in N.T.

αὐτοῦ (adv.), see αὐτός.

αὐτόφωρος (αὐτός and φώρ, *a thief*) ; ἐπ' αὐτοφώρῳ (flagrante delicto), *in the act.*

αὐτόχειρ (probably exclusively literary), *with one's own hand.*

αὐχέω (mostly in poetry), *I speak with proud confidence of, I boast of.*

αὐχμηρός (poetical, lit. *dry and parched*; then *squalid and rough*), *dingy, dusky, obscure, dark, funereal.*

ἀφαιρέω, *I take away.*

ἀφανής, *invisible.*

ἀφανίζω, *I cause to disappear, hide, remove; I disfigure* (probably by leaving unwashed for a long period), Mt. vi 16.

ἀφανισμός, *disappearing, disappearance.*

ἄφαντος (originally poetical), *disappearing, invisible, hidden.*

ἀφεδρών, *a drain, latrine.*

ἀφειδία (lit. *unsparingness*), *severe treatment.*

ἀφελότης, *simplicity.*

ἄφεσις (from ἀφίημι) (remissio), *a sending away, a let-*

ting go, a release; hence (cf. in inscriptions, *remission* from debt or punishment), *remission, forgiveness*.

ἀφή, *a band, fastening* (hence, possibly, *a ligament*).

ἀφθαρσία, *indestructibility, incorruptibility*; hence *immortality*.

ἄφθαρτος, *indestructible, imperishable, incorruptible*; hence *immortal*.

ἀφθορία, (*moral*) *incorruptness, incorruption, purity, freedom from taint*.

ἀφίημι, (a) *I send away*; (b) *I let go* or *away, release, permit to depart*; (c) *I remit, forgive*; (d) *I permit*, followed by the subjunctive with (or without) ἵνα, or with acc. obj. and infin.; ἄφες ἐκβάλω (Mt. vii 4 = Lk. vi 42), *let me (allow me to) cast out*: so also Mt. xxvii 49 = Mk. xv 36, John xii 7.

ἀφικνέομαι (in ordinary use very rare at this time), *I arrive, reach.*

ἀφιλάγαθος, *not loving that which is good.*

ἀφιλάργυρος, *not loving money, not avaricious.*

ἄφιξις, *departure.* (This is the sense required by Ac. xx 29, but as the word comes from ἀφικνέομαι, it ought to mean *arrival.* No certain parallel (except Josephus, *Antiq.* ii 18 fin., where = *departure* or *journey*) for this change of sense has been found.)

ἀφίστημι (a) 1 aor. tr. *I made to stand away, I drew away*, Ac. v 37; *I repelled*; (b) other tenses of act., and mid. *I take up a position away from, I withdraw from, I leave.*

ἄφνω, *suddenly.*

ἀφόβως (literary), *fearlessly.*

ἀφομοιόω, *I make like to.*

ἀφοράω (cf. ἀποβλέπω), *I look away from (something else) to*: ἀφίδω, Phil. ii 23, aspirated from ἀπίδω by analogy with ἀφοράω.

ἀφορίζω, *I rail off, I separate, I place apart.*

ἀφορμή (a) *a starting, a start*; (b) *cause, occasion, opportunity.*

ἀφρίζω, *I foam* (at the mouth).

ἀφρός, *foam* (at the mouth).

ἀφροσύνη, *want of sense, foolishness.*

ἄφρων, *senseless, foolish, inconsiderate.*

ἀφυπνόω (very rare), *I fall asleep.*

ἀφυστερέω, *I withdraw, take away.*

ἄφωνος, *soundless, voiceless, speechless, dumb.*

Ἄχαζ (Ἄχας) (Hebr.), *Achaz*, son of Joatham and father of Hezekiah.

Ἀχαΐα, *the Roman Province Achaia*, governed by a proconsul, and practically conterminous with modern Greece before 1912.

Ἀχαϊκός, *Achaicus*, a Corinthian Christian.

ἀχάριστος, *ungrateful.*

Ἀχείμ (Hebr.), *Acheim*, son of Zadok and father of Eliud.

ἀχειροποίητος (unknown outside N.T.), *not made by hand, not handmade.*

Ἀχελδαμάχ (Aram.), *Acheldamach*, the place where Judas Iscariot committed suicide.

ἀχλύς, *mist.*

ἀχρεῖος, *unprofitable, useless, unworthy.*

ἀχρεόομαι (earlier ἀχρειόομαι) (lit. *I become sour, I turn*, of milk), *I am good for nothing.*

ἄχρηστος, *unprofitable, useless* (a play upon words, with ὀνήσιμος).

ἄχρι, ἄχρις, *as far as, up to, until* ; ἄχρι τοῦ νῦν = adhuc ; ἄχρι οὗ (with or without ἄν) with the subjunctive, *until.*

ἄχυρον, *chaff.*

ἀψευδής, *not guilty of falsehood, truthful.*

ἄψινθος, *wormwood* ; ὁ Ἄψινθος, a star.

ἄψυχος, *lifeless.*

B

Βάαλ (Bahal, properly *Lord*, and so not a proper name), *Baal*, a god worshipped by the Hebrews (in Rom. xi 4 fem., because Jews in reading substituted αἰσχύνη), being the highest god of all the West-Semitic peoples.

Βαβυλών, (a) *Babylon*, the ancient city on the
Euphrates, to which the people of Jerusalem, &c.,
were transported; (b) hence allegorically of Rome,
from the point of view of the Christian people:
Rev. (6 times), 1 Pet. v 13 (probably).

βαθμός, *a step* (of a stairway); hence, *a stage* in a career,
a position.

βάθος (a) *depth*; (b) *a depth, a deep* (also met.).

βαθύνω, *I deepen*.

βαθύς, *deep* (lit. and met.); ὄρθρου βαθέως, *in the depths of
the early morning, while still very early*.

βαΐον, *a palm branch*.

Βαλαάμ (Hebr.) (Balaham), *Balaam*, son of Beor of
Pethor on the Euphrates, a soothsayer in the Old
Testament.

Βαλάκ (Hebr.), *Balac, Balak*, son of Zippor, King of Moab.

βαλλάντιον, *a purse*.

βάλλω (a) *I cast, throw*; intr. *I rush*, Ac. xxvii 14; (b)
often, in the weaker sense (cf. mitto), *I place, put,
drop*; βεβλημένος, *lying in bed*, Mt. viii 14.

βαπτίζω, lit. *I dip, submerge*, but specifically of ceremonial dipping (whether immersion or affusion), *I
baptize*; when the preposition εἰς with a noun in the
accus. follows, it appears to indicate that through
this ceremony the baptized person becomes the
property of the person indicated after εἰς: met.
Mk. x 38.

βάπτισμα, *a dipping, a baptism*: c. gen. μετανοίας, belonging to a change of mental attitude, sign of a change
of mental attitude.

βαπτισμός, *dipping, washing* (of a ceremonial character).

βαπτιστής, *the baptizer, the baptist*, epithet used only of
John, the son of Zechariah and Elizabeth, forerunner
of Jesus.

βάπτω, (a) *I dip*; (b) *I dye*; Rev. xix 13, cf. **δίβαφα**,
twice-dyed garments.

Βαραββᾶς, *Barabbas* (really *Jesus Barabbas*, according
to certain MSS. of Mt. xxvii 17), a highway robber.

Βαράκ (Hebr.), *Barak*, one of the Judges of Israel.

Βαραχίας (Hebr.), *Barachias, Baruch.* His identity is uncertain, perhaps father of the Zacharias killed by the Zealots in the last Jewish War (Josephus, *B.J.* iv 5. 4). See **Ζαχαρίας.**

βάρβαρος, *a foreigner,* one who speaks neither Greek nor Latin : as adj. *foreign.*

βαρέω, *I weight, load, burden,* lit. and met.

βαρέως, *heavily, with difficulty.*

Βαρθολομαῖος (Aram.)(son of Tholmai [= Ptolomaeus]), *Bartholomew,* one of the twelve disciples of Jesus.

Βαριησοῦς (Aram.), *Bar-Jesus* (i. e. son of Jesus), the name of the magician and false prophet at Paphos in Cyprus. He is also called *Elymas.*

Βαριωνᾶς (Aram.), *Bar-jonas,* son of Jonas, the surname of Simon Peter.

Βαρνάβας (Aram.) (son of Nebo), *Barnabas,* a Cypriote Jew, uncle of John Mark ; his other name was Joseph.

βάρος, *a weight, a burden,* lit. or met.: in 1 Thess. ii 7 there may be a play on the derived sense, *authority, dignity.*

Βαρσαββᾶς (Aram.), *Barsabbas,* son of Sabbas, a surname of Joseph (Ac. i 23) and Judas (Ac. xv 22).

Βαρτίμαιος (Aram.), *Bartimaeus,* son of (?) Timaeus.

βαρύς, *heavy, weighty, burdensome,* lit. and met.

βαρύτιμος, *heavy in price, very expensive.*

βασανίζω, *I torture.*

βασανισμός, *torture.*

βασανιστής, *a torturer.*

βάσανος, *torture.*

βασιλεία, *kingship, sovereignty, authority, rule,* especially of God, both in the world, and in the hearts of men ; hence *kingdom,* in the concrete sense ; ἡ βασιλεία τῶν οὐρανῶν perhaps always signifies the *coming* kingdom, but ἡ βασιλεία τοῦ θεοῦ is wider.

βασίλειος, (a) in Lk. vii 25 either masc. *courtiers,* or neut. *palaces*; (b) the LXX intended **βασίλειον** as subst., *a body of kings,* in the passage quoted by

1 Pet. ii 9, but Peter clearly takes βασίλειον as adj., *royal*.

βασιλεύς, *a king*, but in some passages, as 1 Pet. ii 17, clearly to be translated *emperor* : ὁ βασιλεὺς τῶν βασιλέων (βασιλευόντων), *the King of Kings*, an oriental type of phrase, used for the Persian king as overlord of other kings, and in scripture of God.

βασιλεύω, (a) *I rule, reign* ; (b) *I reign over*, c. gen.

βασιλικός, *connected with a king, royal, regal* ; in James ii 8 βασιλικὸς νόμος, a supreme law is referred to, the more important parts of the law : substantivally (a) *an officer in the service of the king* (Herod Antipas), John iv 46, 49 ; (b) ἡ βασιλική (sc. χώρα), *the king's country*, Ac. xii 20.

βασίλισσα, *a queen*.

βάσις (properly, that on which something may rest), *a foot*.

βασκαίνω, *I give the evil eye to, fascinate, bewitch, overpower*.

βαστάζω, (a) *I carry, bear* ; (b) *I carry (take) away*, Mt. iii 11, John xx 15 ; *I pilfer*, John xii 6.

βάτος, *a thorn-bush* : ἐπὶ τοῦ (Lk. τῆς) βάτου, *in the passage about the thorn-bush*, Mk. xii 26, Lk. xx 37.

βάτος (Hebr.), *a batus*, a liquid measure among the Jews, containing 72 sextarii, that is, between eight and nine gallons.

βάτραχος, *a frog*.

βατταλογέω, *I chatter, am long-winded, utter empty words*.

βδέλυγμα, *an abominable thing, an accursed thing*.

βδελυκτός, *abominable, detestable*.

βδελύσσομαι, *I abominate, detest*.

βέβαιος, *firm, stedfast, enduring*.

βεβαιόω, *I confirm, ratify*.

βεβαίωσις, *confirmation, ratification, establishment*.

βέβηλος, *profane, secular* ; *unspiritual, godless, worldly*, Heb. xii 16.

βεβηλόω, *I profane*.

48

Βεεζεβούλ, Βεελζεβούλ, *Beezebul, Beelzebul,* a name of uncertain derivation, the chief of evil spirits among the Jews. The form Beelzebub = god of Flies at Ekron (2 Kings i 2, 3): the better attested form perhaps = the Phoenician Sungod as lord of the heavenly dwelling.

Βελίαρ (originally a Hebrew word = *uselessness, corruption*), *Beliar* (spelt sometimes Belial, Beliab), a demon, among the Jews, and in fact a name for Satan.

βελόνη, *a needle.*

βέλος, *a missile, dart.*

βέλτιον (very rare in this period), an adverb, comparative in form, superlative in meaning, *best.*

Βενιαμείν (Hebr.), *Benjamin,* youngest son of Jacob, founder of one of the twelve tribes of Israel.

Βερνίκη, *Berenice* (Lat.), (born A.D. 29) daughter of Agrippa I and Kypros, and sister of M. Iulius Agrippa II, in whose company she appears, Ac. xxv, xxvi.

Βέροια, *Beroea,* a town of the province Macedonia.

Βεροιαῖος, *belonging to Beroea, Beroean.*

Βεώρ (Hebr.), *Beor,* father of Balaam. (The v.l. Βόσορ has no authority in LXX, and is probably due to textual corruption here).

Βηθαβαρά, *Bethabara,* one reading in John i 28. If the place existed, it was on E. side of Jordan, see **Βηθανία.**

Βηθανία, (a) *Bethany,* the home of Lazarus, Martha, and Mary, near Jerusalem; (b) *Bethany,* beyond Jordan, the reading with the strongest attestation in John i 28, see **Βηθαβαρά.**

Βηθεσδά, see **Βηθζαθά.**

Βηθζαθά, *Bethzatha* (= House of Olives), name of a pool in Jerusalem. (But there is great doubt as to the real form: see G. A. Smith, *Jerusalem,* vol. ii, pp. 564 ff.; J. R. Harris, *Side-Lights on New Testament Research,* lecture ii; F. C. Burkitt, *The Syriac Forms of New Testament Proper Names,* pp. 19 ff.)

Βηθλεέμ

Βηθλεέμ, *Bethlehem,* a town of Judaea.

Βηθσαϊδά, *Bethsaida,* a city of Galilee.

Βηθφαγή, *Bethphage,* a village in the neighbourhood of Jerusalem, on the Mt. of Olives.

βῆμα (from root of ἔβην, *I went*), (a) βῆμα ποδός, the space covered by a step of the foot; (b) *tribunal.*

βήρυλλος, *a beryl,* a precious stone of various colours, the best known being sea-green.

βία, *force.*

βιάζομαι, (a) mid. *I use force, I force my way, I come forward violently,* cf. Mt. xi 12 (where perhaps pass.); (b) pass. *I am forcibly treated.*

βίαιος, *strong, violent.*

βιαστής, *a forceful, violent man.*

βιβλαρίδιον, *a little papyrus roll.*

βιβλίον (libellus, originally a diminutive), *a papyrus roll*: ἀποστασίου, document of divorce, handed by the husband to the wife whom he divorces: ζωῆς, of life, preserved in heaven and containing the names of those who share in [eternal] life.

βίβλος (liber), *a papyrus roll,* with a sacred connotation: ζωῆς, see βιβλίον, which had almost ousted it.

βιβρώσκω, *I eat.*

Βιθυνία, *Bithynia,* a Roman province, NW. of Asia Minor and SW. of the Black Sea.

βίος (uictus), (a) *life*; (b) *manner of life*; *livelihood.*

βιόω, *I live.*

βίωσις, *manner of life.*

βιωτικός, *belonging to ordinary life,* with somewhat contemptuous attitude.

βλαβερός, *injurious.*

βλάπτω, *I injure.*

βλαστάνω, βλαστάω, intr. *I sprout*: tr. *I cause to sprout, make to grow up,* James v 18.

Βλάστος, *Blastus,* chamberlain of King Herod Agrippa I.

βλασφημέω, *I speak evil against, I use abusive* or *scurrilous language about* (God or men).

βλασφημία, *abusive* or *scurrilous language*.

βλάσφημος, *abusive, scurrilous*.

βλέμμα, *look*, the faculty of looking.

βλέπω (primarily physical), *I look, see*; βλέποντες βλέψετε, Hebraistic; βλέπειν ἀπό, *to look away from, to beware of*; βλέπειν μή, *to take care lest*; βλέπειν πῶς, *to take care how*: almost *I find*, Rom. vii 23 (cf. 21).

βλητέον (verbal adj. from βάλλω): sc. ἐστίν, *one must put*.

Βοανηργές, *Boanerges*, a doubtful name of doubtful origin and meaning : see my crit. note.

βοάω, *I shout, call aloud*.

Βοές, see Βοός.

βοή, *a shout*.

βοήθεια, (a) abstr., *assistance*; (b) concr. (a technical term of nautical language), *a help*.

βοηθέω, *I come to the rescue of, come to help, help*.

βοηθός, *helper*.

βόθυνος, *a hole in the earth, ditch*.

βολή, *a casting, throw*: in acc. as measure of distance.

βολίζω, *I cast the line* (for sounding), *I sound*.

Βοός, Βοές (Hebr.), *Boos* or *Boes* (*Boaz*), son of Salmon (Sala) and Rahab, husband of Ruth, father of Iobed.

βόρβορος, *a miry dungeon, hole*.

βορρᾶς, *the north wind*, hence *the north*.

βόσκω, *I feed*.

Βοσόρ, *Bosor*, father of Balaam : but see Βεώρ.

βοτάνη, *fodder, food*.

βότρυς, *cluster* (*bunch*) *of grapes*.

βουλεύομαι, *I deliberate, take counsel*.

βουλευτής, *a member of a* βουλή (*city council*), in N. T. of the συνέδριον, Sanhedrin at Jerusalem.

βουλή, *counsel, deliberate wisdom*.

βούλημα, *will, desire*.

βούλομαι, *I will*.

βουνός (tumulus), *a hillock, hill*.

βοῦς, *an ox*.

βραβεῖον, *a prize*.

βραβεύω, *I decide* (in a conflict between contending forces); hence, *I rule, I administer.*

βραδύνω, *I am slow, I delay*: followed by gen., 2 Pet.iii 9.

βραδυπλοέω, *I sail slowly.*

βραδύς, *slow.*

βραδυτής, *tardiness, dilatoriness.*

βραχίων, *arm.*

βραχύς, *little*: mostly in various adverbial phrases, indicating degree or time.

βρέφος, *infant, babe, bantling, child in arms*: ἀπὸ βρέφους, *from babyhood* (cf. a pueris).

βρέχω, (a) *I wet*; (b) *I rain,* having originally the rain-god (Ζεύς, Jupiter) as subject (cf. Mt. v 45 and Latin pluo): thence, of a shower from the sky other than rain, Lk. xvii 29.

βροντή, *thunder.*

βροχή, *a wetting, rain.*

βρόχος, *a noose.*

βρυγμός, *gnashing, crunching.*

βρύχω, *I gnash, crunch.*

βρύω, *I cause to gush forth, send forth.*

βρῶμα, *food.*

βρώσιμος, *eatable, suitable for food.*

βρῶσις, (a) (abstr.) *eating*; (b) *food*; *a meal*, Heb. xii 16; (c) *rust.*

βυθίζω, *I cause to sink.*

βυθός, *the deep sea.*

βυρσεύς, *a tanner.*

βύσσινος, *of fine-linen, of lawn.*

βύσσος (Semitic origin), *fine-linen.* (Some authorities consider *cotton* to be meant; others *silk.*)

βωμός, *an altar.*

Γ

Γαββαθά, *Gabbatha,* i. e. *Gab Baitha,* 'the ridge (back) of the House', i. e. the Aramaic name for what the Greeks called Λιθόστρωτον, a sort of paved square, on which the procurator had his judgement seat.

Γαβριήλ (Hebr.), *Gabriel*, a messenger of God.

γάγγραινα, *a cancerous sore, a cancer*.

Γάδ (Hebr.), *Gad*, one of the twelve tribes of Israel.

Γαδαρηνός, *Gadarene, belonging to Gadara* (an important Hellenized town, one of the Decapolis, and SE. of the Sea of Galilee), see **Γερασηνός, Γεργεσηνός**.

Γάζα, *Gaza* (mod. ṛazze), an old town in the south of Palestine, on the sea-coast.

γάζα (a Persian loan-word), *treasure*.

γαζοφυλάκιον, *treasury*.

Γάϊος, *Gāïus*, (a) a Corinthian, Rom. xvi 23, 1 Cor. i 14; (b) a Macedonian (?), Ac. xix 29; (c) a citizen of Derbe, Ac. xx 4; (d) an Ephesian (?), 3 John 1. It may be that (b) and (c) or even (b), (c), and (d) are identical.

γάλα, *milk*.

Γαλάτης, *a Galatian* (meaning any inhabitant of the Roman *province* Galatia).

Γαλατία, *Galatia*, a large Roman province in central Asia Minor, comprising the districts of Paphlagonia, Pontus Galaticus, Galatia (in the narrower sense, which some still think is intended in the N.T.), Phrygia Galatica, Lycaonia Galatica, Pisidia and Isaurica. In 2 Tim. iv 10 the reference may be to *Gaul*, even if we read Γαλατίαν.

Γαλατικός, *Galatic*, belonging to the province Galatia: τὴν Φρυγίαν καὶ Γαλατικὴν χώραν, Ac. xvi 6, 'the region which is both Phrygian (racially) and Galatic (by administration)'.

γαλήνη, *a calm*.

Γαλιλαία, *Galilee*, a district towards the southern end of the Roman province Syria.

Γαλιλαῖος, *a Galilaean*, an inhabitant of Galilee.

Γαλλία, *Gaul*, a various reading in 2 Tim. iv 10, indicating one of the four provinces called by this name, which together comprised for the most part the territory of modern France.

Γαλλίων, *Gallio*, Lucius Iunius Gallio, who received

this name by adoption into another family, but was born brother of the philosopher Seneca and originally named L. Annaeus Nouatus; proconsul of the Roman province Achaia from spring A. D. 52 to spring 53.

Γαμαλιήλ (Hebr.), *Gamaliel*, a noted Pharisee, teacher of Saul.

γαμέω, *I marry*, used of either sex.

γαμίζω, *I give in marriage* : this sense probably even in 1 Cor. vii 38, where the older view took it as equal to γαμέω.

γαμίσκομαι, *I am given in marriage* (reading doubtful).

γάμος, *a marriage, wedding, wedding-ceremony* : γάμοι (plur.), *a wedding-feast*.

γάρ, *for* (conj.).

γαστήρ, *belly* : often ἐν γαστρὶ ἔχειν, of a woman, *to be pregnant* (lit. *to have* [a child] *in the belly*).

γε, an enclitic, emphasizing particle (quidem), *at least, indeed, really*, but generally too subtle to be represented in English.

Γεδεών (Hebr.), *Gideon*, one of the Judges of Israel.

γέεννα (Aram.), *gehenna*, and originally *gē ben hinnōm* name of a valley or cavity near Jerusalem, Jer. vii 31, 2 Kings xxiii 10, a place underneath the earth, a place of punishment (retributive or purificatory) for evil.

Γεθσημανεί, *Gethsemani*, a small place between the brook Kidron and the Mount of Olives near Jerusalem.

γείτων, *a neighbour*.

γελάω, *I laugh*.

γέλως, *laughter*.

γεμίζω, *I fill, load*.

γέμω, *I am full of*.

γενεά, *a generation* : in combination with another γενεά, or with αἰών, practically indicates infinity of time.

γενεαλογέομαι, *I am put into a genealogy*.

γενεαλογία, *genealogy*.

γενέσια, *birthday-anniversary feast*.

γένεσις, *birth, creation, beginning*.

γενετή, *birth*.

γένημα (from γίνομαι), of vegetable, never of animal, products (contrast γέννημα), *fruit, crop, produce of the earth*.

γεννάω, *I beget* (of the male), more rarely (e. g. Lk. i 13), (of the female) *I bring forth*.

γέννημα (from γεννάω), of animal, never of vegetable, products (contrast γένημα), *offspring, child*.

Γεννησαρέτ, *Gennesaret*, a fertile district by the lake of Tiberias, which was in consequence sometimes called the Lake of Gennesaret.

γεννητός, *begotten*, used as subst.

γένος, (a) *race*; (b) *kind*.

Γερασηνός, *Gerasene, of Gerasa*, a town on the E. of the Lake of Tiberias. Wherever this people is mentioned, the variants Γαδαρηνός and Γεργεσηνός occur.

Γεργεσηνός, *Gergesene, of Gergesa* (mod. Kursi), a place on a hill on the Lake of Tiberias. It is best perhaps to regard Γερασηνός as a by-form of this word, Γαδαρηνός being a conscious alteration.

γερουσία, *the assembly* or *body of elders*, probably as synonymous with or explicative of συνέδριον and πρεσβύτεροι. (The term γερουσία was often used in such a collective sense in the cities of Asia Minor, cf. Ramsay, *Cities and Bishoprics of Phrygia*, vol. i, p. 64.)

γέρων, *an old man*.

γεύομαι, (a) *I taste*; (b) *I experience*.

γεωργέω, *I work the soil, I cultivate the soil*.

γεώργιον, *a cultivated field*.

γεωργός, *a worker of the soil, husbandman, farmer, farm-labourer*.

γῆ, *the earth, soil, land*.

γῆρας, *old age*.

γηράσκω, *I become old, grow old*.

γίνομαι, *I come into being, am born*, John viii 58, Gal. iv 4, &c.: *I become, come about, happen*. (In aorist ἐγένετο

γινώσκω

over-used by Luke, to give Hebraistic colouring, in various constructions: (1) ἐγένετο ἦλθεν, (2) ἐγένετο καὶ ἦλθεν, (3) ἐγένετο ἐλθεῖν (the latest of the three and non-Hebraistic).)

γινώσκω, *I am taking in knowledge, come to know, learn*: aor. *I ascertained, realized,* but not in John xvii 25, 2 Tim. ii 19.

γλεῦκος, *sweet-wine*, made perhaps from a small specially sweet grape.

γλυκύς, *sweet*.

γλῶσσα, (a) *tongue*, especially as an organ of speech; (b) *tongue, language*; (c) also, usually in the plural, for the unintelligible sounds uttered in spiritual ecstasy.

γλωσσόκομον (a vernacular word), *bag, purse*: some prefer to take as *box, chest*.

γναφεύς, *fuller*.

γνήσιος (lit. *born*), hence *real, true, genuine*; τὸ γνήσιον, *the true, genuine element*.

γνησίως, *truly, genuinely*; *honourably*.

γνόφος, *darkness*.

γνώμη, *opinion, counsel*.

γνωρίζω, *I make known*.

γνῶσις, *knowledge*.

γνώστης, *a knower, expert*.

γνωστός, *known*: subst. *an acquaintance*.

γογγύζω, *I whisper, murmur, grumble* (generally of smouldering discontent).

γογγυσμός, *murmuring, grumbling*.

γογγυστής, *murmurer, grumbler*.

γόης, *a conjuror, juggler, sorcerer*; *a tricky (crafty) deceiver, impostor*.

Γολγοθά, *Golgotha*, a knoll outside the wall of Jerusalem.

Γόμορρα, *Gomorrha*, one of the destroyed cities on the Dead Sea.

γόμος, *a cargo, freight*.

γονεύς, *a parent*.

γόνυ, *a knee*.

γονυπετέω, *I fall on my knees before* (in supplication), *supplicate, entreat.*

γράμμα (littera), *a letter of the alphabet*; collectively, *written* (revelation), Rom. ii 27 : γράμματα (litterae), *writings,* (a) *a written document,* Lk. xvi 6, 7 ; *a letter, an epistle,* Ac. xxviii 21 ; (b) *writings, literature,* John v 47, vii 15, Ac. xxvi 24, 2 Tim. iii 15.

γραμματεύς, (a) in Jerusalem, *a scribe,* one learned in the Jewish Law, a religious teacher ; (b) at Ephesus, *the town-clerk, the secretary of the city,* Ac. xix 35.

γραπτός, *written.*

γραφή, (a) *a writing*; (b) *a passage of scripture* : plur. αἱ γραφαί, *the scriptures* (of the Old Testament, and in 2 Pet. iii 16 also of the New).

γράφω, *I write* : γέγραπται, *it is written, it stands written* (in the scriptures of the Old Testament : so in ordinary life, a formula introducing an unalterable agreement) : = προγράφω, Rom. xv 4.

γραώδης (anilis), *belonging to old women, such as old women tell.*

γρηγορέω (uigilo), (a) *I am awake* (in the night), *watch* ; (b) *I am watchful, on the alert.*

γυμνάζω, *I train by physical exercise* : hence, *train* in widest sense ; with gen. of sphere, 2 Pet. ii 14.

γυμνασία (physical) *exercise,* in a wide sense, 'escarum, balnearum, uenationum et huius modi' (Pelagius).

γυμνιτεύω, *I am habitually* γυμνός, that is, *I wear the under-garment* (χιτών, tunica) *only,* it being the regular practice to wear two garments.

γυμνός, rarely *stark-naked,* generally *wearing only the under-garment* (χιτών), see **γυμνιτεύω** ; γυμνὸς κόκκος, *a simple seed, a seed* per se.

γυμνότης, *nakedness,* cf. γυμνός, γυμνιτεύω.

γυναικάριον (muliercula), *a woman* with all a woman's weakness, *a poor weak woman.*

γυναικεῖος, *belonging to woman, of woman.*

γυνή, *a* (married) *woman, a wife* : so even in Mt. v 28 : voc. γύναι, Lk. xxii 57, John ii 4, *my lady.*

57

Γώγ

Γώγ, *Gog*, a name borrowed from Ezekiel (xxxviii 2 ff.,
where = prince over Mesech and Thubal), to indicate a race or races to be led astray by Satan at the
end of the thousand years.
γωνία, *a corner*.

Δ

δαιμονίζομαι, *I am under the power of an evil-spirit* or
demon.
δαιμόνιον, *an evil-spirit, demon*.
δαιμονιώδης, *demon-like, such as demons have*.
δαίμων, *an evil-spirit, a demon*, much less common than
the diminutive δαιμόνιον.
δάκνω, *I bite*; hence, *I backbite*, or *harm seriously*.
δάκρυ, δάκρυον, *a tear*.
δακρύω, *I shed tears, weep*.
δακτύλιος, *a finger-ring*.
δάκτυλος, *a finger*: the picturesque δακτύλῳ of Lk. xi 20
is represented by πνεύματι in Mt. xii 28.
Δαλμανουθά, *Dalmanutha*: nothing is known of name or
place, and text is probably corrupt (a conjecture of
Burkitt in *Amer. Journ. Theol.* xv (1911) 174).
Δαλματία, *Dalmatia*, a province of the Roman Empire,
E. of the Adriatic, a later name for part of what was
earlier called *Illyricum* (Rom. xv 19).
δαμάζω, *I tame, subdue*, involving obedience and restraint.
δάμαλις, *a heifer*.
Δάμαρις, *Damaris*, an Athenian woman.
Δαμασκηνός, *a Damascene, an inhabitant of Damascus*.
Δαμασκός, *Damascus*, an ancient city of Coele-Syria.
δανείζω (δανίζω), *I lend*; mid. δανείζομαι, *I borrow*.
δάνειον (δάνιον), *a loan*.
Δανιήλ (Hebr.), *Daniel*, loosely called a 'prophet'.
δανιστής, *a lender, creditor*.
δαπανάω, *I spend*.

58

δαπάνη, *cost, expense.*

Δαυείδ (Hebr.), *David,* King of Israel, to whose name the Old Testament collection of Psalms was attached.

δέ (autem), a weak adversative particle, generally placed second in its clause, *but, on the other hand:* and. See μέν.

δέησις, *a requesting, a begging, request.*

δεῖ (necesse est), *it is necessary, inevitable;* less frequently (oportet), *it is a duty,* τὰ μὴ δέοντα, *what is improper, wrong:* δέον (ἐστίν) = δεῖ, Ac. xix 36, 1 Pet. i 6.

δεῖγμα, *an example, type.*

δειγματίζω, *I hold up as an example.*

δείκνυμι, δεικνύω, *I point out, show.*

δειλία, *cowardice.*

δειλιάω, *I shrink, am fearful.*

δειλός, *cowardly, timid.*

δεῖνα: ὁ δεῖνα, *so and so, such an one,* where the name of the person is known but not used.

δεινῶς, *terribly.*

δειπνέω, *I dine.*

δεῖπνον, *a dinner, an afternoon* or *evening meal.*

δεισιδαιμονία, *superstition.*

δεισιδαίμων, *respectful of what is divine, religious* perhaps, rather than *superstitious* (the usual meaning).

δέκα, *ten.*

δεκάπεντε, *fifteen.*

Δεκάπολις, *Decapolis,* meaning a group or district of ten cities (of the Greek type) in Palestine, mostly SE. of the Lake of Tiberias. The names and number vary in ancient authorities.

δεκατέσσαρες, *fourteen.*

δεκάτη, *a tenth part, a tithe.*

δέκατος, *tenth.*

δεκατόω, *I tithe, I collect tithe from.*

δεκτός, *acceptable.*

δελεάζω, *I allure* (by a bait).

δένδρον, *a tree.*

δεξιολάβος

δεξιολάβος, a word of uncertain meaning, indicating some class of soldier (cf. Nestle in *Archiv für lateinische Lexikographie*, Bd. xii, 581–2).

δεξιός, *on the right hand, right hand, right.*

δέομαι, *I request, beg.*

δέον, see **δεῖ.**

δέος, *fear.*

Δερβαῖος, *Derbean, belonging to Derbe.*

Δέρβη, *Derbe,* a town in Lycaonia and in the southern part of the Roman province Galatia.

δέρμα, *a hide, skin.*

δερμάτινος, *made of hide, leathern.*

δέρω, *I flay, flog, beat.*

δεσμεύω, *I bind.*

δέσμη, *a bond.*

δέσμιος, *bound, captive, in chains*; sometimes substantivally *prisoner, captive.*

δεσμός, plur. sometimes **δεσμά,** *a bond, chain*; in Ac. xxiii 29, xxvi 31 (= uincula), the reference is to the form of 'capital' punishment involving loss of freedom and work in chains in the quarries.

δεσμοφύλαξ, *a prison governor, gaoler.*

δεσμωτήριον, *a prison, gaol.*

δεσμώτης, *a prisoner, captive.*

δεσπότης, *a master,* particularly a master and owner of slaves, *lord.*

δεῦρο, (originally *hither,* hence) (a) exclamatory, *come*; (b) temporal, *now, the present,* Rom. i 13.

δεῦτε (plur. of **δεῦρο**), *come hither, come, hither,* an exclamatory word.

δευτεραῖος, adj. where Eng. requires adv., *on the second day, on the next day.*

δευτερόπρωτος, a ghost-word which has crept into the text of many authorities at Lk. vi 1, by mistake.

δεύτερος, *second*: (τὸ) δεύτερον is used adverbially, *in the second place, for the second time.*

δέχομαι, *I receive, welcome.*

δέω, *I bind.*

δή, (a) in a clause expressing demand : *so, then*, 1 Cor. vi 20 ; (b) *indeed*, Lk. ii 15, &c. ; (c) *truly*, Mt. xiii 23.

δηλαυγῶς (from δῆλος and αὐγή), *with perfect clearness* (but see τηλαυγῶς).

δῆλος, *clear, manifest.*

δηλόω, *I show, make clear, reveal.*

Δημᾶς (a pet form, probably of Δημήτριος), *Demas*, a helper of St. Paul in Rome.

δημηγορέω, *I make a public speech, I address a multitude.*

Δημήτριος, *Demetrius*, a silversmith of Ephesus.

δημιουργός, *a constructor, builder.*

δῆμος (populus), properly *the people*, especially the citizens of a Greek city in popular assembly (ἐκκλησία), but in N. T. = *multitude, rabble.*

δημόσιος (publicus), *public* : **δημοσίᾳ**, adv. (publice) *publicly.*

δηνάριον, *a denarius*, a small Roman silver coin, weighing in Nero's time 53 grs. Its value and purchasing power varied from time to time.

δήποτε (δή ποτε), *even at that time*, only in the interpolation, John v 4.

δήπου (δή που), *of course*, qualifying and yet strengthening the assertion.

διά, (a) c. gen. *through* : *throughout* (διὰ παντός, *always*) ; *by the instrumentality of* : denoting mediate and not original authorship, e. g. Mt. i 22, John i 3, 1 Cor. viii 6 ; (b) c. acc. *through*, Lk. xvii 11 (?) ; *on account of, by reason of, for the sake of, because of.*

διαβαίνω, *I cross.*

διαβάλλω, *I slander* : merely *I complain of* (without idea of malice), Lk. xvi 1.

διαβεβαιόομαι, *I assert emphatically.*

διαβλέπω, *I see thoroughly.*

διάβολος (adj. used oftener as noun), *slanderous* (1 Tim. iii 11, 2 Tim. iii 3, Tit. ii 3) ; almost always ὁ Διάβολος, *the Slanderer* (par excellence), *the Devil.*

διαγγέλλω, *I announce throughout* the world, *I spread the news of.*

δια γίνομαι

διαγίνομαι, *I pass* (of time).
διαγινώσκω, *I learn thoroughly, I determine* (Ac. xxiv 22).
διάγνωσις (cognitio), *investigation and decision.*
διαγογγύζω, *I murmur greatly, I continue murmuring.*
διαγρηγορέω, *I awake out of sleep, I am thoroughly awake.*
διάγω (either tr. or intr.), *I spend time, pass time, live.*
διαδέχομαι, *I receive in my turn.*
διάδημα, *a chaplet, crown.*
διαδίδωμι, *I offer here and there, distribute.*
διάδοχος, *a successor.*
διαζώννυμι, *I gird myself,* by pulling up the tunic and allowing a fold to fall over the belt (ζώνη).
διαθήκη, (a) = συνθήκη, *a covenant* between two parties ; (b) (the ordinary, everyday sense [found a countless number of times in papyri]) *a will, testament,* Gal. iii 15, 17, Heb. ix 16. See my *Text and Canon,* p. 157, n. 2.
διαίρεσις, *division, distribution.*
διαιρέω, *I divide, distribute.*
διακαθαίρω, *I clean thoroughly.*
διακαθαρίζω, *I clean thoroughly.*
διακατελέγχομαι, *I effectively* (*utterly*) *refute* (*confute*).
διακονέω (ministro), *I wait at table* (particularly of a slave who pours out wine to the guests); *I serve* (generally).
διακονία (ministerium), *waiting at table* ; in a wider sense, *service, ministration.*
διάκονος (minister), *a waiter, servant* : then of any one who performs any service, *an administrator,* &c.
διακόσιοι, *two hundred.*
διακούω, *I hear throughout,* of a judicial hearing.
διακρίνω, *I separate, distinguish, discern* one thing *from* another ; διακρίνομαι, *I doubt, hesitate, waver.*
διάκρισις, *distinguishing* ; hence, *deciding, passing sentence on* (Rom. xiv 1).
διακωλύω, *I obstinately prevent.*

διαλαλέω, I *interchange talk*; of conversation passing from mouth to mouth.

διαλέγομαι, I *converse*, Mk. ix 34; elsewhere, I *address, preach, lecture.*

διαλείπω, I *cease, give over, give up.*

διάλεκτος, *language, speech.*

διαλιμπάνω, a by-form of διαλείπω.

διαλλάσσομαι, I *become reconciled to, I reconcile myself with.*

διαλογίζομαι, I *reason* (*with*), *debate* (*with*), *consider.*

διαλογισμός, a *calculation, reasoning, thought, movement of thought, deliberation, plotting.*

διαλύω, I *break up, disperse.*

διαμαρτύρομαι, I *give solemn evidence, I testify* (*declare*) *solemnly.*

διαμάχομαι, I *strive greatly.*

διαμένω, I *remain throughout.*

διαμερίζω, I *divide up into parts, break up*; I *distribute.*

διαμερισμός, *breaking up; discord, hostility.*

διανέμω, I *divide into portions, distribute*; I *spread abroad.*

διανεύω, I *nod continually.*

διανόημα, a *reasoning, thought, cogitation.*

διάνοια (*process of reasoning* in Plato), *understanding, intellect, mind.*

διανοίγω, I *open up.*

διανυκτερεύω, I *spend the whole night.*

διανύω, I *finish, complete.*

διαπαντός, see διά.

διαπαρατριβή, *perpetual wrangling.*

διαπεράω, I *cross over.*

διαπλέω, I *sail over* (*across*).

διαπονέομαι, I *am greatly troubled.*

διαπορεύομαι, I *journey through* (*past*).

διαπορέω, I *am in trouble, doubt, difficulty.*

διαπραγματεύομαι, I *gain by business* (*trading*).

διαπρίω (lit. I *saw through*), I *cut to the quick* (with indignation and envy).

διαρπάζω, I *plunder, rob thoroughly.*

63

διαρρήσσω, *I tear asunder.*

διασαφέω, *I make clear, explain.*

διασείω (concutio), *I blackmail, extort from.*

διασκορπίζω, *I scatter.*

διασπάω, *I tear apart, burst.*

διασπείρω, *I scatter (like seed).*

διασπορά, lit. *scattering abroad of seed* by the sower: hence *dispersion,* used especially of the Jews who had migrated and were scattered over the ancient world. In James i 1 and 1 Pet. i 1 the reference may be to the New Israel, the Christians.

διαστέλλομαι, *I give a commission (instructions), I order.*

διάστημα, *an interval.*

διαστολή, *distinction, separation.*

διαστρέφω, *I pervert.*

διασώζω, *I save (rescue) through* (some danger): διασ. πρός (Ac. xxiii 34), *I bring safely to,* so διεσώθησαν εἰς (1 Pet. iii 20), *escaped into.*

διαταγή, *ordaining, ordinance, disposition.*

διάταγμα, *a commandment.*

διαταράσσω, *I disturb greatly.*

διατάσσω, *I command.*

διατελέω (act. and) mid. *I continue.*

διατηρέω, *I keep safe, hold fast.*

διατί = διὰ τί.

διατίθεμαι, (a) *I appoint, make* (of a covenant); (b) *I make* (a will) (regular in papyri), Heb. ix 16, 17.

διατρίβω, *I tarry, continue, stay* in a place.

διατροφή, *nourishment, food.*

διαυγάζω, *I dawn* (of the light coming *through* the shadows).

διαυγής, *through which light passes, transparent.*

διαφέρω, (a) tr. *I carry through, hither and thither* ; (b) intr. *I am different, I differ,* sometimes c. gen. : hence c. gen. *I surpass, I excel.*

διαφεύγω, *I flee through, I escape.*

διαφημίζω, *I spread about* (by *word* of mouth).

διαφθείρω, *I destroy, waste* ; hence met. *I corrupt.*

διαφθορά, *destruction, dissolution, corruption.*

διάφορος, *differing, different;* hence *excellent.*

διαφυλάσσω, *I guard securely, I preserve,* or *guard through* (a danger), *save.*

διαχειρίζομαι, *I lay my hands upon,* and so, *I slay, kill.*

διαχλευάζω, *I mock* (*scorn*) *greatly,* with words and gesture.

διαχωρίζομαι, *I separate myself from, I part from.*

διδακτικός, *able to teach, apt to teach.*

διδακτός, *taught.*

διδασκαλία, *teaching.*

διδάσκαλος, *teacher.*

διδάσκω, *I teach.*

διδαχή, *teaching.*

δίδραχμον, *a double-drachma, two drachmae,* a Greek silver coin, roughly equal to the modern two-franc-piece in value, but greater in purchasing power. In the time of Christ 1 drachma roughly = 1 denarius = $\frac{1}{4}$ shekel: δίδραχμον, the yearly temple-tax thus = $\frac{1}{2}$ shekel.

Δίδυμος, *the Twin.*

δίδωμι, *I offer, give;* elliptically used Rev. ii 23 : (Hebraistic = τίθημι), *I put, place,* Rev. iii 8.

διεγείρω, *I wake out of sleep ; I arouse,* in general.

διενθυμέομαι, *I weigh in my mind, ponder.*

διέξοδος, *a going out in various directions, a parting ;* hence, *the issue* of a street, where it leads out of the city into the country.

διερμηνευτής, *an interpreter.*

διερμηνεύω, *I translate, interpret, explain.*

διέρχομαι, *I go* (*come, journey*) *all the way through* : in Ac. seems frequently to imply, *I itinerate, evangelize as I go.*

διερωτάω, *I inquire for.*

διετής (bimus), *two years old.*

διετία, *a period of two years, two years.* (According to ancient practice this means any period between one and two years.)

δ ι η γ έ ο μ α ι

διηγέομαι, *I relate, narrate.*
διήγησις, *a narrative.*
διηνεκής, *continuous*: εἰς τὸ διηνεκες, in perpetuum.
διθάλασσος, *between two seas, which has sea on both sides.*
διϊκνέομαι, *I pass through (to), come through (to).*
διΐστημι: διαστήσαντες (Ac. xxvii 28) tr. with τὸ πλοῖον understood, *having moved (the ship) some distance*: διαστῆναι, intr. *to be distant from, to be separated from; to pass away.*
διϊσχυρίζομαι, *I assert emphatically.*
δικαιοκρισία, *just judging, just judgement.*
δίκαιος, *just*; especially, *just* in the eyes of God, *righteous*: οἱ δίκαιοι in Mt. *the elect* (a Jewish idea): κρίνω τὸ δίκαιον, *I give just judgement,* Lk. xii 57.
δικαιοσύνη (usually if not always in Jewish atmosphere), *justice, justness: righteousness* (cf. δίκαιος): δικαιοσύνη θεοῦ strictly, *righteousness of which God is the source* or *author,* but practically, *a divine righteousness* and equivalent to βασιλεία τοῦ θεοῦ.
δικαιόω, *I make δίκαιος (righteous), I defend the cause of, plead for the righteousness (innocence) of, I acquit, justify*; hence, *I regard as δίκαιος (righteous).*
δικαίωμα, *(an argument, a pièce justificative,* hence) *a thing pronounced (by God) to be δίκαιος (just, the right)*; or *the restoration* of a criminal, a fresh chance given him; *a righteous deed* (e. g. Rom. v 18).
δικαίως, *justly, righteously.*
δικαίωσις, *justifying, justification, a process of absolution.*
δικαστής, *a judge.*
δίκη, (a) (originally *custom, usage*: hence) *right, justice,* Ac. xxviii 4, where rather *Justice* (the goddess); (b) *process of law, judicial hearing*; (c) *execution of sentence, punishment, penalty,* 2 Thess. i 9, Jude 7.
δίκτυον, *a net.*
δίλογος, *double-tongued.*
διό (= δι᾿ ὅ, *on account of which thing*), *wherefore.*
διοδεύω, *I travel through.*

66

δοκιμάζω

Διονύσιος, *Dionysius,* an Athenian.

διόπερ (δι' ὅπερ), an emphatic διό.

διοπετής, *fallen from the sky.*

διόρθωμα, *a correction, reform.*

διόρθωσις, *amendment, improvement* (originally *right ordering*; then *bettering*).

διορύσσω, *I dig through, break through.*

Διόσκουροι (= Διὸς κοῦροι, *boys of Zeus*), the *Dioscuri,* Castor and Pollux, sons of Zeus and Leda, and patrons of sailors.

διότι (= διὰ ὅ τι), *wherefore*; = ὅτι Rom. viii 21 (v. l.).

Διοτρέφης, *Diotrephes.*

διπλόος, *double.*

διπλόω, *I double.*

δίς, *twice.*

δισμυριάς = δὶς μυριάς.

διστάζω, *I doubt.*

δίστομος (lit. *twain-mouthed*; hence of a sword, as a drinker of blood), *two-edged.*

δισχίλιοι, *two-thousand.*

διυλίζω, *I strain, put through a sieve.*

διχάζω, *I make to differ from, I make to be hostile.*

διχοστασία, *division* (between persons).

διχοτομέω, *I cut in two.*

διψάω, *I thirst.*

δίψος, *thirst.*

δίψυχος (lit. *of two souls, of two selves*), *double-minded, wavering.*

διωγμός, *persecution.*

διώκτης, *a persecutor.*

διώκω, *I pursue*; hence, *I persecute.*

δόγμα, *a decree.*

δογματίζομαι. *I subject myself to regulations,* or *I am decree-ridden.*

δοκέω (uideor), *I seem, am thought*; δοκεῖ impers. c. dat. (placet), *it seems good, it is resolved by.*

δοκιμάζω, *I put to the test, I prove, examine*: in Rom. ii 18, Phil. i 10 either *I distinguish by testing,* or, more probably, *I approve after testing*: *I think fit*, Rom. i 28.

δοκιμασία, *testing, proving.*

δοκιμή, *approvedness*; hence, *character.*

δοκίμιον (neut. of δοκίμιος *genuine*, as opposed to *alloyed, counterfeit*), *what is genuine, the approved part, the pure part.*

δόκιμος, *approved.*

δοκός, *a beam.*

δόλιος, *treacherous, deceitful.*

δολιόω, *I act deceitfully, treacherously.*

δόλος, *deceit, guile, treachery.*

δολόω, *I adulterate* (cf. ἄδολος).

δόμα, *a gift.*

δόξα, *glory*, an especially divine quality, the unspoken manifestation of God; in James ii 1 it is in apposition to Ἰησοῦ Χριστοῦ, and is personified (cf. 1 Cor. ii 8, Ac. vii 2, and the Shekinah of Targums and post-canonical Jewish writings).

δοξάζω, *I glorify, bestow glory on*: τὸν θεόν, *I acknowledge the glory of God.*

Δορκάς, the Greek name of Tabitha, *Dorcas* (lit. *gazelle*), (δορκάς dicitur a uidendo; δορκατικόν etenim uisus acutioris est, Ambros. *expos. ps.* cxviii 6. 12 § 1).

δόσις, *giving* (from God).

δότης, *giver.*

δουλαγωγέω, *I enslave.*

δουλεία, *slavery.*

δουλεύω, *I serve as a slave, I am a slave.*

δούλη, *a female slave.*

δοῦλος, (a) (as adj.) *enslaved, subject*; (b) (as noun) *a (male) slave.*

δουλόω, *I enslave.*

δοχή, *a reception, party.*

δράκων, *a serpent.*

δράσσομαι, *I take hold of, grasp.*

δραχμή, *a drachma*, a Greek silver coin, corresponding nearly to the modern *franc.*

δρέπανον, *a sickle.*

δρόμος, *a run, a course* (in running).

Δρούσιλλα, *Drusilla* (born A.D. 39), daughter of Herod Agrippa I and his cousin Kypros, wife, first of Azizos, King of Emesa, and then of Antonius Felix, procurator of Judaea.

δύναμαι, (a) *I am powerful, I have (the) power*; (b) *I am able, I can.*

δύναμις, (a) *physical power, force, might*; (b) in plur., *powerful deeds, deeds showing* (physical) *power, marvellous works.*

δυναμόω, *I empower, fill with power.*

δυνάστης (*a man who rules by force,* lit.), *a ruler, potentate*: Ac. viii 27 in appos., seems = *courtier, member of the court.*

δυνατέω, *I am powerful, I have power, I am able.*

δυνατός, (a) of persons, *powerful, able*; (b) of things, *possible.*

δύνω, *I sink* (intr.).

δύο, *two*: δυὸ δυό, *two by two*; ἀνὰ (κατὰ) δύο, *two by two*: ἀνὰ δύο δύο in some MSS of Luke x 3 is a mistaken fusion of the two phrases.

δυσβάστακτος, *difficult to carry.*

δυσεντέριον, *dysentery.*

δυσερμήνευτος, *difficult to interpret.*

δύσκολος, *difficult.*

δυσκόλως, *with difficulty.*

δυσμή, *a setting* (of the sun); hence *the West*: for the plur. cf. *occasus.*

δυσνόητος, *hard to understand.*

δυσφημέω, *I am badly spoken of, I have a bad reputation.*

δυσφημία, *evil repute.*

δώδεκα, *twelve*: οἱ δώδεκα, the usual way in which *the Twelve* disciples of Jesus are referred to.

δωδέκατος, *twelfth.*

δωδεκάφυλον, *the Twelve Tribes* (of Israel).

δῶμα, *the roof* (of a house), *the top of the house.*

δωρεά, *a (free) gift, a gift (without repayment).*

δωρεάν

δωρεάν (acc. of δωρεά used as adv., cf. *gratis* abl. plur.
of *gratia*), *as a free gift, without payment, freely,
gratis*.
δωρέομαι, *I give, grant, donate*.
δώρημα, *a gift*: in James i 17 (*of God*).
δῶρον, *a gift*.

E

ἔα, an interjection, *ho!* It is supposed to imply surprise,
fear and indignation.
ἐάν, (a) introducing a clause, *if*, with subjunctive, but
1 Thess. iii 8, 1 John v 15 have the indicative; (b) (an
usage beginning about 133 B.C.) within a clause,
modifying, generalizing, ὅς, ὅστις, ὅσος, ὁσάκις, ὅπου, οὗ,
exactly as ἄν does in Attic Greek: thus ὅς = *who*, ὅς
ἐάν, *whosoever*, &c.
ἐάνπερ, *if indeed*.
ἑαυτοῦ, &c., *self, selves*; for all three persons, singular
(not first person) and plural, according to context,
*ourselves; yourself, yourselves; himself, herself, itself,
themselves*.
ἐάω, *I allow, permit, leave*.
ἑβδομήκοντα, *seventy*.
ἑβδομηκοντάκις, *seventy times*.
ἕβδομος, *seventh*.
Ἔβερ (Hebr.), *Eber*, father of Phalek and son of Sala.
Ἑβραῖος, *a Hebrew*, particularly one who speaks
Hebrew (Aramaic), cf. Ac. vi 1; Ἑβραῖος ἐξ Ἑβραίων,
a Hebrew descended from Hebrews (Phil. iii 5).
Ἑβραΐς, *Hebrew*, or rather *Aramaic*.
Ἑβραϊστί, *in the Hebrew*, or rather, *in the Aramaic
dialect*.
ἐγγίζω, *I come near, approach*.
ἐγγράφω, see ἐνγράφω.
ἔγγυος, *a surety, security*.
ἐγγύς, *near*.

ἐγείρω, (a) *I wake, arouse*; (b) *I raise up*; intr. in imperative, ἔγειρε, ἐγείρεσθε, *wake up!*: passive sometimes = *I rise*, e. g. Mk. xvi 6.

ἔγερσις, *a waking up.*

ἐγκ., see ἐνκ.

ἐγκαλέω, *I bring a charge against.*

ἐγκαταλείπω, *I leave in the lurch, I abandon* (one who is in straits), *I desert.*

ἔγκλημα, *an accusation, charge.*

ἐγκομβόομαι, *I clothe myself* (originally, *I tie round in a knot*).

ἐγκράτεια, *self-mastery, self-restraint, self-control, continence.*

ἐγκρατεύομαι, *I exercise self-control, I am continent.*

ἐγκρατής, *self-controlled.*

ἐγκρύπτω, *I hide* (*within*).

ἐγχρίω, *I besmear, anoint.*

ἐγώ, *I*: τί ἐμοὶ (ἡμῖν) καὶ σοί; quid mihi (nobis) tecum? *What have I* (*we*) *to do with thee?*, but in John ii 4 ἐμοὶ καὶ σοί may be simply equal to ἡμῖν; τὸ (τὰ) κατ᾽ ἐμέ, *so far as I am concerned*: in letters ἡμεῖς often alternates with ἐγώ without real difference of meaning.

ἐδαφίζω, *I dash to the ground.*

ἔδαφος, *ground.*

ἑδραῖος (stabilis) (lit. *seated*), *firm, stedfast.*

ἑδραίωμα, *a foundation.*

Ἑζεκίας (Hebr.), *Hezekiah*, son of Achas (Ahaz), father of Manasseh, and king of Judah (727–686 [?] b. c.).

ἐθελοθρησκεία (cf. ἐθελοδουλεία), *service* (*worship*) *of the will, worship of self*, practically, *worship of the angels.*

ἐθέλω, see θέλω.

ἐθίζω, *I accustom*: τὸ εἰθισμένον, *the custom.*

ἐθνάρχης, *ethnarch, tribal lord*, a subordinate ruler.

ἐθνικός (represents a word which in Biblical Hebrew means *nation*, but in Rabbinic Hebrew = *non-Jew*) (gentilis), *a Gentile*, a non-Jew.

ἐθνικῶς, *in the manner of Gentiles.*

71

ἔθνος

ἔθνος (originally, a rustic or village people as opposed to those dwelling in organized cities or πόλεις), *a race, people* (usually outside the privileged Jewish people, but also sometimes in the singular for it) (sometimes = the inhabitants of a Roman province): τὰ ἔθνη (gentes), *the nations* outside Judaism, *the Gentiles*.

ἔθος, *a custom*.

εἰ, *if*: but in strong statements, approaching oaths in character, and as the first word in an interrogative clause, it is probably a mere graphic equivalent, first appearing second century B.C., of ἦ [and should be written εἶ], and in the former case = *verily, indeed, assuredly* (sometimes negative [Semitic], *assuredly not*, Mk. viii 12, Heb. iii 11), while in the latter it is merely a particle asking a question. [The Latin translators, however, rendered interrogative εἰ by *si*.] εἰ μή (nisi); *but only*, e.g. Lk. iv 26 f., John xv 4, Ac. xxvii 22, Rev. xxi 27; in Mk. vi 8 probably due to a misreading of an Aramaic word = *and not*: εἰ δὲ μή, εἰ δὲ μήγε (Aramaism?), (alioqui, si minus, sin autem, &c.), *otherwise*: εἴπερ (= εἰ περ) a more emphatic εἰ, *if indeed*.

εἰδέα, *appearance*.

εἶδα, **εἶδον**, 1 and 2 aor. respectively, *I saw*, cf. ὁράω: ἰδὼν εἶδον, a Hebraistic repetition.

εἶδος, *visible form, shape, appearance, outward show*; in 1 Thess. v 22 = *kind, species, class*.

εἰδωλεῖον, *a temple for (containing) an image* (of a god).

εἰδωλόθυτος (of meat), *sacrificed to an image* (of a god).

εἰδωλολατρεία, *service (worship) of an image* (of a god).

εἰδωλολάτρης, *a server (worshipper) of an image* (of a god).

εἴδωλον (simulacrum), *an image of a god*.

εἰκῆ, used both with reference to antecedent causes and purposes for the future, *without a cause*; *purposelessly, in vain, for nothing*.

εἴκοσι, *twenty*.

εἴκω, *I yield*.

72

εἰκών (imago), *image, likeness, bust.*

εἰλικρίνεια, *purity.*

εἰλικρινής (sincerus) (originally *unmixed*), *pure, uncon-taminated.*

εἰλίσσω, see ἐλίσσω.

εἰμί, *I am, exist.* Note periphrasis with participles, the special frequency of which in the imperfect is due to the Aramaic basis of the language. ὁ ἦν ungrammatically, in Rev., where an aor. pcpl. would be expected.

εἵνεκεν, see ἕνεκα.

εἶπα, see εἶπον.

εἴπερ, see εἰ.

εἶπον, 2 aor., εἶπα 1 aor. *I spoke, said*: ὡς ἔπος εἰπεῖν, *one might almost say* (*almost, about*).

εἰρηνεύω, *I am peaceful, I keep the peace, I am at peace.*

εἰρήνη, *peace, undisturbedness*: invocation of peace a common Jewish farewell (Mk. v 34, &c.), in the Hebraistic sense of *the health* (*welfare*) of an individual.

εἰρηνικός, *making for peace, productive of peace.*

εἰρηνοποιέω, *I make peace.*

εἰρηνοποιός, *peace-making, peace-maker.*

εἰς, (a) *into; till; for;* (b) εἰς τό c. infin. generally final, but also expressing tendency, result, e.g. Rom. xii 3, 2 Cor. viii 6, Gal. iii 17, content of command or entreaty, e.g. 1 Thess. ii 12, or simply = explanatory infinitive, 1 Thess. iv 9; (c) encroaches on ἐν and = *in,* e.g. John i 18, Ac. vii 12, 2 Cor. xi 10, 1 John v 8: εἰς ἑκατόν, &c., *a hundredfold.*

εἷς, *one;* καθ᾽ εἷς, *each single one, one by one*: sometimes no whit different from τις (Mk. xiv 10), and sometimes too = πρῶτος, *first.*

εἰσάγω, *I lead in, bring in.*

εἰσακούω, *I hear.*

εἰσδέχομαι, *I welcome in.*

εἴσειμι, *I go in, enter* (originally, *I shall go in*).

εἰσέρχομαι, *I go in.*

εἰσκαλέω, mid. *I call in* (to my house).

εἴσοδος, (abstr.) (*act of*) *entering, entrance, entry*: concrete, *the entrance* itself, Heb. x 19 (cf. 20), 2 Pet. i 11.

εἰσπηδάω, *I leap into, rush into*.

εἰσπορεύομαι, *I journey in*(*to*), *I go in*(*to*).

εἰστρέχω, *I run in*(*to*).

εἰσφέρω, *I carry* (*bring*) *in*.

εἶτα, *then, thereafter, next* (marking a fresh stage).

εἴτε (siue), lit. *and if*: **εἴτε . . . εἴτε** (siue . . . siue), *whether . . . or*.

εἶτεν = **εἶτα**.

εἴτις = **εἴ τις**.

εἴωθα, *I am accustomed*: τὸ εἰωθός, *custom, what was customary*.

ἐκ, **ἐξ**, *from out, out from among. from*, suggesting from the interior outwards; ἐξ Ἑβραίων, *descended from Hebrews*, Phil. iii 5: with gen. of price, Mt. xx 2, Ac. i 18; in partitive phrase, as subject of sentence, John xvi 17; cf. the periphrasis οἱ ἐξ ἐριθείας, Rom. ii 8.

ἕκαστος (quisque), *each* (of more than two); εἷς ἕκαστος, *each individual*; plur. ἕκαστοι, &c., *each class, group*.

ἑκάστοτε, *on each occasion*.

ἑκατόν, *a hundred*; εἰς ἑκατόν, see **εἰς**.

ἑκατονταετής, *a hundred years old*.

ἑκατονταπλασίων, *a hundredfold*.

ἑκατοντάρχης (-ος) (centurio, see **κεντουρίων**), *a centurion* of the Roman army.

ἐκβαίνω, *I go out*.

ἐκβάλλω, *I throw* (*cast, put*) *out*; *I banish*, Gal. iv 30, 3 John 10; *I bring forth, I produce*, Mt. xii 35.

ἔκβασις, (a) *a way out, escape*, 1 Cor. x 13; (b) *result*, Heb. xiii 7.

ἐκβολή (iactura), *a throwing out, a jettisoning* of cargo, to lighten a ship.

ἔκγονος, *descended*, hence subst. *a descendant*.

ἐκδαπανάω, *I spend* (*give out*) *completely*.

ἐκδέχομαι, *I wait for, expect*.

ἔκδηλος, *perfectly evident, manifest.*

ἐκδημέω, *I am away from the* δῆμος, *from my parish, from home.*

ἐκδίδωμι, *I give out, let*: middle, *I let out for my own advantage,* Mk. xii 1.

ἐκδιηγέομαι, *I give a complete narrative of.*

ἐκδικέω, *I give justice over, defend, avenge, vindicate*

ἐκδίκησις, (a) *defence, avenging, vindication, vengeance*; (b) *full (complete) punishment,* 2 Thess. i 8, 1 Pet. ii 14.

ἔκδικος, *avenging, an avenger.* (The word occurs frequently in the sense of a special *advocate* [*champion*] of a city.)

ἐκδιώκω, *I drive out.*

ἔκδοτος, *given up, delivered up.*

ἐκδοχή, *waiting, expectation.*

ἐκδύω, *I put off, take off, strip off,* with acc. of person or garment or both.

ἐκεῖ (illic), (a) *there, yonder*; (b) *thither, there.*

ἐκεῖθεν (illinc), *thence, from that place.*

ἐκεῖνος (ille), *that, yonder* (of what is distant, or great): in 1 John usually = Christ.

ἐκεῖσε (illuc), (a) *thither,* Ac. xxi 3; (b) *there,* Ac. xxii 5.

ἐκζητέω (exquiro), *I seek out.*

ἐκζήτησις, *a seeking out, searching questioning.*

ἐκθαμβέομαι, *I am greatly astonished.*

ἔκθαμβος, *full of astonishment.*

ἐκθαυμάζω, *I wonder greatly.*

ἔκθετος, *exposed* (to the elements).

ἐκκαθαίρω, *I clean (cleanse) out,* 1 Cor. v 7; *I clean thoroughly,* 2 Tim. ii 21.

ἐκκαίομαι, *I burn (with lust).*

ἐκκεντέω, *I pierce through* (or *deeply*).

ἐκκλάω, *I break off.*

ἐκκλείω, *I shut out, exclude.*

ἐκκλησία, (literally, *a calling out*; then) *an assembly, meeting of assembly,* Ac. xix 39; (a) *a community, congregation,*

ἐκκλίνω

church, society (first used in LXX for *the congregation of Israel*), the assembly of Christians in *one* city or community; in Mt. xvi 18, xviii 17 the body of Palestinian adherents of the Messiah is intended; (b) much more rarely, in a developed sense, especially with ὅλη, *the Church* (the whole body of Christians in the world).

ἐκκλίνω (*I bend away from*, literally), *I fall away from, I turn away* (from).

ἐκκολυμβάω, *I swim out* (of the water).

ἐκκομίζω (effero), *I carry out* (of the city gate for burial).

ἐκκοπή (ἐνκοπή), *a block, check, obstacle*.

ἐκκόπτω, *I cut out* (*off, away*).

ἐκκρέμαμαι (-ομαι), c. gen. *I hang upon* (met.).

ἐκλαλέω, *I speak out, tell out*.

ἐκλάμπω, *I shine forth* (*out*).

ἐκλανθάνομαι, *I quite forget*.

ἐκλέγομαι, *I pick out for myself, I choose*.

ἐκλείπω, intr. *I fail utterly: I am in a state of eclipse* (of the sun) Lk. xxiii 45.

ἐκλεκτός, *chosen out, selected*, sometimes as substantive, of those chosen out by God for the rendering of special service to Him (of the Hebrew race, particular Hebrews, the Messiah, and the Christians): an adj. in 2 John 1, 13.

ἐκλογή, *choosing out, selecting, choice* (by God): in Ac. ix 15 a Hebraistic genitive, equivalent to ἐκλεκτόν.

ἐκλύομαι, *I am unstrung, become weak, fail*.

ἐκμάσσω, *I wipe* (*off*) *thoroughly*.

ἐκμυκτηρίζω, *I mock greatly*.

ἐκνεύω (lit. *I bend the head aside*, to avoid a blow), *I retire, withdraw*.

ἐκνήφω, *I am thoroughly sober* (in mind).

ἑκούσιος, *willing:* κατὰ ἑκούσιον, *with right good will*.

ἑκουσίως, *willingly, with the will*.

ἔκπαλαι, *from of old, long since*.

ἐκπειράζω, *I put to a thorough test*.

ἐκπέμπω, *I send out*.

ἐκπερισσῶς, *most exceedingly, with exceeding emphasis.*

ἐκπετάννυμι, *I spread (stretch) out.*

ἐκπηδάω, *I leap (rush) out.*

ἐκπίπτω, *I fall out, I fall off, I fall away*: hence, in nautical language, *I fall off* from the straight course: of flowers, *I fade away, wither away.*

ἐκπλέω, *I sail out* (of harbour), *I sail away.*

ἐκπληρόω, *I fill completely, I fulfil in every particular (to the utmost), I make good.*

ἐκπλήρωσις, *completion, fulfilment.*

ἐκπλήσσομαι, *I am thunderstruck, astounded.*

ἐκπνέω (lit. *I breathe out*), *I breathe my last, I expire.*

ἐκπορεύομαι, *I journey out; I come forth.*

ἐκπορνεύω, *I am guilty of fornication* (the force of ἐκ is uncertain).

ἐκπτύω (cf. Fr. *conspuer*), *I spit upon, disdain.*

ἐκριζόω, *I root out, root up.*

ἔκστασις (properly, *distraction* or *disturbance* of mind caused by a shock), *bewilderment.*

ἐκστρέφω, *I pervert.*

ἐκσῴζω, *I save completely*, v. l. in Ac. xxvii 39.

ἐκταράσσω, *I disturb (trouble) greatly (exceedingly).*

ἐκτείνω, *I stretch out (forth).*

ἐκτελέω, *I complete, bring to completion, carry out, perform.*

ἐκτένεια, *earnestness, strenuousness.*

ἐκτενής, *intent, constant, strenuous.*

ἐκτενῶς, *earnestly, strenuously.*

ἐκτίθημι, (a) (expono) *I expose* a child; (b) mid. *I set forth, expound, explain.*

ἐκτινάσσω, *I shake off*; mid. *I shake off from myself.*

ἕκτος, *sixth.*

ἐκτός, (a) adv. (1) *without, outside*; (2) *except*; (3) τὸ ἐκτός, substantivally, *the outside*; (b) prep. c. gen. *outside, apart from.*

ἐκτρέπω (lit. *I turn out from*): mid. and pass. *I turn aside* (from the right road), *I wander*, and with an obj. *I remove from myself*, 1 Tim. vi 20.

ἐκτρέφω

ἐκτρέφω, *I nourish, nurture.*

ἔκτρομος, *trembling greatly.*

ἔκτρωμα, (strictly *a lifeless abortion*) *an untimely birth.*

ἐκφέρω, *I bring out, carry out,* sometimes (effero) out of the city for burial; *I bring forth, bear,* Heb. vi 8.

ἐκφεύγω, *I flee out, away, I escape*: with an acc. *I escape* something.

ἐκφοβέω, *I terrify exceedingly.*

ἔκφοβος, '*exceedingly afraid.*

ἐκφύω, *I put forth, cause to sprout.*

ἐκχέω, *I pour out* (liquid or solid), *I shed.* See ἐκχύννω.

ἐκχύννω, *I pour out, I shed,* cf. ἐκχέω: pass. *I am swept on, rush* or *I surrender,* Jude 11.

ἐκχωρέω, *I go out.*

ἐκψύχω, *I breathe my last, I die.*

ἑκών, *willing, willingly.*

ἐλαία (olea), *an olive tree*: see ἐλαίων.

ἔλαιον (oleum), *olive-oil*: ἔλαιον ἀγαλλιάσεως, *oil of enjoyment,* the oil with which the heads of guests at banquets are anointed, Heb. i 9.

Ἐλαιών (oliuetum), *Olive-grove, Olive-yard,* probably the right text in Lk. xix 29, xxi 37, as well as Ac. i 12.

Ἐλαμείτης, *an Elamite,* one of a people living to the north of the Persian Gulf in the southern part of Persia.

ἐλάσσων (less correct ἐλάττων), *less, smaller*: *poorer, inferior,* John ii 10: ἔλαττον (adv.), *less.*

ἐλαττονέω, *I have less, I lack.*

ἐλαττόω, *I make less (inferior).*

ἐλαύνω, (a) tr. *I drive (on), propel*: (b) intr. *I row,* Mk. vi 48, John vi 19.

ἐλαφρία (leuitas), *levity, fickleness.*

ἐλαφρός (leuis), *light.*

ἐλάχιστος, *least, smallest* (Mt., 1 Cor. xv 9), but perhaps oftener in the weaker sense, *very little, very small* (Lk., 1 Cor. iv 3, vi 2, James): ὁ ἐλαχιστότερος, *the smallest, the least important*: εἰς ἐλάχιστόν ἐστιν, *it matters very little*: ἐλάχιστον, adv. *a very little.*

Ἐλεάζαρ (Hebr.), *Eleazar*, son of Eliud, and father of Matthan.

ἐλεάω, see ἐλεέω.

ἐλεγμός, *reproof*.

ἔλεγξις, *rebuke, reproof*.

ἔλεγχος, *a proof* : possibly *a persuasion*.

ἐλέγχω, (a) *I reprove, rebuke* : (b) *I expose, show to be guilty*, John iii 20, 1 Cor. xiv 24, Eph. v 11, 13, James ii 9.

ἐλεεινός, *merciful, pitiful*.

ἐλεέω (ἐλεάω), *I pity*.

ἐλεημοσύνη, abstr. *alms-giving, charity* : concr. *alms, charity*.

ἐλεήμων, *pitiful, merciful*.

Ἐλεισάβετ (Hebr.), *Elisabeth*, mother of John the Baptizer.

ἔλεος, *pity, mercy*.

ἐλευθερία, *freedom, liberty*, especially *a state of freedom* from slavery.

ἐλεύθερος, *free* (opposite of *enslaved*, cf. 1 Cor. xii 13).

ἐλευθερόω, *I free, set free, liberate*.

ἔλευσις, *coming, arrival*.

ἐλεφάντινος, *made of ivory*.

Ἐλιακείμ (Hebr.), *Eliakim*, son of Abiud and father of Azor (Mt. i 13), son of Melea and father of Jonam (Lk. iii 30).

ἔλιγμα, *a roll*.

Ἐλιέζερ (Hebr.), *Eliezer*, son of Joreim and father of Joshua.

Ἐλιούδ (Hebr.), *Eliud*, son of Acheim, and father of Eleazar.

Ἐλισάβετ, see Ἐλεισάβετ.

Ἑλισαῖος, *Helisaeus*, grecized form of *Elisha*.

ἐλίσσω, *I roll, roll up*.

ἑλκόομαι, *I am covered with sores*.

ἕλκος (ulcus), *a (festering) sore*.

ἑλκύω, *I drag, draw, pull*.

ἕλκω, *I drag, draw, pull*.

Ἑλλάς, *Hellas*, the native name for *Greece*.

Ἕλλην

Ἕλλην, *a Hellene*, the native word for *a Greek*: it is, however, a term wide enough to include all Greek-speaking (i. e. educated) non-Jews.

Ἑλληνικός, *Greek*: ἡ Ἑλληνικὴ (γλῶσσα), *the Greek language.*

Ἑλληνίς (fem.), *Greek*; see Ἕλλην.

Ἑλληνιστής, *a Hellenist, Grecian Jew*, a Greek-speaking Jew, that is one who can speak Greek only and not Hebrew (or Aramaic).

Ἑλληνιστί, *in the Greek language.*

ἐλλογάω (ἐλλογέω), *I put down (set) to some one's account, reckon, impute.*

Ἐλμαδάμ (Hebr.), *Elmadam, father of Kosam, son of Er.*

ἐλπίζω (ἐλπίζω), *I hope, hope for* : the substantive following ἐν, εἰς, ἐπί with dat. or acc., is the ground of the hope, that which makes hope possible.

ἐλπίς (oftener probably ἐλπίς), *hope.*

Ἐλύμας, *Elymas*, the name of the sorcerer at Paphos (the form of the name is doubtful : some MSS read Ἑτοιμᾶς, *Son of the Ready*).

ἐλωί (Aramaic), *my God* (form of word is doubtful).

ἐμαυτοῦ, *of myself.*

ἐμβαίνω, *I embark.*

ἐμβάλλω, *I cast in, throw in.*

ἐμβάπτω, act. and mid. *I dip in.*

ἐμβατεύω, (*I enter on, take possession of,* hence) technical expression connected with the pagan Mysteries, *I enter, set foot on* (the inner shrine, after the first initiation). It indicates the final act in mystic ceremonial, the entrance on a new life in presence of the god.

ἐμβιβάζω, tr. *I embark, put on board.*

ἐμβλέπω, *I look into (upon).*

ἐμβριμάομαι, *I groan* (with the notion of coercion springing out of displeasure, anger, indignation, antagonism), *I express indignant displeasure*, with dat. of person with whom it is felt, Mt. ix 30, Mk. i 43, xiv 5: absol. John xi 33, 38.

ἐμέω, I vomit.

ἐμμαίνομαι, I am madly enraged with.

Ἐμμανουήλ (Hebr.), Emmanuel, a Messianic title derived from Isa. vii 14 = God with us.

Ἐμμαούς, Emmaus (Ammaus), a village not far from Jerusalem.

ἐμμένω, I remain (abide) in, Ac. xxviii 30 : hence met. Heb. viii 9 : with plain dative, I abide by, maintain, Ac. xiv 22, Gal. iii 10.

Ἐμμώρ (Hebr.), Emmor, Hamor, a man whose sons sold a field at Shechem to Jacob.

ἐμός, mine (predominates in John).

ἐμπ. see also ἐνπ.

ἐμπαιγμονή, mockery.

ἐμπαιγμός, mockery.

ἐμπαίζω, I mock.

ἐμπαίκτης, a mocker.

ἐμπί(μ)πλημι, ἐμπι(μ)πλάω, I fill up, fill.

ἐμπί(μ)πρημι, ἐμπρήθω, I burn, set on fire : but forms from -πρήθω = I cause to swell, hence pass. I suffer inflammation, Ac. xxviii 6 (v. l.).

ἐμπίπτω, I fall in, am cast in.

ἐμπλέκω, I enfold, entangle.

ἐμπλοκή, braiding.

ἐμπορεύομαι, I travel as a merchant, engage in trade: c. acc. I traffic in, make gain or business of.

ἐμπορία, trading, trade, trafficking, business.

ἐμπόριον, a place of traffic, mart, market, market-house.

ἔμπορος, a merchant, trader.

ἐμπρήθω, see ἐμπί(μ)πρημι.

ἔμπροσθεν, in front, before the face : sometimes made a substantive by the addition of the article ; usually c. gen. in front of, before the face of.

ἐμπτύω, I spit upon.

ἐμφανής, manifest, visible.

ἐμφανίζω, I make visible (manifest); hence, act. I report (inform) against, Ac. xxiv 1, xxv 2, 15 ; pass. (quasi-technical) I appear before.

ἔμφοβος

ἔμφοβος, *full of fear, terrified.*
ἐμφυσάω, *I breathe into, breathe upon.*
ἔμφυτος, *inborn, ingrown, congenital, natural.*
ἐν, (a) of place, *in*; ἐν τοῖς, see ὁ: ἐν Χριστῷ, of mystic indwelling; (b) = εἰς, *into,* e. g. Mt. x 16; (c) of time, *in, during, at*; (d) of instrument, (*armed*) *with,* Lk. xxii 49, 1 Cor. iv 21, &c.; (e) *amounting to,* Ac. vii 14 (cf. Mk. iv 8 bis); (f) *consisting in,* Eph. ii 15; (g) *in the department of,* cf. 1 Cor. vi 2; (h) *in the judgement of,* cf. 1 Cor. xiv 11; (i) Hebraistic use, Mt. x 32, Lk. xii 8. For ἐν ᾧ, see ὅς.
ἐναγκαλίζομαι, *I take (fold) in my arms.*
ἐνάλιος (rather a poetical word), of creatures, *living in the sea.*
ἔναντι, *before, in the presence of.*
ἐναντίον, *before, in the presence of*; *in the eyes of*: see also τοὐναντίον.
ἐναντίος, *opposite, opposed, contrary*: ἐξ ἐναντίας (adv.), *opposite*; ὁ ἐξ ἐναντίας, *the adversary.*
ἐνάρχομαι, *I begin (in).*
ἔνατος, *ninth.*
ἐνγράφω, *I write (in), inscribe.*
ἐνδεής, *in need, needy.*
ἔνδειγμα, (*a thing proved,* hence) *a plain token (sign, proof).*
ἐνδείκνυμι (in the middle voice ἐνδείκνυμαι only), *I show forth.*
ἔνδειξις, *a showing, proof, demonstration.*
ἔνδεκα, *eleven.*
ἐνδέκατος, *eleventh.*
ἐνδέχομαι, ἐνδέχεται, impers., *it is possible.*
ἐνδημέω, *I am in* my δῆμος (*parish*), *I am at home.*
ἐνδιδύσκω, (somewhat rare) (of clothing, *I put on* another): mid. *I put on* (myself).
ἔνδικος, *just.*
ἐνδοξάζω (*I make* ἔνδοξος), *I glorify, acknowledge the glory belonging to* (cf. δόξα), *recognize as glorious.*
ἔνδοξος, *glorious.*

ἔνδυμα, *a garment, dress.*

ἐνδυναμόω, *I fill with* δύναμις *(power)* (almost = δυναμόω).

ἐνδύνω, *I enter into.*

ἔνδυσις, *putting on* (of a garment).

ἐνδύω, *I put on, clothe* (another): mid. *I clothe* (myself), *dress*: hence, metaphorically, of acquiring qualities; = ἐπενδύομαι, 2 Cor. v 3.

ἐνδώμησις, *roofing, coping.* (So probably, from δῶμα = *roof*, but most interpret *building*.)

ἐνέδρα (insidiae), *ambuscade*; hence *plot, treachery, fraud.*

ἐνεδρεύω, *I lie in wait* (*ambush*) *for, seek to entrap* (hence *I defraud, deceive*).

ἐνειλέω, *I wrap up, roll up in* (something).

ἔνειμι, *I am in* (*within*): τὰ ἐνόντα, probably *the contents* (of the dish), or perhaps *what you can*, but the words are obscure and may be a mistranslation of an Aramaic original.

ἕνεκα, ἕνεκεν, εἵνεκεν, *for the sake of, on account of*: οὗ (neut.) εἵνεκεν, *on account of which, wherefore*, Lk. iv 18; τίνος ἕνεκα, *on account of what, wherefore, why*, Ac. xix 32.

ἐνενήκοντα, *ninety.*

ἐνεός (= ἄνεως), *speechless, dumb, unable to speak.*

ἐνέργεια, *working, action productive of* ἔργον (concrete *work*), *activity*: in the N.T. confined to superhuman activity.

ἐνεργέω, (a) intr. *I am at work, work*; (b) tr. *I work*, the acc. expressing 'that which is worked', *effect*. In N.T. the word is generally connected with miraculous interpositions; (c) in the passive always with non-personal subject, as ἐνεργεῖν always with personal, *I am made operative* (*effective*), *I am made to produce my appropriate result, I am set in operation, I am made to work.* Mid. absent from N.T.

ἐνέργημα, *a working.*

ἐνεργής, *effective, productive of due result.*

ἐνευλογέω, *I bless* (of God) (ἐν is considered to have instrumental force).

ἐνέχω

ἐνέχω, (a) *I have a grudge against, I am angry (with)*: in Mk. vi 19 the Sahidic translates 'I am angry with', the Vulgate 'insidior'; in Lk. xi 53 δεινῶς ἐνέχειν is translated by the Sahidic 'to provoke him', by the Vulgate 'grauiter insistere'; (b) pass. or mid. *I am entangled, entangle myself* (in 2 Thess. i 4 text doubtful).

ἐνθάδε, *here, in this place.*

ἔνθεν, *hence, from this place.*

ἐνθυμέομαι, *I meditate upon, reflect upon.*

ἐνθύμησις, *inward thought, meditation*; plur. *thoughts.*

ἔνι (ἐνί, Ionic form of ἐν), *is in (among)*: οὐκ ἔνι, *there is* (or *can be*) *no room for.*

ἐνιαυτός, *a year.*

ἐνίστημι: only in the intr. tenses, *I impend, am at hand, am present*: perf. pcpl. ἐνεστηκώς (ἐνεστώς) as adj. *present.*

ἐνισχύω, *I strengthen within, I fill with strength.*

ἐνκάθετος, *a snare-setter, spy.*

ἐνκαίνια, *festival of dedication* of the Temple, to celebrate the re-dedication of the Temple by Judas Maccabeus in 164 B.C., held at Jerusalem about the middle of December.

ἐνκαινίζω, (*I restore* or *carry out anew*, then) *I dedicate.*

ἐνκακέω, ἐκκακέω (from κακός in the sense of *cowardly*) (very rare outside the Bible), *I lose heart.*

ἐνκατοικέω, *I am settled among, dwell among.*

ἐνκαυχάομαι, *I boast in (because of)* something.

ἐνκεντρίζω, *I graft.*

ἐνκοπή, ἐκκοπή, *obstacle, check, hindrance.*

ἐνκόπτω, (*I introduce an obstacle sharply in the way of a moving object*, cf. Eng. colloquial 'I strike in') *I block, check, hinder.*

ἐνκρίνω, *I judge (reckon) to belong to, I class with.*

ἔνκυος, *pregnant.*

ἐννέα, *nine.*

ἐννεύω, *I make a sign to by nodding.*

ἔννοια (*intelligence, thought*), *intention, purpose.*

84

ἐντρυφάω

ἔννομος, (a) *legal, statutory, duly constituted*, Ac. xix 39 ; (b) *under the law, obedient to the law*, 1 Cor. ix 21.

ἔννυχα, *in the night.*

ἐνοικέω, *I dwell in, am settled (stationary) in.*

ἐνορκίζω (a strengthened ὁρκίζω), c. dupl. acc. *I adjure* some one *by*, *I solemnly appeal to* some one *by.*

ἑνότης, *oneness, unity.*

ἐνοχλέω, *I disturb, torment* (Heb. xii 15 is from the LXX, where ἐνοχλῇ appears to be a corruption for ἐν χολῇ, *in gall*).

ἔνοχος (obnoxius), *involved in*, hence *liable*, generally with dat. (or gen.) of the punishment.

ἐνπεριπατέω, *I walk among.*

ἐνπνέω (lit. *I breathe in*), *I breathe of, breathe.*

ἔνταλμα, *an injunction, ordinance.*

ἐνταφιάζω, *I embalm, prepare for burial.*

ἐνταφιασμός, *embalming, preparation* of corpse *for burial.*

ἐντέλλομαι, *I give orders* (*injunctions, instructions, commands*).

ἐντεῦθεν (hinc), *hence, from this place* ; ἐντεῦθεν καὶ ἐντεῦθεν (hinc et illic), *on this side and on that*, cf. Rev. xxii 2.

ἔντευξις (lit. *approaching* the king, hence a technical term), *a petition.*

ἔντιμος, (*held precious*, hence) *precious; honoured, honourable* in rank, &c., Lk. xiv 8.

ἐντολή, *an ordinance, injunction, command.*

ἐντόπιος, *belonging to the place, native, resident.*

ἐντός, *within, inside* (so also Lk. xvii 21) ; τὸ ἐντός, *the inside.*

ἐντρέπω, (a) *I turn to confusion, put to shame*, e.g. 1 Cor. iv 14, 2 Thess. iii 14, Tit. ii 8 ; (b) mid. c. acc., meaning *I reverence*, e. g. Mk. xii 6, Heb. xii 9.

ἐντρέφω, *I nourish (sustain) on.*

ἔντρομος, *trembling.*

ἐντροπή (from ἐντρέπω), *shame.*

ἐντρυφάω, *I revel (in).*

85

ἐντυγχάνω, (a) *I meet, encounter*; hence, (b) *I call (upon)*, *I make a petition, I make suit, supplication,* cf. ἔντευξις.

ἐντυλίσσω, *I wrap up, roll round, envelop.*

ἐντυπόω, *I engrave.*

ἐνυβρίζω, *I insult, outrage.*

ἐνυπνιάζομαι, *I dream* (*see visions*) *in my sleep.*

ἐνύπνιον, *a dream, vision.*

ἐνώπιον (vernacular, attested from saec. ii B. c.), *before the face of, in the presence of; in the eyes of.*

Ἐνώς (Hebr.), *Enos,* son of Seth, and father of Cainam.

ἐνωτίζομαι (from ἐν and οὖς), *I take into my ear, give ear to.*

Ἐνώχ, Ἑνώκ (Hebr.), *Enoch,* son of Jaret and father of Mathusala: Jude 14 refers to the apocryphal *Book of Enoch.*

ἕξ, *six.*

ἐξαγγέλλω, *I announce publicly, proclaim.*

ἐξαγοράζω, *I buy out, buy away from, ransom*: mid. *I purchase out, buy, redeem.*

ἐξάγω, *I lead out,* sometimes to death, execution (duco).

ἐξαιρέω, *I take out, remove*; sometimes (mid.) *I choose,* sometimes *I rescue.*

ἐξαίρω, *I remove.*

ἐξαιτέομαι, *I beg earnestly for*: aor. = *I have procured to be given up to me* (Field).

ἐξαίφνης (ἐξέφνης, colloquially), *suddenly.*

ἐξακολουθέω, *I follow closely, adhere to.*

ἐξακόσιοι, *six hundred.*

ἐξαλείφω, *I wipe away, obliterate.*

ἐξάλλομαι, *I leap up* (for joy).

ἐξανάστασις, *rising up and out, resurrection.*

ἐξανατέλλω, *I rise* (*spring*) *up out* (of the ground).

ἐξανίστημι, (a) in tr. tenses, *I raise up, cause to grow*; (b) in intr. tenses, *I rise up.*

ἐξαπατάω, *I deceive.*

ἐξάπινα, *suddenly.*

ἐξαπορέομαι, *I am at my wits' end, I despair*: c. gen. *about,* 2 Cor. i 8.

ἐξαποστέλλω, *I send away out, I send forth* (a person qualified for a task).

ἐξαρτίζω, (a) *I fit up, equip, furnish, supply,* 2 Tim. iii 17; (b) *I accomplish, finish,* Ac. xxi 5.

ἐξαστράπτω (corusco), *I flash forth like lightning.*

ἐξαυτῆς (= ἐξ αὐτῆς τῆς ὥρας), *immediately.*

ἐξεγείρω, *I raise up, arouse.*

ἔξειμι (originally, *I shall go out*), *I go out* (*away*), *depart.*

ἐξέλκω (lit. *I draw out* of the right place, or *I draw aside* out of the right way), *I entice.*

ἐξέραμα, *vomit, purge.*

ἐξεραυνάω, *I search diligently, I examine carefully* (*minutely*).

ἐξέρχομαι, *I go out.*

ἔξεστιν, impers. *it is permitted* (*allowed*), sometimes followed by acc. et inf.: ἐξόν ἐστιν = ἔξεστιν, the ἔστιν being understood in Ac. ii 29, 2 Cor. xii 4.

ἐξετάζω (indicates precise and careful inquiry), *I examine, question, inquire at.*

ἐξηγέομαι, (*I interpret*) *I relate, expound, explain; make declaration* (John i 18).

ἑξήκοντα, *sixty.*

ἑξῆς (deinceps), *next in order:* ἡ ἑξῆς (sc. ἡμέρα), *the next day, the following day:* τῷ ἑξῆς (Lk. vii 11, v. l.), perhaps = τῷ ἑξῆς χρόνῳ, *at the period immediately following.*

ἐξηχέω, *I sound out* (*forth*) (referring either to the clearness or to the loudness of the sound).

ἕξις, *condition, state,* especially *good condition* of body or soul.

ἐξίστημι, ἐξιστάω, ἐξιστάνω (lit. *I remove from a standing position*), (a) in tr. tenses (including ἐξέστακα), *I astonish, amaze;* (b) in intr. tenses, *I am astonished, amazed; I am out of my mind, I am mad,* Mk. iii 21, 2 Cor. v 13.

ἐξισχύω, *I have strength for* (a difficult task).

ἔξοδος, (a) *going out, departure* from a place; (b) (excessus) *death,* Lk. ix 31, 2 Pet. i 15.

ἐξολεθρεύω

ἐξολεθρεύω, *I destroy utterly, annihilate, exterminate.*

ἐξομολογέω, (a) *I consent fully, agree out and out,* Lk. xxii 6 ; (b) *I confess, admit, acknowledge* (cf. the early Hellenistic sense of the middle, *I acknowledge* a debt) ; (c) in certain passages there is a difficulty as to the sense: in Mt. xi 25 (Lk. x 21) the Vulgate (with the Sahidic) renders by *confiteor,* but modern scholars prefer either *I give thanks* or *I praise.*

ἐξόν, see **ἔξεστιν.**

ἐξορκίζω, *I exorcize, cast out by appeal to a god.*

ἐξορκιστής, *an exorcist, a caster out of evil spirits* by the use of names or spells.

ἐξορύσσω, (a) *I dig out* : hence, *I open up* ; (b) *I gouge,* Gal. iv 15.

ἐξουδενέω, another (inferior) spelling of ἐξουθενέω.

ἐξουδενόω (an inferior spelling is ἐξουθενόω) = ἐξουθενεω.

ἐξουθενέω, *I set at nought, ignore, despise.*

ἐξουσία, (a) *power, authority, weight,* especially *moral authority, influence* ; in 1 Cor. xi 10 the *authority* which the wearing of the veil gives the woman, making her sacrosanct ; c. gen. indicates *over* any one ; (b) in a quasi-personal sense, derived from later Judaism, of *a spiritual power,* 1 Pet. iii 22, and hence of *an earthly power* (e. g. Lk. xii 11 and often, in combination with ἀρχή).

ἐξουσιάζω, *I exercise* (*wield*) *power* (*authority*), c. gen., *over* : pass. 1 Cor. vi 12, *I am ruled.*

ἐξοχή, *projection, prominence* : οἱ κατ᾽ ἐξοχήν, *the prominent persons, the chief men.*

ἐξυπνίζω, *I wake* out of sleep.

ἔξυπνος, *awake* out of sleep.

ἔξω, (a) adv. *without* ; in ὁ ἔξω, &c. the adv. is equivalent to an adjective, τὰς ἔξω πόλεις, *foreign cities,* Ac. xxvi 11, ὁ ἔξω ἄνθρωπος, *the outer* (*physical*) *nature,* 2 Cor. iv 16, especially οἱ ἔξω, *the outsiders, the non-Christians* ; (b) prep. c. gen. *outside.*

ἔξωθεν, (a) *from outside, from without* ; (b) *outside,* equivalent to ἔξω, both as adv. and as prep. (Mk.

88

vii 15, Rev. xi 2, xiv 20, &c.); τὸ ἔξωθεν, *the outside*,&c., οἱ ἔξωθεν = οἱ ἔξω.

ἐξωθέω, *I push out, thrust out*: εἰς αἰγιαλὸν ἐξῶσαι, *to drive the ship upon the beach*, Ac. xxvii 39.

ἐξώτερος, *outmost*.

ἔοικα, *I am like, resemble*.

ἑορτάζω, *I take part in a festival, keep a feast* (allegorically).

ἑορτή, *a festival, feast*, periodically recurring: ποιεῖν ἑορτήν, Ac. xviii 21 = ἑορτάζειν.

ἐπαγγελία, *a promise*: see τέκνον·

ἐπαγγέλλομαι, (a) *I promise*; (b) *I profess*, 1 Tim. ii 10, vi 21.

ἐπάγγελμα, *a promise*.

ἐπάγω, *I bring upon*.

ἐπαγωνίζομαι, *I contend for*.

ἐπαθροίζομαι, *I crowd upon* (some one), *press around*.

Ἐπαίνετος, *Epaenetus*, a Christian in Rome.

ἐπαινέω, *I praise, commend*.

ἔπαινος, *praise*.

ἐπαίρω, *I raise, lift up*.

ἐπαισχύνομαι, *I am ashamed of*.

ἐπαιτέω, *I beg, am a beggar*.

ἐπακολουθέω, *I follow close after, I accompany, dog*; *I promote*, 1 Tim. v 10; hence *I endorse* [Mk.] xvi 20.

ἐπακούω, *I listen to, hear*.

ἐπακροάομαι, *I listen to, hearken to*.

ἐπάν, *whensoever*.

ἐπάναγκες, adv. used as adj. *necessary, inevitable, obligatory*.

ἐπανάγω, (a) nautical, *I put out* (from the shore), (lit. *I take up* a ship *on to* the high seas); (b) *I go up*, possibly *I go up again, return*.

ἐπαναμιμνήσκω, *I remind*, possibly *I remind again*.

ἐπαναπαύομαι, *I rest upon*.

ἐπανέρχομαι, *I return*.

ἐπανίστημι, intr. tenses, *I rise against*.

ἐπανόρθωσις, *setting straight (right) again.*

ἐπάνω, (a) adv. *on the top, above*; (b) prep. *on the top of, above, over, on*: met. of rule, *over*, Lk. xix 17, &c.; *above, more than*, Mk. xiv 5, 1 Cor. xv 6.

ἐπάρατος, *accursed, cursed.*

ἐπαρκέω, *I do service, render help.*

ἐπαρχεία, the official equivalent of Lat. prouincia, *sphere of duty, province.*

ἐπάρχειος (a v. l. in Ac. xxv 1), *belonging to the province*: τῇ ἐπαρχείῳ (understand ἐξουσίᾳ), *the power over the province, the province.*

ἔπαυλις, *a farm, estate.*

ἐπαύριον, *to-morrow.*

Ἐπαφρᾶς (the pet form of Ἐπαφρόδιτος), *Epaphras, Epaphroditus*, a Colossian Christian, in captivity with Paul in Rome.

ἐπαφρίζω, *I foam out* (a metaphor from the seaweed and refuse borne on the crest of waves).

Ἐπαφρόδιτος, see Ἐπαφρᾶς.

ἐπεγείρω, *I arouse, stimulate.*

ἐπεί, (a) *after*, Lk. vii 1 (v. l.), Ac. xiii 46 (v. l.); (b) *for, since*; (c) *otherwise*, Rom. xi 6. 22, 1 Cor. v 10, &c.

ἐπειδή, (a) *when*, Lk. vii 1; (b) *since.*

ἐπειδήπερ, *since.*

ἐπεῖδον, *I looked upon, regarded.*

ἔπειμι, in the participle ἐπιοῦσα, *coming on, next*: τῇ ἐπιούσῃ (understand ἡμέρᾳ), *next day.*

ἐπεισαγωγή, *bringing in, introduction, importation.*

ἐπεισέρχομαι, *I come (in) upon.*

ἔπειτα, *then, thereafter, afterwards.*

ἐπέκεινα, *beyond.*

ἐπεκτείνομαι, *I strain after.*

ἐπενδύομαι, *I put on* (as a garment).

ἐπενδύτης, *a coat, outer wrap.*

ἐπέρχομαι, *I come upon*, sometimes with hostility.

ἐπερωτάω = ἐρωτάω simply, *I ask, question.*

ἐπερώτημα = ἐρώτημα, *a request.*

ἐπέχω, (a) tr. *I hold forth*; (b) intr. (νοῦν being understood) *I mark, pay attention* (*heed*)*, note,* Ac. iii 5, I Tim. iv 16 : *I delay,* Ac. xix 22.

ἐπηρεάζω, *I insult, treat wrongfully, molest.*

ἐπί, (a) c. gen. locally, *on, upon*; and so met. of that *on* which anything rests, e. g. ἐπ' ἀληθείας, *in truth* : of authority *over,* e.g. Mt. xxiv 45: *concerning,* Gal. iii 16: *in presence of,* e. g. Mt. xxviii 14 : *at, in,* Mk. xii 26 : *in* (*at*) *the time* (*period*) *of,* e. g. Mk. ii 26 ; (b) c. dat. *on, upon* : *near,* e. g. Mt. xxiv 33 : *on the basis* (*ground*) *of,* e. g. Mt. iv 4 : *on account of,* e. g. Lk. v 5, ἐφ' ᾧ (= ἐπὶ τούτῳ, ὅ, τι), *in view of the fact that* : *over* (cf. under (a)), Lk. xii 44 : *against,* Lk. xii 52 : *in addition to,* e. g. 2 Cor. vii 13 : *in, at,* ἐπὶ τούτῳ, *meantime,* John iv 27 : *for, with a view to,* cf. Ac. v 35 ; (c) c. acc. locally, *on, upon,* generally after verbs indicating motion, but afterwards more widely used, both lit. and met., ἐπὶ τὸ αὐτό, *in the same place, together, in all,* cf. Ac. i 15, ii 47 : *near, to, towards* (after word expressing motion, and then more widely), both lit. and met. : *against* : *in addition to* (cf. under (b)), Phil. ii 27: of number or degree attained, *as far as,* e. g. ἐπὶ πλεῖον, ἐφ' ὅσον : of charge, rule, or power *over* : *concerning,* e. g. Lk. xxiii 28 : *on account of, with a view to,* Mk. xv 24, John xix 24 : of time, *for, during,* e. g. Lk. iv 25 : of time, *about,* e. g. Lk. x 35.

ἐπιβαίνω, (a) *I set foot on, I step on*; (b) *I mount* (a horse)*, board* (a vessel).

ἐπιβάλλω, (a) *I throw upon, cast over,* 1 Cor. vii 35, Rev. xviii 19 (v.l.); (b) *I place upon*; (c) *I lay,* with τὴν χεῖρα (τὰς χεῖρας), either with innocent, or with hostile, intent (= inicere manum [manus]) ; (d) intr. *I strike upon,* Mk. iv 37 ; (e) intr. τὸ ἐπιβάλλον μέρος, *the share that falls to* (*belongs to*) *one,* Lk. xv 12 ; (f) intr. ἐπιβαλὼν ἔκλαιεν, *he set to and wept,* Mk. xiv 72.

ἐπιβαρέω, *I put a burden on, burden.*

ἐπιβιβάζω, *I place upon* (a horse, mule).

ἐπιβλέπω, *I look with favour on.*

ἐπίβλημα, *something put on, a patch*

ἐπιβουλή

ἐπιβουλή, *a plot.*

ἐπιγαμβρεύω, *I take to wife after.*

ἐπίγειος, (a) *on the earth, belonging to the earth* (as opposed to the sky); (b) in a spiritual sense, *belonging to the earthly sphere, earthly* (as opposed to heavenly) (opp. ἐπουράνιος in both senses).

ἐπιγίνομαι, *I come on, supervene.*

ἐπιγινώσκω, *I come to know* by directing my attention to (ἐπί) him or it, *I perceive, discern, recognize*: aor. *I found out.*

ἐπίγνωσις, *knowledge* of a particular point (directed towards a particular object); *perception, discernment, recognition; intuition.*

ἐπιγραφή, *an inscription.*

ἐπιγράφω, *I write upon, inscribe.*

ἐπιδείκνυμι, *I show, display, point out, indicate; I prove, demonstrate,* Ac. xviii 28, Heb. vi 17.

ἐπιδέχομαι, *I welcome.*

ἐπιδημέω, *I am resident* (temporarily, in a foreign city).

ἐπιδιατάσσομαι, *I make an additional testamentary disposition, I furnish with additions.*

ἐπιδίδωμι, (a) tr. *I hand in;* (b) intr. *I give way* (to the wind), Ac. xxvii 15.

ἐπιδιορθόω, *I put besides into a state of order, I put in order.*

ἐπιδύω, *I sink, set.*

ἐπιείκεια, *considerateness, forbearance, fairness.*

ἐπιεικής, *forbearing, fair, reasonable.*

ἐπιζητέω, *I seek after, search for, make inquiries about.*

ἐπιθανάτιος, *at the point of death, doomed to death.*

ἐπίθεσις, *laying on.*

ἐπιθυμέω, *I desire, long;* ἐπιθυμίᾳ ἐπιθυμεῖν, Hebraistic, *to long eagerly,* Lk. xxii 15.

ἐπιθυμητής, *a longer after, luster after.*

ἐπιθυμία, *eager* (*passionate*) *desire, passion:* see ἐπιθυμέω.

ἐπικαθίζω, *I sit.*

ἐπικαλέω, (a) *I call* (*name*) *by a supplementary* (*addi-*

tional, alternative) *name*; (b) mid. *I call upon, appeal to, address.*

ἐπικάλυμμα, *a covering, pretext.*

ἐπικαλύπτω, *I put a cover on, cover up.*

ἐπικατάρατος, *on whom a curse has been invoked, accursed.*

ἐπίκειμαι, (a) c. dat. or c. ἐπί et dat. *I am placed upon, am laid upon, lie upon, am imposed*; *I press upon*, Lk. v 1; (b) absol. *I press hard,* Ac. xxvii 20; *I am insistent, insist,* Lk. xxiii 23.

ἐπικέλλω, *I beach, run aground, drive* a ship *on to.*

Ἐπικούρειος, *an Epicurean,* one who holds the tenets of Epicurus (341–270 B.C.).

ἐπικουρία, *succour* (against foes), *help.*

ἐπικρίνω, *I give decision, decide.*

ἐπιλαμβάνομαι, *I lay hold of, take hold of, seize* (sometimes with beneficent, sometimes with hostile, intent).

ἐπιλανθάνομαι, *I forget.*

ἐπιλέγομαι, (a) mid. *I choose for myself,* Ac. xv 40; (b) pass. *I am named.*

ἐπιλείπω, *I fail, leave behind.*

ἐπιλείχω, *I lick.*

ἐπιλησμονή, *forgetting,* in James i 25 a Hebraistic gen. = *that forgets.*

ἐπίλοιπος, *remaining, that is left over.*

ἐπίλυσις, *solution, explanation, interpretation.*

ἐπιλύω, *I explain.*

ἐπιμαρτυρέω, *I call to witness.*

ἐπιμέλεια, *care, attention.*

ἐπιμελέομαι, *I care for, attend to.*

ἐπιμελῶς, *carefully, attentively.*

ἐπιμένω, (a) *I remain, tarry*; (b) c. dat. *I remain in, persist in.*

ἐπινεύω, *I consent.*

ἐπίνοια, *thought.*

ἐπιορκέω, ἐφιορκέω, *I take an oath, swear.*

ἐπίορκος, *perjuring, a perjurer.*

ἐπιούσιος (from ἡ ἐπιοῦσα [ἡμέρα]), *belonging to the morrow.*

93

ἐπιπίπτω, *I fall upon*; *I press upon*, Mk. iii 10.

ἐπιπλήσσω, *I reprove*.

ἐπιποθέω, *I long for, strain after, desire greatly*.

ἐπιπόθησις, *eager longing* (*desire*).

ἐπιπόθητος (desiderabilis, desiderantissimus), *longed for, missed*.

ἐπιποθία, *longing, eager desire*.

ἐπιπορεύομαι, *I journey* (*to*).

ἐπιράπτω, *I sew* (*on*).

ἐπιρίπτω, *I throw* (*cast*) (*upon*).

ἐπίσημος, *notable, conspicuous*.

ἐπισιτισμός, *provision, nourishment, food*.

ἐπισκέπτομαι, (a) *I look out*, Ac. vi 3 ; (b) *I visit*.

ἐπισκευάζομαι, *I equip* (horses).

ἐπισκηνόω, *I raise a tent* (*over*).

ἐπισκιάζω, *I overshadow, envelop*.

ἐπισκοπέω, *I exercise oversight* (*care*).

ἐπισκοπή, (a) *visitation* (of judgement), Lk. xix 44, 1 Pet. ii 12 ; (b) *oversight, supervision, overseership*.

ἐπίσκοπος (used as an official title in civil life), *overseer, supervisor, ruler*, especially used with reference to the supervising function exercised by an elder or presbyter of a church or congregation, and therefore (at first) practically synonymous with πρεσβύτερος.

ἐπισπάω (lit. *I draw over*), mid. *I undo the effects of circumcision on myself.*

ἐπισπείρω, *I sow above* (*over*), *I resow*.

ἐπίσταμαι, *I know, understand*.

ἐπίστασις, *caballing* (*conspiring*) *against*.

ἐπιστάτης, *master, teacher* (cf. Dalman, *Words of Jesus*, Eng. tr., p. 276).

ἐπιστέλλω, *I enjoin*, generally *in writing, I write*.

ἐπιστήμων, *knowing* by experience (personal acquaintance).

ἐπιστηρίζω, *I prop up, uphold, support, confirm*.

ἐπιστολή, *a letter, dispatch*.

ἐπιστομίζω, *I muzzle, silence*.

ἐπιστρέφω, (a) tr. *I turn* (*back*) *to* (*towards*); (b) intr.

94

I turn (*back*) (*to* [*towards*]); *I come to myself*, Lk. xxii 32.

ἐπιστροφή, *a turning* (*to God*).

ἐπισυνάγω, *I collect, gather together*.

ἐπισυναγωγή, *gathering* (*collecting*) *together, assembling*.

ἐπισυντρέχω, *I run together to* (*towards*).

ἐπισφαλής, *dangerous*.

ἐπισχύω, *I persist, insist*.

ἐπισωρεύω, *I heap up*.

ἐπιταγή, *instruction, command, order, authority* (often of a god).

ἐπιτάσσω, *I give order, command*.

ἐπιτελέω, *I complete, accomplish, perfect*.

ἐπιτήδειος, *necessary*.

ἐπιτίθημι, *I place upon, lay on* : with ὄνομα, *I add, give in addition*.

ἐπιτιμάω, (a) *I rebuke, chide, censure*; (b) c. ἵνα, *I warn*.

ἐπιτιμία, *punishment*.

ἐπιτρέπω, *I allow, permit*.

ἐπιτροπεύω, *I act as* ἐπίτροπος (*procurator*) *over*, v. l. Lk. iii 1.

ἐπιτροπή, *commission*.

ἐπίτροπος, (a) (procurator) *a steward*; (b) (tutor) *a guardian* (appointed for an 'infant' [under 14 perhaps] by the father or by a magistrate), Gal. iv 2.

ἐπιτυγχάνω, *I attain, obtain*.

ἐπιφαίνω, *I appear* (as of a light in the heavens [cf. Ac. xxvii 20] or from the heavens).

ἐπιφάνεια, *appearing, manifestation* (of a conspicuous intervention from the sky on behalf of a worshipper).

ἐπιφανής, *manifest*.

ἐπιφαύσκω, *I shine upon*.

ἐπιφέρω, *I bring forward* (*against*).

ἐπιφωνέω, *I call out, shout*; c. dat. *against*, Ac. xxii 24.

ἐπιφώσκω, of the next day, *I draw on*.

ἐπιχειρέω, *I take in hand, I attempt*.

ἐπιχέω, *I pour on*.

ἐπιχορηγέω, *I supply, provide* (perhaps lavishly).

ἐπιχορηγία, *supply, provision, equipment.*

ἐπιχρίω, *I besmear, anoint.*

ἐποικοδομέω, *I build upon* (*above*) *a foundation.*

ἐπονομάζω, *I name, impose a name on.*

ἐποπτεύω, *I am an eyewitness of, behold.*

ἐπόπτης (originally of one initiated into the mysteries, but also found of *a surveyor, supervisor*), *an eyewitness.*

ἔπος, *a word*: ὡς ἔπος εἰπεῖν (a literary phrase), *one might almost say,* modifying a statement, Heb. vii 9.

ἐπουράνιος (opp. ἐπίγειος), *heavenly, in heaven*: ἐν τοῖς ἐπουρανίοις, *in the heavenly sphere,* the sphere of spiritual activities.

ἑπτά, *seven*: οἱ ἑπτά, *the seven* ('deacons' of Ac. vi 3–6).

ἑπτάκις, *seven times*: ἑπτάκις τῆς ἡμέρας, *seven times in the day.*

ἑπτακισχίλιοι, *seven thousand.*

ἑπταπλασίων, *sevenfold.*

Ἔραστος, *Erastus,* steward of Corinth, a Christian.

ἐραυνάω (a form of ἐρευνάω not known before 1st cent. A.D.), *I search*: = ἐξεραυνάω, 1 Pet. i 11.

ἐργάζομαι, (a) *I am at work, I work*; (b) tr. *I produce by work, put in force, give operation to, realize,* e.g. Mt. vii 23 ; c. cogn. acc. ἔργον, ἔργα, Mt. xxvi 10, &c. ; c. acc. βρῶσιν, *I work for,* John vi 27.

ἐργασία, *working, activity, work, service, trade, business, gains of business*: δὸς ἐργασίαν (da operam), *take pains to, see to it that you,* Lk. xii 58 ; *performance, practice,* Eph. iv 19.

ἐργάτης, *a field-labourer*; then, *a labourer, workman* in general.

ἔργον, (a) *work, labour* (in the physical, originally in the agricultural, sphere); (b) moral *action, deed,* hence with adjectives or genitives defining its character.

ἐρεθίζω, *I stir up,* 2 Cor. ix 2 : *I arouse to anger, provoke,* Col. iii 21.

ἐρείδω, *I strike* ; *I run aground* (of a ship).

ἐρεύγομαι, (lit. *I belch forth,* hence) *I utter, declare.*

ἐρημία, *a desert place, a desert.*

ἔρημος (the Latin *heremus* may be due to false analogy with *heres, hereticus,* &c.), adj. *desert*; hence, ἡ ἔρημος (sc. χώρα), *the desert,* to the E. and S. of Palestine : of a person, *deserted, abandoned, desolate,* Gal. iv 27.

ἐρημόω, (a) *I make desolate, bring to desolation, destroy, waste*; (b) of a person, *I strip, rob.*

ἐρήμωσις, *making into a desert, wasting, desolating, desolation.*

ἐρίζω, *I strive.*

ἐριθεία, (*the seeking of followers and adherents by means of gifts, the seeking of followers,* hence) *ambition, rivalry.*

ἔριον, *wool.*

ἔρις, *strife.*

ἐρίφιον, *a goat,* or *kid.*

ἔριφος, *a goat.*

Ἑρμᾶς, *Hermas,* a Roman Christian.

ἑρμηνεία, *translation, interpretation.*

ἑρμηνευτής, *translator, interpreter.*

ἑρμηνεύω, (a) *I translate*; (b) *I interpret* the meaning of, Lk. xxiv 27 (v. l.).

Ἑρμῆς, (a) *Hermes,* the messenger and herald of the Greek gods, or rather the corresponding Lycaonian deity : to him also corresponded the Latin Mercurius, Ac. xiv 12 ; (b) *Hermes,* a Roman Christian.

Ἑρμογένης, *Hermogenes,* a faithless Christian at Rome.

ἑρπετόν, *a creeping creature, reptile,* especially *a serpent.*

ἐρυθρός, *red.*

ἔρχομαι, (a) *I go*: with acc. of extent, ὁδόν; (b) *I come*: εἰς ἑαυτὸν ἐλθών, *having come to himself, having come to his right mind, 'having reasoned with himself'* (Sahidic), Lk. xv 17.

ἐρῶ, *I shall say*: c. acc. pers. ὑμᾶς εἴρηκα φίλους, *I have called you friends,* John xv 15, ἄρχοντα οὐκ ἐρεῖς κακῶς, *thou shalt not speak evilly of a leader,* Ac. xxiii 5, cf. Rom. iv 1 (v. l.); cf. εἶπον.

ἐρωτάω, (a) *I ask* (a question), *I question*; (b) (= αἰτέω) *I request, make a request to, I pray.*

ἐσθής, *clothing*.

ἔσθησις, *a garment*.

ἐσθίω, ἔσθω, tr. and intr. *I eat, I am eating*; *I take a meal*: aor. φαγεῖν, *to eat*, but in Rev. x 10 = καταφαγεῖν.

Ἐσλεί (Hebr.), *Eslei*, son of Naggai and father of Nahum.

ἔσοπτρον, *a mirror, looking-glass* (made of highly polished metal).

ἑσπέρα, *evening*.

ἑσπερινός, *in the evening, belonging to the evening, evening*.

Ἑσρώμ, Ἑσρών (Hebr.), *Hesrom, Hesron*, son of Phares, father of Aram (Arnei).

ἔσχατος (ultimus), *last*: ἔσχατον, neut. acc. as adv., *at the last, finally*; ἐπ' ἐσχάτου, *at the end*; ἕως ἐσχάτου, *till the end*.

ἐσχάτως: ἐσχάτως ἔχειν, *to be at the extremity, to be 'in extremis', to be at the last gasp*.

ἔσω, (adv.) *within, inside*, with verbs either of rest or of motion: ὁ ἔσω ἄνθρωπος, *that part of man which is spiritual*; οἱ ἔσω, *those within* (the church), *members of the church*, 1 Cor. v 12; (prep.) *within, to within, inside*, Mk. xv 16.

ἔσωθεν, (a) *from within, from inside*; (b) *within, inside*: τὸ ἔσωθεν, *the inner part, the inner element*.

ἐσώτερος, *inner*: τὸ ἐσώτερον, *the part that is within*, c. gen.

ἑταῖρος, *companion, comrade*.

ἑτερόγλωσσος, *speaking another language*.

ἑτεροδιδασκαλέω, *I teach different things*, that is, *different from the true* or *necessary teaching*.

ἑτεροζυγέω, *I am yoked with one different from myself, unequally yoked*.

ἕτερος (alter), (a) of two, *another, a second*: ἐν ἑτέρῳ (sc. ψαλμῷ), Heb. v 6; ὁ ἕτερος, *the other, the second*, τῇ ἑτέρᾳ (sc. ἡμέρᾳ), *on the second day*, Ac. xx 15, xxvii 3; ἕτεροι, *others, another group*; (b) sometimes it does not differ from ἄλλος (alius), being used of more than two, *other, different,* cf. Lk. viii 6–8, 2 Cor. xi 4 : in Gal. i 6 f. ἕτερος appears to mean *another of the same kind,* as contrasted with ἄλλος, *another of a different kind.*

ἑτέρως, *differently.*

ἔτι (adhuc), (a) of time, *still, yet* ; *even now* : οὐκ ἔτι, *no longer,* and similarly with other negatives ; (b) of degree, *even* ; *further, more, in addition.*

ἑτοιμάζω, *I make ready, prepare.*

ἑτοιμασία, (in LXX, *a stand, base,* but also) *readiness* (of bearer of good tidings).

ἕτοιμος, *ready, prepared* : ἐν ἑτοίμῳ ἔχοντες, *being ready,* 2 Cor. x 6, cf. **ἑτοίμως.**

ἑτοίμως, *readily* : ἑτοίμως ἔχειν, *to be ready.*

ἔτος, ἔτος, *a year* : κατ᾽ ἔτος (καθ᾽ ἔτος), *annually* ; ἀπὸ or ἐξ ἐτῶν followed by a number (Fr. *depuis,* Germ. *seit,* English *for*), lit. *from . . . years.*

εὖ (bene), adv. *well* : as interj. *well done! bravo!*

Εὖα, Εὕα (Hebr.), *Eva, Eve,* wife of Adam, the first man.

εὐαγγελίζω, but far oftener mid. εὐαγγελίζομαι, *I bring good news, I preach good tidings,* with or without an obj., expressing either the persons who receive the good news or the good news itself (the good news being sometimes expressed as a person, e.g. Ac. v 42).

εὐαγγέλιον, τό, *the good news* of the coming of the Messiah, *the gospel* : the gen. after it expresses sometimes the giver (God), sometimes the subject (the Messiah, &c.), sometimes the human transmitter (an apostle).

εὐαγγελιστής, *a missionary* (an occurrence on a pagan inscription = priest of Εὐάγγελος, that is, of Ἑρμῆς, is found).

εὐαρεστέω, *I give pleasure to, I please* (perhaps with the added idea of *rendering good service to,* cf. ἀρέσκω).

εὐάρεστος, *well-pleasing* (especially to God).

εὐαρέστως, *in a well-pleasing way.*

Εὔβουλος

Εὔβουλος, *Eubulus*, a Christian with St. Paul in Rome.

εὖγε, interj. *well done! bravo!*

εὐγενής (generosus), (a) *of noble birth, of high birth*; (b) *noble* in nature, Ac. xvii 11.

εὐδία, *fair weather, good weather*.

εὐδοκέω, *I am well-pleased*, c. acc. expressing *with*, Mt. xii 18, &c.; *I think it good, am resolved* (a characteristic word of Jewish Greek).

εὐδοκία, (a) *good-will* (*good-pleasure*), *favour, feeling of complacency* of God to man: ἄνθρωποι εὐδοκίας (Hebraistic), *men with whom God is well-pleased*, Lk. ii 14; (b) *good-pleasure, satisfaction, happiness, delight* of men, e. g. 2 Thess. i 11, though even in such passages there may be a latent reference to (divine) approval.

εὐεργεσία, *good action, well-doing, benefiting, kind service*.

εὐεργετέω, *I do good deeds, perform kind service, benefit*.

εὐεργέτης, *Benefactor*, an honorary title of kings and governors.

εὔθετος, *fitted, suitable*: absol. Heb. vi 7.

εὐθέως, *immediately*.

εὐθυδρομέω, *I run a straight course*.

εὐθυμέω, *I keep up spirit, am of good courage*.

εὔθυμος, *in good spirits*.

εὐθύμως, *with good courage*.

εὐθύνω, (a) *I make straight* (of the direction, not the surface, of a road); (b) *I steer*, James iii 4.

εὐθύς, adj. (a) *straight*, of direction, as opposed to crooked (σκολιός); (b) met. *upright*.

εὐθύς, adv. *immediately*: characteristic of Mk.

εὐθύτης, *straightness, uprightness*.

εὐκαιρέω, *I have a good* (*favourable*) *opportunity, I have leisure*.

εὐκαιρία, *a good opportunity, an opportunity*.

εὔκαιρος, *opportune, timely, suitable*: in Mk. vi 21 perhaps = *empty, holiday, festal*.

εὐκαίρως, *opportunely, in season, conveniently*.

εὔκοπος, *easy.*

εὐλάβεια, *caution, care*; then *anxiety, fear* (in a good sense); then almost *piety.*

εὐλαβέομαι (cf. εὐλάβεια), *I am anxious,* περί, *about.*

εὐλαβής, (lit. *handling well*, hence) *cautious, circumspect*; hence *God-fearing, pious.*

εὐλογέω, (lit. *I speak well of,* opp. *I abuse, curse*) *I bless*; εὐλογημένος, of a man, *blessed* (by God; contrast εὐλογητός): εὐλογῶν (or ἐν εὐλογίᾳ) εὐλογῶ (Hebraistic), *I bless abundantly.*

εὐλογητός (used only of God), *blessed* (as entitled to receive blessing from man).

εὐλογία, *blessing.*

εὐμετάδοτος, *willingly sharing, ready to impart.*

Εὐνίκη, *Eunice,* mother of Timothy.

εὐνοέω, *I have good-will.*

εὔνοια, *good-will.*

εὐνουχίζω, *I make into a eunuch, emasculate, castrate.*

εὐνοῦχος, (a) *a chamberlain, keeper of the bed-chamber* of an Eastern potentate, *eunuch,* Ac. viii: hence, as such were castrated, (b) *a eunuch, a castrated person.*

Εὐοδία, *Euodia, Evodia,* or rather *Euhodia,* a Christian woman of Philippi.

εὐοδόομαι, *I have a happy (successful) journey*: hence *I prosper,* with the acc. in 1 Cor. xvi 2 expressing the concrete sign of prosperity.

εὐπάρεδρος, *promotive of fit waiting on.*

εὐπειθής, *compliant.*

εὐπερίστατος, *easily surrounding, easily encircling.*

εὐποιία, *good doing, doing of good.*

εὐπορέομαι, *I am prosperous.*

εὐπορία, *wealth, gain.*

εὐπρέπεια (with a notion of stateliness or majesty), *glory.*

εὐπρόσδεκτος, *well-received, acceptable, welcome.*

εὐπροσωπέω, *I look well, I make a fair show* (a good outward appearance, and so win good opinion).

Εὐρακύλων, *Euraquilo,* an East-north-east wind.

εὑρίσκω (reperio), *I find,* especially after searching ; but in Phil. iii 9 possibly *I surprise.*

εὐρύχωρος, *broad.*

εὐσέβεια, *piety* (towards God), *godliness.*

εὐσεβέω, *I am dutiful, pious* : c. acc. pers. *towards* one who has the right to it, man or God.

εὐσεβής, *pious, God-fearing.*

εὐσεβῶς, *piously.*

εὔσημος, *with clear meaning.*

εὔσπλαγχνος, *tender-hearted, merciful.*

εὐσχημόνως, *becomingly, decorously.*

εὐσχημοσύνη, *comeliness.*

εὐσχήμων, (a) *comely, seemly, decorous* ; (b) *of honourable position* (in society).

εὐτόνως, *vehemently, powerfully.*

εὐτραπελία, *versatility* (especially of speech) ; *facetiousness, raillery.*

Εὔτυχος, *Eutychus,* a young hearer of St. Paul at Troas.

εὐφημία, *good reputation.*

εὔφημος, *well reported of.*

εὐφορέω, *I bear well, I bring a good harvest.*

εὐφραίνω, *I cheer, make glad* : generally mid. or pass. *I am glad* ; *I make merry, revel, feast.*

Εὐφράτης, *the Euphrates,* boundary river of the province Syria.

εὐφροσύνη, *gladness.*

εὐχαριστέω, *I give thanks* : pass. 3 sing. *is received with thanks,* 2 Cor. i 11.

εὐχαριστία, *thankfulness, gratitude.*

εὐχάριστος, *thankful.*

εὐχή (uotum), *a prayer* comprising *a vow,* as was usual ; *a prayer* ; *a vow.*

εὔχομαι, *I pray.*

εὔχρηστος, *useful, serviceable.*

εὐψυχέω, *I am of good cheer.*

εὐωδία, *a sweet smell.*

εὐώνυμος (lit. *well-named,* to avoid the evil omen

attaching to the left), *on the left-hand side, left*: ἐξ
εὐωνύμων, *on the left.*

ἐφάλλομαι, *I leap upon.*

ἐφάπαξ (ἐφ᾽ ἅπαξ), *once, once for all.*

Ἐφέσιος, *Ephesian, of Ephesus.*

Ἔφεσος, *Ephesus*, a coast city, capital of the Roman
province Asia.

ἐφευρετής, *a finder out, discoverer.*

ἐφημερία, *a class* of priests who served for a stated
number of days.

ἐφήμερος, *for the day, for a day.*

ἐφικνέομαι, *I reach as far as.*

ἐφίστημι: in intr. tenses and passive, *I come upon
(suddenly* or *unexpectedly) and stand by*: met. *I press
forward,* 2 Tim. iv 2.

ἐφνίδιος, a phonetic spelling of αἰφνίδιος.

Ἐφραΐμ, *Ephraim,* a city of uncertain situation.

ἐφφαθά (Aramaic, meaning) *be opened up.*

ἐχθές, *yesterday.*

ἔχθρα, *enmity, hostility.*

ἐχθρός, *an enemy.*

ἔχιδνα, *a serpent, snake*: in Ac. xxviii 3 probably
Coronella leopardinus, a constrictor snake like
a viper without poison-fangs, which fixes its small
teeth into the skin, but is harmless.

ἔχω, (a) tr. *I hold, have, possess*; ἔσχον, generally, *I got,
received, acquired,* ἔσχηκα, *I possessed*; ἔχω τι κατά
(εἰς), *I have* a ground of complaint *against*; ἐν γαστρὶ
ἔχειν, *to have* (a child) *in the womb*; with double
acc., the second being in the pred. (with or without
εἰς), *to have* so and so *as . . . , to regard* so and so *as* (cf.
Mk. xi 32); with obj. indicating time (cf. Fr. avoir) *to
be* so and so days &c. *old*; (b) c. infin. *I am able*;
(c) c. adv. equal to εἰμί with corresponding adjective;
(d) intr. κατὰ κεφαλῆς ἔχων, *having* a covering *over the
head, with head covered,* 1 Cor. xi 4; (e) Mid. *I am
neighbouring, I am next to,* e. g. Mk. i 38, τῇ ἐχομένῃ
(sc. ἡμέρᾳ), *next day,* Lk. xiii 33, cf. Ac. xiii 44 (v. l.), &c.

ἕως, (a) conj. *until*: followed by the indic. where
a definite time in the past is indicated; with or without οὗ or ὅτου, and followed by the subjunctive aorist
with, or without, ἄν or ἐάν, indicating an indefinite
time, *until ... shall have*, e. g. ἕως ἂν πάντα γένηται,
until all shall have happened, Mt. v 18; (b) prep. *as
far as, up to, as much as, until*, both in local and
temporal connexions, both with nouns in gen. and
with adverbs (or prepositions).

Z

Ζαβουλών (Hebr.), *Zebulon*, one of the sons of Jacob, and
founder of one of the twelve tribes.

Ζακχαῖος, *Zacchaeus*, a Jewish tax-gatherer.

Ζαρά (Hebr.), *Zara*, son of Judah and Thamar.

ζαφθανεί (Hebr. in contrast to the Aram. σαβαχθανεί),
hast forsaken.

Ζαχαρίας (Hebr.), *Zechariah*: (a) a priest referred to in
2 Chron. xxiv 20 as a son of Jehoiada, in most copies
of Mt. xxiii 35, and some of Lk. xi 51, perhaps confused with Zechariah the prophet, who was son of
Berechiah (Zech. i 1) (but see also **Βαραχίας**); (b)
another priest, father of John Baptist.

ζάω, *I live*; ἑαυτῷ ζῆν, *to be one's own master*.

ζβέννυμι, a graphic variety of σβέννυμι.

Ζεβεδαῖος, *Zebedee*, father of the disciples James and
John.

ζεστός, *boiling hot*.

ζεῦγος, *a yoke, team*; hence *a pair*.

ζευκτηρία, *a band, a fastening*.

Ζεύς, *Zeus*, the Greek god of the sky in all its mani-
festations, corresponding to the Roman Jupiter and
to the leading god of the native Lycaonians, &c.

ζέω (lit. *I boil, I am boiling*), *I burn* (in spirit).

ζηλεύω, *I am zealous*.

ζῆλος (masc. and neut.), (a) *eagerness, zeal, enthusiasm*;
(b) *jealousy, rivalry*.

ζηλόω, (a) intr. *I am jealous*; (b) tr. *I am jealous of*, with acc. of a person; *I am eager for, I am eager to possess*, with acc. of a thing.

ζηλωτής, *one who is eagerly devoted to* a person or a thing, *a zealot*.

ζημία, *loss*.

ζημιόω, *I inflict loss* (*damage*) *upon, I fine, I punish*, sometimes with the acc. of the penalty, even when the verb is passive.

Ζηνᾶς (pet form of Ζηνόδοτος or Ζηνόδωρος), *Zenas*, a lawyer in Rome.

ζητέω (quaero), *I seek, search for*.

ζήτημα (quaestio), *a question, subject of inquiry*.

ζήτησις, *questioning*.

ζιζάνιον (lolium); in plur. *darnel*.

Ζμύρνα, the correct spelling of Σμύρνα.

Ζοροβάβελ (Hebr.), *Zerubbabel* (flourished 6th cent. B.C.), son of Salathiel, according to one of three traditions, all of which agree on Davidic descent, and father of Abiud and Resa.

ζόφος, *darkness, murkiness*.

ζυγός, *a yoke*; hence met. (a Jewish idea) of a *heavy burden*, comparable to the heavy yokes resting on the bullocks' necks.

ζύμη, *leaven, ferment*, both lit. and met.

ζυμόω, *I leaven*.

ζωγρέω, *I capture alive* or *I capture for life*.

ζωή, *life*, both of physical (present) and of spiritual (particularly future) existence; sometimes, e.g. Mk. x 17, = Hebrew *ḥayyīm* (a plural form) = *all the days you are alive* (nearer to βίος than ζωή), of a place in the New Age.

ζώνη, *a girdle, belt, waistband*; because the purse was kept there, also *a purse*.

ζώννυμι, *I gird, I put on the girdle*, especially as preparatory to active work; in John xxi 18 there is a *double entendre*, the second occurrence referring to *binding* by another.

ζωογονέω

ζωογονέω, *I preserve alive* (lit. *bring to birth*).

ζῶον, *an animal*.

ζωοποιέω, *I make* that which was dead *to live*.

H

ἤ, (a) *or*, both in rel. and interrog. clauses : in interrog.
sentences we ought perhaps sometimes to accent ἦ
(cf. εἰ) and regard simply as an interrogative particle,
not to be translated ; (b) *than*, sometimes almost
otiose after πρίν; ἀλλ' ἤ (Lk. xii 51, 2 Cor. i 13) should
be ἄλλ' ἤ (i. e. ἄλλο ἤ), *nothing but*; ἦ γάρ in Lk. xviii
14 (v. l.) is corrupt.

ἡγεμονεύω, *I govern*.

ἡγεμονία, *rule, authority*.

ἡγεμών (praeses, a very wide word), *a* (Roman) *governor*.

ἡγέομαι, (a) *I lead* : ὁ ἡγούμενος (as subst.), *the leader* ;
(b) (cf. duco) *I think, I am of opinion*.

ἡδέως, *gladly, pleasantly*.

ἤδη, *already* ; *now at length, now after all this waiting*
Rom. i 10.

ἤδιστα, see ἡδέως.

ἡδονή, *pleasure, a pleasure*, especially sensuous pleasure.

ἡδύοσμον, *mint, peppermint*.

ἦθος, *a habit*.

ἤκω, *I have come*, but other tenses are translated as if
the present meant *I come*.

Ἡλεί (ἠλεί) (Hebr., as contrasted with the Aram. ἐλωί),
my God.

Ἡλεί (Hebr.), *Heli*, the father of Joseph, husband of
Mary, according to Lk.

Ἡλείας (Ἡλείας) (Hebr.), *Elias, Elijah*, the prophet.

ἡλικία, *age, term of life* ; *full age*, ἡλικίαν ἔχει, *he has
come to maturity*, John ix 21, 23, cf. Eph. iv 13 ;
stature, only in Lk. xix 3.

ἡλίκος (quantus), rel. and interrog. *of which size, of what
size*, e.g. in James iii 5 ἡλίκον means *how small*, ἡλίκην,

106

how much, just as *quantus* sometimes = *quantulus*. Context determines the sense in each case.

ἥλιος, *the sun* ; μὴ βλέπων τὸν ἥλιον, equivalent to *stone-blind*, Ac. xiii 11.

ἧλος, *a nail*.

ἡμέρα (dies), *a day*, the period from sunrise to sunset ; (ἡ) ἡμέρα κρίσεως, ἡ ἡμέρα ἐκείνη, ἡ ἡμέρα τοῦ κυρίου, *the judgement day*, coinciding with the end of the world, according to late Jewish belief ; τῇ τρίτῃ ἡμέρᾳ, &c., *on the third day, after two days*, so διὰ τριῶν ἡμερῶν, Mt. xxvi 61, &c. ; νύκτα καὶ ἡμέραν, *through night as well as day* ; νυκτὸς καὶ ἡμέρας, *by night as well as day*, imply merely *before dawn* as well as *during the day* ; (τὸ) καθ᾽ ἡμέραν, *day by day, each day* ; πάσας τὰς ἡμέρας (vernacular phrase), *perpetually*, Mt. xxviii 20.

ἡμέτερος, *our*.

ἡμιθανής, *half-dead*.

ἥμισυς (dimidius), *half* ; (τὸ) ἥμισυ, τὰ ἡμίσια (ἡμίσεια, elsewhere unparalleled ; usual form ἡμίση), *the half*.

ἡμίωρον, *half an hour*, but see ὥρα.

ἡνίκα, *when* ; ἡνίκα ἄν, *whensoever*.

ἥπερ, an intensified ἤ, *than*.

ἤπιος, *gentle*.

Ἤρ (Hebr.), *Er*, son of Joshua and father of Elmadam.

ἤρεμος, *undisturbed*.

Ἡρώδης, *Herod* : three persons are indicated by this name, (a) '*Herod the King*', '*Herod the Great*', Herod I (73–4 B.C.), Mt. ii *passim*, Lk. i 5, Ac. xxiii 35 ; (b) '*Herod, the Tetrarch*', son of (a), Herod Antipas, ruled 4 B.C.–A.D. 39 ; (c) '*Herod the King*', Agrippa I, grandson of (a), brother of Herodias (10 B.C.–A.D. 44), ruled A.D. 37–44, Ac. xii *passim*.

Ἡρωδιανοί, *the Herodians, the partisans of Herod* (Antipas).

Ἡρῳδιάς, *Herodias* (died after A.D. 40), daughter of Aristobulus and granddaughter of Herod I, wife, first, of her uncle Herod, second, of his half-brother, her uncle Herod Antipas.

'Ηρῳδίων

'Ηρῳδίων, *Herodion*, a Christian in Rome, a 'relative' of St. Paul.

'Ησαΐας (Hebr.), *Esaias, Isaiah*, the prophet.

'Ησαῦ (Hebr.), *Esau*, elder son of Isaac the patriarch, brother of Jacob.

ἡσσάομαι, see ἡττάομαι.

ἥσσων (sometimes ἥττων under the influence of ἡττάομαι), *less* ; *worse*.

ἡσυχάζω, *I am quiet, I keep quiet, I rest* ; *I am silent*.

ἡσυχία, *quietness* ; *silence*.

ἡσύχιος, *quiet*.

ἤτοι, *or of course*.

ἡττάομαι, *I am defeated, I am worsted, I am made inferior*.

ἥττημα, *a defeat* (*failure*).

ἠχέω, *I make a sound, give forth a sound, sound* (when struck).

ἦχος, (a) *a sound* ; (b) *a rumour*, Lk. iv 37.

Θ

Θαδδαῖος (Aram. = *Theodotus* or some similar name), *Thaddaeus*, one of the twelve disciples (v. l. Λεββαῖος).

θάλασσα, (a) *the sea*, in contrast to the land (γῆ): τὸ πέλαγος τῆς θαλάσσης (tautol.), *the depth of the sea*, Mt. xviii 6 ; (b) *a particular sea* or *lake*, e.g. *the sea of Galilee* (*Tiberias*), *the Red Sea*.

θάλπω, (properly *I warm*, then) *I cherish*.

Θάμαρ (Hebr.), *Thamar, Tamar*, mother of Phares and Zara by Judah, son of Jacob.

θαμβέω, pass. *I am amazed* (almost *terrified*).

θάμβος, *astonishment, amazement* (allied to terror or awe).

θανάσιμος (mortifer), *deadly*.

θανατηφόρος, *death-bringing, deadly*.

θάνατος, *death*, physical or spiritual ; θάνατοι appears to mean *risks to life*, 2 Cor. xi 23 ; ὁ δεύτερος θάνατος (ὁ θάνατος ὁ δεύτερος), the death of the spiritual part in man, practically annihilation of personality.

θανατόω, *I put to death*.

θάπτω, *I bury*.

Θαρά (Hebr.), *Thara, Terah*, the father of Abraham.

θαρρέω, *I am courageous, I am of good cheer*, a by-form of θαρσέω.

θαρσέω, only in the imperative, *be of good cheer*, a by-form of θαρρέω.

θάρσος, *courage*.

θαῦμα, (a) concr., *a marvel, a wonder*; (b) abstr., *wonder*.

θαυμάζω, (a) intr. *I wonder*; cognate acc. θαυμάζειν θαῦμα μέγα, Rev. xvii 6, *to wonder very greatly*; (b) tr. *I wonder at, admire*.

θαυμάσιος, *wonderful*.

θαυμαστός, *to be wondered at, wonderful*.

θεά, *a goddess*.

θεάομαι (specto), *I behold*.

θεατρίζω, *I make a public show of, I expose to public shame*.

θέατρον, (a) *a theatre*, a semi-circular stone building, generally open to the sky; (b) *a spectacle*, 1 Cor. iv 9.

θεῖον, *brimstone, sulphur*.

θεῖος, *divine*; τὸ θεῖον, *the divine, the divine nature*, Ac. xvii 29.

θειότης (diuinitas), *divinity*.

θειώδης, *of brimstone, sulphurous*.

θέλημα, *an act of will, will*; plur. *wishes, desires*; τὸ θέλημα τοῦ θεοῦ, *the will of God*, sometimes as a will to be recognized, sometimes as a will to be obeyed.

θέλησις, *willing, will*.

θέλω, (a) intr. *I will*; οὐ θέλω, *I refuse*; θέλειν ἐν, *to fix one's will on, to stick resolutely to*, Col. ii 18; followed by subj. with, or without, ἵνα, *I will that*; (b) tr. *I wish, desire*.

θεμέλιος (properly an adj. *belonging to the foundation*, with λίθος understood), *a foundation stone*; plur. neut. θεμέλια is used, Ac. xvi 26.

θεμελιόω, *I found*, lit. and met.

θεοδίδακτος, *taught by the god*.

θεομάχος, *fighting against the god*.

θεόπνευστος, *inspired by the god, due to the inspiration of the god*.

θεός, (a) *a god* or *goddess*, John x 34, 35, Ac. vii 40, xiv 11, xix 26, 37, 1 Cor. viii 5, Gal. iv 8 ; (b) *the god*. The word is an appellative. The Christian, like the Jew and many pagans, avoided *naming* his God, and referred to him as *the* god.

θεοσέβεια, *reverence for the god*.

θεοσεβής, *devout, religious*.

θεοστυγής, *hating the god*.

θεότης (deitas), *deity, godhead*.

Θεόφιλος, *Theophilus*, a friend of Luke of equestrian rank, to whom the Gospel and Acts are dedicated.

θεραπεία, *care, attention* (Lk. xii 42), especially *medical attention (treatment)* (Lk. ix 11); hence almost *healing* (Rev. xxii 2). In Lk. xii 42 may, however, be taken as abstr. for concr. (cf. seruitia), *the slaves*.

θεραπεύω, *I care for, attend, serve, treat*, especially of a physician ; hence *I heal*, sometimes with ἀπό, *of*.

θεράπων, *a servant, slave*.

θερίζω, *I reap*.

θερισμός, *reaping, harvest*.

θεριστής, *a reaper, harvester*.

θερμαίνομαι, *I warm myself*.

θέρμη, *heat*.

θέρος, *summer*.

Θεσσαλονικεύς, *a man of Thessalonica*.

Θεσσαλονίκη, *Thessalonica* (modern *Saloniki*), an important city of the Roman province Macedonia.

Θευδᾶς, *Theudas*, a Jewish pretender of date about 4 B.C., otherwise unknown.

θεωρέω (specto), *I behold, look at*.

θεωρία (spectaculum), *a sight*.

θήκη, *a scabbard, a sheath*.

θρλάζω, (a) *I give suck* ; (b) *I suck*.

Θυάτειρα

θῆλυς, *female*.

θήρα, *hunting, entrapping*.

θηρεύω, *I hunt, I seek to catch* or *entrap*.

θηριομαχέω, *I fight with wild beasts* (i. e. wild beasts in human form).

θηρίον, properly *a wild beast*, hence any *animal*.

θησαυρίζω, *I store up, I treasure up, I save*.

θησαυρός, *a store-house* for precious things; hence *a treasure, a store*.

θιγγάνω, *I touch*.

θλίβω, (a) *I make narrow* (strictly *by pressure*), Mt. vii 14; *I press upon*, Mk. iii 9; (b) *I persecute, press hard*.

θλῖψις, *persecution, affliction, distress*.

θνήσκω, *I am dying*: perf. τέθνηκα, *I am dead*; τεθνηκώς, *dead*.

θνητός, *mortal*.

θορυβάζω, *I disturb greatly*.

θορυβέω, *I disturb greatly, I terrify, I strike with panic*.

θόρυβος, (a) *din, hubbub, confused noise*, Ac. xxi 34, cf. Mk. v 38; (b) *riot, disturbance*.

θραύω, *I crush*.

θρέμμα, (lit. *a nursling*, hence probably) plur. *cattle* (rather than *household, slaves*).

θρηνέω, *I lament*.

θρησκεία (underlying sense, *reverence* or *worship* of the gods), *worship* as expressed in ritual acts, *religion*.

θρῆσκος (religiosus) (refers probably to a careful observance of religious restrictions), *religious* (probably in a limited sense), James i 26.

θριαμβεύω, (properly, *I lead* one as my prisoner *in a triumphal procession*, hence) *I lead around, I make a show (spectacle) of*.

θρίξ, *a hair*; plur. *hair*.

θροέω, *I disturb, agitate*.

θρόμβος, *a clot*.

θρόνος, *a* (king's) *throne, seat*.

Θυάτειρα, *Thyatira*, a city of the old district Lydia, in the Roman province Asia.

θυγάτηρ, *a daughter*; hence (Hebraistic?), of any female *descendant*, however far removed, Lk. i 5, xiii 16; even of one unrelated, *my young lady*, Mk. v 34, &c.

θυγάτριον, *a little (young) daughter*.

θύελλα (procella), *a storm, tempest*.

θύϊνος, *of the sandarach* (so-called *citron*) *tree*.

θυμίαμα, *incense*.

θυμιατήριον, (ordinarily *censer*, but) either the *altar of incense* (Exod. xxx 1–10), or the *shovel*, on which the high-priest poured the coals, when he entered the Holy of Holies on the Day of Atonement (Lev. xvi 12).

θυμιάω, *I burn incense*.

θυμομαχέω, (lit. *I fight desperately*, hence) *I am furiously angry with*.

θυμόομαι, *I am full of angry passion*.

θυμός, *an outburst of passion, wrath*.

θύρα, (a) *a door*; (b) met. *an opportunity*, Ac. xiv 27, 1 Cor. xvi 9, &c.

θυρεός (scutum), the heavy oblong Roman *shield*.

θυρίς, *a window-sill*.

θυρωρός (ostiarius), *door-keeper, porter*.

θυσία, abstr. and concr., *sacrifice; a sacrifice*.

θυσιαστήριον, *an altar* (for sacrifice).

θύω, *I sacrifice*, generally an animal; hence *I kill*.

Θωμᾶς, *Thomas*, also called Didymus, one of the Twelve.

θώραξ, *a breastplate, corslet, cuirass*.

I

Ἰάειρος, *Jaïrus*, a Jewish ruler of the synagogue.

Ἰακώβ (Hebr.), *Jacob*, (a) the patriarch, son of Isaac; (b) father of Joseph, the husband of Mary, according to Mt. i 15, 16.

Ἰάκωβος. *Jacobus* (Ital. *Giacomo*, Span. and Welsh *Iago*, Fr. *Jacques*), *James*, (a) the Small, son of Alphaeus, and one of the Twelve, Mt. x 3, xxvii 56, Mk. ii 13 (v. l.),

iii 18, xv 40, xvi 1, Lk. vi 15, xxiv 10, Ac. i 13;
(b) brother of Jesus, Mt. xiii 55, Mk. vi 3, Ac. xii 17,
xv 13, xxi 18, 1 Cor. xv 7, Gal. i 19, ii 9, 12, James
i 1 (?), Jude 1; (c) father (?) of Jude, Lk. vi 16, Ac.
i 13; (d) son of Zebedee, and brother of John, one
of the Twelve, killed A. D. 44; (e) a late Egyptian (?)
author, if not to be identified with (b), James i 1.

ἴαμα, *a healing, a curing.*

Ἰαμβρῆς, *Jambres*, a sorcerer at the court of the Pharaoh
(*v. l.* Μαμβρῆς).

Ἰανναί (Hebr.), *Jannai*, an ancestor of Jesus, son of
Joseph, and father of Melchi.

Ἰαννῆς, *Jannes*, a sorcerer at the court of the Pharaoh
(*v. l.* Ἰαμνῆς).

ἰάομαι, *I heal*, generally of physical, sometimes of
spiritual, disease.

Ἰάρετ (Hebr.), *Jareth*, son of Maleleel and father of
Enoch.

ἴασις, *healing.*

ἴασπις, *jasper.*

Ἰάσων, *Jason*, a Christian of Thessalonica, perhaps the
same as the 'relative' of St. Paul in Rom. xvi 21.

ἰατρός, *a physician.*

ἴδε, *behold!* (originally imper. of εἶδον and accented ἰδέ).

ἴδιος (ἴδιος) (proprius), *one's own, belonging to one,
private, personal*: οἱ ἴδιοι, *one's own people, one's own
family*, John i 11; ὁ ἴδιος, possibly *his own* (son),
Ac. xx 28; τὰ ἴδια, *one's own home, one's own property*,
John i 11, &c.; ἰδίᾳ, κατ' ἰδίαν (καθ' ἰδίαν) (possibly sc.
ὁδόν), *privately, apart, in private, by oneself, individually.*

ἰδιώτης, (priuatus, *unofficial*, hence) *an amateur, an un-
professional man, a layman.*

ἰδού (originally the imper. of εἰδόμην and accented ἰδού),
interjection, *behold! lo!* Its excessive frequency is
a Semitism.

Ἰδουμαία, *Idumaea, Edom*, a district of Arabia, immediately S. of Judaea.

ἱδρώς, *sweat, perspiration.*

Ἰεζάβελ (Zezabel, Old Latin and Armenian), *Jezebel,* name given to a false prophetess of Thyatira, possibly borrowed from the name of Ahab's wife, queen of Israel (1 Kings xvi 31, &c.).

Ἱεράπολις, *Hierapolis,* a city of the Lycus valley in Phrygia, near Laodicea and Colossae.

ἱερατεία, *the duty (office) of a priest.*

ἱεράτευμα, *act or office of priesthood.*

ἱερατεύω, *I serve as priest.*

Ἰερειχώ (Ἱερειχώ), *Jericho, Hiericus,* a city a little north of the Dead Sea.

Ἱερεμίας (Hebr.), *Jeremiah,* Old Testament prophet (wrote about 603–586 B.C.).

ἱερεύς, *a priest,* one who offers sacrifice to a god (in Jewish and pagan religions; of Christians only metaphorically).

ἱερόθυτος, *slain as sacred, slain in sacrifice.*

ἱερόν, *a temple,* either the whole building, or specifically the outer courts, open to worshippers: contrast ναός.

ἱεροπρεπής, *like those employed in sacred service.*

ἱερός, *sacred.*

Ἱεροσόλυμα, the Greek form of the Hebrew name *Jerusalem.*

Ἱεροσολυμείτης, *an inhabitant of Jerusalem,* see Ἱερουσαλήμ.

ἱεροσυλέω, *I rob temples.*

ἱερόσυλος, *a robber of temples,* but possibly simply *sacrilegious.*

ἱερουργέω, *I sacrifice.*

Ἱερουσαλήμ (Aramaic form), *Jerusalem,* the capital of Palestine: hence, *Judaism,* Gal. iv 25, and allegorically, *Christendom, the Christian Church,* Gal. iv 26, &c.

ἱερωσύνη (earlier ἱερεωσύνη, from ἱερεύς), the abstract notion of the *priestly office.*

Ἰεσσαί (Hebr.), *Jesse,* son of Obed (Iobed), and father of King David.

Ἰεφθάε (Hebr.), *Jephthah,* one of the Judges of Israel.

Ἰεχονίας (Hebr.), *Jechoniah*, son of Josiah and father of Salathiel.

Ἰησοῦς, *Jesus*, the Greek form of Joshua, and the human name of our Saviour (see Χριστός). The name is generally contracted thus, ῙῨ, ῙῩῩ, in MSS., as a sign of sanctity.

Ἰησοῦς, (a) according to certain MSS. one of the names of Barabbas, the robber, Mt. xxvii 16, 17; (b) *Joshua*, Moses' successor as leader of the children of Israel, Ac. vii 45, Heb. iv 8; (c) an ancestor of our Lord, Lk. iii 29; (d) *Jesus*, who was also called Justus, an early Christian, with St. Paul, Col. iv 11 (Philem. 23, if Amling's emendation Ἰησοῦς be accepted). In these cases the name is not contracted.

ἱκανός, (a) *considerable, sufficient*, of number, quantity, time: ἐξ ἱκανῶν χρόνων (*v. l.* ἱκανοῦ), *already for a long time*, Lk. xxiii 8 (cf. viii 27), ἐφ᾽ ἱκανόν, *for a sufficiently long time*, Ac. xx 11; ἱκανόν ἐστιν, *enough* of this subject, Lk. xxii 38 (cf. 2 Cor. ii 6); τὸ ἱκανὸν ποιεῖν τινι (satis facere alicui), *to satisfy one, to give him no ground of complaint*, Mk. xv 15, τὸ ἱκανὸν λαμβάνω (satis accipio), *I get surety* (*security*), Ac. xvii 9; (b) of persons, *sufficiently strong* (*good*, &c.), *worthy, suitable*, with various constructions.

ἱκανότης, *sufficiency, ability, power.*

ἱκανόω, *I make sufficient, I make fit.*

ἱκετηρία (originally ἱ. ῥάβδος, the olive branch held in the hand of the suppliant), *supplication, entreaty.*

ἰκμάς, *moisture.*

Ἰκόνιον, *Iconium*, a Phrygian city of the Roman province Galatia (mod. Konia).

ἱλαρός, *cheerful.*

ἱλαρότης, *cheerfulness.*

ἱλάσκομαι, (a) c. dat. *I have mercy on, I show favour to*; (b) tr. with obj. of sins, *I forgive.*

ἱλασμός, *a propitiation* (of an angry god).

ἱλαστήριον (original idea, *propitiation* of an angry god), (a) *a sin offering*, by which the wrath of the deity

ἵλεως

shall be appeased, *a means of propitiation*, Rom. iii 25;
(b) *the covering* of the ark, which was sprinkled with
the atoning blood on the Day of Atonement (Hebr.
Kappôreth), Heb. ix 5.

ἵλεως, *propitious, forgiving*, Heb. viii 12 : ἵλεώς σοι =
ἵλεως εἴη σοι ὁ θεός, *may the god be favourable to you,
God be merciful to you, may God help you, God forbid!*
Mt. xvi 22.

Ἰλλυρικόν, *Illyricum*, a Roman province, afterwards
called Dalmatia, bounded by Pannonia on the N.,
Macedonia on the S., Moesia on the E., and the
Adriatic Sea on the W.

ἱμάς, *a thong, strap*, (a) for binding a man who is to be
flogged, Ac. xxii 25 ; (b) for fastening a sandal or shoe.

ἱματίζω, *I clothe, I provide clothing for*.

ἱμάτιον, a long flowing *outer garment*.

ἱματισμός, a collective word, *raiment, clothing*.

ἵνα, (A) in statements : (a) indicating purpose, *in order
that* ; (b) indicating a command or wish, Mk. v 23,
vi 25, x 35, 51, John xvii 24, 1 Cor. vii 29, 2 Cor. viii 7,
Gal. ii 10, Eph. v 33 ; (c) indicating consequence, *so
that*, e. g. Rom. xi 11 ; (d) a mere introduction to
a noun clause, *that*, e. g. John xvii 3 ; (B) in interrogations : ἵνα τί (ut quid), *why ? wherefore ?*

Ἰόππη, *Joppa*, a coast town of Judaea, WNW. of Jerusalem.

Ἰορδάνης (a long), *Jordan*, a great river flowing due S.
and bounding Galilee, Samaria, and Judaea on the E.

ἰός (cognate with Latin *uirus*), *poison*; hence *rust*,
James v 3.

Ἰούδα, see Ἰούδας.

Ἰουδαία, *Judaea*, a Roman province, capital Jerusalem.

Ἰουδαΐζω, *I live as a Jew* (in religion, ceremonially).

Ἰουδαϊκός, *Jewish, Judaic*.

Ἰουδαϊκῶς, *in the manner of Jews* (religiously, ceremonially).

Ἰουδαῖος, *Jewish*.

Ἰουδαϊσμός, *the Jewish religion, Judaism*.

Ἰούδας (Hebr.), (a) *Judah*, son of Jacob, the tribe founded
by him, and the country occupied by it, Mt. i 2, 3, ii 6,
Lk. i 39 (but some think Ἰούδα the name of the city,
modern *Yutta*), iii 33, Heb. vii 14, viii 8, Rev. v 5,
vii 5; (b) *Judas*, Iscariot (son of Simon), the disciple
who betrayed Jesus; (c) *Jude*, the brother of Jesus,
Mt. xiii 55, Mk. vi 3, Jude 1 (?); (d) *Jude*, an ancestor
of Jesus, Lk. iii 30; (e) *Jude* (son of James), the
apostle, Lk. vi 16, John xiv 22, Ac. i 13; (f) *Judas*,
a Galilean rebel about 4 B.C., Ac. v 37; (g) *Judas*,
a resident of Damascus, Ac. ix 11; (h) *Judas*, sur-
named Barsabbas, a leading Christian and 'prophet'
sent by the Jerusalem church to Antioch, Ac. xv 22–
34, perhaps identical with (g).

Ἰουλία, *Julia*, a Roman Christian, probably a slave or
freedwoman of the Imperial household.

Ἰούλιος, *Julius*, a Roman centurion on special service.

Ἰουνία, *Junia*, a Roman Christian.

Ἰοῦστος, *Justus*, (a) a surname of Joseph Barsabbas,
one of the two nominated to fill Judas' place as apostle,
Ac. i 23; (b) Titius *Justus*, a Corinthian Christian,
Ac. xviii 7; (c) surname of Jesus, a Christian with
St. Paul in Rome.

ἱππεύς, *a horse-soldier, a mounted soldier, a cavalryman.*

ἱππικός, adj. used as collective subst. *cavalry.*

ἵππος, *a horse.*

ἶρις, *a rainbow.*

Ἰσαάκ (Hebr.) (better Ἰσάκ), *Isaac*, the patriarch.

ἰσάγγελος, *like the angels.*

Ἰσκαριώθ, *Iscariot*, the surname of Judas the Betrayer,
which would seem to indicate the place from which
he came (*v. l.* Σκαριώθ).

Ἰσκαριώτης, the graecized form of Ἰσκαριώθ, *Iscariot*
(*v. l.* in John vi 71, xii 4, xiv 22 ἀπὸ Καρυώτου, *from
Karyotes*).

ἴσος (ἴσος), *equal, equivalent, identical:* τὰ ἴσα, *the equivalent*, Lk. vi 34; ἴσα, adverbially, *on an equality,*
Phil. ii 6 (if text be sound).

ἰσότης

ἰσότης, *equality; equality of treatment, fairness.*

ἰσότιμος, *equally privileged, equal.*

ἰσόψυχος, *likeminded.*

Ἰσραήλ (Ἰστραήλ) (Hebr.), *Israel,* surname of Jacob, then the Jewish people, the people of God.

Ἰσραηλείτης (Ἰστραηλείτης), *an Israelite,* one of the chosen people Israel, a Jew.

Ἰσσαχάρ (Hebr.), *Issachar,* one of the sons of Jacob and founder of a tribe of Israel.

ἰστάνω (form appearing first in 3rd cent. B. C.), ἵστημι, (a) tr. in tenses of the active mood (including new perf. -έστακα), except 2 aor. and perf. (form ἔστηκα) and plup., *I make to stand, I set up: I weigh (pay),* Mt. xxvi 15; (b) intr. in 2 aor. and perf. (form ἔστηκα) and plup., also mid. and pass., *I am set up, I am made to stand, I stand, I take an erect position, I stand firm*: = ἀντιστῆναι, Eph. vi 13.

ἱστορέω, *I visit, see* (some person or object of importance) (rendered 'inspicio' in one inscription).

ἰσχυρός, *strong* (originally and generally of physical strength); *powerful.*

ἰσχύς, *strength* (absolutely).

ἰσχύω, *I have strength, I am strong, I am in full health and vigour* (opp. κακῶς ἔχω) Mt. ix 12; and so *I am able,* sometimes followed by the inf. or εἰς c. acc. to indicate the purpose for which the strength is used, e. g. Mt. xxvi 40, v 13; c. acc. adverbially, qualifying the strength, τι ἰσχύει, *has any validity (value),* Gal. v 6, cf. Heb. ix 17, πάντα ἰσχύω, *I have all strength (power),* Phil. iv 13, πολὺ ἰσχύει, *has great power,* James v 16.

ἴσως, *perhaps* (cf. Eng. *likely*).

Ἰταλία, *Italy.*

Ἰταλικός, *Italic,* the name of a cohort forming part of the Syrian army.

Ἰτουραῖος, *Ituraean,* an adjective applied to a district (χώρα), also called Trachonitic, about 60 miles E. of the Sea of Galilee, and partly inhabited by the nomad tribe called Ituraeans (Ἰτουραῖοι).

118

ἰχθύδιον, *a little fish.*

ἰχθύς, *a fish.*

ἴχνος (uestigium), *a track, footstep.*

Ἰωάθαμ (Hebr.), *Joatham,* son of Ozias and father of Achaz.

Ἰωάνα (Ἰωάννα) (Hebr.), *Joanna, Johanna,* wife of Chuza, Herod's steward.

Ἰωανάν (Hebr.), *Joanan, Johanan,* one of the ancestors of Jesus.

Ἰωάννης, Ἰωάνης (Hebr.), *Johannes, John* : (a) the Baptizer, son of Zacharias and Elizabeth ; (b) son of Zebedee and brother of James ; (c) the writer of the Apocalypse, by very many identified with (b) ; (d) also called Mark, cousin of Barnabas, generally regarded as author of the second Gospel, Ac. xii, xiii, xv; (e) the father of Simon Peter and Andrew, John i, xxi ; (f) (*v. l.* Ἰωνάθας, i. e. Jonathan, son of Annas, who succeeded Caiaphas) otherwise unknown, unless to be identified with Johanan ben Zacchai, president of the Great Synagogue after A. D. 70.

Ἰώβ (Hebr.), *Job,* the hero of the Old Testament book of that name.

Ἰωβήδ (Ὠβήδ) (Hebr.), *Jobed, Obed,* son of Boaz and Ruth, father of Jesse, and grandfather of David.

Ἰωδά (Hebr.), *Jodah,* an ancestor of Jesus.

Ἰωήλ (Hebr.), *Joel,* the Old Testament prophet.

Ἰωνάμ (Hebr.), *Jonam,* an ancestor of Jesus.

Ἰωνᾶς (Hebr.), *Jonah,* the Old Testament prophet.

Ἰωράμ (Hebr.), *Joram,* son of Jehoshaphat and father of Ozias.

Ἰωρείμ (Hebr.), *Jorim,* an ancestor of Jesus.

Ἰωσαφάτ (Hebr.), *Jehoshaphat,* king of Judah, son of Asaph, father of Joram, an ancestor of Jesus.

Ἰωσείας (Hebr.), *Josiah,* king of Judah, son of Amos and father of Jechoniah.

Ἰωσῆς (Hebr.), *Joses,* son of Mary, sister of Mary, the mother of Jesus ; see Ἰωσήφ (d).

Ἰωσήφ (Hebr.), *Joseph* : (a) son of Jacob the patriarch, John

Ἰωσήχ

iv 5, Ac. vii 9, 13, 14, 18, Heb. xi 21, 22, Rev. vii 8;
(b) husband of Mary; (c) of Arimathaea, rich member of the Sanhedrin, Mt. xxvii 57, 59, Mk. xv 43, 45,
Lk. xxiii 50, John xix 38; (d) see Ἰωσῆς, which is
a by-form of Ἰωσήφ, and add Mt. xiii 55, xxvii 56;
(e) an ancestor of Jesus, Lk. iii 24; (f) another
ancestor of Jesus, Lk. iii 30; (g) also called Barsabbas and Justus, one of the two nominated to fill
the place of the Betrayer Judas among the apostles,
Ac. i 23; (h) another name of Barnabas of Cyprus,
cousin of Mark, colleague of St. Paul.

Ἰωσήχ (Hebr.), *Josech*, an ancestor of Jesus.

ἰῶτα, *yod*, the Hebrew or rather Aramaic letter which
was smallest of all.

Κ

κἀγώ, contracted from καὶ ἐγώ, *I also, I too.*

καθά (i. e. καθ᾽ ἅ, *according to which things*), *as.*

καθαίρεσις (destructio), *taking down, razing, destroying.*

καθαιρέω, (a) *I take down, pull down*; (b) *I depose*, Lk.
i 52, cf. 2 Cor. x 4, c. gen. *I diminish* aught *from,*
Ac. xix 27; (c) *I destroy*, Ac. xiii 19.

καθαίρω, *I cleanse, purify.*

καθάπερ (i. e. καθ᾽ ἅπερ, *according to which things*), *even
as.*

καθάπτω, *I lay hold of, I fasten on to*, of a snake with
short teeth harmless to the skin.

καθαρίζω (alternative spelling καθερίζω, perhaps = καθαι-
ρίζω, but it occurs only in augmented and redupli-
cated forms and has been otherwise explained)
(purgo), *I make clean*, literally, ceremonially, or
spiritually, according to context, ἀπό c. gen. being
sometimes added, of the dirt removed.

καθαρισμός, *cleansing, purifying, purification*, literal,
ceremonial, or moral.

καθαρός (purus), *clean, pure, unstained*, either literally
or ceremonially or spiritually; καθαρὸς ἀπό, *unstained
by.*

καθαρότης, *cleanness.*

καθέδρα, *a seat, chair.*

καθέζομαι, *I am sitting, I sit, I am seated.*

καθεξῆς (deinceps), *in order, in succession* : ἐν τῷ καθεξῆς (sc. χρόνῳ), *in the time immediately after, just after,* Lk. viii 1 ; οἱ καθεξῆς, *those who followed,* Ac. iii 24.

καθεύδω, *I am sleeping* (*asleep*), *I sleep.*

καθηγητής, *a leader, a teacher.*

καθήκω, impers. καθήκει, *it is fitting* : τὰ μὴ καθήκοντα (a technical phrase of the Stoic philosophy), *what is unfitting.*

κάθημαι, *I am seated, I sit* : καθήμενος, *seated, sitting.*

καθημερινός, *daily.*

καθίζω, (a) tr. *I make to sit, I set* ; (b) intr. aor. *I sat down.*

καθίημι, *I let down.*

καθίστημι, καθιστάνω, in the tr. tenses (see ἵστημι), *I set, establish, appoint, constitute, make* ; *I conduct,* Ac. xvii 15 : καθίσταται, *shows itself, acts its part,* James iii 6.

καθό (i. e. καθ᾽ ὅ, *according to which thing*), *as, according as.*

καθόλου (i. e. καθ᾽ ὅλου), *at all.*

καθοπλίζω, tr. *I arm completely, I arm cap-à-pie.*

καθοράω, *I see clearly.*

καθότι (i. e. καθ᾽ ὅ, τι [neut. of ὅστις], cf. καθό, καθά), (a) *in proportion as, according as,* Ac. ii 45, iv 35 ; (b) *because,* Lk. i 7, xix 9, Ac. ii 24, xvii 31.

καθώς, *according to the manner in which, in the degree that, as.*

καθώσπερ, *according to the very manner in which, even as.*

καί, *and* ; sometimes modifying a following word, *even.*

Καϊάφας (Καϊαφᾶς) (Old Latin and Sahidic Καίφας), *Caiaphas,* Jewish high priest.

Καΐν (Hebr.), *Cain,* son of Adam and Eve and brother of Abel.

Καϊνάμ (Καϊνάν) (Hebr.), *Cainam,* one of the ancestors of Jesus.

καινός (recens), *fresh, new.*

καινότης, *freshness, newness.*

καίπερ, *although.*

καιρός, *fitting season, season, opportunity, occasion, time*: πρὸς καιρόν, *for a time.*

Καῖσαρ, *Caesar,* a surname of the gens Iulia, which became practically synonymous with *the Emperor* for the time being: in the Gospels it refers always to Tiberius (A. D. 14–37) except in Lk. ii 1 to Augustus (23 B. C.–A. D. 14); in Ac. xvii 7 to Claudius (A. D. 41–54), in Ac. xxv–xxviii, Phil. iv 22 to Nero (A. D. 54–68).

Καισάρεια, *Caesarea,* (a) *Caesarea of Philip* (Lk. iii 1), Mt. xvi 13, Mk. viii 27, otherwise called *Caesarea Panias,* a city in Phoenice at the foot of Mt. Hermon, by the source of the Jordan; (b) *Caesarea of Strato* (a king of Sidon) or *of Palestine,* on the coast of Palestine, about 60 miles NNW. of Jerusalem.

καίτοι, *and yet.*

καίτοιγε, *and yet.*

καίω, tr. *I ignite, I light, I burn,* lit. and met.

κἀκεῖ (contraction of καὶ ἐκεῖ), *and there, and yonder.*

κἀκεῖθεν (contraction of καὶ ἐκεῖθεν), *and thence, and from there.*

κἀκεῖνος (contraction of καὶ ἐκεῖνος), *and he, and that.*

κακία, (a) *evil* (i. e. trouble, labour, misfortune), Mt. vi 34; (b) *wickedness,* Ac. viii 22; (c) *vicious disposition, malice, spite.*

κακοήθεια, *evilmindedness,* the tendency to put the worst construction on everything.

κακολογέω, *I speak evil of* (not so strong a word as βλασφημέω).

κακοπάθεια, *experience of evil, suffering.*

κακοπαθέω, *I am ill-treated.*

κακοποιέω, *I do evil.*

κακοποιός, *an evil-doer*: in 1 Pet. iv 15 probably = maleficus, *a sorcerer, magician,* or *poisoner.*

κακός, *bad, evil,* in the widest sense.

κακοῦργος (lit. *an evil-worker*), *a criminal.*

κακουχέω, *I treat evilly.*

κακόω, *I treat badly.*

κακῶς, *badly, evilly* : κακῶς ἔχω, see ἔχω.

κάκωσις, *ill-treating, ill treatment.*

καλάμη, *stubble.*

κάλαμος, *a reed* ; *a reed-pen,* 3 John 13.

καλέω, (a) *I call, summon, invite* ; (b) *I call, name* : ἐπί, *after,* Lk. i 59.

καλλιέλαιος, *a cultivated olive-tree.*

κάλλιον, see καλῶς.

καλοδιδάσκαλος, *a teacher of that which is noble* (*honourable*).

καλοποιέω, *I do the noble* (*honourable*) *thing.*

καλός (honestus), *beautiful,* as an outward sign of the inward *good, noble, honourable* character; *good, worthy, honourable, noble,* and seen to be so.

κάλυμμα, *a covering,* especially a covering of head and face, *a veil.*

καλύπτω, *I veil, hide, conceal, envelop.*

καλῶς, *well, nobly, honourably* ; *in a good place,* James ii 3 : compar. κάλλιον ; καλῶς ποιήσεις, especially with aor. participle, is idiomatic for *please,* 3 John 6, cf. Ac. x 33, Phil. iv 14, 2 Pet. i 19.

κάμηλος, includes both *camel* and *dromedary.*

κάμινος, *a furnace.*

καμμύω, *I close.*

κάμνω, (a) *I am weary,* Heb. xii 3 ; (b) *I am ill,* James v 15.

κάμπτω, *I bend.*

κἄν (= καὶ ἄν, καὶ ἤν), *and if* ; *even if.*

Κανᾶ, *Cana,* a town in Galilee.

Καναναῖος, *a Cananaean,* a (former) adherent of the party of Zealots (= ζηλωτής).

Κανδάκη, *the Candace,* a dynastic name for queens of the Ethiopians in Abyssinia.

κανών (lit. *a level, ruler*), (a) *rule, regulation,* Gal. vi 16 ; (b) *a measured* (*defined*) *area, province.*

καπηλεύω, *I hawk, trade in, deal in for purposes of gain.*

καπνός, *smoke*.

Καππαδοκία, *Cappadocia*, a large Roman province in the central eastern part of Asia Minor.

καρδία (Lat. cor, Hebr. lēb, lēbab), (A) lit. *the heart*, as an organ of the body ; (B) *mind* covers the non-physical sense best : (a) *personality, character, inner life* (illa uis qua cogitationes fiunt, Augustine, *De nat. et orig. animae* iv 6 § 7), e. g. 1 Cor. xiv 25, 1 Pet. i 22 ; (b) *emotional state*, e. g. Rom. ix 2 ; (c) *mind, intellect*, e. g. Rom. i 21 ; (d) *will, volition, intention*, e. g. Rom. ii 5.

καρδιογνώστης, *a knower of the inner life* (*character*).

καρπός (fructus), (a) *fruit*, generally vegetable, sometimes animal (e. g. Lk. i 42, Ac. ii 30) ; (b) met. *fruit, deed, action, result*, Mt. iii 8, Lk. iii 8, James iii 17 f., &c. ; (c) *profit, gain*, Rom. i 13, &c.

Κάρπος, *Carpus*, a Christian of Troas.

καρποφορέω (fructifico), act. and mid. *I bear fruit*.

καρποφόρος, *fruit-bearing*.

καρτερέω, *I persevere, endure*.

κάρφος, *a dry stalk* ; *a chip of wood*.

κατά, (A) c. gen. : (a) *against*, Mt. xii 30 ; (b) *down from*, Mt. viii 32, κατὰ κεφαλῆς, *down over the head, on the head*, 1 Cor. xi 4 ; (c) *throughout*, Lk. iv 14, xxiii 5, Ac. ix 31, x 37, always with ὅλος ; ἡ κατὰ βάθους πτωχεία, *deep* (*abject*) *poverty*, 2 Cor. viii 2 ; (d) in oaths, *by*, Mt. xxvi 63, Heb. vi 13, 16 ; (B) c. acc. (lit. *down along*) : (a) *over against*, Ac. ii 10, xvi 7 ; (b) *among*, νόμος ὁ καθ' ὑμᾶς, *the law among you, your law*, Ac. xviii 15, cf. xvii 28, xxvi 3, Eph. i 15, Col. iv 7, &c. ; (c) with distributive force, (τὸ) καθ' ἡμέραν, *daily, day by day, each day*, κατὰ ἑορτήν, *at each feast*, Mt. xxvii 15, Mk. xv 6, κατὰ ἑκατόν, *by hundreds*, Mk. vi 40, ungrammatically εἷς κατὰ (καθ') εἷς, Mk. xiv 19, [John] viii 9 (contrast Eph. v 33), τὸ δὲ καθ' εἷς (καθεῖς), *singly, with reference to each individual*, Rom. xii 5, &c. ; (d) *according to, by way of*, Mt. ii 16, καθ' ὅσον, &c. ; in titles of Gospels, κατά practically indicates the author ; (e) various adverbial phrases : τὸ κατ᾽ ἐμέ, *as far as in me lies*, with πρόθυμος, Rom. i 15, cf. τὸ κατὰ σάρκα, Rom. ix 5, &c. ; κατ᾽ (καθ᾽) ἰδίαν (ἰδίαν) (opp. δημοσίᾳ), *privately, by oneself, individually*, Mt. xiv 13, &c. ; κατὰ μόνας, *alone*, Mk. iv 10, Lk. ix 18 ; κατὰ πρόσωπον, in a Hebraistic periphrasis, *in the presence of*, Lk. ii 31, Ac. iii 13, cf. xxv 16.

καταβαίνω, *I go down, I come down*, either from the sky or from higher land.

καταβάλλω (cf. iacere), (a) mid. *I lay*, of a foundation, Heb. vi 1 (cf. **καταβολή**) ; (b) met. *I cast down*, 2 Cor. iv 9.

καταβαρέω, *I burden, oppress.*

καταβαρύνω, *I weigh down, make heavy.*

κατάβασις, *descent.*

καταβιβάζω, *I bring down, I cause to go down.*

καταβολή, (a) *foundation*, only in Mt. xiii 35 without κόσμου (add. v. l.) ; (b) *depositing, sowing, deposit*, σπέρματος, technically used of the act of conception, Heb. xi 11.

καταβραβεύω, of the umpire in a contest, *I decide against, take part against, condemn* (perhaps with the idea of *assumption, officialism*).

καταγγελεύς, *a reporter, announcer, proclaimer, herald, setter forth.*

καταγγέλλω, *I announce.*

καταγελάω, *I laugh at, ridicule.*

καταγινώσκω, *I condemn* ; κατεγνωσμένος, *reprehensible*, Gal. ii 11.

κατάγνυμι, *I break.*

καταγράφω, *I write* (*down*).

κατάγω, *I lead down, I bring down*, either from a high place on land to a lower (or actually to the sea-coast), or from the high seas to land.

καταγωνίζομαι (debello), *I subdue* (in warfare).

καταδέω, *I bind up.*

κατάδηλος, *quite clear.*

καταδικάζω, *I condemn.*

καταδίκη, *sentence of condemnation, condemnation.*

καταδιώκω, *I hunt down.*

καταδουλόω, *I enslave.*

καταδυναστεύω, *I overpower, quell*; *I treat harshly.*

κατάθεμα, *an accursed thing.*

καταθεματίζω, *I curse.*

καταισχύνω, *I shame, disgrace, bring to shame, put to utter confusion.*

κατακαίω, *I burn down.*

κατακαλύπτομαι, *I veil myself, I cover my head.*

κατακαυχάομαι, *I boast against.*

κατάκειμαι, *I recline* (at table); more often, *I keep my bed, I am lying ill* (in bed).

κατακλάω, *I break up.*

κατακλείω, *I shut up.*

κατακληρονομέω, *I give as an inheritance.*

κατακλίνω, *I cause to recline* at table; mid. (and pass.) *I recline* at table.

κατακλύζω, *I flood over, overwhelm.*

κατακλυσμός, *a flood.*

κατακολουθέω, *I follow after.*

κατακόπτω, *I beat.*

κατακρημνίζω, *I throw down a precipice.*

κατάκριμα, *punishment following condemnation, penal servitude.*

κατακρίνω, *I condemn.*

κατάκρισις, *condemnation.*

κατακύπτω, *I stoop down, I look down.*

κατακυριεύω, *I exercise lordship over, I overpower.*

καταλαλέω, *I speak evil of.*

καταλαλιά, *evil-speaking, backbiting, detraction.*

κατάλαλος, *speaking against*; *a backbiter.*

καταλαμβάνω, (A) act. (a) *I seize tight hold of, arrest, catch, capture, appropriate,* Mk. ix 18, [John] viii 3, 4, Rom. ix 30, 1 Cor. ix 24, Phil. iii 12, 13 ; (b) *I overtake,* John i 5, vi 17 (v. l.), xii 35, 1 Thess. v 4 ; (B) mid. aor. *I perceived, comprehended.*

καταλέγω, *I enter in a list, register.*

καταλείπω, *I leave behind*; *I desert, abandon.*

καταλιθάζω, *I stone down, stone to death, overwhelm with stones.*

καταλλαγή, *reconciliation.*

καταλλάσσω, *I reconcile.*

κατάλοιπος, *left behind*; οἱ κατάλοιποι (reliqui), *the rest, the remainder.*

κατάλυμα, *an inn, lodging.*

καταλύω (lit. *I loosen thoroughly*), (a) tr. *I break up, overthrow, destroy*, both lit. and met., ὁ καταλύων, *you would-be destroyer (of)*, Mt. xxvii 40; (b) *I unyoke, unharness* a carriage horse or pack animal; hence *I put up, I lodge, I find a lodging*, Lk. ix 12, xix 7.

καταμανθάνω, *I understand, take in a fact about.*

καταμαρτυρέω, *I give evidence against.*

καταμένω, *I wait*, Ac. i 13; *I stay*, πρός, *with*, 1 Cor. xvi 6.

καταναλίσκω, *I consume utterly.*

καταναρκάω, (properly a medical term, *I stupefy*; hence) *I burden, encumber.*

κατανεύω, *I nod, make a sign.*

κατανοέω, *I understand, take in a fact about, take knowledge of, take notice of, perceive*; *I detect*, Lk. xx 23; *I master*, Ac. vii 31.

καταντάω, (a) *I come down*, either from high land to lower (or actually to the sea-coast), or from the high seas to the coast; hence met. *I reach* (my destination), Ac. xxvi 7, Eph. iv 13, Phil. iii 11; (b) of property, *I come down* (*descend*) by inheritance to an heir, 1 Cor. x 11, xiv 36.

κατάνυξις, *deep sleep, torpor, insensibility.*

κατανύσσομαι. met. *I am pierced, stung.*

καταξιόω, *I deem* (*count*) *worthy.*

καταπατέω, lit. and met. *I trample down.*

κατάπαυσις (in O.T. of *the rest* attained by the settlement in Canaan), *resting, rest.*

καταπαύω, (a) tr. *I cause to rest, bring to rest*; c. gen. *I cause to refrain*, Ac. xiv 18; (b) intr. *I rest*, Heb. iv 4, 10.

καταπέτασμα

καταπέτασμα (lit. *that which is spread out downwards, that which hangs down*), *curtain*, of that which separated the Holy of Holies from the outer parts of the temple at Jerusalem, also of an outer curtain at the entrance to the Holy Place in the same temple; the latter is strictly denoted by κάλυμμα; yet Heb. ix 3 speaks of the former as τὸ δεύτερον καταπέτασμα.

καταπίνω, (a) (originally of liquids, extended to solids) *I drink up, swallow, gulp down*; *I gobble*; (b) pass. lit. and met. *I drown, am drowning.*

καταπίπτω, *I fall down.*

καταπλέω, *I sail down* (from the high seas to the shore).

καταπονέω, *I illtreat*; pass. *I am getting the worse.*

καταποντίζομαι, *I am submerged, I drown.*

κατάρα, *cursing*; *a curse.*

καταράομαι, *I curse*; κατηραμένοι, *having become the subjects of a curse*, Mt. xxv 41.

καταργέω, (a) *I make idle (inactive), I make of no effect, I annul, abolish, bring to naught*; (b) with ἀπό, *I discharge, sever, separate from.*

καταριθμέω, *I number.*

καταρτίζω, (a) *I fit (join) together*, Mk. i 19, Mt iv 21; met. *I compact together*, 1 Cor. i 10; (b) act. and mid. *I prepare, I perfect*, for his (its) full destination or use, *I bring into its proper condition* (whether for the first time, or after a lapse).

κατάρτισις, *restoration.*

καταρτισμός, *bringing to a condition of fitness, perfecting.*

κατασείω, *I shake* (the hand) up and *down, I wave*; intr. *I beckon* for silence.

κατασκάπτω, *I dig down.*

κατασκευάζω, *I build, construct, prepare, make.*

κατασκηνόω, *I encamp, take up my quarters, tabernacle, dwell.*

κατασκήνωσις, *a dwelling.*

κατασκιάζω, *I overshadow.*

κατασκοπέω, *I spy out.*

κατάσκοπος, *a spy.*

καταψύχω

κατασοφίζομαι, *I circumvent by trickery.*

καταστέλλω, *I quieten.*

κατάστημα (a man's outward bearing, including *gait, posture, expression of countenance, dress,* &c., involving the idea of *calmness* and *composure*), *demeanour, deportment.*

καταστολή, *garb, clothing.*

καταστρέφω, *I overturn.*

καταστρηνιάω, *I exercise my youthful vigour against.*

καταστροφή, *destruction,* material or spiritual.

καταστρώννυμι, *I scatter on the ground.*

κατασύρω, *I drag (down).*

κατασφάζω, *I slaughter.*

κατασφραγίζω, *I seal* and thus close.

κατάσχεσις, abstr., (permanent) *possession.*

κατατίθημι, (a) (depono) *I lay down, deposit*; (b) mid. χάριν, χάριτα, *I lay down* or *deposit a favour,* with the view of receiving one in return, *I seek favour.*

κατατομή, a word-play with περιτομή, *a cutting up, spoiling.*

κατατρέχω, *I run down.*

καταφέρω, (a) *I bring down,* ψῆφον, *the pebble* into the urn, i.e. *I give my vote*; αἰτίωμα, *I bring a charge against*; (b) *I oppress*; καταφερόμενος, *being gradually oppressed, becoming oppressed,* Ac. xx 9, κατενεχθείς, *being borne down, overcome,* Ac. xx 9.

καταφεύγω (confugio), *I flee for refuge* (implying that the refuge is reached); aor. indicates moment of arrival.

καταφθείρω, *I destroy, I corrupt.*

καταφιλέω, *I kiss affectionately.*

καταφρονέω, *I despise, scorn,* and show it by active insult.

καταφρονητής, *a despiser.*

καταχέω, *I pour (down) over.*

καταχθόνιος, *under the earth, subterranean.*

καταχράομαι (abutor), *I use to the full, I use up.*

καταψύχω, *I cool, I refresh.*

κατείδωλος

κατείδωλος, *full of images* of gods.
κατέναντι, adv. and prep. c. gen. *opposite, in front (of)*.
κατενώπιον, prep. *before the face of*.
κατεξουσιάζω, *I have (exercise) power (authority) over*.
κατεργάζομαι, *I work out* ; *I produce, accomplish*.
κατέρχομαι, *I come down* from sky to earth, or from high land to lower land (or to the coast), or from the high seas to the shore : pcpl. qualitative in James iii 15.
κατεσθίω, κατέσθω (comedo, deuoro), *I eat up, I eat till it is finished* (cf. καταπίνω) : so aor. καταφαγεῖν.
κατευθύνω, (a) *I make straight*, 1 Thess. iii 11 ; (b) met. *I put in the right way, I direct*.
κατευλογέω, *I bless*.
κατεφίστημι, aor. intr. *I set upon*.
κατέχω, (a) *I hold fast, bind, arrest* ; (b) *I take possession of, lay hold of*, Lk. xiv 9 ; (c) *I hold back, detain, restrain*, Lk. iv 42, Rom. i 18, 2 Thess. ii 6, 7, Philem. 13 ; (d) *I hold a ship* (sc. τὴν ναῦν), *keep its head*, Ac. xxvii 40.
κατηγορέω (accuso), *I accuse, charge* ; *I prosecute*.
κατηγορία, *a charge, an accusation*.
κατήγορος, *a prosecutor, an accuser*.
κατήγωρ (an abbreviated vulgar form of κατήγορος), *an accuser*.
κατήφεια, *a downcast countenance* as a sign of sorrow, *gloominess, gloom, dejection*.
κατηχέω, *I instruct orally*.
κατιόομαι, *I am rusted*.
κατισχύω, (a) *I have strength against, I prevail against*, Mt. xvi 18 ; (b) *I prevail*, Lk. xxiii 23 ; (c) *I have strength, I am able*, c. infin., Lk. xxi 36.
κατοικέω, *I dwell in* (implying a more permanent settlement than παροικέω), *I settle in, I am established in* (permanently).
κατοίκησις, *dwelling, abode*.
κατοικητήριον, *a habitation, dwelling-place*.
κατοικία, *dwelling, habitation*.

κατοικίζω, *I take up a dwelling,* but probably κατῴκισεν is an itacistic error for κατῴκησεν (from κατοικέω), as κατοικίζω is properly transitive.

κατοπτρίζομαι, mid. for act., *I mirror, reflect*: elsewhere mid. = *I gaze upon myself in a mirror.*

κάτω, (a) *down, below,* also *downwards*; (b) compar. κατωτέρω, *lower, under, less,* of a length of a time, Mt. ii 16.

κατώτερος, compar. adj. *lower,* Hebraistic, with ref. to Sheol.

Καῦδα, *Cauda* (mod. *Gaudho*), an island twenty-three miles south of the Western end of Crete (*v. l.* Κλαῦδα, see my apparatus).

καῦμα, *burning heat, heat.*

καυματίζω, tr. *I burn, I scorch.*

καῦσις, *burning.*

καυσόω, tr. *I burn* (perhaps by internal heat).

καυστηριάζω, *I cauterize, I burn with a hot iron*: hence met. *I sear.*

καύσων, *the East wind* of Palestine, *the Simoom,* which blows from February to June.

καυχάομαι, *I boast; I glory (exult) proudly.*

καύχημα, *a boasting, a ground of boasting (glorying, exultation).*

καύχησις, *boasting; glorying, exultation.*

Καφαρναούμ, *Capharnahum* (the form *Capernaum* appears to be a conscious alteration made in Syria not earlier than the fourth century), perhaps modern *Tell Ḥum.*

κέδρος, *a cedar*: in John xviii 1 τῶν Κέδρων is probably due to a popular misunderstanding of the original name τοῦ Κεδρών (*Kidron,* 1 Kings ii 37, &c.), especially as cedars grew in the vicinity.

κεῖμαι, a perf. used instead of the perf. pass. of τίθημι, *I have been placed (put, laid),* hence, *I lie:* the former sense explains the construction with εἰς and acc.

κειρία, a kind of *girdle* made of cords: *a bandage.*

κείρω, *I shear, I cut the hair of*; mid. *I cut my own hair, I have my hair cut.*

Κείς (Hebr.), *Kish*, father of Saul, king of Israel.

κέλευσμα, *a word of command, a call*.

κελεύω, *I command, I order*.

κενοδοξία (cenodoxia), *vainglory*.

κενόδοξος, *vainglorious*.

κενός, (a) *empty* ; (b) met. *empty* (in moral content), *vain, ineffective, foolish, worthless* ; εἰς κενόν, *in vain, to no purpose* ; (c) *false, unreal, pretentious, hollow*, Eph. v 6, Col. ii 8, James ii 20.

κενοφωνία, *a worthless utterance*.

κενόω, (a) *I empty*, Phil. ii 7 ; (b) *I deprive of content; make unreal*.

κέντρον, *a goad*.

κεντυρίων (Lat., = Gk. ἑκατοντάρχης), *a centurion*, an officer commanding about a hundred infantry in the Roman army.

Κεγχρεαί, *Cenchreae*, the harbour town of Corinth on the Saronic Gulf.

κενῶς, *falsely*.

κεραία (variation κερέα), *a little hook, an apostrophe* on letters of the alphabet, distinguishing them from other like letters, or *a separation stroke* between letters.

κεραμεύς, *a potter*.

κεραμικός, *of clay, made by a potter*.

κεράμιον, *an earthenware pitcher*.

κέραμος, *a tile* ; οἱ κέραμοι, practically *the roof*.

κεράννυμι, *I mix*.

κέρας, (a) *a horn* ; (b) as a symbol of strength, κέρας σωτηρίας, *a powerful support of salvation*, Lk. i 69 ; (c) a dwarfed *column* set upon or at the corner of an altar, with ritual significance, Rev. ix 13.

κεράτιον, *a husk (pod) of the carob* (siliqua graeca).

κερδαίνω, *I gain* : ὕβριν καὶ ζημίαν, *I gain injury and loss*, i. e. *I gain by shunning injury and loss, I do not suffer (I am spared) injury and loss*, Ac. xxvii 21.

κέρδος, *gain*.

κερέα, see κεραία.

κέρμα, *a small coin* : plur. *small change*.

κλάδος

κερματιστής, properly *a changer of* large into smaller *coins, a money-changer*.

κεφάλαιον, (a) *the chief matter, the main point*, Heb. viii 1 ; (b) *a sum* of money, Ac. xxii 28.

κεφαλαιόω, see **κεφαλιόω**.

κεφαλή, (a) *head*, κατὰ κεφαλῆς ἔχων, see **κατά**; (b) met. κεφαλὴ γωνίας, *a corner stone*, uniting two walls, Mk. xii 10 and parallels ; *head, ruler, lord*, 1 Cor. xi 3, &c.

κεφαλιόω, *I wound in the head*.

κεφαλίς, (lit. *little head*, then the *knob* at the end of the wooden core of a roll of papyrus, then) *a roll*.

κημόω (from κῆμος, *a muzzle*), *I muzzle*.

κῆνσος (Latin census), *poll-tax*.

κῆπος, *a garden*.

κηπουρός, *keeper of a garden*.

κηρίον, *a honeycomb*.

κήρυγμα, *a proclamation*.

κῆρυξ, *a herald, proclaimer*.

κηρύσσω, *I proclaim, herald, preach*.

κῆτος, *a sea monster, a huge sea fish*.

Κηφᾶς, *Cephas* (Aram. for *rock*), the new name given to Simon, the disciple.

κιβωτός, (properly *a wooden box*, hence) *the Ark*, in which Noah sailed.

κιθάρα, *a harp*.

κιθαρίζω, intr. and tr., *I play on the harp, I harp*, with acc. of the tune.

κιθαρῳδός, *a harpist*.

Κιλικία, *Cilicia*, a Roman province between the Taurus range of mountains and the coast in the SE. corner of Asia Minor, linked up with the province of Syria.

κινδυνεύω, *I am in danger*, sometimes c. infin. *of . . .*

κίνδυνος, *danger, peril, risk*.

κινέω, tr. *I move* ; *I stir, excite*.

κίνησις, *moving, stirring*.

κιννάμωμον (a Semitic word), *cinnamon*.

κλάδος, *a branch* of a tree.

133

κλαίω, *I weep*; c. acc. or ἐπί c. acc. *I weep for, mourn.*

κλάσις, *breaking.*

κλάσμα, *a fragment.*

Κλαῦδα, see Καῦδα.

Κλαυδία, *Claudia*, a Christian woman in Rome; if historical, probably a freedwoman of the imperial household.

Κλαύδιος, (a) *Claudius*, the fourth of the Roman Emperors, Tiberius Claudius Caesar Augustus Germanicus, who ruled A.D. 41–54; (b) *Claudius* Lysias, a tribune at Jerusalem.

κλαυθμός, *weeping.*

κλάω, *I break.*

κλείς, *a key.*

κλείω, *I shut.*

κλέμμα, *a theft.*

Κλεόπας, *Cleopas*, one of the two companions of the risen Jesus from Jerusalem to Emmaus.

κλέος, *glory, fame.*

κλέπτης, *a thief.*

κλέπτω, *I steal*; ὁ κλέπτων, *the stealer*, Eph. iv 28.

κλῆμα, *a branch.*

Κλήμης (Latin, = Clemens), *Clement*, a fellow-worker of St. Paul in Rome.

κληρονομέω, *I inherit, I obtain (possess) by inheritance.*

κληρονομία, *an inheritance, an heritage*, regularly the gift of God to His chosen people, in O.T. the Promised Land, in N.T. a possession viewed in one sense as present, in another as future.

κληρονόμος, *an heir, an inheritor* : cf. κληρονομία.

κλῆρος, (a) *a lot*; (b) *a portion* assigned, Ac. i 17, viii 21, xxvi 18, Col. i 12; hence, a portion of the people of God assigned to one's care, *a congregation*, 1 Pet. v 3.

κληρόω, lit. *I choose by lot, I appoint by lot*; hence *I assign*; mid. *I assign to myself, choose*; pass. *I am assigned, I am chosen* as God's portion (κλῆρος), Eph. i 11.

κλῆσις, *a calling, invitation, summons* of God to the religious life; sometimes, e. g. Phil. iii 14, 2 Thess. i 11, Heb. iii 1, it may include a reference to the final issue of this invitation.

κλητός, *called, invited, summoned* by God to the religious life.

κλίβανος, *an oven, a furnace.*

κλίμα, a small geographical division, district, or *territory,* a portion of a χώρα (which see).

κλινάριον, *a couch* or *litter* of a sick person.

κλίνη, *a couch, a bed,* alike a mere mat (e. g. Mt. ix 2, 6), and a more elaborate structure (e. g. Mk. iv 21); possibly *a bier* in Rev. ii 22.

κλινίδιον, *a couch* or *litter* of a sick person.

κλίνω, (A) tr. (a) *I rest, recline* (even in John xix 30); *I bend, incline*; (b) (inclino) *I cause to give ground, I make to yield,* Heb. xi 34; (B) intr. of the day, *declines, approaches its end,* Lk. ix 12, xxiv 29.

κλισία, properly *a dining couch*; hence *a group of diners.*

κλοπή, *thieving, theft.*

κλύδων, *rough water, roughness of water*; κ. θαλάσσης *a rough sea,* James i 6.

κλυδωνίζω, *I toss as in a storm at sea.*

Κλωπᾶς, *Clopas,* husband of one Mary, who stood by the cross.

κνήθω, *I rub, tickle* : κνηθόμενοι τὴν ἀκοήν, *with ears itching* with eagerness to hear pleasant things, 2 Tim. iv 3.

Κνίδος, *Cnidus,* a town on the coast of Caria (SW. Asia Minor) near the island of Cos.

κοδράντης (Latin, = quadrans), *a quadrans,* the smallest Roman copper coin, a quarter of an *as,* the sixteenth part of a *sestertius.*

κοιλία, *belly, abdomen,* a general term covering any organ in the abdomen, e. g. stomach, womb : ἐκ κοιλίας μητρός, *from birth.*

κοιμάομαι, *I fall asleep, I am asleep,* sometimes of the sleep of death (e. g. Mt. xxvii 52).

κοίμησις

κοίμησις, *sleeping*, followed by constituent gen. τοῦ ὕπνου, *which is slumber*.

κοινός, (a) *common, shared*; (b) Hebraistic use (in contrast to ἅγιος), *profane*; *dirty, unclean, unwashed*, Mk. vii 2, Ac. x 14, 28, xi 8, Rom. xiv 14, Heb. x 29, Rev. xxi 27.

κοινόω (cf. κοινός), (a) *I make unclean, I pollute*; (b) mid. *I regard (treat) as unclean*, Ac. x 15, xi 9.

κοινωνέω, (a) *I share, communicate, contribute, impart*, Rom. xii 13, Gal. vi 6; (b) *I share in, I have a share of, I have fellowship with*, c. gen. or dat.

κοινωνία, (lit. *partnership*) (a) *contributory help*, Ac. ii 42, Rom. xv 26, 2 Cor. viii 4, ix 13, Heb. xiii 16; (b) *sharing in*, Phil. i 5, iii 10, Philem. 6, cf. (c); (c) spiritual *fellowship*, a *fellowship* in the spirit, 1 Cor. i 9, x 16, 2 Cor. vi 14, xiii 13, Gal. ii 9, Phil. ii 1, 1 John i 3, 6, 7 (frequently outside N.T., of the marriage relationship).

κοινωνικός, *willing to share*.

κοινωνός, *a sharer*; *a partner*.

κοίτη, (a) *a bed*, Lk. xi 7; (b) *a marriage bed*, Heb. xiii 4; κοίτην ἔχειν ἐκ, *to conceive seed from*, Rom. ix 10 : κοῖται plur. *repeated* (immoral) *sexual intercourse*, Rom. xiii 13.

κοιτών (cubiculum), *bed-chamber* : ὁ ἐπὶ τοῦ κοιτῶνος (cubicularius), *chamberlain*.

κόκκινος, *crimson*, dyed with Kermes (coccum), the female coccus of the Kermes oak.

κόκκος, *a grain*.

κολάζω, *I punish*; mid. *I cause to be punished*.

κολακεία (adulatio), *flattery*, with a view to advantage or gain.

κόλασις, *punishing, punishment*, perhaps with the idea of *deprivation*, 1 John iv 18.

κολαφίζω, *I strike with the fist*; hence, *I maltreat violently*.

κολλάω (lit. *I glue*): hence, mid. and pass. *I join myself closely, I cleave, I adhere (to), I keep company*

136

(with), of friendly intercourse ; of inanimate objects, Lk. x 11.

κολλούριον, *eye-salve.*

κολλυβιστής (from κόλλυβος, *a commission paid on exchange*), *a money-changer*, who changed heathen into Jewish money, for payment into the Temple treasury.

κολλύριον, correct spelling of κολλούριον.

κολοβόω (lit. *I maim, mutilate*), *I cut short, shorten, abbreviate.*

Κολοσσαί, *Colossae*, a town of the Roman province Asia, in the Lycus valley, near Laodicea and Hierapolis.

κόλπος, (a) sing. and plur. *bosom*; (sinus) the overhanging fold of the garment used as a pocket, Lk. vi 38 ; (b) *a bay, gulf*, Ac. xxvii 39.

κολυμβάω, (properly *I dive* ; hence) *I swim.*

κολυμβήθρα (lit. a *diving* or *swimming place*), *a pool.*

κολωνία (Latin, = colonia), *a colony*, a city settlement of Roman (soldier) citizens ; *a garrison city.*

κομάω, *I wear the hair long, I allow the hair to grow long.*

κόμη, *hair, long hair.*

κομίζω, (a) act. *I convey, bring*, Lk. vii 37 ; (b) mid. *I receive back, I receive* what has belonged to myself but has been lost, or else promised but kept back, or *I get* what has come to be my own by earning, *I recover.*

κομψῶς (colloquial), *nicely, finely, bravely.*

κονιάω, *I whitewash.*

κονιορτός, *dust.*

κοπάζω, *I cease, drop.*

κοπετός (planctus), *beating of the breast* or *head* in lamentation, *lamentation.*

κοπή (caedes), *slaughter.*

κοπιάω, (a) *I grow weary*, Mt. xi 28, John iv 6, Rev. ii 3 ; (b) *I toil, work with effort* (of bodily and mental labour alike).

κόπος, (a) *trouble* ; κόπους (κόπον) τινὶ παρέχειν, *to give* κοπρία

trouble to one, to annoy one; (b) *toil, labour, laborious toil*, involving weariness and fatigue.

κοπρία, *manure.*

κόπριον, *manure.*

κόπτω, (a) *I cut, I cut off,* Mt. xxi 8, Mk. xi 8; (b) mid. (plango) *I beat my breast* or *head* in lamentation, *I lament, mourn,* sometimes with acc. (ἐπὶ c. acc.) of person whose loss is mourned.

κόραξ, *a raven.*

κοράσιον (colloquial), *a little girl, a young girl; a girl.*

κορβάν (Aramaic), *a gift.*

κορβανᾶς, *the temple treasure.*

Κορέ (Hebr.), *Korah* (Num. xvi 1 ff.).

κορέννυμι, *I fill, sate, glut, feed full.*

Κορίνθιος, *Corinthian, of Corinth.*

Κόρινθος, *Corinth,* in NE. Peloponnese, the capital of the Roman province Achaia.

Κορνήλιος, *Cornelius,* a centurion of the Roman army, stationed at Caesarea (b).

κόρος (Hebr.), *a (dry) measure,* equivalent to ten Attic μέδιμνοι or 120 gallons.

κοσμέω, *I put into order; I decorate, deck, adorn.*

κοσμικός, *earthly, worldly* (belonging to the present, earthly world as opposed to the heavenly and future).

κόσμιος, *orderly, virtuous.*

κοσμίως, *in an orderly, virtuous manner; modestly.*

κοσμοκράτωρ, *ruler of this world,* that is, of the world as asserting its independence of God; used of the angelic or demonic powers controlling the sublunary world, cf. ἀρχή, ἐξουσία, στοιχεῖον.

κόσμος (mundus), (a) *the universe, the world,* the sum-total of created things; (b) a Jewish conception; the word has acquired a bad sense in Isaiah (e. g. xiii 11), the sum of the fierce surrounding heathen nations, the powers of the heathen world, at once destructive and corruptive. Hence, *the world* as apart from God its Creator, the world as self-sufficient, consequently running counter to its Creator, and thus evil

138

in its tendency, cf. John, 1 John (e. g. ii 15), James
(e. g. iv 4), 2 Pet. ii 20; (c) sometimes seems not
different from, *the* inhabited *world*; (d) *adornment*,
1 Pet. iii 3.

Κούαρτος, *Quartus*, a Christian, brother of Erastus the
Corinthian. Cf. ἀδελφός.

κούμ (κοῦμι) (Aramaic), *arise*.

κουστωδία (Latin, = custodia), concr., *a guard*.

κουφίζω, *I lighten*.

κόφινος (cophinus), a stiff wicker *basket*.

κράβαττος (grabattus), *a bed, mattress, mat* of a pcor
man. (Spelling κράβακτος in Egyptian documents.)

κράζω, *I cry aloud, shriek*.

κραιπάλη (crapula), *surfeiting*.

κρανίον, *the skull*.

κράσπεδον, *the fringe, the edge*.

κραταιόομαι, *I become strong*.

κραταιός, *strong, powerful*.

κρατέω, *I lay hold of, take possession of, obtain*, c. gen.
and (much oftener) c. acc.

κράτιστος (egregius), *most excellent*, an official epithet,
used in addressing a Roman of high rank, and in
the second century one of equestrian (as distinguished
from senatorial) rank.

κράτος, Divine *might, rule, power*, except in Heb. ii 14.

κραυγάζω, *I cry aloud, shout*.

κραυγή, (a) *a shout, cry, clamour*; (b) *outcry, clamour-
ing* against another, Eph. iv 31.

κρέας (caro), *flesh* : plur. (carnes) *pieces of flesh, kinds of
flesh*.

κρείσσων (also κρείττων), *better*.

κρεμάννυμι (pendo), *I hang, I suspend*; mid. (pendeo)
I am hanging, I hang.

κρεπάλη (a variety of κραιπάλη).

κρημνός, *a crag, precipice*.

Κρής, *a Cretan, an inhabitant of Crete*.

Κρήσκης (Latin, = Crescens), *Crescens*, a Christian,
coadjutor of St. Paul.

Κρήτη

Κρήτη, *Crete*: see **Κυρήνη**.
κριθή, *barley*.
κρίθινος, *made of barley*.
κρίμα, (a) *a judgement, a verdict*; sometimes implying an *adverse verdict, a condemnation*; (b) *a case at law, a lawsuit*, 1 Cor. vi 7.
κρίνον, *a lily* growing wild, variously identified with the red anemone, the white lily, the sword lily.
κρίνω, (a) *I judge*, whether in a law-court or privately: sometimes with cognate nouns κρίμα, κρίματι, κρίσιν, emphasizing the notion of the verb; (b) *I decide, I think (it) good*, c. infin. Ac. iii 13, xv 19, &c. (cf. Ac. xxvii 1).
κρίσις, *judging, judgement*; generally *divine judgement: accusation*, Jude 9.
Κρίσπος, *Crispus*, ruler of the synagogue at Corinth, converted and baptized by St. Paul.
κριτήριον, (a) *a law-court*, James ii 6; (b) *a law-case* before an arbiter.
κριτής, *a judge*.
κριτικός, *able to judge*.
κρούω (pulso), *I beat* a door with a stick, to gain admittance.
κρύπτη (κρυπτή), *a hidden place*, cf. κρυπτός.
κρυπτός, *hidden, secret*: τὰ κρυπτά, as subst. *the hidden (secret) things (parts), the inward nature (character)*; ἐν [τῷ] κρυπτῷ, *in the secret place, in the hidden sphere, inwardly*.
κρύπτω, *I hide, conceal*.
κρυσταλλίζω, *I am clear as crystal*.
κρύσταλλος, *crystal*.
κρυφαῖος, *hidden, secret*: ἐν τῷ κρυφαίῳ = ἐν τῷ κρυπτῷ.
κρυφῆ, *in secret, secretly*.
κτάομαι, (a) *I acquire, win, get, purchase, buy*; (b) *I possess*, 1 Thess. iv 4.
κτῆμα, *a piece of landed property, a field*, Ac. v 1; plur. *possessions, property*, possibly *landed property, property in land* in Mk. x 22, Mt. xix 22, as it is in Ac. ii 45.

κτῆνος, *a beast of burden* (generally, a horse or mule), either for riding or for carrying loads on its back, or for yoking to a cart or carriage.

κτήτωρ, *a possessor, owner.*

κτίζω, *I create, found, make,* always of God.

κτίσις (often of the *founding* of a city), (a) abstr., *creation* ; (b) concr., *creation, creature, institution.* Always of Divine work.

κτίσμα, *a created thing, a creature,* of God.

κτίστης (often of the *founder* of a city), *creator,* God.

κυβεία, (lit. *playing with dice, gaming,* hence) *trickery, sleight.*

κυβέρνησις (lit. *steering, piloting*), *governing, government,* supposed to refer to such duty as was, later at least, performed by any presbyter or by that presbyter who was ἐπίσκοπος.

κυβερνήτης, *a steersman, a pilot.*

κυκλεύω, *I encircle, invest, enclose.*

κυκλόθεν, *in a circle round, round about.*

κύκλος, *a circle* : dat. κύκλῳ as adv., *in a circle, round about.*

κυκλόω, *I encircle, invest, surround.*

κυλισμός, *rolling, wallowing.*

κυλίω, tr. *I roll* : mid. intr. *I roll.*

κυλλός (debilis), *maimed.*

κῦμα, *a wave.*

κύμβαλον, *a cymbal.*

κύμινον (a Semitic word), *cummin,* a plant used as a spice.

κυνάριον, *a house dog,* possibly with a touch of contempt.

Κύπριος, *Cypriote, belonging to Cyprus.*

Κύπρος, *Cyprus.*

κύπτω, *I stoop.*

Κυρηναῖος, *belonging to Cyrene.*

Κυρήνη, *Cyrene,* a district W. of Egypt on the Mediterranean coast, forming with Crete a Roman province.

Κυρήνιος, Publius Sulpicius *Quirinius* (ob. A.D. 21),

who conducted two censuses of the province Syria,
one in 8, 7, or 6 B.C., Lk. ii 2, as plenipotentiary of
the Emperor, and another as *legatus pro praetore* in
A.D. 7, Ac. v 37.

κυρία, *a lady* : voc. *my lady*, an address of courtesy.

κυριακός (dominicus), *of the Lord* (κύριος), *special to the
Lord* : δεῖπνον, supper (dinner) for church members,
combined with the Eucharist : ἡμέρα, Sunday (cf. Fr.
dimanche, Span. domingo, Ital. domenica). [In
constitutional law means *imperial.*]

κυριεύω, *I rule* ; c. gen. *I rule over, lord it over, master*.

κύριος (dominus), (a) *an owner* of property, particularly
of slaves (δοῦλοι), *a lord, master* (cf. 1 Pet. iii 6) : plur.
οἱ κύριοι (domini), *master and mistress*, Mt. xv 27 (?),
Lk. xix 33, Ac. xvi 16, 19, and perhaps elsewhere ;
(b) weaker sense, in the vocative, as a polite address,
κύριε, *sir* !, κύριοι, *gentlemen, sirs*, Ac. xvi 30, cf. κυρία ;
(c) of Divine beings, κύριος, *Lord*, without article,
generally refers to God, whereas ὁ κύριος, *the Lord*,
generally refers to Jesus, the Messiah (cf. Ac. ii 34).
In this sense the word connotes that these Divine
Beings are absolute rulers (kings) of the whole world,
and that we are their slaves (subjects). As the term
was also applied to oriental sovereigns and to the
Roman Emperors (particularly frequently in Nero's
case) in the same sense, it focussed the deadly rivalry
between the two powers (cf. Ac. xxv 26).

κυριότης, (a) abstr., *lordship*, 2 Pet. ii 10 ; (b) concr.,
divine or *angelic lordship, domination, dignity*, Eph.
i 21, Col. i 16, Jude 8, usually with reference to
a celestial hierarchy.

κυρόω, *I ratify, confirm*.

κύων, *a dog* : universally despised in the East, and thus
the name is applied contemptuously to persons,
Phil. iii 2, Rev. xxii 15 (cf. Mt. xv 26).

κῶλον (membrum), *a limb* : plur. (membra) *bodies*.

κωλύω, *I prevent, debar, hinder* : c. infin. *from* doing so
and so.

κώμη (uicus), *a village.*

κωμόπολις, a city which in constitution has only the status of a village.

κῶμος (comissatio), *a revel, a revelling,* such as took place at the gathering of the grapes.

κώνωψ, *a gnat, mosquito,* referred to proverbially as something small.

Κῶς, *Cos,* an island in the Aegean Sea, SW. of Asia Minor.

Κωσάμ (Hebr.), *Cosam,* son of Elmadam and father of Addei.

κωφός, *dumb.*

Λ

λαγχάνω, (a) *I obtain (receive) by lot, my lot (turn) is*; (b) *I cast lots,* John xix 24.

Λάζαρος ('Ελεάζαρος in old Western documents), *Lazarus, Eliezer,* (a) the beggar, Lk. xvi 20 ff.; (b) the brother of Martha and Mary, of Bethany, John xi, xii.

λάθρα (**λάθρᾳ**), *secretly.*

λαῖλαψ, *a sudden storm, a squall.*

λακτίζω, *I kick.*

λαλέω, (*I talk, chatter* in classical Greek, but in N.T. a more dignified word) *I speak; I say.*

λαλιά, (in classical Greek *babble, chattering*) *speech, talk; manner of speech.*

λαμά (Hebr.), *why.*

λαμβάνω, (a) *I receive, get*: πρόσωπον λαμβάνειν τινός (Hebraistic), lit. *to receive the face of, to accept the person of,* i. e. *to favour specially*; (b) *I take*: συμβούλιον λαβεῖν, *to deliberate,* Mt. xii 14; (c) = παραλαμβάνω, John i 12.

Λάμεχ (Hebr.), *Lamech,* son of Methuselah and father of Noah.

λαμπάς, *a lamp, a lantern.*

λαμπρός, *shining, glossy, bright.*

λαμπρότης, *brightness.*

λαμπρῶς

λαμπρῶς, *sumptuously.*

λάμπω, *I shine.*

λανθάνω, *I am hidden (concealed), I lie hid, I escape notice*, sometimes with acc. of person from whom concealment takes place, Ac. xxvi 26, 2 Pet. iii 8: with participles (classical constr.), I do so and so *unconsciously, unknown to myself, I shut my eyes to* so and so, Heb. xiii 2.

λαξευτός, *hewn* out of the rock.

Λαοδίκεια, *Laodicea*, a city in the Lycos valley in the Roman province Asia, near Colossae and Hierapolis.

Λαοδικεύς, *a Laodicean, an inhabitant of Laodicea.*

λαός, (a) *a people*, characteristically of God's chosen people, first the Jews, then the Christians; (b) sometimes, but rarely, *the people, the crowd*, e.g. Lk. ix 13, xx 6.

λάρυγξ, *the throat.*

Λασέα, another spelling of Λασαία, *Lasaea*, a city in Crete, about the middle of the S. coast.

λάσκω, *I burst asunder with a loud noise.*

λατομέω, *I hew* (of stone).

λατρεία, *service* rendered to God, perhaps simply *worship.*

λατρεύω, *I serve*, especially God, perhaps simply *I worship.*

λάχανον, *a vegetable.*

Λεββαῖος, *Lebbaeus*, a pet-name, a v. l. for Thaddaeus, one of the twelve disciples of Jesus. The full form of the name is not known.

λεγιών (Latin, = legio), properly a division of the Roman army, numbering about 6,000 infantry with additional cavalry (cf. Mt. xxvi 53): hence, *a very large number.*

λέγω (denoting speech in progress), (a) *I say, speak; I mean; I mention, tell;* (b) *I call, name*, especially in the pass., e.g. Mt. i 16, John i 38, but also act., e.g. Mk. x 18; (c) *I tell, I command*, e.g. Mt. v 34, 39, Rom. ii 22.

λεῖμμα, *a remnant, a remainder.*

λεῖος, *smooth.*

λείπω (earlier, *I leave behind, abandon*), (a) *I am wanting*; τὰ λείποντα, *what is defective*, Tit. i 5 ; (b) mid. e.g. c. gen. *I come behind* (in a race), *I am left behind in, I fall short of* (some standard), *I am wanting in.*

λειτουργέω, *I act in the public service, I render service, I minister*, in the widest sense, Rom. xv 27, of some special public religious service, Ac. xiii 2 : but also of the service of priests and levites, Heb. x 11.

λειτουργία, *public service* in the widest sense, 2 Cor. ix 12, Phil. ii 30: *service* as of priest or levite ritual, Lk. i 23, Phil. ii 17, Heb. viii 6, ix 21.

λειτουργικός, *given to serving (ministration), ministering.*

λειτουργός, *minister, servant*, of an official character; of priests and levites, Heb. viii 2.

λεμά (Aramaic), *why.*

λεντίον (Latin, = linteum), *a towel.*

λεπίς, *a scale, a scaly substance* thrown off from the body,

λέπρα, *leprosy.*

λεπρός, *a leprous person, a leper.*

λεπτόν, *a small piece of money*, probably *the smallest piece of money* = ½ quadrans (κοδράντης, which see).

Λευεί, Λευείς (Hebr.), *Levi*, (a) an ancestor of Jesus, Lk. iii 24; (b) another ancestor of Jesus, Lk. iii 29; (c) third son of Jacob, the patriarch, and founder of a tribe named after him, Heb. vii 5, 9, Rev. vii 7 ; (d) son of Alphaeus, and called also Matthew, a revenue officer and one of the twelve disciples of Jesus.

λευείτης, *a levite*, properly a man of the tribe of Levi ; hence, *a priest's assistant, an under priest,* as the members of that tribe were charged with this duty.

λευειτικός, *belonging to the tribe of Levi, levitical.*

λευκαίνω, *I whiten.*

λευκοβύσσινος, *of white fine linen* (but see βύσσος).

λευκός, *white.*

λέων, *a lion* : ἐκ τῆς φυλῆς Ἰούδα applied to Jesus, Rev.

v 5 (after Gen. xlix 9) : in 2 Tim. iv 17 used proverbially for very great danger.

λήθη, *forgetfulness.*

λῆμψις, *receiving.*

ληνός, *a winepress* : hence met. Rev. xiv 19, xix 15.

λῆρος, *folly, nonsense, idle talk.*

λῃστής, *a robber, brigand, bandit.*

λίαν, *very ; very much, exceedingly.*

λίβανος (Semitic word), *frankincense, incense.*

λιβανωτός, *a censer.*

Λιβερτῖνος (Latin, = libertinus), *a freedman,* one of the
class of manumitted slaves. A synagogue at Jerusalem appears to have been reserved for them.

Λιβύη, *Libya, Africa* (in the modern sense).

λιθάζω, *I stone.*

λίθινος, *made of stone.*

λιθοβολέω, *I stone, I cast stones (at).*

λίθος, *a stone*: met. of Jesus as the chief stone in
a building, &c., Ac. iv 11, &c.

λιθόστρωτος, *paved with stone.*

λικμάω, *I crush to powder.*

λιμήν, *a harbour, port.*

λῖμμα, an itacistic spelling of λεῖμμα.

λίμνη, *a lake.*

λιμός, *a famine.*

λίνον, *flax ; linen.*

Λίνος, *Linus,* a Christian in Rome.

λιπαρός, (lit. *fat*) *rich, sumptuous.*

λίτρα (libra), *a Roman pound,* of about twelve ounces,
327½ grammes.

λίψ (Africus), *the south-west wind,* and thus the quarter
from which it comes.

λογεία, λογία (from λογεύω, ‘ I collect ’), *a collection,
collecting* (of money), particularly of an irregular
local contribution for religious purposes.

λογίζομαι (properly of an accountant, book-keeper, *I
count, reckon up*), (a) *I reckon, count, put down* to
one’s account, τι or τινί τι, Rom. iv 6, 1 Cor. xiii 5,

2 Cor. v 19, 2 Tim. iv 16 ; also with εἴς τι = *as some-thing, as of some value*, e. g. Ac. xix 27, Rom. iv 3, Gal. iii 6 ; (b) *I number, class* amongst, [Mk.] xv 28, Lk. xxii 37 ; (c) *I reckon up accounts, I weigh arguments, I deliberate*, Mk. xi 31 (v.l.) ; (d) hence *I consider, weigh*, John xi 50, 2 Cor. x 11, Phil. iv 8, Heb. xi 19 ; (e) *I think, I judge*, often ; (f) *I decide, determine*, 2 Cor. x 2.

λογικός, (a) *reasonable, rational*, Rom. xii 1 ; (b) *meta-phorical*, as contrasted with literal, 1 Pet. ii 2 (so perhaps also in Rom. xii 1).

λόγιον, plur. *oracles, divine responses* or *utterances* (it can include the entire O. T. scriptures) ; in Rom. iii 2 mainly of the promises in the Old Testament ; in Heb. v 12 probably of Jesus' teaching.

λόγιος, *eloquent*.

λογισμός, *reasoning, thinking*.

λογομαχέω, *I battle with (for) words*.

λογομαχία, *a battling with (for) words, a battle of words*.

λόγος (speech in progress) (sermo, uerbum, ratio), (a) *a word, an utterance, speech, discourse, saying*, frequently of God through his messengers ; the gen. expresses either this origin or the subject of the word ; διὰ λόγου, *by spoken word, by word of mouth* ; ὁ λόγος, the Gospel news, e. g. Lk. i 2, Ac. xiv 25 ; (b) *the personalized Word* or *Divine utterance*, a conception of Palestinian or Alexandrian theology, referred by the Fourth Evangelist to Jesus the Messiah, John i 1, 14 ; (c) *an account*, Ac. xx 24, 1 Pet. iv 5 ; hence (d) *reason, a reason*, 1 Pet. iii 15 : κατὰ λόγον, *rightly, deservedly*, Ac. xviii 14 ; (e) *analogy*, ἐπέχειν λόγον τινός, *to correspond to, be analogous to, be instead of* something, Phil. ii 16.

λόγχη, *a long lance*.

λοιδορέω, *I revile* a person *to his face, I abuse insult-ingly*.

λοιδορία, *reviling, abuse*.

λοίδορος, *a railer, reviler, abuser*.

λοιμός

λοιμός (pestis), (a) *a pestilence*; (b) *a pestilent fellow*, Ac. xxiv 5.

λοιπός (reliquus), (a) *left, left behind*, οἱ λοιποί, *the remainder, the rest, the others*; (b) adverbial phrases, acc. neut., λοιπόν, τὸ λοιπόν, *for the rest, now, already*; temporal gen., τοῦ λοιποῦ (sc. χρόνου), *henceforth*.

Λουκᾶς, *Lucas, Luke*, an abbreviated pet-form either of Λουκανός, as the Old Latin Bible gave in the title of the Third Gospel, or of Λούκιος, as some moderns have thought, Christian physician and writer of the Third Gospel and Acts.

Λούκιος, *Lucius*, (a) of Cyrene, an early Christian, in the church of Antioch, Ac. xiii 1, by some identified with the evangelist Luke; (b) a Christian with Paul at Corinth, by some identified with (a), Rom. xvi 21.

λουτρόν, *a bath* (of the water, not the vessel), *water for washing, washing*.

λούω (literally or merely ceremonially), *I wash, bathe* (the body): mid. of *washing, bathing one's self*.

Λύδδα, *Lydda, Diospolis, Lod* (modern *Ludd*), a city on the way to Joppa within a day's journey of Jerusalem.

Λυδία, *Lydia*, a lady resident of Philippi, native of Thyatira in Lydia (Asia Minor), and engaged in the clothing trade.

Λυκαονία, *Lycaonia, the country of the Lykaones*, a district of Asia Minor, comprised within the Roman province Galatia and including the cities Derbe and Lystra.

Λυκαονιστί, *in the Lycaonian language*.

Λυκία, *Lycia*, a small Roman province on the south coast of Asia Minor.

λύκος, *a wolf*, or perhaps *a jackal*: often applied to persons of wolfish proclivities.

λυμαίνομαι, *I ravage, harry, devastate*.

λυπέω, *I pain, grieve, vex*.

λύπη, *pain, grief*.

Λυσανίας, *Lysanias*, tetrarch of Abilene.

Λυσίας, Claudius *Lysias,* a Roman tribune of the soldiers in Jerusalem.

λύσις, *dissolution, release.*

λυσιτελέω, impers. 3 sing. *it is advantageous to, it profits.*

Λύστρα, *Lystra,* a Lycaonian city in the southern part of the Roman province Galatia.

λύτρον, *the purchasing money* for manumitting slaves, *a ransom, the price of ransoming;* especially *the sacrifice by which expiation is effected, an offering of expiation.*

λυτρόω (originally, *I deliver* captives from robbers or enemies in war *by payment, I manumit* or *liberate* a slave from slavery), *I ransom, liberate, deliver.*

λύτρωσις (in O. T. *ransoming from imprisonment for debt,* or *from slavery, release from national misfortune,* &c.), *liberation, deliverance, release* (cf. λυτρόω).

λυτρωτής, *a ransomer, a liberator.*

λυχνία, *a lampstand.*

λύχνος, *a lamp.*

λύω (soluo), (a) *I unloose, loose, loosen, untie, release,* Mk. i 7, &c.: thus *I break* (in a phrase where the time order of the two processes is inverted), Rev. v 2 ; (b) met. *I break, destroy, set at naught, contravene;* sometimes merely, *I declare* a law *to be not binding,* John v 18 ; *I break up* a meeting, Ac. xiii 43 ; *I annul,* 1 John iv 3 (v. l.).

Λωΐς, *Lois,* grandmother of Timothy.

Λώτ (Λώθ) (Hebr.), *Lot,* nephew of Abraham.

M

Μαάθ (Hebr.), *Maath, Mahath,* an ancestor of Jesus.

Μαγαδάν, *Magadan.* The reading and the site are uncertain. Two views are held with regard to the latter, (a) that it was in the Decapolis near Gerasa ; (b) that it was at Meğdel on the western bank of the Sea of Galilee.

Μαγδαληνός, *a Magdalene, of Magdala,* a place identical with modern Meğdel, near Tiberias : see **Μαγαδάν** (b).

Μαγεδών, *Magedon,* the second part of the name, Ἄρ Μαγεδών (*Har Magedon*), perhaps *Megiddo.*

μαγεύω, *I practise sorcery* or *magic.*

μαγία, *sorcery, magic.*

μάγος, *a sorcerer, a magician, a wizard.*

Μαγώγ (Hebr.), *Magog,* sometimes as name of a people, sometimes as name of a country in O.T. (Gen. x 2, Ezek. xxxviii 2, xxxix 6), probably the Scythians ; hence, used in apocalyptic literature.

Μαδιάμ (Hebr.), *Madiam, Midian,* generally taken to mean or to include the peninsula of Sinai.

μαθητεύω, *I make disciples, I make into disciples* : followed by dat. of instrument, Mt. xiii 52.

μαθητής, *a learner, disciple, pupil.*

μαθήτρια, *a woman disciple.*

Μαθθαῖος, *Matthaeus, Matthew,* a revenue officer, then one of the twelve disciples of Jesus.

Μαθθάν (Hebr.), *Matthan,* son of Eleazar and father of Jacob, an ancestor of Jesus.

Μαθθάτ (Ματθάτ) (Hebr.), *Matthat,* son of Levi and father of Jorem, an ancestor of Jesus.

Μαθθίας, *Matthias,* elected one of the Twelve in room of the deceased Judas.

Μαθουσάλα (Hebr.), *Methuselah,* son of Enoch and father of Lamech.

μαίνομαι (furo), *I am raving mad, I speak as a madman.*

μακαρίζω, *I deem* (*declare*) *happy.*

μακάριος, *happy, to be envied.*

μακαρισμός, *felicitation, regarding as happy* or *enviable.*

Μακεδονία (Hebr.), *Macedonia,* a Roman province north of Achaia (Greece).

Μακεδών, *a Macedonian,* an inhabitant of the Roman province Macedonia.

μάκελλον (Latin, = macellum), *meat-market.*

μακράν (procul), adv. sometimes used adjectivally, *at a distance, far away.*

μακρόθεν, *from a (long) distance*, often in the tautological expression ἀπὸ μακρόθεν = μακρόθεν, ἀπὸ μακράν (cf. Lk. xviii 13).

μακροθυμέω, *I defer my anger, I am long-suffering*, i. e. the opposite of short- or quick-tempered.

μακροθυμία, *long-suffering*.

μακροθύμως, *with long-suffering, patiently*.

μακρός, (a) *long*: acc. neut. plur. as adv. *long*, Mk. xii 40, Lk. xx 47; (b) *distant*.

μακροχρόνιος, *long-timed, long-lived*.

μαλακία (malacia), *weakness, illness*.

μαλακός (mollis), (a) *soft*, (τὰ) μαλακά, as substantive, *soft material*; (b) of persons, *soft, voluptuous, effeminate* (really = cinaedus, pathicus).

Μαλελεήλ (Hebr.), *Maleleel, Malelehel*, one of the ancestors of Jesus.

μάλιστα (superlative, see **μᾶλλον**), *most of all, especially*.

μᾶλλον (comparative, see **μάλιστα**), *more, rather*.

Μάλχος (Aram. *Malchu*), *Malchus*, a slave of the high-priest at Jerusalem.

μάμμη, *a grandmother*.

μαμωνᾶς (Aramaic, with cognate words in Hebrew and Punic), *riches, money, possessions, property*.

Μαναήν (grecized form of Aramaic *Menahem*), *Manaen*, probably a member of Herod Antipas' court.

Μανασσῆς (Hebr.), *Manasseh*, (a) son of Joseph, founder of a tribe of Israel, Rev. vii 6; (b) son of Hezekiah and father of Amon (Amos).

μανθάνω, *I learn*; with adjectives or nouns, *I learn* to be so and so, 1 Tim. v 13; with acc. of person who is the object of knowledge, Eph. iv 20; aor. sometimes *to ascertain*, Ac. xxiii 27, Gal. iii 2.

μανία (furor), *raving madness*.

μάννα (Hebrew), *manna*, the supernatural food eaten by the Israelites in the desert: of spiritual food, Rev. ii 17.

μαντεύομαι, *I practise soothsaying*, suggesting the fraud involved in the practice.

μαραίνω

μαραίνω: pass. *I die, I wither* (like the grass).
μαρὰν ἀθά (Aramaic), either *Our Lord hath come,* or
Our Lord cometh (will come, is at hand).
μαργαρίτης (margarita), *a pearl.*
Μάρθα, *Martha,* sister of Mary and Lazarus of Bethany.
Μαρία, Μαριάμ (the former is the grecized form), *Mary,*
Miriam, (a) the mother of Jesus; (b) of Magdala,
which epithet is always attached (except John xx 11,
16 where it is unnecessary; (c) sister of Martha and
Lazarus, Lk. x 39, 42, John xi, xii 3; (d) mother of
James and Joseph (or Joses), Mt. xxvii 56, Mk. xv 40,
and presumably in Mk. xv 47, xvi 1, Lk. xxiv 10;
wife of Clopas, John xix 25. Also referred to in Mt.
xxvii 61, xxviii 1; (e) mother of John Mark, Ac. xii
12; (f) a Christian in Rome, Rom. xvi 6.
Μᾶρκος, *Marcus, Mark,* who also had the Hebrew
name John, son of Mary [(e) above], nephew of Barnabas, coadjutor of Barnabas, Saul (Paul), and Peter.
μάρμαρος (marmor), *marble.*
μαρτυρέω, *I witness, I bear witness, I give evidence, I*
testify, c. dat. pers. or quality, in one's favour, in
favour of; c. acc. cognate, μαρτυρίαν, ὁμολογίαν, practically otiose; in the passive, *I am witnessed to, I am*
borne witness to, sometimes with nom. and dependent
infin. (impersonal, 3 John 12), corresponding to the
act.; Rev. i 2, xxii 16, 18, 20.
μαρτυρία, *witness, evidence, testimony.*
μαρτύριον, *witness, evidence* (of recovery, Mt. viii 4, Mk. i
44, Lk. v 14: so of other occurrences or thoughts):
ἡ σκηνὴ τοῦ μαρτυρίου, *the tent* of the congregation, *the*
tent of meeting of God with His people, because it
contained the ark and the tablets *of the testimony* to
the covenant between God and his people, cf.
Exod. xxv 9, 10.
μαρτύρομαι, (properly, *I call* (summon) *to witness,* and
then, absolutely) *I testify, I protest, I asseverate;*
(obtestor) *I conjure, solemnly charge,* 1 Thess. ii 12,
Eph. iv 17.

μάρτυς, *a witness, eye-* or *ear-witness*. In Ac. xxii 20, Rev. ii 13 it approaches the ecclesiastical sense of *martyr*, i. e. one who gives public testimony to his faith before a tribunal, and suffers the penalty.

μασάομαι, *I gnaw.*

μασθός, see μαστός.

μαστιγόω (uerbero), *I flog, scourge*, the victim being strapped to a pole or frame, see μάστιξ.

μαστίζω, *I flog, scourge*, see μάστιξ.

μάστιξ (flagrum), (a) *a scourge, lash*, of leathern thongs with pieces of metal sewn up in them, Ac. xxii 24, Heb. xi 36 ; (b) met. *severe pains (sufferings)* sent by God.

μαστός, *a breast*, especially *a nipple* of a woman's breast.

ματαιολογία, *vain speaking, foolish talking.*

ματαιολόγος, *speaking vain things.*

ματαιόομαι, *I am made vain, ineffective, godless.*

μάταιος, *vain, unreal, ineffectual, unproductive*: practically *godless.*

ματαιότης, *vanity, emptiness, unreality, purposelessness, ineffectiveness, instability.*

μάτην, *in vain, in an unreal way.*

Ματθάτ (Hebr.), *Matthat*, an ancestor of Jesus.

Ματταθά (Hebr.), *Mattathah*, an ancestor of Jesus.

Ματταθίας (Hebr.), *Mattathias*, an ancestor of Jesus.

μάχαιρα, *a sword*: met. of the spirit, Eph. vi 17.

μάχη, (earlier, *a battle, conflict*, perhaps in James iv 1 ; hence) in the sphere of words, &c., *strife, contention, quarrel.*

μάχομαι, *I engage in battle, I fight*: hence *I strive*, John vi 52.

μεγαλεῖος : τὰ μεγαλεῖα (magnalia), *the mighty deeds.*

μεγαλειότης, *(divine) majesty* or *magnificence.*

μεγαλοπρεπής, *magnificent, superb, transcendent.*

μεγαλύνω, (a) *I enlarge, lengthen*, Mt. xxiii 5 ; (b) *I increase, magnify.*

μεγάλως, *greatly*: compar. μεῖζον.

μεγαλωσύνη, (*divine*) *majesty*; in Heb. i 3, viii 1, a sort of substitute for the divine Name.

μέγας, *large, great*, in the widest sense: see **μειζότερος, μείζων, μέγιστος**.

μέγεθος, *greatness*.

μεγιστάν (megistan), *a great one, a lord, a courtier, a satrap*. (The word has an oriental flavour and belongs to late Greek.)

μέγιστος (elative superlative, practically obsolete and only literary), *very great*: see **μέγας** (positive), **μείζων** (comparative and superlative).

μεθερμηνεύω, *I translate* (from one language into another).

μέθη, *deep drinking, drunkenness*.

μεθιστάνω, μεθίστημι, *I cause to change its place, I move out of its place, I translate, transfer, remove*.

μεθοδεία (from **μέθοδος**, *a way of search after something, an inquiry; a method*), *scheming, craftiness*.

μεθύσκομαι, *I become intoxicated with wine, I become drunk*.

μέθυσος (originally, *tipsy*), *a drunkard*.

μεθύω, *I am intoxicated with wine, I am drunk*.

μεῖζον, see **μεγάλως**.

μειζότερος, μείζων, (a) compar. *greater* (3 John 4); (b) superl. *greatest*, Mt. xiii 32, xxiii 11, 1 Cor. xiii 13, &c.

μέλας, *black*: τὸ μέλαν (atramentum), *ink*, 2 Cor. iii 3, 2 John 12, 3 John 13.

Μελεά (Hebr.), *Meleah*, one of the ancestors of Jesus.

μέλει, impersonal, *it is a care, it is an object of anxiety*, c. dat. of the person: personal, διὸ μελήσω, *wherefore I will take care*, true text in 2 Pet. i 12 (Field).

μελετάω, *I devise, plan; practise, exercise myself in*.

μέλι, *honey*.

μελίσσιος, *belonging to bees, coming from bees*.

Μελίτη (Μελιτήνη), *Malta*.

μέλλω, (a) c. infin. *I am about to, I intend*; (b) absol., in present participle, *coming, future*: so τὸ μέλλον, *the future*, εἰς τὸ μέλλον (sc. ἔτος), *next year*, Lk. xiii 9, τὰ

μέλλοντα, *the things that are to be* (*come to pass*).　See
μέλει.

μέλος (membrum, but wider in sense than κῶλον), *a bodily
organ, limb, member*.

Μελχεί (Hebr.), *Melchi,* one of the ancestors of Jesus.

Μελχισεδέκ (Hebr.), *Melchisedek,* king and priest of
Salem (Gen. xiv 18–20).

μεμβράνα (Latin, = membrana), *a parchment leaf,*
perhaps for notes.

μέμφομαι, *I blame.*

μεμψίμοιρος, *blaming one's lot* or *destiny, discontented.*

μέν, an untranslatable particle, generally answered by
δέ (sometimes by ἀλλά, πλήν), each of the two introducing a clause intended to be contrasted with the
other.　[The μέν is very often omitted as compared
with classical Greek.]　Other uses are (a) μέν followed
by καί (e. g. Lk. viii 5), where an additional detail is
given, not explicitly contrasted with the earlier, (b)
μέν followed by no contrasting particle in the following clause (e. g. πρῶτον μέν, almost *at the very first,*
Rom. i 8, 1 Cor. xi 18), and (c) μὲν οὖν, for the most
part in narrative passages, where the μέν brings the
accompanying noun or pronoun into relief, without
any contrast being expressed by a following δέ (e. g.
Ac. i 6), (1) where what has preceded is summed up
on the way to the relation of some new detail, or (2)
where it acts as the introduction to a further occurrence : but see μὲν οὖν for another use.

Μεννά (Hebr.), *Menna,* one of the ancestors of Jesus.

μὲν οὖν, μενοῦν, μὲν οὖν γε, μενοῦνγε, especially in an
answer, strengthening or correcting, *nay more, nay
rather.*

μενοῦν, μενοῦνγε, see μὲν οὖν.

μέντοι (originally a strengthened μέν), (a) *indeed, really,*
James ii 8 ; (b) *yet, however, nevertheless.*

μένω, *I remain, abide, wait* ; c. acc. *I wait for, await.*

μερίζω, *I divide into parts, I divide, I part, I share, I
distribute* ; mid. *I go shares, I share* (with others ;

in this case with Paul, Apollos, Cephas), *I take part in a partitioning*, 1 Cor. i 13; *I distract*, 1 Cor. vii 34.

μέριμνα, *care, worry, anxiety*.

μεριμνάω, *I am over-anxious*; c. acc. *I am anxious about, I care for*.

μερίς, (a) (a sense amply attested outside) *a part, division* of a country, Ac. xvi 12; (b) *a share, portion*.

μερισμός, (a) *a distributing, a distribution*, Heb. ii 4; (b) *a parting, dividing, severance, separation*.

μεριστής, *a divider, partitioner, distributor*.

μέρος, *a part, portion*: τὰ μέρη, territorially, *the region*; adv. phrases are ἀπὸ μέρους, ἐκ μέρους, *in part, partly*, ἀνὰ μέρος, κατὰ μέρος, *part by part, each part separately, in detail*; *a party*, Ac. xxiii 9.

μεσημβρία (lit. *midday*, hence, the position of the sun at midday), *the south*.

μεσιτεύω, *I mediate, interpose*; but probably in Heb. vi 17 rather *I am surety, I give bail*.

μεσίτης, (a) *a mediator, intermediary*, 1 Tim. ii 5; (b) *a go-between, arbiter, agent* of something good, Gal. iii 19, 20, Heb. viii 6, ix 15, xii 24.

μεσονύκτιον, *midnight*, the middle of the period between sunset and sunrise.

Μεσοποταμία, *Mesopotamia, the Country between the* (two) *Rivers*, i. e. the Euphrates and the Tigris.

μέσος, *middle, in the middle*, sometimes followed by the genitive of the whole area referred to; adverbial (with or without gen.) are μέσου (acc. neut.), ἀνὰ μέσον (elliptical in 1 Cor. vi 5), κατὰ μέσον, ἐν [τῷ] μέσῳ, *in the middle, before them all*, ἐκ μέσου, *from the midst*.

μεσότοιχον, *mid-wall*.

μεσουράνημα, *mid-heaven, the middle of heaven*.

μεσόω, *I am in the middle* of my course.

Μεσσίας (Hebrew), *Messiah, the Anointed One*, generally translated into Greek as Χριστός.

μεστός, *full*; met. (cf. πλήρης) almost *tainted, diseased with*, Mt. xxiii 28, Rom. i 29.

μεστόω, *I fill*.

μετά, (a) c. gen. *with, in company with* : merely, *in connexion with*, Lk. i 58 ; (b) c. acc. (1) *behind, beyond, after,* of place ; (2) *after,* of time, with nouns, neut. of adjectives, or τό c. infin.

μεταβαίνω, *I change my place* (*abode*), *I leave, I depart, I remove.*

μεταβάλλω : mid. *I change my mind.*

μετάγω (usually *transfer, transport,* and met., to a better mind), *I turn about, I change the position of.*

μεταδίδωμι (lit. *I offer by way of change, I offer so that a change* of owner is produced), *I share* ; sometimes merely, *I impart.*

μετάθεσις, (a) *change, transformation,* Heb. vii 12, xii 27 ; (b) *removal,* Heb. xi 5.

μεταίρω, *I change my position, remove.*

μετακαλέω : mid. *I summon to myself, I send for.*

μετακινέω, tr. *I move away, I dislodge.*

μεταλαμβάνω, (a) c. gen. *I take a share* (*part*) *of, I share in, I partake of* ; (b) c. acc. *I take after* (*later*) or *I take instead,* Ac. xxiv 25.

μετάλημψις, *partaking of, sharing in.*

μεταλλάσσω, *I transform, alter.*

μεταμέλομαι (lit. *I change* one *care* or *interest* for another), *I change my mind* (generally for a better).

μεταμορφόω, *I change a form* (involving a change of inmost nature ; contrast the creatures described in Ovid's *Metamorphoses*) ; mid. c. acc. *I assume* something *through a change,* 2 Cor. iii 18.

μετανοέω, *I change my mind, I change the inner man* (particularly with reference to acceptance of the will of God by the νοῦς (mind) instead of rejection) : with ἀπό or ἐκ, the giving up definitely of the courses denoted by the following words is indicated.

μετάνοια, *a change of mind, a change in the inner man* : ἀπό indicates what is given up in this change, Heb. vi 1.

μεταξύ, (prep.) *between* : μεταξὺ σοῦ καὶ αὐτοῦ μόνου (Aramaic idiom), *privately,* Mt. xviii 15, μεταξὺ ἀλλή-

μεταπέμπομαι

λων, *in their mutual intercourse*, Rom. ii 15; (adv.)
with ὁ in the sense *the next, the next after* (because
between the present and the one after that), Ac. xiii 42,
ἐν τῷ μεταξύ (sc. χρόνῳ), *meantime, meanwhile*, John
iv 31.

μεταπέμπομαι, *I send for, summon.*

μεταστρέφω, *I turn, change.*

μετασχηματίζω, *I change the outward appearance* (*the
dress, the form of presentment*) of something; *I transfer
by a fiction, adapt.*

μετατίθημι, (a) *I transfer*, Ac. vii 16, Heb. xi 5; mid.
I go over to another party, *I desert*, Gal. i 6; (b)
I change, Heb. vii 12.

μετατρέπω, tr. *I turn, change.*

μετέπειτα, *thereafter.*

μετέχω, *I have a share of, I participate in, I share.*

μετεωρίζομαι, *I am* μετέωρος, i.e. *suspended, anxious*,
Lk. xii 29.

μετοικεσία, *transportation, deportation*, followed by genitive of reference, Βαβυλῶνος.

μετοικίζω, *I transport.*

μετοχή, *sharing, partnership.*

μέτοχος, *a sharer, partner*; c. gen. *in* something.

μετρέω, *I measure.*

μετρητής, *a measure*, about 39·39 litres or 8¾ gallons.

μετριοπαθέω, *I feel moderately*, with particular reference
to displeasure at men's sin.

μετρίως (*modice*), *moderately*: οὐ μετρίως, *greatly, exceedingly.*

μέτρον, *a measure*, whether lineal (e.g. Rev. xxi 15) or
cubic (e.g. Lk. vi 38): ἐκ μέτρου (Aramaic idiom?),
in scanty measure.

μέτωπον, *forehead.*

μέχρι, μέχρις, (conjunction) with or without οὗ, the ἄν
(ἐάν) being omitted in N.T. examples, with aor. subj.,
until . . . shall have . . .: (preposition) *as far as*;
until.

μή, negative particle, *not, that . . . not* (*lest*), &c., used

158

generally, instead of οὐ the negative of fact (expressed by the indicative), where there is some indefiniteness about the action or occurrence referred to (expressed by other moods), either because it is in the future, or because it is in an interrogative clause (a feature of everyday language), or because it is in an indefinite relative, or a conditional, optative, or final clause, &c. Sometimes c. indic. to be translated by *perhaps*, Lk. xi 35, Col. ii 8 (cf. Heb. iii 12), Gal. iv 11 (but also with subjunctive as in classical Greek, Mt. xxv 9, v.l.). οὐ μή, (a) c. indic. future or, far more often, with subjunctive aorist, in a statement, a very emphatic negative, *assuredly not*. It occurs for the most part in passages coming from the O.T. and sayings of Christ (both from Semitic originals), where words of decisive tone are especially in place. In this construction the prohibition refers to the future, 'do not' (in future), as contrasted with μὴ ποίει, meaning 'desist from'; the latter is sometimes durative: (b) c. subjunct. aor. in interrog. clause, *not*, Lk. xviii 7, John xviii 11. μή ποτε, see μήποτε; μή που, see μήπου.

μήγε, see εἰ δὲ μήγε under εἰ.

μηδαμῶς, *not at all*.

μηδέ (neue, neque), generally after a preceding μή, *nor . . . either*.

μηδείς (also another Hellenistic orthography μηθείς, Ac. xxvii 33), (a) adj. *no*, in agreement with nouns; (b) each gender used as a noun, *no person, nothing*. Its use with respect to that of οὐδείς corresponds to that of μή with respect to that of οὐ.

μηδέποτε, *not at any time*.

μηδέπω, *not yet*.

Μῆδος, *a Mede, a Median*, from East of Assyria.

μηθείς, see μηδείς.

μηκέτι, *no longer*.

μῆκος, *length*.

μηκύνω, *I lengthen*.

μηλωτή, *sheep's* (sometimes *pig's*) *hide, sheepskin.*

μήν, noun, *a* (lunar) *month.*

μήν, adverb, expressing emphasis, mostly in the formulae of oaths, *assuredly, in very truth.*

μηνύω, (a) *I reveal, make known* : in a law-court, *I lay information, I inform,* John xi 57, Ac. xxiii 30 ; (b) *I make known, I point out,* Lk. xx 37, 1 Cor. x 28.

μήποτε (= μή ποτε), *lest at any time, lest*: then weakened, *whether perhaps, whether at all* ; in a principal clause, *perhaps.*

μήπου (= μή που), *lest anywhere.*

μήπω, *not yet.*

μήπως (= μή πως), *lest in any way.*

μηρός, *thigh.*

μήτε (= μή τε), *nor*: μήτε... μήτε, *neither ... nor,* sometimes also oftener than twice (e. g. James v 12).

μήτηρ, *a mother*: sometimes also of one who is *as a mother,* who takes the place of a mother, Mk. iii 34, 35, &c., John xix 27, Rom. xvi 13, Gal. iv 26, 1 Tim. v 2, Rev. xvii 5.

μήτι (μή strengthened by the addition of the acc. neut. of τις (indefinite) as adv.), (a) with εἰ : thus εἰ μήτι = εἰ μή, *if not, unless,* Lk. ix 13, εἰ μήτι ἄν, *unless in a given case,* 1 Cor. vii 5 ; (b) in questions, expecting a negative answer, cf. Mt. vii 16, *can it be that?* suggesting impossibility.

μήτιγε, a modified μήτι, in elliptical construction, *not to speak of.*

μήτις = μή τις.

μήτρα, *the womb.*

μητραλῴας, *a matricide.*

μιαίνω, met. *I stain, pollute, defile.*

μίασμα, *a pollution, a defilement.*

μιασμός, *pollution, defilement.*

μῖγμα, *a mixture.*

μίγνυμι, *I mix.*

μικρόν, (neut. of adj. as) noun and adv. *a little,* both of space and of time as well as of size, degree : in

John xiv 19, &c., understand ἐστιν or ἔσται after μικρόν.

μικρός, (a) *small*: superl. μικρότερος, *smallest*, in Mk. xv 40 possibly *junior*; (b) of time, *short*; see μικρόν.

Μίλητος, *Miletus*, a city on the coast of the Roman province Asia.

μίλιον (Latin, = milium, a false singular formed from milia [passuum], *a thousand double paces*), *a Roman mile*, measuring 1478·5 mètres.

μιμέομαι, *I imitate*.

μιμητής, *an imitator*.

μιμνήσκομαι, mid. and pass. (memoror), *I remember*: the passive forms sometimes have passive sense, from active μιμνήσκω (memoro), *I call to mind, I recall, I mention*, Ac. x 31, Rev. xvi 19.

μισέω, *I hate*.

μισθαποδοσία (lit. *repayment of price* or *payment of price due*), *reward*, Heb. x 35, xi 26: in the sense, *due punishment*, Heb. ii 2.

μισθαποδότης (see μισθαποδοσία), *a rewarder*.

μίσθιος (mercennarius), *a paid worker, a hired servant, a hireling* (contrasted with a slave).

μισθόομαι, *I hire, engage*.

μισθός (merces), (a) *pay, wages, salary*; (b) *reward, recompense*.

μίσθωμα, *a rented apartment* or *flat*.

μισθωτός, *hired, engaged* for wages.

Μιτυλήνη (earlier Μυτιλήνη, as in the best MSS of the Vulgate), *Mitylene*, the capital of the island of Lesbos in the northern Aegean sea.

Μιχαήλ, *Michahel, Michael*, an archangel.

μνᾶ (a Semitic word), *a mina*, a Greek money unit = 100 δραχμαί, or about £4.

Μνάσων, *Mnason*, an early Christian, native of Cyprus, resident at a place between Caesarea and Jerusalem.

μνεία, *remembrance, recollection, mention; commemoration*, Rom. xii 13 (v.l.).

μνῆμα, *a tomb, monument*.

μνημεῖον, *a tomb, monument.*

μνήμη, *memory,* or *mention.*

μνημονεύω, *I remember; I hold in remembrance; I make mention of,* Heb. xi 22.

μνημόσυνον, *reminder, memorial; a remembrance offering,* Ac. x 4.

μνηστεύω, *I betroth.*

μογιλάλος, (lit. *speaking with difficulty,* hence) *dumb.*

μόγις, *with difficulty; scarcely, hardly.*

μόδιος (Latin, = modius), a dry measure, the chief corn unit, nearly two English gallons.

μοιχαλίς, (a) *an adulteress* (that is, a married woman who commits adultery), Rom. vii 3, 2 Pet. ii 14; (b) Hebraistically extended to those who worship any other than the true God (Yahweh).

μοιχάομαι, *I commit adultery,* not only of a married woman but of a married man (see Mt. xix 9, v.l., Mk. x 11).

μοιχεία, *adultery.*

μοιχεύω, *I commit adultery* (of a man with a married woman, but also (Lk. xvi 18) of a married man).

μοιχός, *an adulterer,* that is, a man who is guilty with a married woman.

μόλις (uix), *with difficulty, hardly.*

Μολόχ (Hebr.), *Moloch,* a god worshipped by several Semitic peoples (name is properly appellation = king).

μολύνω, *I soil, stain, pollute,* literally and morally.

μολυσμός, *staining, contamination, pollution.*

μομφή (lit. *blame, fault-finding*), *a complaint, fault.*

μονή, (a) abstr., μονὴν ποιεῖσθαι, *to stay, to dwell,* John xiv 23; (b) concr., *lodging, dwelling-place, room.*

μονογενής, of children, *only-born, only.*

μόνον, acc. sing. neut. of μόνος, used as adv., *only.*

μόνος, *alone*: κατὰ μόνας = κατ᾽ ἰδίαν, *by himself.*

μονόφθαλμος, *one-eyed, with one eye only.*

μονόω, *I leave alone (solitary).*

μορφή, *form,* implying essential character as well as outline. It suggests unchangeableness, as contrasted with σχῆμα (= figure, fashion). In Phil. ii 6 the reference is to the pre-incarnate Christ with divine attributes.

μορφόω, *I form, shape* (of the development of the embryo into the fully formed child).

μόρφωσις, a mere *form, outline.*

μοσχοποιέω, *I make* a model of *a calf.*

μόσχος, *a calf.*

μουσικός, *a musician,* but probably in some narrower sense in Rev. xviii 22.

μόχθος, *struggle, hardship,* involved in continued *labour.*

μυελός, *marrow.*

μυέω, (*I initiate* into the Mysteries, hence) *I habituate.*

μῦθος, *an idle tale, fable, fanciful story.*

μυκάομαι, *I roar.*

μυκτηρίζω (properly, *I turn up the nose* as a sign of contempt), *I sneer at, disdain.*

μυλικός, *belonging to a mill.*

μύλινος, *a mill-stone.*

μύλος, *a mill.*

Μύρα, Μύρρα, *Myra,* a port in Lycia, SW. Asia Minor.

μυριάς, a group of *ten thousand, a ten thousand.*

μυρίζω, *I anoint.*

μυρίοι, *ten thousand* : also used for a very large number.

μύρον (a Semitic word), *anointing-oil ; ointment.*

Μύρρα, see **Μύρα.**

Μυσία, *Mysia,* a country in the NW. of the Roman province Asia (and of Asia Minor).

μυστήριον, *a secret,* Mk. iv 11 and parallels: also (a) a symbol containing *a secret* meaning, Rev. xvii 5, cf. Eph. v 32 ; (b) the meaning of such a symbol, Rev. i 20, xvii 7 ; (c) as the counterpart of ἀποκάλυψις, *a secret* to be revealed, *the secret purpose* of God in His dealings with man, *a Divine secret,* especially the inclusion of the Gentiles as well as the Jews in the scope of the Messiah's beneficent reign ; (d) the sum of the Christian faith, 1 Tim. iii 9, 16.

μυωπάζω

μυωπάζω, *I half-close the eyes, I blink.*
μώλωψ, *a weal*, left on the body by scourging.
μωμάομαι, *I calumniate, slander.*
μῶμος, *a blemish* (a 'Hebraic' sense peculiar to Biblical Greek; the classical sense is *blame*).
μωραίνω (from μωρός) (infatuo): (a) *I make foolish, I turn to foolishness*; (b) *I taint*, and thus *make useless*, Mt. v 13, Lk. xiv 34.
μωρία, *foolishness.*
μωρολογία, *foolish talking.*
μωρός, (a) adj. *foolish*; (b) noun *a fool.*
Μωυσῆς, *Moses* (the form nearer Hebrew found in oldest Latin Bible and Vulgate), *Moyses*, the lawgiver of the Hebrews, thus regarded as the author of the Pentateuch, where the laws are preserved (cf. 2 Cor. iii 15, &c.).

N

Ναασσών (Hebr.), *Naasson*, son of Aminadab and father of Salmon (Sala), and one of the ancestors of Jesus.
Ναγγαί (Hebr.), *Naggai*, one of the ancestors of Jesus.
Ναζαρά (the Greek form, declined), Ναζαρέτ (the native form, not declined), *Nazareth*, a city of Galilee, where Jesus lived before His ministry.
Ναζαρηνός, *of Nazareth, a Nazarene.*
Ναζωραῖος, commonly interpreted to mean, *of Nazareth, Nazarene*, the ω being nearer to the Syriac form *Natsoreth.*
Ναθάμ (Hebr.), *Nathan*, son of David, and an ancestor of Jesus.
Ναθαναήλ, *Nathanael, Nathanahel*, of Cana in Galilee, an early disciple.
ναί, *yes*, sometimes made a substantive by prefixing the article τό.
Ναιμάν, *Naaman*, commander-in-chief of the army of a king of Syria in the ninth century B.C. (2 Kings v).
Ναΐν, Ναΐμ, *Nain*, a city SW. of the Sea of Galilee.

ναός, *a temple, a shrine*, that part of the temple where the god himself resides (contrast ἱερόν); so also figuratively.

Ναούμ (Hebr.), *Naum, Nahum*, an ancestor of Jesus.

νάρδος (Hebr., borrowed into Persian and Sanscrit), *spikenard*, a perfume made originally from the *Nardostachys Jatamansi* growing on the Himalayas.

Νάρκισσος, *Narcissus*, a resident in Rome in Nero's time.

ναυαγέω (naufrago), (a) *I am shipwrecked*; so (b) figuratively, *I come to ruin*.

ναύκληρος, *a captain (master) of a ship*.

ναῦς (literary), *a ship, a vessel*, Ac. xxvii 41 only (an almost obsolete word, rare in the vernacular; see πλοῖον).

ναύτης, *a sailor*.

Ναχώρ (Hebr.), *Nachor*, one of the ancestors of Jesus.

νεανίας (iuuenis), *a young man, a man in his prime* (used even of a man of 40).

νεανίσκος, *a youth*.

Νεάπολις, see νέος.

νεκρός, (a) adj. *dead, lifeless*; hence met.; (b) noun *a dead body, a corpse*, ἐκ [τῶν] νεκρῶν, *from among the dead*.

νεκρόω, lit. and met. *I make (cause) to be dead; I make as dead*.

νέκρωσις, (a) *putting to death*, 2 Cor. iv 10; (b) *dead or lifeless condition*, Rom. iv 19.

(νεομηνία, Ionic, probably not used by N.T. writers), νουμηνία (Attic), *a new moon*. (So *numenia* occurs in good Latin MSS.)

νέος, (a) *young*; (b) *new, fresh*; Νέα πόλις, *Neapolis, New City*, the harbour town of Philippi.

νεότης, *youth, youthfulness*.

νεόφυτος (lit. *newly planted*), *newly converted* to Christianity.

νεύω, *I nod, make a sign*.

νεφέλη, *a cloud*.

Νεφθαλείμ, *Naphthali*, son of Jacob, founder of a tribe which occupied territory.

νέφος, (lit. *a cloud*, hence) *a dense crowd*.

νεφρός, *a kidney* (as a general emotional centre).

νεωκόρος (lit. *temple-sweeper*), *temple-warden*; an honorary title.

νεωτερικός, *associated with youth* (*younger men*), *youthful*.

νή, with an acc. of adjuration, *by*.

νήθω (a vulgar and late form of **νέω**, neo), *I spin*.

νηπιάζω, *I am childish* (*infantile*).

νήπιος (infans), *an infant, a child*.

Νηρεί (Hebr.), *Nerei*, an ancestor of Jesus.

Νηρεύς, *Nereus*, a Christian in Rome.

νησίον, *a little island, an islet*.

νῆσος, *an island*.

νηστεία, *fasting*.

νηστεύω, *I fast*.

νῆστις, *fasting, without food*.

νηφάλιος, *sober, not intoxicated* (with wine).

νήφω (lit. *I am sober*), *I am calm* (*vigilant*).

Νίγερ, *Niger*, another name of Symeon, a Christian at Antioch.

Νικάνωρ, *Nicanor*, one of the original seven 'deacons' in the church at Jerusalem.

νικάω, *I conquer* (transferred from battle to other conflicts).

νίκη, *victory*.

Νικόδημος, *Nicodemus*, a rich Jewish follower of Jesus, and member of the Sanhedrin.

Νικολαΐτης, *a Nicolaitan, a follower of Nicolaus* (a heretic at Ephesus).

Νικόλαος, *Nicolaus*, a Jewish proselyte of Antioch, one of the original seven 'deacons' in the church at Jerusalem.

Νικόπολις, *Nicopolis*, probably the city near Actium in Epirus, N. W. Greece.

νῖκος (a later variety of **νίκη**, dating from about the middle of first century B.C.), *victory*.

Νινευείτης, *a Ninevite, an inhabitant of Nineveh* or *Ninus*, a city on the Tigris in Assyria.

νιπτήρ, *a basin*.

νίπτω, *I wash*; mid. *I wash my own* (hands, &c.).

νοέω, *I understand, conceive, apprehend*; aor. possibly *realize*, John xii 40, Eph. iii 4.

νόημα, *a thought*; *a design*.

νόθος, *a bastard, an illegitimate son*.

νομή, (a) *pasture*; (b) ἔχειν νομήν, *to spread*, 2 Tim. ii 17.

νομίζω, *I think, suppose*.

νομικός, (a) adj. *connected with law, about law*, Tit. iii 9; (b) noun *a lawyer, one learned in the Law* (i.e. in the Gospels), *one learned in the Old Testament scriptures* (like γραμματεύς), *a scribe*; *a jurist*, Tit. iii 13.

νομίμως (legitime), *in a legitimate way, according to law and regulation*.

νόμισμα, *a coin*.

νομοδιδάσκαλος, (a) *a teacher of the Law, one learned in the Law* (i.e. the Old Testament), = γραμματεύς, νομικός; (b) *a teacher of laws*, probably with reference to heretics of ascetic tendency, 1 Tim. i 7.

νομοθεσία, *legislation* (at Sinai), *enactment of the Law*.

νομοθετέω, (a) *I ordain, lay down, give the sanction of law to, enact*, Heb. viii 6; (b) *I base legally, I regulate, I direct*.

νομοθέτης, *a legislator*.

νόμος, (a) *the Law*, and so sometimes = the body of moral and ceremonial enactments forming the basis of Judaism; especially as set forth in the Old Testament; *the Old Testament*; but also ὁ νόμος καὶ οἱ προφῆται, Mt. vii 12, &c., as a description of the content of the Old Testament, though as strictly interpreted the phrase excludes the 'writings' (namely Psalms, Proverbs, Job, Song of Songs, Ruth, Ecclesiastes, Esther, Daniel, Ezra, Nehemiah, Chronicles); (b) *a power to legislate, a sense of law, something with legislative authority*, e. g. Rom. vii 23, viii 2, Gal. vi 2; (c) *a law, an ordinance*, Rom. vii 2, James i 25, ii 8.

νοσέω

νοσέω, *I am diseased*, hence of mental or spiritual disease.

νόσημα, *a disease, a trouble*.

νόσος, *a disease, a malady*.

νοσσιά (syncopated from **νεοσσία**), *a nestling, a young bird in the nest*.

νοσσίον, *a nestling, a young bird in the nest*; see **νοσσιά**.

νοσσός, *a nestling, a young bird, a young one*.

νοσφίζω: mid. *I separate for myself, I set apart for myself, I annex, appropriate for my own benefit, purloin, peculate*.

νότος, *the south wind*; hence *the south*.

νουθεσία, *a warning, admonition*.

νουθετέω, *I admonish, warn*.

νουμηνία, see **νεομηνία**.

νουνεχῶς, *reasonably, sensibly*.

νοῦς (a non-Semitic Greek term, meaning in Plato *reason, intuition*, sometimes in the LXX taking the place of the commoner καρδία as a rendering of Hebrew *lēb*), *the intellectual faculty* of the natural man, applicable to God or Christ (Rom. xi 34, 1 Cor. ii 16), employed in practical judgement, capable of being good or evil, and of being regenerated, *the mind, the reason, the reasoning faculty*.

Νύμφα, *Nympha*, a woman's name, if we read Νύμφαν and αὐτῆς in Col. iv 15, as we probably should; otherwise, Νυμφᾶν will be the accusative of the masculine name Νυμφᾶς, a pet form of Νυμφόδωρος, *Nymphas, Nymphodorus*.

νύμφη, νύνφη, (a) *a bride*; hence, in the symbolism of Rev., the New Jerusalem, the Lamb's Bride; (b) *a daughter-in-law*, Mt. x 35, Lk. xii 53.

νυμφίος, *a bridegroom*: name applied to the Messiah, Mk. ii 19, 20 and parallels.

νυμφών, *a wedding chamber*; οἱ υἱοὶ τοῦ νυμφῶνος (a Semitism), *the wedding guests*, the Messiah being spoken of as bridegroom, Mk. ii 19 and parallels, cf. νυμφίος.

νῦν (nunc), *now, at present*, sometimes with article preceding, τὸ νῦν, τὰ νῦν, governed at times by prepositions, ἀπό, ἕως, ἄχρι.

νυνί (originally a more emphatic νῦν), *now*.

νύξ, (a) *night*: νυκτός, διὰ νυκτός, *by night, sometime during the night*, see also ἡμέρα; (b) met. 1 Thess. v 5, &c.

νύσσω, *I prick*.

νυστάζω, *I sleep, slumber*; met. 2 Pet. ii 3.

νυχθήμερον, *a night and a day* (not necessarily more than the latter part of a night and the earlier part of the succeeding day).

Νῶε (Hebr.), *Noah*.

νωθρός, *blunt, dull*, hence spiritually; *sluggish, remiss, slack*.

νῶτος (dorsum), *the back*.

Ξ

ξενία (hospitium), *a lodging*, or rather, abstr., *hospitality*.

ξενίζω, (a) *I entertain* a stranger; (b) *I startle, bewilder*, Ac. xvii 20, 1 Pet. iv 4, 12.

ξενοδοχέω, *I receive (entertain) strangers*.

ξένος, (a) adj. *foreign*, Ac. xvii 18; *strange, unusual*, Heb. xiii 9, 1 Pet. iv 12; (b) noun (hospes) *a stranger, a foreigner* (either one belonging to another community in the same country, or to another country); *a resident alien*, without city rights, Ac. xvii 21, Eph. ii 19, Heb. xi 13; c. gen. *a stranger to*, Eph. ii 12; *a host (guest) friend*, the word indicating the reciprocal relationship, which was a sacred one, Rom. xvi 23.

ξέστης (Latin, = sextarius), properly a Roman dry measure, rather less than a pint: referred to rather as a household *utensil* than as a measure.

ξηραίνω, *I dry up; parch*.

ξηρός, *dry*: ἡ ξηρά (arida), *dry land*, as opposed to sea, &c.; *dried up, withered, parched*; in generalizing neuter, Lk. xxiii 31.

ξύλινος, *made of wood.*

ξύλον, *wood, a piece of wood*; hence, *a club, a staff,*
Mk. xiv 43, 48 and parallels; *the trunk of a tree,* used
to support the cross-bar of a cross in crucifixion,
Ac. v 30, &c.; *a tree,* Lk. xxiii 31, *ζωῆς,* the fruit of
which gives life, Rev. ii 7, xxii 2, 14, 19.

ξυράομαι, *I shave* my head.

O

ὁ, ἡ, τό, originally a demonstrative pronoun, as in *τοῦ
γένος ἐσμέν, we are descended from Him,* Ac. xvii 28,
cf. *ὁ μέν . . . ὁ δέ (ἄλλος δέ), the one . . . the other.* But in
the following phrases some word is understood, *ὁ τινός,
the son of* so and so, cf. Mt. iv 21, *ἡ τινός, the daughter
(wife) of* so and so, *ἐν τοῖς τινός, in the house of* so and
so, Lk. ii 49; then, the definite article, by which the
following word is defined more precisely or exactly than
it would otherwise be (but it is often omitted, for example, after a preposition, even where a definite place
is intended, cf. *ἐν οἴκῳ, in the house,* Mk. ii 1, *ἐν ἀγορᾷ, in
the market-place,* Lk. vii 32, *ἐν συναγωγῇ, in church,*
John vi 59, xviii 20). It is thus found (a) with
common nouns, e. g. *ὁ ἀγρός, the* field (*ἀγρός, a* field),
(in Tit. ii 13 the absence of *τοῦ* before *σωτῆρος* shows
that Christ Jesus is our great God and Saviour), and
(b) sometimes also with proper nouns, where it was
equivalent to pointing out a man, and was popular
in origin; with the vocative, commonest where
translated from Semitic; (c) with adjectives, e. g. *ὁ
ἄλλος, the* other (*ἄλλος, an* other), *ὁ αὐτός, the same*
(*αὐτός, he, self*), *ὁ πᾶς, πᾶς ὁ, the whole* (*πᾶς, every*); (d)
with numerals, e. g. *ὁ εἷς, the* one (*εἷς, one*), *ὁ πρῶτος,
the* first, *the* former (*πρῶτος, first*); (e) with participles, e. g. *τοῖς καθημένοις, those* seated, Mt. iv 16, cf.
instances where a participle may be regarded as
understood, e. g. *Σαῦλος ὁ καὶ Παῦλος, Saul who*

was also called Paul, Saul, otherwise Paul, Ac.
xiii 9; (f) with the infinitive, making it a substantive, and so capable of being governed by prepositions: see below also; (g) with adverbs, e. g. τὸ
πέραν, *the other side* (πέραν, *beyond*), τὸ νῦν, τὰ νῦν;
(h) with interjections, e. g. τὸ ἀμήν, ἡ οὐαί; (i) with
a clause or phrase, e. g. τὸ οὐ φονεύσεις, *the command Thou shalt do no murder,* Mt. xix 18. **The
genitive** sing. neut. τοῦ with the infinitive is used in
three special ways (like ἵνα), (1) as in classical Greek,
indicating purpose, final, telic, *in order that*: never
in Paul; (2) indicating consequence, epexegetic, *so
that, so as to, with the result that,* e. g. Rom. i 24, vii
3, viii 12, 1 Cor. x 13, Rev. xii 7; (3) introducing
a noun clause, indicating content, in no way different
from τό, Mt. xxi 32, Lk. xvii 1, Ac. x 25, James v 17.

ὀγδοήκοντα, *eighty.*

ὄγδοος, *eighth.*

ὄγκος, (properly *bulk, mass,* hence) *a burden.*

ὅδε (hic), *this here, this;* also as pronoun.

ὁδεύω, *I am on a journey.*

ὁδηγέω, *I lead, guide.*

ὁδηγός, *a guide.*

ὁδοιπορέω, *I am on a journey, I journey.*

ὁδοιπορία, *journeying, travelling, travel.*

ὁδοποιέω, *I journey* (a Latinism (?), = iter facere: in
careful Greek it would mean, *I build (pave) a road).*

ὁδός, (a) (uia) *a road;* (b) (iter) *a journey;* hence met.
a way of life, a course of conduct, and ἡ ὁδός, **the** *way*
of life, *Christianity,* Ac. ix 2, &c.

ὀδούς, *a tooth.*

ὀδυνάομαι, *I suffer acute pain,* physical or mental.

ὀδύνη, *acute* mental *pain.*

ὀδυρμός, *mourning, grieving.*

Ὀζείας (Hebr.), *Ozeias, Uzziah,* son of Joram and father
of Joatham, and king of Judah from about 785 to
746 B. C., an ancestor of Jesus.

ὄζω, intr. *I smell, am fetid.*

ὅθεν

ὅθεν (unde), (a) local, *whence, from which place*; (b) inferential, *wherefore*.

ὀθόνη (a word of Semitic origin), *a sheet*, made of fine linen.

ὀθόνιον, *a bandage, a wrapping* (see ὀθόνη).

οἶδα, (a) (scio), *I know* a fact; perhaps, *I remember*, 1 Cor. i 16, 2 Cor. xii 3; c. infin. *I know how to*; (b) (noui), *I know (am acquainted with)* a person.

οἰκεῖος (from οἶκος, *household, family*), *of one's family, intimate*, 1 Tim. v 8; hence met.

οἰκέτεια (familia), *household* of slaves.

οἰκέτης (famulus), *a household slave, a slave*.

οἰκέω, *I dwell*, lit. and met.; c. acc. *I inhabit*.

οἴκημα, *a prison* (euphemism for δεσμωτήριον).

οἰκητήριον (habitaculum), *a dwelling-place*, lit. and met.

οἰκία, *a house* (strictly *the whole house*, see οἶκος): of Heaven, John xiv 2; also met. *property, belongings*, Mk. xii 40 and parallels; *household*, John iv 53; of the body, 2 Cor. v 1, 2.

οἰκιακός, *a member of one's household*.

οἰκοδεσποτέω, *I am (master or) mistress of a house*.

οἰκοδεσπότης, *a master of a house, a head of a house* (possibly a play upon words with Βεεζεβούλ).

οἰκοδομέω, *I build* (a house); hence met.

οἰκοδομή, (a) abstract, *building, the operation (process) of building*, sometimes transitional, without being strictly concrete, 1 Cor. iii 9, 2 Cor. v 1, Eph. ii 21, iv 12, 16, 29 (here perhaps = *improvement*); met. *upbuilding, edification*; (b) concrete, *a building*, Mk. xiii 1, 2, Mt. xxiv 1.

οἰκοδόμος, *a house-builder, a builder*.

οἰκονομέω, *I am a steward, I do the work of a steward*.

οἰκονομία, *household management, stewardship, the office of a steward*; hence met. of any position of trust or the duties of that position, *provision, arrangement, dispensation* (even God being sometimes regarded as steward).

οἰκονόμος (dispensator), (a) *a steward* (commonly

172

a superior slave of tried character, who looked after the accounts of a household; hence met. 1 Cor. iv 1, 2, Tit. i 7, 1 Pet. iv 10; (b) apparently, *City Steward* or *Treasurer*, Rom. xvi 23; (c) perhaps not to be separated from (a), (curator) *a guardian, a legal guardian*, Gal. iv 2. In any case he manages the property of the 'infant' till the age of 25, perhaps.

οἶκος (strictly *a set of rooms*, see οἰκία), (a) *a house*, the material building; οἶκος τοῦ θεοῦ, the Temple at Jerusalem, Mk. ii 26, &c. (referred to in Mt. xxiii 38); hence met.; (b) *a household, family*; οἶκος Ἰσραήλ, Ἰακώβ, Δαυείδ (Hebraic, note the omission of the article).

οἰκουμένη (properly present pcpl. pass. of οἰκέω, with γῆ understood, *the land that is being inhabited, the land in a state of habitation*), *the inhabited world*, that is, *the Roman world* (orbis terrarum), for all outside it was regarded as of no account.

οἰκουργός, *a house-worker, a housekeeper*, v. l.

οἰκουρός, *a keeper at home; a housekeeper*.

οἰκτείρω (Attic οἰκτίρω), *I pity*.

οἰκτιρμός, *pity, mercy*: the frequency of the plural is due to Hebraic influence (the corresponding Hebrew word has the same meaning in the plural).

οἰκτίρμων, *pitiful, merciful*.

οἶμαι, οἴομαι, *I think*: c. infin. the underlying idea is that of purpose, Phil. i 17.

οἰνοπότης, *an excessive wine-drinker*.

οἶνος, *wine*; met. Rev. (except vi 6, xviii 13), where almost otiose.

οἰνοφλυγία, *sottishness*, steeping of oneself in wine.

οἴομαι, see οἶμαι.

οἶος (qualis), properly correlative to τοιοῦτος, the combined expression meaning *of such a kind as*, 1 Cor. xv 48; by itself, both rel. and indirect interrog., *such as, of what kind (character)*: οὐχ οἶον δὲ ὅτι, Rom. ix 6, is equivalent to a strong negative, *not of course* (lit. *it is not so that*).

ὀκνέω

ὀκνέω, *I shrink (from), I hesitate, I am afraid.*

ὀκνηρός, *timid*; *slothful*: ἐμοὶ οὐκ ὀκνηρόν, a kind of epistolary formula, *I do not hesitate.*

ὀκταήμερος, *eight days old.*

ὀκτώ, *eight.*

ὄλεθρος, *ruin, doom, destruction.*

ὀλιγοπιστία, *smallness of belief (faith).*

ὀλιγόπιστος, *of little faith (belief).*

ὀλίγος (ὀλίγος), (a) especially in the plural, *few*; (b) in the singular, *small*; hence, of time, *short*, of degree, *light, slight, little*: πρὸς ὀλίγον, *to a slight degree,* 1 Tim. iv 8, *for a short time,* James iv 14; ἐν ὀλίγῳ, *in brief compass, in brief, in few words, briefly* (cf. 1 Pet. v 12), Eph. iii 3, Ac. xxvi 28 (perhaps = *in very short time*); ὀλίγον (acc. neut.), adverbially, of space, *a little,* Mk. i 19, Lk. v 3, of time, *for a short (little) time,* Mk. vi 31, 1 Pet. i 6 (but more probably, *to a little amount*), v 10, Rev. xvii 10.

ὀλιγόψυχος, *pusillanimous, of small courage.*

ὀλιγωρέω (contemno), *I hold in low esteem, I make light of.*

ὀλίγως, *slightly, just.*

ὀλοθρευτής, *the destroying angel* (cf. Num. xvi 41 ff.).

ὀλοθρεύω: ὁ ὀλοθρεύων, *the Destroyer, the destroying angel* (cf. Exod. xii 23, and ὀλοθρευτής).

ὁλοκαύτωμα, *a burnt offering.*

ὁλοκληρία, *perfect (unimpaired) health.*

ὁλόκληρος (properly a word of Greek ritual, of either victim for sacrifice or priest, *free from bodily defect*), *complete* (in every part), *entire, whole.*

ὀλολύζω (onomatopoeic), *I howl.*

ὅλος (totus), *whole, all*: δι' ὅλου, *throughout, for its whole extent, quite, entirely,* John xix 23.

ὁλοτελής, *complete, rounded off.*

Ὀλυμπᾶς (pet form of Ὀλυμπιόδωρος probably), *Olympas,* a Christian man in Rome.

ὄλυνθος, *an unripe fig.*

ὅλως (omnino), (a) *entirely, altogether, at all*; (b) *actually,* 1 Cor. v 1; *absolutely,* 1 Cor. vi 7, xv 29.

ὄμβρος, *a rain-storm.*

ὀμείρομαι (perhaps a nursery word, derived from a word indicating 'remembrance'), *I long for,* c. gen.

ὁμιλέω, *I consort with, associate with, commune with;* particularly, *I talk (converse) with,* Ac. xx 11.

ὁμιλία, *intercourse, companionship, conversation.*

ὁμίχλη, *a mist.*

ὄμμα, *an eye.*

ὄμνυμι, ὀμνύω, *I swear, I take an oath:* sometimes with cognate acc. or with dat.: with acc., or with κατά c. gen., of the power invoked or appealed to, *by,* James v 12, Heb. vi 13, 16.

ὁμοθυμαδόν, *with one mind, with one accord.*

ὁμοιάζω, *I am like.*

ὁμοιοπαθής, *of like feelings,* almost, *of like nature.*

ὅμοιος, *like.*

ὁμοιότης, *resemblance:* understand ἡμῶν in Heb. iv 15, cf. vii 15.

ὁμοιόω, *I make like, liken; I compare.*

ὁμοίωμα (originally, *a thing made like* something else), *likeness,* or rather *form.* (In fact ὁμοίωμα (concrete) differs from ὁμοιότης (abstract) much as simulacrum differs from similitudo.)

ὁμοίως, *in a similar way, similarly, in the same way.*

ὁμοίωσις, *making like; likeness* (cf. Gen. i 26).

ὁμολογέω (originally, *I agree with the statement* of another), (a) *I promise,* Mt. xiv 7, Ac. vii 17; (b) *I confess* (confiteor); (c) *I publicly declare* (profiteor), cf. 1 John ii 23, iv 3, sometimes with the Aramaic and Syriac construction, ἐν c. dat. equivalent to an acc., Mt. x 32, Lk. xii 8, of confessing allegiance to Jesus before an earthly law-court: c. cognate acc. 1 Tim. vi 12; (d) a Hebraism, *I praise, celebrate,* Heb. xiii 15 (cf. ἐξομολογέομαι).

ὁμολογία, *a confession* (the act rather than the contents or substance) of faith in Christ: 1 Tim. vi 12 refers either to that at baptism or to that at ordination:

ὁμολογουμένως

1 Tim. vi 13 is referred by Pelagius to John xviii 37, not inappropriately.

ὁμολογουμένως, *admittedly.*

ὁμότεχνος, *of the same trade.*

ὁμοῦ (simul), *together.*

ὁμόφρων, *of one mind* (*intent, purpose*).

ὅμως, *nevertheless.*

ὄναρ, *a dream.*

ὀνάριον, *an ass* (a conversational diminutive).

ὀνειδίζω, *I reproach.*

ὀνειδισμός, *a reproaching, a reproach.*

ὄνειδος, *a reproach.*

Ὀνήσιμος (originally adj. *useful,* hence the play upon words in Philem. 10, 11, and very common as slave name), *Onesimus,* a slave of Philemon, a Christian of Colossae.

Ὀνησίφορος, *Onesiphorus,* a Christian of the province of Asia. (An Onesiphorus, probably intended to be the same person, comes into the *Acts of Paul*).

ὀνικός, *connected with an ass;* μύλος ὀνικός, an upper mill-stone so heavy that it requires an ass to turn it (in contrast to the ordinary handmill).

ὀνίνημι, tr. *I profit*: pass. c. gen. *I have joy of.*

ὄνομα, (a) *a name*; but as, according to Hebrew notions, the name is something inseparable from the person to whom it belongs, something of his essence, and therefore in the case of the God specially sacred, it is often used Hebraistically in the sense of (b) *person, personality, power, authority, character* (cf. Ac. i 15, Rev. iii 4, xi 13) ; in some passages it is in consequence best left untranslated altogether : εἰς τὸ ὄνομά τινος is a vernacular phrase, however (see [d]); (c) *a title of rank* (*dignity*), Eph. i 21, Phil. ii 9; (d) (nomen, ratio), *account, reason, pretext,* Mk. ix 41, 1 Pet. iv 16 ; similarly εἰς ὄνομα, Mt. x 41, 42 = *qua, as*; (e) *reputation,* Rev. iii 1.

ὀνομάζω, *I name, give a name to.*

ὄνος, *an ass.*

ὄντως, *really, actually*.

ὄξος (posca), *vinegar of wine* (Num. vi 3), *vinegar*, the drink of field-labourers and private soldiers.

ὀξύς, (a) *sharp*; (b) *swift, express*, Rom. iii 15.

ὀπή, *a crevice* (in a rock); *a cave*.

ὄπισθεν, adv. and prep., *behind*; in Rev. v 1 the reverse (outer) side of the papyrus roll, where the fibres are vertical, is referred to: this was seldom written on, and only from motives of economy.

ὀπίσω, adv. and prep., *behind*; *after*: εἰς τὰ ὀπίσω (Mk. xiii 16) = ὀπίσω (Mt. xxiv 18), cf. Lk. ix 62.

ὁπλίζω, tr. *I arm*; mid. *I arm myself*: especially of defensive armour (breastplate, shield, &c.).

ὅπλον; especially plur. ὅπλα (properly arma, also tela), *defensive armour* (Rom. xiii 12), but also *offensive armour, weapons, arms* (John xviii 3): sometimes met.

ὁποῖος (qualis), corresponding to τοιοῦτος (talis), rel. and indirect interrog., *of which kind*; *of what kind, what sort of*. This word was dying out in N.T. times.

ὁπότε (in classical Greek *whenever*), *when*, Lk. vi 3 (v. l. ὅτε).

ὅπου, *where*, also *whither*; ὅπου ἄν (ἐάν), *wheresoever*, also *whithersoever*.

ὀπτάνομαι, *I appear, I am seen* (by), *I let myself be seen* (by).

ὀπτασία, *a vision*; *an appearance*.

ὀπτός, *broiled*.

ὀπώρα, *autumn*; hence *fruit*.

ὅπως, with the subjunctive, with or without ἄν, *in order that*; *that* (especially after ἐρωτάω).

ὅραμα (literally, *something seen*), *a sight, a vision*.

ὅρασις, *a sight, a vision*: ὁράσει (specie), *in appearance*, Rev. iv 3.

ὁρατός, *to be seen, visible*.

ὁράω, *I see*; hence, like γεύω, widened in sense to mean, *I experience* (Lk. iii 6, &c.): ὅρα (ὅρατε) μή, (uide, uidete ne), *see that* you do *not* . . ., *beware of doing so and so; beware lest.*

ὀργή, *anger, wrath, passion* ; *the settled feeling of anger* (cf. Eph. iv 31), particularly, τοῦ θεοῦ, of God, *the hostility* to sin: ἡ μέλλουσα (ἐρχομένη) ὀργή also refers to the divine wrath, and has a definite eschatological reference; occasionally also without epithet, of the divine wrath, e. g. Rom. iii 5, v 9, ix 22, xiii 5, 1 Thess. ii 16.

ὀργίζομαι, *I am angry.*

ὀργίλος (iracundus), *irascible.*

ὀργυιά, *a fathom* (six feet).

ὀρέγομαι, *I hanker after, I seek (long) for, I am eager for, I aspire to.*

ὀρεινός, ὀρινός; ἡ ὀρεινὴ (sc. γῆ), *the mountain (mountainous) country (region), the highlands.*

ὄρεξις, *eagerness, strong desire.*

ὀρθοποδέω, (strictly, *I am an* ὀρθόπους [*a man with straight feet*], and therefore πρός = *with reference to*; but it is possible that we ought to take it) *I go straight,* πρός, *to.*

ὀρθός, *straight, erect* (perhaps with reference to recovery of health, cf. 'non *erigit* aegros . . . Bacchus,' Lucan, *B. C.* iv 378), Ac. xiv 10; met. *that goes in the right direction,* Heb. xii 13.

ὀρθοτομέω, perhaps, *I cut* (or *carve*) *according to rule* (and thus, *I define* according to the norm of the Gospel); if the metaphor be from drawing furrows (understanding τὴν γῆν), then it may be, *I cultivate, I am occupied with.*

ὀρθρίζω, *I rise early, I come in the morning.*

ὀρθρινός, *belonging to the morning*; hence, equivalent to adv., *in the morning, early.*

ὄρθρος, *dawn, early morning, day-break.*

ὀρθῶς, *rightly.*

ὁρίζω, (lit. *I bound, fix a limit*; hence) *I fix, determine, define*; *I fix upon, appoint, designate.*

ὀρινός, less correct spelling of ὀρεινός.

ὅς—ἥ—ὅ

ὅριον; plur. ὅρια (fines), *territory, district.*

ὁρκίζω, with double acc., of the one adjured and of the one in the name of whom he is adjured, *I adjure.*

ὅρκος, *an oath* (see ὀμνύω).

ὁρκωμοσία, *the swearing of an oath, the taking of an oath.*

ὁρμάω, *I rush.*

ὁρμή, *a sudden movement, an impulse,* communicated by the hand, James iii 4; *inclination,* hostile *intention, instigation.*

ὅρμημα, *a mighty impulse* (*impetus*).

ὄρνεον (originally, *a little bird*), *a bird.*

ὄρνιξ (originally a Doric form, given by MSS ℵDW, and less common than ὄρνις), *a bird.*

ὄρνις, *a bird.*

ὁροθεσία (originally, *a laying down [fixing] of a boundary*), *a boundary.*

ὄρος, *a mountain.*

ὀρύσσω, *I dig.*

ὀρφανός, *orphaned; an orphan;* hence *friendless,* John xiv 18.

ὀρχέομαι, *I dance.*

ὅς—ἥ—ὅ, definite relative pronoun, *who, which;* ὅς ἄν (ἐάν) with subjunctive, *whosoever;* ὅς is sometimes equal to the classical ὅστις, Mt. x 26, xxiv 2, Lk. xii 2, Ac. xix 35, &c.; it is frequently attracted into the case of its antecedent, the latter being sometimes omitted; sometimes the attraction is inverse, that is, the antecedent is attracted into the case of the relative, e.g. Mt. xxi 42, Lk. xii 48, Ac. x 36, 1 Cor. x 16; sometimes the demonstrative pronoun is pleonastically added in the relative clause, a colloquial Greek use, the frequency of which is probably suggested by Semitic usage, e.g. Mk. i 7, vii 25 (cf. xiii 19), Lk. iii 16, John i 27, Ac. xv 17, 1 Pet. ii 24 (v. l.), Rev. iii 8, vii 2, 9, xiii 8, 12, xx 8 (either a Hebrew or an Aramaic source is generally presumed); ὅς μὲν...ὅς δέ, *the one...the other,* or *one...*

179   N 2

ὁσάκις

another; ἀφ᾽ οὗ, ἀφ᾽ ἧς, since (where ἡμέρας or ὥρας can
be supplied) 2 Pet. iii 4 ; ὅ ἐστιν can introduce relative
clauses containing interpretations, whatever be the
gender and number of the antecedent, e. g. Mk. xii 42,
xv 22 ; ἐν ᾧ, in that, because, Rom. ii 1, viii 3, Heb. ii
18 ; wherefore, Heb. vi 17 ; as long as, while, Mk. ii
19, Lk. v 34, John v 7 ; until, Lk. xix 13 (= ἐς ὅ); ἐφ᾽
ᾧ, see ἐπί ; ἐφ᾽ ὃ πάρει, to the task for which you have
come !, Mt. xxvi 50 (a command, not a question);
ἄχρι, ἕως, μέχρις οὗ (lit. up to the point at which), until;
ἀνθ᾽ ὧν, οὗ εἵνεκεν, οὗ χάριν, on account of which, wherefore ; ὅ, as 'cognate' acc., Rom. vi 10, Gal. ii 20.

ὁσάκις, always with ἐάν and subjunctive, as often as, as
many times as.

ὅσιος, (a) holy, pious (implying the right relation to
God); τὰ ὅσια, the pieties, the pious deeds, Ac. xiii 34 :
(b) (Hebrew Chāsīd means not only godly, pious,
but also beloved of Yahweh), ὁ ὅσιος, the Holy One
(i. e. the Messiah).

ὁσιότης, holiness, piety.

ὁσίως, religiously, piously.

ὀσμή, odour ; generally met. in connexion with εὐωδίας
(from O.T.), originally of the sweet smelling odour of
sacrifice, and then widely used.

ὅσος (originally correlative to τοσοῦτος, cf. Heb. x 25),
(quantus) relative and indirect interrogative adj., as
great as ; how great : of time, as long as, Mk. ii 19 :
ὅσος ἐάν (ἄν) generalizes, (quantuscumque) how great
soever, plur. as many soever as : ὅσοι = πάντες οἵ (quot,
later Latin quanti), how many, as many as : ἐφ᾽ ὅσον,
as long as, e. g. Mt. ix 15 ; to the degree that, inasmuch
as, e. g. Mt. xxv 40, Rom. xi 13 : καθ᾽ ὅσον, in proportion as, Heb. iii 3, vii 20, ix 27 : ὅσον ὅσον, a little (cf.
English so so).

ὀστέον, a bone.

ὅστις (rare except in the nominative), either generic,
who, as other like persons, which, as other like things,
or essential, who, by his (her) very nature, which, by
180

its very nature. There is a tendency (seen in the Ionic dialect and also in colloquial Greek) to weaken ὅστις to the sense of ὅς, cf. Mt. xxvii 62, Lk. ii 4, x 42, but examples are very rare: ὅστις ἄν (ἐάν) = ἐάν τις, with subjunctive, *whosoever* (it is doubtful whether the ἄν should be omitted, cf. Mt. x 33, James ii 10): ὅ,τι, short for τί ὅ,τι (= τί γέγονεν ὅτι, John xiv 22), *why*, Mk. ii 16 (v. l.), ix 11, 28 (v. l.), John viii 25 (but in this passage ὅτι can be read, ' do you reproach me *that* . . .'): examples of τί ὅ, τι (or ὅτι) are Mk. ii 16 (v. l.), Lk. ii 49 : ἕως ὅτου, *until* the time at *which*, *until*.

ὀστράκινος, *made of pottery, of earthenware.*

ὄσφρησις, *sense of smell.*

ὀσφύς, sing. and plur., *the loins, the middle*, mentioned in two connexions, first as the quarter from which comes the male seed (Hebraism Ac. ii 30, &c.), and second as the part of the body round which the girdle is placed, when the flowing robes are girt higher with a view to travel or work (cf. Lk. xii 35); hence also met., 1 Pet. i 13 (the negation of mental slackness is referred to).

ὅταν, *whensoever, whenever, as often as*, followed by the indic., in case of repeated events in the past (thus it is incorrectly used=*when* in Rev. viii 1, &c.), but also like ἐάν with pres. and fut. indic., usually with variations in the reading, Mk. xi 25, xiii 7, Lk. xi 2, xiii 28, John vii 27 : followed by subjunctive, where frequency in the future is referred to, the subjunctive present being strictly equivalent to the Latin pres. subjunctive or fut. indicative (conative, continuous, or iterative), while the subjunctive aorist (punctiliar) corresponds to the fut. perf. indic. In Mk. xi 19 perhaps *when*.

ὅτε, *when, at which time*, used especially with all tenses of the indicative : only once with subjunctive, *the time when*, Lk. xiii 35 (v. l.).

ὅτι (a development of ὅ,τι, neuter of ὅστις, which see), most often, either *because, for*, or, after a verb or other word of saying (perhaps under influence of Aramaic in Mk.) or thinking, *that*, introducing a noun clause; an ellipsis of δῆλον in 1 Tim. vi 7, 1 John iii 20; so ὡς ὅτι pleonastically, 2 Cor. v 19, xi 21, 2 Thess. ii 2, where the expressions are equivalent to ὡς with the participle: ὅτι sometimes also introduces a piece of direct speech, e. g. John x 36, and so perhaps in Mk. ii 16, ix 11, 28, John viii 25 (see under ὅστις): ὅτι with infin., Ac. xxvii 10, is due to forgetfulness. A Hebraistic weakening of the force of causal ὅτι is seen in Mt. viii 27, Mk. i 27 (v. l.), iv 41, Lk. iv 36, viii 25, John ii 18 (xiv 22), Heb. ii 6, &c.: τί ὅ,τι (ὅτι), see ὅστις: οὐχ ὅτι = οὐ λέγω ὅτι, *not that*, John vi 46, vii 22, 2 Cor. i 24, Phil. iv 11, &c., with which compare οὐχ οἷον ὅτι, *it is not so that, it is by no means the case that*, Rom. ix 6. In Mk. viii 24 ὅτι is a mistranslation of an Aramaic word which should have been rendered οὕς.

οὗ, relative adverb, *where*; also *whither*.

οὔ, interjection, *no!* an accented form of οὐ.

οὐ, so before consonants: regularly οὐκ before smooth breathings and οὐχ before rough breathings, *not*, the proper negative for a denial of a fact, used generally with the indicative, as μή is with other moods, but sometimes with the participle, it being closely related to the indic. and coming also under the rule that οὐ negatives a single word rather than a clause: οὐ with future indic. in a question is equivalent to an imperative: for οὐχ ὅτι see ὅτι: οὐ ... πᾶς is Hebraistic = οὐδείς, Lk. i 37, &c.: for οὐ μή see under μή.

οὐά (uah), an interjection expressing real or ironical wonder.

οὐαί (uae), adv., *woe*, c. dat. or acc., sometimes in Rev. made a noun ἡ οὐαί (= ? ἡ κραυγὴ οὐαί); expresses rather a statement than a wish or imprecation, *distress comes (will come) upon*.

οὐδαμῶς, *in no way, in no respect, not at all*.

οὐδέ, *nor . . . either, nor . . . at all* ; *not even.*

οὐδείς (οὐθείς), adj. and noun, *no* ; *no one* (masc. fem.), *nothing* (neut.).

οὐδέποτε, *not at any time, never.*

οὐδέπω, *not yet either, not yet, not as yet, never before.*

οὐθείς, later form of οὐδείς, occurring first in 378 B.C. and with more or less frequency until its disappearance before A.D. 200.

οὐκέτι, *no longer, no more.*

οὐκοῦν, (in a question) *not really ?*

οὖν, adv. or conjunction, properly in causal connexion, *therefore,* but also freely of a mere temporal connexion, continuing a narrative, *then,* for example, in the combined expression μὲν οὖν (see under μέν); it sometimes indicates the return to the narrative after some digression, John iv 45, vi 24, 1 Cor. viii 4, xi 20 : ἄρα οὖν is a strengthened οὖν.

οὔπω, *not yet.*

οὐρά, *a tail.*

οὐράνιος, *in heaven, belonging to heaven, heavenly, from heaven.*

οὐρανόθεν, *from heaven, from the sky.*

οὐρανός (caelum), *the sky, the heaven* : as later Jewish cosmology conceived of a series of heavens one above the other (sometimes three, sometimes seven), the plur. (caeli) is sometimes used, where we should use the singular, and numbers are even attached to individual strata (e. g. 2 Cor. xii 2). Heaven was conceived as the special realm and abode of the Deity, hence the word is constantly used in connexion with Him, and almost as equivalent to the divine name ; cf. the practical equivalence of ἡ βασιλεία τῶν οὐρανῶν, the kingdom (rule) *from heaven,* of *divine* origin, a phrase which may be in origin purely eschatological (so Mt.) with ἡ βασιλεία τοῦ θεοῦ, God Himself being the ruler, Mt. xii 28, xix 24 (v. l.), xxi 31, 43, Mk., Lk., Paul.

Οὐρβανός, *Urbanus,* a Christian in Rome, fellow-worker of St. Paul.

Οὐρίας (Hebr.), *Uriah*, husband of Bathsheba, the mother of Solomon.

οὖς, *an ear*.

οὐσία, *property*.

οὔτε : οὔτε ... οὔτε, *neither ... nor*; οὐ ...οὔτε ... οὔτε, *not ... neither ... nor*; sometimes the other clause is positive, e. g. John iv 11, 3 John 10.

οὗτος—αὕτη—τοῦτο, demonstrative adj. and pron., *this*; *he, her, it* : αὕτη (Hebraistic) = τοῦτο, Mt. xxi 42 : τοῦτ᾽ ἔστιν (id est, Fr. ça veut dire, Germ. das heisst), *which means, meaning, actually, in reality* (cf. 1 Pet. iii 20): ἐκ τούτου, *for this reason*, John vi 66 (possibly, *from that time onwards*), xix 12, *by this mark, by this means*, 1 John iv 6 ; ἐν τούτῳ, *for this reason*, John xvi 30, Ac. xxiv 16, *by this mark, by this means*, 1 John iii 19 ; ἐπὶ τούτῳ, *meantime*, John iv 27 ; τούτου χάριν, *on this account*; κατὰ ταῦτα, *in the same way*, Lk. vi 23 v. l., xvii 30 v. l. : καὶ τοῦτο (idque), *and that too*; *especially*; καὶ ταῦτα, *and indeed*. A special sense = *as it is called*, Heb. ix 11.

οὕτως (sic), *in this way (manner), thus, so, under these circumstances*; used sometimes with εἶναι, γίνεσθαι, where a part of τοιοῦτος would be expected (cf. ἔχω), Mt. i 18, xix 10, &c.

οὐχί, a more emphatic form of οὐ (οὐκ, οὐχ), *not*; *no, not so*; also = nonne, in a question, expecting a positive answer.

ὀφειλέτης, (a) *a debtor, one who owes, one who is indebted*; (b) *one who has sinned against* another (an Aramaism, see ὀφείλημα), *a sinner*, Lk. xiii 4.

ὀφειλή, *a debt, what is owing (due)*: the mutual obligation of married life, 1 Cor. vii 3.

ὀφείλημα, (a) *a debt*; (b) in Aramaic the same word indicates a debt and a sin ; hence *a sin* (probably as that for which we owe reparation to God or to another person).

ὀφείλω (debeo), *I owe*: c. infin. *I ought*.

ὄφελον (in origin an aorist of ὀφείλω, with augment dropped), *I would that.*

ὄφελος, *advantage, gain.*

ὀφθαλμοδουλεία, *enslavement to the eye,* the subjection that waits upon a glance of a master's eye.

ὀφθαλμός, (a) *an eye*: (b) ὀφθαλμὸς πονηρός (a Semitic idiom), *envy, ill will,* Mt. xx 15, Mk. vii 22 ; (c) met. ' the mind's *eye* ' (Shakespeare), Eph. i 18.

ὄφις, *a serpent.*

ὀφρύς, (properly *the brow*; hence) *the brow, a ridge* (of a mountain).

ὀχετός, *a water-pipe,* Mk. vii 19 (v.l.).

ὀχλέω, *I trouble, torment, worry.*

ὀχλοποιέω, *I gather a crowd.*

ὄχλος (turba, plebs), *a crowd* of men, *a mob, a multitude*: the plur. much affected by Matthew (Semitism ?) does not differ in meaning from the singular (cf. iv 25).

ὀχύρωμα, *a bulwark, a bastion*: hence, met.

ὀψάριον, (conversational diminutive of ὄψον, *seasoning* [especially *fish*] taken as a relish with bread : hence) *a relish*; then especially, *a fish.*

ὀψέ, *late* : sometimes c. gen. either *late on* or *after.*

ὀψία, of a period never earlier than sunset; *early evening.*

ὄψιμος, *late* in the year (opposite to πρόϊμος).

ὄψιος, *late,* Mk. xi 11 (v.l.).

ὄψις, (a) *the face*; (b) *the features, the outward appearance,* John vii 24.

ὀψώνιον, especially plur. ὀψώνια, (*rations* : then) soldier's *pay,* Lk. iii 14, cf. 1 Cor. ix 7 : *pay, wages, salary, reward* in general, Rom. vi 23, 2 Cor. xi 8 ; *charges,* 1 Cor. ix 7.

Π

παγιδεύω, *I ensnare, I entrap.*

παγίς, *a snare* (especially for catching birds : perhaps a net thrown over one): hence, met., of moral snares.

πάγος

πάγος : see Ἄρειος.

πάθημα, properly colourless, *an experience* : but most commonly, *an evil experience, evil treatment, suffering*, e. g. τὰ εἰς Χριστὸν παθήματα, *the sufferings destined for Messiah*, 1 Pet. i 11.

παθητός (passibilis), *capable of suffering*.

πάθος, (properly *experience, feeling* ; hence) *passion, lustfulness, lust* (as a state or condition).

παιδαγωγός (pedagogus), *a boy-leader*, a slave or freed- man who attends and guards a boy to and from (sometimes also in) school, and looks after his moral character especially, *a tutor*.

παιδάριον (formerly a diminutive), either *a boy* or *a slave*.

παιδεία, *discipline*.

παιδευτής, *one who disciplines*, *a trainer* ; almost *a chas- tiser*, Heb. xii 9.

παιδεύω, (a) *I discipline, educate, train* ; (b) more severely, *I chastise*.

παιδία, a less correct spelling of παιδεία.

παιδιόθεν, *from childhood, from early boyhood*.

παιδίον, (a) *a little boy, a child* (from birth onwards); hence affectionately, of those grown up ; (b) (com- pare the use of *boy* in parts of Africa) *a slave*, Lk. xi 7 (according to an interpretation in Augustine).

παιδίσκη, *a female slave, a maidservant, a maid*.

παίζω, *I play, I sport* (includes singing and dancing).

παῖς, (a) *a male child, a boy* ; (b) (cf. παιδίον) *a male slave, a servant* ; thus *a servant of* God, especially as a title of the Messiah (from Isa. xli–liii) Ac. iv 27, 30 ; (c) *a female child, a girl*, Lk. viii 51, 54.

παίω, *I strike*.

πάλαι, *long ago*, almost weakened to *already* in Mk. xv 44.

παλαιός, *old* ; ὁ παλαιὸς ἄνθρωπος (perhaps Hebraism), one's *former character* (*personality*). The word and its derivatives bear a derogatory sense.

παλαιότης, *oldness*.

παλαιόω, *I make old, I antiquate* ; *I wear out* ; *I treat as past*, Heb. viii 13 ; pass. *I fall to the past*, Heb. viii 13.

πάλη, *wrestling, a wrestling bout* ; hence *a struggle, a conflict.*

πάλιν (iterum, rursus), *again*, properly of a return over the same course in the reverse direction (rursus), but also used of a repetition of the same journey in the same direction (iterum) ; it may also be used of any number of times ; in Mk. xv 13 perhaps an unsuitable mistranslation of an Aramaic word of much wider signification, *further, thereupon* ; εἰς τὸ πάλιν = πάλιν, 2 Cor. xiii 2.

παλινγενεσία, (a) an eschatological term (used by Pythagoreans and Stoics, found in Josephus of the rebirth of the fatherland after the exile, and in Philo of the re-birth of the earth after the flood), in Mt. xix 28 for the current conception of the Messianic renewal of the world or of the people Israel, *rebirth* ; (b) *rebirth* of the individual life following on or typified in baptism, Tit. iii 5.

Παμφυλία, *Pamphylia*, a Roman province on the south coast of Asia Minor.

πανδοχεῖον, *an inn, khan, hotel.*

πανδοχεύς, *an innkeeper, landlord, hotel-manager.*

πανήγυρις, *a festival assembly.*

πανοικεί, *with all (his) household.*

πανοπλία, *armour.*

πανουργία, (a) *cleverness*, usually with the idea that it is evil ; (b) *cunning, craftiness*, Lk. xx 23.

πανοῦργος, *crafty* (playfully used).

πανπληθεί, adv. lit. *with the whole crowd*, almost equivalent to a subject of the sentence.

πανταχῆ, *everywhere.*

πανταχοῦ, *everywhere.*

παντελής ; εἰς τὸ παντελές (omnino), *utterly, at all*, Lk. xiii 11 ; in Heb. vii 25 either *entirely*, or, more probably, *for ever, finally.*

πάντῃ, *in every way.*

πάντοθεν (undique), *from all sides, from all quarters*; *on all sides.*

παντοκράτωρ, *ruler of all, ruler of the universe*; the LXX introduced κύριος (θεὸς) παντοκράτωρ as a translation of *Lord of Hosts.*

πάντοτε, *at all times, always.*

πάντως, *entirely*; *in any case*; (after a negative) *at all*; *assuredly, to be sure.*

παρά, (a) c. acc. *by, beside, near*, without difference between 'where?' (properly παρὰ τίνι) and 'whither?': not with persons: (*not in accordance with*, opp. κατά) *against, contrary to*, Rom. i 26, xi 24, 2 Cor. viii 3 (*over*); *differently from*, Gal. i 8 (cf. 1 Cor. iii 11); *more than*, sometimes with comparative, Lk. xiii 2, 4, Rom. i 25, xii 3, xiv 5; *less*, 2 Cor. xi 24; οὐ παρὰ τοῦτο κτλ., *this is no reason that &c.*, 1 Cor. xii 15; (b) c. gen. *from the side of, from*, only with persons; οἱ παρ᾽ αὐτοῦ, *his family, his relations*, Mk. iii 21 (in papyri generally = *his agents, his representatives*), τὰ παρ᾽ ἑαυτῆς, *her money, her wealth*, Mk. v 26, cf. Lk. x 7, Phil. iv 18; (c) c. dat. *by, beside*, answering the question 'where?', with the exception of John xix 25 only of persons, not of immediate proximity, but *in the house of* any one (apud, Fr. *chez*), Lk. xix 7, John i 39, Ac. x 6, *among* a people, Rev. ii 13; *in the eyes of*, e.g. παρὰ τῷ θεῷ, *in the judgement of*, Rom. xii 16, &c.

παραβαίνω, (a) *I fall away, take a false* step, Ac. i 25; (b) *I overstep, transgress.*

παραβάλλω, *I cross over, I strike across.*

παράβασις, *transgression; a transgression.*

παραβάτης (lit. an overstepper), *a transgressor, a lawbreaker.*

παραβιάζομαι, *I urge, press.*

παραβολεύομαι, *I expose myself* (to danger).

παραβολή, *a similitude, allegory, parable, emblematic allusion*: in Heb. xi 19 ἐν = *as.*

παραιτέομαι

παραγγελία, *a command, an injunction*; *a precept, rule of living,* 1 Thess. iv 2.

παραγγέλλω, *I command, I charge*; παραγγελίᾳ παραγγέλλειν (Hebraism), *to charge strictly,* Ac. v 28.

παραγίνομαι, (a) *I come on the scene, I appear, I come*; (b) with words expressing destination, *I present myself at, I arrive at, I reach.*

παράγω, (a) *I pass by,* Mt. xx 30, Mk. xv 21, &c.; (b) *I vanish, disappear,* 1 Cor. vii 31, in which sense the passive is used, 1 John ii 8, 17 (the verb being originally transitive); (c) *I depart,* Mt. ix 9, 27 (the text is doubtful in both passages, and therefore this meaning is questionable); (d) almost, *I walk,* Mk. i 16, ii 14, xv 21 (?)

παραδειγματίζω, *I put to open shame.*

παράδεισος, a quarter of heaven conceived by the later Jews to be in or just above the 'third heaven', *paradise* (lit. *an enclosed orchard* or *garden with fruit trees*).

παραδέχομαι, *I receive (welcome) favourably.*

παραδίδωμι, *I hand over, I pledge*; *I hand down, deliver*; *I betray.*

παράδοξος, *unexpected*; hence *wonderful.*

παράδοσις, originally abstract, *handing over,* generally concrete, *that which is handed down, a tradition* (whether of written or of oral teaching).

παραζηλόω, *I make jealous, I provoke to jealousy.*

παραθαλάσσιος, *by the sea (lake), on the coast.*

παραθεωρέω, *I look past, overlook, neglect.*

παραθήκη (depositum), *a deposit* (properly of money or valuables deposited with a friend for safe-keeping, while the owner is abroad).

παραινέω, *I admonish, advise.*

παραιτέομαι, (a) *I beg* from another, Mk. xv 6 (v.l.), Heb. xii 19 (cf. (b)); (b) (deprecor), *I beg off from, I seek to turn away* (from myself) *by entreaty*; hence, *I give an excuse, I excuse myself, I beg to be excused,* Lk. xiv 18, 19, Heb. xii 25; *I decline, refuse, object to,* Ac. xxv 11, 1 Tim. iv 7, v 11, 2 Tim. ii 23, Tit. iii 10.

189

παρακαθέζομαι, *I sit beside.*

παρακαλέω, (a) *I ask, beseech*; (b) *I exhort*; (c) *I comfort.*

παρακαλύπτω, *I conceal, veil.*

παράκειμαι, *I rest with.*

παράκλησις, *an appeal*, which according to circumstances may be either hortatory, *exhortation*, or consolatory, *consolation*: in Lk. ii 25 it seems to have a quasi-technical sense, with reference to the coming of the Messiah.

παράκλητος (aduocatus), (originally passive in sense, *one called in* for support, *one summoned* as support, but this idea drops into the background: in the technical legal sense it never occurs, but in writings prior to the N.T. has the general sense, *one who speaks in favour of another, an intercessor, helper*: it tends thus to have an active sense, and was borrowed by Hebrew and Aramaic) *helper*; *consoler* (corresponding to the name Menahem given to the Messiah).

παρακοή, *disobedience.*

παρακολουθέω, *I accompany, follow closely*, both lit. and met., *I investigate*; *I result* [Mk.] xvi 17 (v. l).

παρακούω, (a) *I hear carelessly* or *incidentally*, or *I pretend not to hear*, Mk. v 36; (b) *I refuse to hear*; *I disobey.*

παρακύπτω, *I stretch forward the head to catch a glimpse* (especially through a window or door, sometimes inwards, oftener outwards: fig. it implies a rapid, hasty, and cursory glance), *I look, peep, peer in* (*at*); *I look down.*

παραλαμβάνω, *I take* from, *I receive* from, or, *I take* to, *I receive* (apparently not used of money, see ἀπέχω); *I take with* me.

παραλέγομαι (lego), *I coast along, sail along.*

παράλιος, *on the sea-coast, on the sea-board*: ἡ παράλιος (sc. χώρα), *the coast country.*

παραλλαγή, *a variation*; hence, *a periodic change* of a heavenly body.

παραλογίζομαι, *I deceive, beguile.*

παραλυτικός, *a paralytic*, a more colloquial word than παραλελυμένος, the medical term (cf. Lk. v 24).

παραλύω : in the passive, παραλελυμένος, *one who has become loosened* (*unstrung*), *one whose power of movement has gone, paralysed, a paralytic.*

παραμένω, *I remain beside, I stand by*; hence equivalent to, *I serve* (as a free man), cf. perhaps Phil. i 25, James i 25; *I remain in* office, Heb. vii 23; *I persevere* in the law, James i 25.

παραμυθέομαι, *I encourage, comfort, console.*

παραμυθία, *encouragement, comfort, consolation.*

παραμύθιον, *consolation.*

παρανομέω, *I contravene a statute* (*law*).

παρανομία, *a breach of a statute* (*law*).

παραπικραίνω, absol. *I embitter, provoke, irritate.*

παραπικρασμός, *embitterment, provocation, irritation.*

παραπίπτω, *I fall back* (into the unbelieving and godless ways of the old time).

παραπλέω, *I sail past* (without stopping there).

παραπλήσιον, *in a manner like.*

παραπλησίως, *correspondingly, in like manner.*

παραπορεύομαι, *I go past*, Mk. xi 20, xv 29 (= Mt. xxvii 39): *I go*, apparently a colloquial or incorrect use, Mk. ii 23 (v.l.), ix 30 (v. l.).

παράπτωμα (delictum), *a falling away, a lapse, a slip, a false step, a trespass.*

παραρέω, (lit. *I flow past, I glide past*, hence) *I am lost, I perish*, or merely, *I drift away* (*I fall away*) *from duty* (or *the way of salvation*).

παράσημος, *a figure-head.*

παρασκευάζω, *I prepare*; mid. *I prepare, make preparations*, 1 Cor. xiv 8.

παρασκευή, *the day of preparation, the day before the sabbath, Friday.*

παρατείνω, *I prolong.*

παρατηρέω, act. and mid. (a) *I watch carefully, keep my eye on* (as a cat does a mouse); absol. *I watch*

παρατήρησις

my *opportunity*, Lk. xx 20; (b) *I observe, keep*, Gal.
iv 10.

παρατήρησις, *a watching* for.

παρατίθημι, (a) (adpono) *I set* (especially a meal) *before,
I serve*; (b) (depono) act. and mid., *I deposit* with,
I entrust to.

παρατυγχάνω, *I come by chance, I am by chance* in a certain
place.

παραυτίκα, adv. with force of adj., *present, immediate.*

παραφέρω, *I turn aside, I cause (suffer) to pass by*, Mk.
xiv 36, Lk. xxii 42; *I carry away, remove*, lit. or
met.

παραφρονέω, *I am out of my senses.*

παραφρονία, *madness.*

παραχειμάζω, (hiberno), *I spend the winter, I winter.*

παραχειμασία, *spending the winter, wintering.*

παραχρῆμα, *immediately.*

πάρδαλις, *a leopard.*

παρεδρεύω, (adsideo), *I have my seat beside, I attend.*

πάρειμι, *I am present*; *I have come, arrived* (hence with
εἰς, πρός).

παρεισάγω, *I introduce from the side.*

παρείσακτος, *introduced (imported) from the side.*

παρεισδύω, *I creep in.*

παρεισέρχομαι, *I come in from the side.*

παρεισφέρω, *I bring in (import) from the side, I
smuggle.*

παρεκτός, (a) adv. used as adj., *outside, without, left
over*; (b) prep., *apart from.*

παρεμβάλλω, *I throw (raise) up beside.*

παρεμβολή, (castra), *a camp*, either a fixed camp
(statiua castra), occupied possibly for centuries,
a fort, castle, like that at Jerusalem, or a marching-
camp, according to context; hence, *the army*
occupying such, Heb. xi 34.

παρενοχλέω, *I trouble*, or perhaps, *I trouble further.*

παρεπίδημος, *a stranger* settled in a town or region for
a time without making it his permanent residence,

192

a sojourner : so in a spiritual sense of those who are on the earth for a time, whose real home is heaven.

παρέρχομαι, tr. and intr. *I pass by, I pass* : sometimes practically, *I pass out of sight, I disappear* : c. acc. (cf. *παραβαίνω*) *I transgress* : intr. *I approach, come up to,* Lk. xii 37, xvii 7. [Ac.] xxiv 7.

πάρεσις (from *παρίημι*), *overlooking, suspension, remission* of punishment for.

παρέχω, act. and mid. *I offer, provide, confer, afford, give, bring, show, cause* : κόπους (κόπον) τινὶ παρέχειν, *to cause one trouble.*

παρηγορία, *a consolation.*

παρθενία, *maidenhood, virginity.*

παρθένος, *a maiden, a virgin*; hence (Rev. xiv 4), extended to men who have not known women : in 1 Cor. vii 25–38, the word must have its usual sense, and refer to women living in merely spiritual wedlock with men. In Mt. i 23 παρθένος is an inaccurate translation (due to LXX) of a Heb. word in Isa. vii 14 meaning *a female adolescent, a young woman of marriageable age,* whether married or not, rightly translated by Theodotion and Aquila νεᾶνις.

Πάρθος, *a Parthian,* an inhabitant of the country beyond the Eastern boundary of the Roman Empire between the Caspian Sea and the Persian Gulf.

παρίημι, (a) *I let pass, neglect, omit,* Lk. xi 42; (b) *I slacken, weary,* Heb. xii 12.

παριστάνω, παρίστημι, (a) in the transitive tenses, *I cause to come to and stand beside* ; *I bring* ; *I present, offer, commend* ; *I introduce* (one person to another) ; *I prove by argument,* Ac. xxiv 13 ; (b) in the intransitive tenses, *I come up to and stand by,* sometimes with the idea of thus providing support (cf. 2 Tim. iv 17).

Παρμενᾶς (a pet form of Παρμενίδης), *Parmenas,* one of the original seven 'deacons' at Jerusalem.

πάροδος, *way-by, passage.*

παροικέω, *I sojourn* (*in*), as a resident stranger.

παροικία, *a sojourn* in a foreign city or land; so also in the spiritual sense (cf. παρεπίδημος), 1 Pet. i 17.

πάροικος (adj. and noun) (= μέτοικος), *a stranger, sojourner*, in a land not his own, *a non-citizen*, with limited rights: so, metaphorically, of the Christian resident on the earth, whose real home is in heaven, Eph. ii 19, 1 Pet. ii 11.

παροιμία (from παρά and οἶμος, *beside the common way*), *a veiled speech* in which particularly high thoughts are concealed, *a cryptic saying, an allegory*; *a proverb* (2 Pet. ii 22).

πάροινος, *one given too much to wine, an excessive drinker*.

παροίχομαι, *I have passed*.

παρομοιάζω, *I resemble*.

παρόμοιος, *like, similar*.

παροξύνω, *I arouse to anger, I provoke*.

παροξυσμός, (a) *irritation of mind, sharp feeling, indignation*; (b) *spurring, incitement*, Heb. x 24.

παροργίζω, *I provoke to anger*.

παροργισμός (generally act. *provocation*), *the state of feeling provocation, wrath*.

παροτρύνω, *I urge on*.

παρουσία (in ordinary Greek = *presence; arrival*; also, technical term with reference to *the visit* of a king or some other official, *a royal visit*), (a) *presence*, as opposed to 'absence', 1 Cor. xvi 17, 2 Cor. vii 6, 7 (cf. x 10), Phil. i 26, ii 12; (b) a technical eschatological term, representing a word used by Jesus Himself, *the presence, coming, arrival, advent* of the glorified Messiah, to be followed by a permanent residence with His people (so, in 2 Thess. ii 9, of that of the Lawless One).

παροψίς, *a bowl, dish*.

παρρησία, *boldness, freedom, liberty*, shown especially *in speech*; ἐν παρρησίᾳ, μετὰ παρρησίας, *quite openly* (opposite to 'secretly').

παρρησιάζομαι, *I speak boldly, I am bold of speech*.

πᾶς, adj. in the sing. without the article, *every, every kind of*; in the sing. with the article preceding or following, *the whole, all the*; in the plur. without the article, *all*; in the plur. with the article following, *all the*: pronoun masc. *every one*, neut. *everything*; πάντες, *all, everybody*, πάντα, *all things*; οὐ πᾶς, &c., *not all*, i. e. *only some*, e. g. Mt. xix 11, John xiii 10, Rom. x 16, but also (like πᾶς κτλ. . . . . οὐ) Hebraistically, especially when words intervene between οὐ and πᾶς, &c. (translation Greek), = *none, no*, Mt. xxiv 22, Mk. xiii 20, Lk. i 37, Ac. xx 25, Rom. iii 20, Gal. ii 16, 2 Pet. i 20, 1 John ii 21, Rev. vii 16, xxi 27, xxii 3: πάντες οὐ = οὐ πάντες, 1 Cor. xv 51: διὰ παντός ('semper', 'omne tempus', 'per omnia', Ambr. *expos. ps. cxviii* 5 22, 6 30), *continually, continuously, always*: κατὰ πάντα, *in everything, in every respect*, Ac. iii 22, xvii 22, &c.

πάσχα (Hebrew, Aramaic), *the feast of passover, the paschal meal*, which took place on the night of full moon after the spring equinox, that is the night between 14th and 15th Nisan. On the afternoon of 14th Nisan before sunset the *paschal lamb*, also called τὸ πάσχα (so met., 1 Cor. v 7), was sacrificed.

πάσχω, *I am acted upon* in a certain way, *I experience* certain treatment, e. g. Mt. xvii 15 (v.l.): hence (by a development from the original use), *I experience ill treatment*, &c., *I suffer*, e. g. Mt. xvii 12.

Πάταρα, *Patara*, a town on the coast of the Roman province Lycia.

πατάσσω, *I strike* (as, with a sword).

πατέω, tr. and intr. *I tread*; *I trample upon*.

πατήρ, (a) *father* in the strict sense, e. g. Mt. ii 22; (b) any male *ancestor*, e. g. Mt. iii 9; (c) *The Father*, used of God as the creator of all beings (cf. Eph. iii 14, 15), the fountain and origin of all life, and, among other beings, of our Lord Jesus Christ, who is in a special sense ὁ υἱός, *the Son*, of the Father (cf. especially John). He is sometimes spoken of as the Heavenly Father, the Father in the

Heavens (e.g. Mt. v 16), as distinguished from earthly fathers. Other epithets, such as τῆς δόξης, τῶν οἰκτιρμῶν, τῶν φώτων, are attached to the Name, some of them under the influence of Hebrew, expressing not only that He is the author of these signs or qualities, but that they bear a likeness to Him; thus πατὴρ τῆς δόξης = *glorious Father*.

Πάτμος, *Patmos*, a small rocky island in the Aegean sea, SW. of Ephesus.

πατριά, a group of persons united by descent from a common father or ancestor, *a family, a tribe.*

πατριάρχης, *a ruler of a family* (or *tribe*), given as an honorary title to David (Ac. ii 29) as ancestor of the race of Jewish kings.

πατρικός, *belonging to the fathers* (*ancestors*).

πατρίς (patria), *native city, native town, native place.*

Πατρόβας, *Patrobas*, a Christian in Rome.

πατρολῴας, *a parricide, a murderer of his father.*

πατροπαράδοτος, *handed down by* (*from*) *one's ancestors, inherited.*

πατρῷος, *belonging to ancestors, ancestral.*

Παῦλος, *Paulus, Paul*, (a) the third part (cognomen) of the full Roman name of the Apostle, the other two parts of which (Gaius Iulius?) are now unknown; (b) the third part (cognomen) of the full name of the proconsul of Cyprus, the first part of which seems to be unknown, Ac. xiii 7.

παύω, (a) act. *I cause to cease*, 1 Pet. iii 10; (b) mid. *I cease.*

Πάφος, *Paphos*, a city at the western end of Cyprus.

παχύνω, *I thicken*: used with καρδία, of obtuseness of mind, *it has become obtuse.*

πέδη, *a fetter.*

πεδινός, *level, low-lying.*

πεζεύω, *I go by land.*

πεζῇ, *on foot* or *by land.*

πεζός, *on foot* or *by land.*

πειθαρχέω, *I obey* one in authority.

πειθός, *persuasive*.

πείθω, (a) (suadeo) *I urge, I apply persuasion, I seek to persuade, I exercise suasion*; (b) 2 perf. and pluperf., *I trust, ἐπί, in*; (c) mid. or pass. (I admit suasion to myself), *I am persuaded*; hence, *I believe*: hence also, c. dat., *I obey*.

Πειλᾶτος, *Pilatus, Pilate*, the third name (cognomen) of the procurator of Judaea, whose first name (prae-nomen) is unknown.

πεινάω, *I hunger*, either lit. or met.: c. acc. *I hunger for*.

πεῖρα, *an attempt, a trial*; πεῖραν λαμβάνειν, *to have experience of*.

πειράζω, (a) *I make trial of, try, test, explore*; God *tests* man by means of suffering or in some other way, man *tests* God by seeking how far it is possible to go on disobeying Him, without provoking his anger; (b) a secondary neutral or evil sense, *I tempt*, Mt. iv 1, Mk. i 13, Lk. iv 2, 1 Cor. vii 5, James i 13 (second occurrence), 14: if trial fails, the result is moral evil: the agency of Satan is interposed, the same process being carried on for God's good purpose and *his* evil purpose; thus ὁ πειράζων comes to indicate the intermediary, *the Tempter*, Mt. iv 3, 1 Thess. iii 5; (c) c. inf. *I try, attempt*.

πειράομαι, *I try, attempt*.

πειρασμός (from πειράζω, which see), (a) *trial, proba-tion, testing, being tried*; (b) *temptation*, Mk. xiv 38 and parallels, Mt. vi 13, Lk. iv 13; (c) in Gal. iv 14 the reading τὸν πειρασμόν (without ὑμῶν or other addition) has been taken, on the analogy of modern popular Greek usage, = *the devil, the demonic power* as the cause of the Apostle's infirmity.

πεισμονή, *persuasion*, both *the act of persuasion* and *the being persuaded*.

πέλαγος, *the open sea*: in Mt. xviii 6 the use of the two words for sea produces a more impressive effect.

πελεκίζω, *I behead with an axe*.

πέμπτος, *fifth*.

πέμπω, *I send*.

πένης, *poor*.

πενθερά, *a mother-in-law*.

πενθερός, *a father-in-law*.

πενθέω, *I mourn*.

πένθος, *mourning, sorrow*.

πενιχρός, *poor*.

πεντάκις, *five times*.

πεντακισχίλιοι, *five thousand*.

πεντακόσιοι, *five hundred*.

πέντε, *five*.

πεντεκαιδέκατος, *fifteenth*.

πεντήκοντα, *fifty*.

πεντηκοστή (originally sc. ἡμέρα; lit. *the fiftieth day* from 14th Nisan, the date of the Passover Feast), *Pentecost*, a Feast of the Jews, *Whitsuntide*.

πεποίθησις, *confidence, trust*.

περαιτέρω (compar. of πέρα, *beyond*), *further, beyond that*.

πέραν (ultra), *beyond, on the other side of, across*; sometimes elliptically used, πέραν = (ἀπὸ) τῆς πέραν, Mk. iii 8 (Mt. iv 25), πέραν = τῆς πέραν, Mk. x 1: τὸ πέραν, as substantive, *the other side, the country beyond*.

πέρας, (a) *a boundary, limit*; (b) *an end*, Heb. vi 16.

Πέργαμον (possibly the other form Πέργαμος, *Pergamus*, was intended), *Pergamum*, an important city of the Roman province Asia.

Πέργη, *Perga*, a city on the river Cestrus in the Roman province Pamphylia.

περί, (a) c. gen., oftenest, *concerning, about* (in such phrases as 'to speak, know, care, &c., about'); at the beginning of a clause, *with regard to*, e.g. 1 Cor. vii 1: *on account of* (with κρίνεσθαι, ἐνκαλεῖν, ἐρωτᾶν, &c.), whence it often passes into the meaning *for* and becomes identical with ὑπέρ, e.g. Mt. xxvi 28, 1 Cor. i 13 (ὑπέρ is nearly always a textual variant in such cases); so with verbs of feeling (= ἐπί c. acc. or dat.), *over*: περὶ αὐτοῦ, *with him*, Lk. ii 27, seems incorrect (= περὶ αὐτόν, αὐτῷ, ἐν αὐτῷ); (b) c. acc., local and temporal, *about*, οἱ περὶ αὐτόν Mk. iv 10, Lk. xxii 49, *his disciples*, but οἱ περὶ Παῦλον, Ac. xiii 13, *Paul and his company* (according to the classical idiom): used to indicate the circumstances of the action or of the effort, e. g. with ἐπιθυμίαι, Mk. iv 19: Paul in his later epistles uses it = *concerning,touching*, e. g. Phil. ii 23.

περιάγω, (a) tr. (1) *I carry about*, (2) *I go about*; (b) intr. *I go about*.

περιαιρέω, (a) *I strip off, I strip from, I take away*; (b) *I cast off, cut adrift*, Ac. xxvii 40 ; in Ac. xxviii 13, if the text be right, the word must be rendered in the same way, *I cast off, I cast loose*.

περιάπτω, *I light, ignite.*

περιαστράπτω, *I flash (gleam) around* like lightning.

περιβάλλω, *I cast around*, Lk. xix 43 (v. l.); *I wrap* a garment *about, I put on*: hence mid. *I put on* to myself, *I clothe myself, I dress.*

περιβλέπομαι, *I look round on, survey.*

περιβόλαιον, *a wrapper, mantle.*

περιδέω, *I bind (tie) around.*

περιεργάζομαι, *I am active around, I am a busy-body.*

περίεργος, (a) *inquisitive, prying, a busybody*; (b) *curious, magical*, Ac. xix 19.

περιέρχομαι, intr. and tr., *I go round, I move about* (περιερχόμενοι, *strolling*, Ac. xix 13); *I make a circuit, tack*, Ac. xxviii 13 (v. l.).

περιέχω, (a) *I contain* (of a book *containing* subject matter): hence, impersonal, *it stands (has its content) thus*, 1 Pet. ii 6; (b) *I encompass, surround; I get hold of, seize.*

περιζώννυμι, *I gird round*: mid. *I gird myself*, generally for active work or travel.

περίθεσις, *a putting around* (or *on*).

περιΐστημι

περιΐστημι: in intr. tenses, *I surround*; *I stand clear of*, 2 Tim. ii 16, Tit. iii 9.

περικάθαρμα, *a rinsing* of a dirty vessel.

περικαλύπτω, *I veil round, I cover over*; *I conceal*.

περίκειμαι, *I am placed around* something; *I have had* something *placed around* me, Ac. xxviii 20, Heb. v 2.

περικεφαλαία, *a helmet*.

περικρατής, *mastering, gaining control over*.

περικρύπτω, *I conceal, hide* (by putting something *around* it).

περικυκλόω, *I encircle, invest*.

περιλάμπω, *I shine around*.

περιλείπω, *I leave behind*.

περίλυπος, *deeply pained* (*grieved*).

περιμένω, *I await* the happening of something.

πέριξ, *round about, in the neighbourhood*.

περιοικέω, *I dwell around* (*near*).

περίοικος, *neighbouring*; *a neighbour*.

περιούσιος, *of* (*for*) *one's own* (*special, private*) *possession*.

περιοχή, *a clause, sentence, short passage*.

περιπατέω, (a) *I walk*: hence, (b) Hebraistically, in an ethical sense, *I conduct my life, I live*.

περιπείρω, *I pierce round about* (on all sides).

περιπίπτω, *I fall into, I fall in with, I meet with, I come upon accidentally, I chance upon, I light upon*.

περιποιέομαι, *I make my own, I acquire* (*get*) *for myself, I gain for myself*; in Lk. xvii 33 perhaps, *I preserve alive*.

περιποίησις, *acquiring, obtaining, possessing, possession, ownership*.

περιραίνω, *I sprinkle round about, I sprinkle over*.

περιρήγνυμι, *I rend all round, I tear off*.

περισπάω, *I distract, trouble greatly*.

περισσεία, *excrescence*; *superabundance, superfluity*.

περίσσευμα, *what is in excess*; *overflow, superabundance, superfluity*.

περισσεύω, (a) intr. *I exceed* the ordinary (the necessary), *I abound, I overflow*; *I am left over*; hence met.:

(b) tr. *I cause to abound*, Mt. xiii 12, Lk. xv 17, 2 Cor. iv 15 (?), ix 8, Eph. i 8, 1 Thess. iii 12.

περισσός, *over and above, excessive, abundant, overflowing*; *superfluous*. Practically a synonym for πλείων (cf. Mt. v 37), especially in the comparative περισσότερος: ἐκ περισσοῦ, *superabundantly, exceedingly*.

περισσοτέρως, *more exceedingly, to a greater degree*: see περισσός.

περισσῶς, *exceedingly*, so perhaps Ac. xxvi 11 ; but usually *more* (cf. περισσός), with reference to what precedes.

περιστερά, *a dove*.

περιτέμνω (circumcido), *I cut round* the foreskin, *I circumcise*.

περιτίθημι, *I place around*; *I put about* (*upon*), *I clothe with*.

περιτομή (circumcisio), *circumcision* (see περιτέμνω); οἱ ἐκ περιτομῆς, *the party of circumcision, the party advocating circumcision*, the rigorist Christian Jews: sometimes met. (as in O. T.), of that *chastening* of the heart (mind) which leads to heartier service to God, e. g. Rom. ii 29.

περιτρέπω, *I turn round, I turn, change*.

περιτρέχω, *I run round* (*around*).

περιφέρω, *I carry around* (*about*); *I swing round*, Eph. iv 14.

περιφρονέω, *I lightly esteem*; *I despise*.

περίχωρος, *neighbouring*; ἡ περίχωρος (sc. γῆ), *the neighbouring country, the neighbourhood, surroundings*.

περίψημα, *that which is scraped off round* anything, *a scraping*.

περπερεύομαι, *I show myself off*; *I am boastful* (*a braggart*).

Περσίς, *Persis*, name of a Christian lady in Rome.

πέρυσι, adverb, *the previous year, last year*.

πετεινός, *flying*: neut. πετεινόν, *a bird*.

πέτομαι, *I fly.*

πέτρα, *rock, solid rock, native rock*, rising up through
the earth, which trips up the traveller, Rom. ix 33,
1 Pet. ii 8; in Mt. xvi 18, of such faith as Peter
has just shown; in 1 Cor. x 4, allegorically interpreted.

Πέτρος, *Petros, Peter* (a Greek name meaning 'rock',
a translation of the Aramaic name Κηφᾶς, given to
Symeon (Simon) by our Lord). .

πετρώδης, *rocky.*

πήγανον, *rue*, a plant used for flavouring, garnishing
dishes, &c.

πηγή, *a spring, a fountain*: *a well*, John iv 6.

πήγνυμι, *I fix, pitch*; *I erect.*

πηδάλιον, *a helm, rudder.*

πηλίκος, *how large, how great.*

πηλός, *mud*; *clay.*

πήρα, *a bag* (to hold food, &c.), *a wallet, a travelling
bag*, perhaps especially *a collecting bag* (such as
beggar-priests of pagan cults carried).

πῆχυς, *the fore-arm*; hence, *a cubit*, about a foot and
a half: used as a measurement of time in Mt. vi 27
(Lk. xii 25), to indicate any extension.

πιάζω (a Doric form; contrast πιέζω), *I take hold of,
seize, apprehend, catch, arrest, grasp.*

πιέζω, *I press down.*

πιθανολογία, *persuasive speech.*

πιθός, an inferior spelling of πειθός.

πικραίνω, *I make bitter* (*tart, sour*): mid. *I am embittered, I show quick temper.*

πικρία, *bitterness, sourness*; hence met., *an embittered
(resentful) spirit*, which refuses reconciliation, Eph.
iv 31.

πικρός, *bitter*, lit. and met.

πικρῶς, *bitterly.*

πίμπλημι, *I fill.*

πίμπρημι, *I cause to swell*: passive, *I become inflamed,
I am swollen.*

πινακίδιον, *a little* waxed *tablet*, on which to write with iron pen.

πίναξ, *a flat dish.*

πίνω, *I drink.*

πιότης, *fatness.*

πιπράσκω, *I sell.*

πίπτω, *I fall.*

Πισιδία, *Pisidia*, a country of Asia Minor, being the south-western part of the Roman province Galatia.

Πισίδιος, *Pisidian*, or rather, *near Pisidia*; see Ἀντιό-χεια.

πιστεύω, (a) *I believe*, with various constructions : c. dat., *I believe* a person, or a statement made by a person (to be true) : εἰς (ἐπί) c. acc., ἐν (ἐπί) c. dat., *I place (repose) my trust* on either God or the Messiah, *I rely* on them, *I commit my life* to them, *I believe in*, *I believe on*, *I cast myself upon* them as stable and trustworthy, with energy of faith : ἐν is sometimes = *in the sphere of*, Mk. i 15 (cf. Rom. i 9, 2 Cor. viii 18, x 14, 1 Thess. iii 2, &c.) ; (b) c. acc. and dat., *I entrust* (so in passive construction, 1 Thess. ii 4, 1 Tim. i 11).

πιστικός, probably = *genuine, pure.*

πίστις, (a) *faith, belief, trust*, generally of the leaning of the entire human personality upon God or the Messiah in absolute trust and confidence in His power, wisdom, and goodness. The older meaning, *intellectual conviction* of certain truths, is often present. (In Eph. i 15 [shorter text] εἰς = *among*) ; (b) with the article, *the faith* (in Lk. xviii 8 perhaps *the necessary faith* or *the faith that perseveres*), *the Christian faith*, Ac. vi 7, xiii 8, xvi 5, xxiv 24, Gal. i 23, iii 23, vi 10, Eph. iv 13, Jude 3, 20, &c. ; (c) as a psychological faculty, Heb. xi 1 ; (d) *integrity, faithfulness, trustworthiness, loyalty*, Mt. xxiii 23, Rom. i 17 (?), Gal. v 22, 2 Tim. iv 7 ; (e) *a guarantee*, Ac. xvii 31.

πιστός, *faithful, trusty, trustworthy, reliable* : οἱ πιστοί, *the Christians.*

πιστόω, *I make sure, I convince, I give assurance to.*

πλανάω, (a) *I cause to wander*: hence, in the moral sense, *I cause to err*; (b) pass. *I wander*; hence *I err.*

πλάνη, *wandering from the way*, and so metaphorically, *error* (perhaps sometimes actively, *deceit*).

πλανήτης, *wandering* (probably of shooting stars).

πλάνος, adj., *misleading, deceiving*: as subst. *a deceiver.*

πλάξ, *a tablet.*

πλάσμα, *a moulded thing*; *a created thing, a creature.*

πλάσσω, *I mould* out of clay; *I create.*

πλαστός (finctus), *made up, fictitious.*

πλατεῖα (sc. ὁδός), *a public square* (as in modern Greek, Lat. platea, cf. Fr. place, Germ. Platz, Span. plaza, Ital. piazza); generally taken as *an open street, a street.*

πλάτος, *breadth.*

πλατύνω, *I broaden, I make broad*: met., of the growth of tenderness and love, 2 Cor. vi 11, 13.

πλατύς, *broad.*

πλέγμα, *plaiting, braiding, dressing* the hair.

πλεῖστος, superlative of πολύς, *very large*: plur. *very many* (*numerous*); adv. τὸ πλεῖστον, *at the most*, 1 Cor. xiv 27.

πλείων, πλέων, comparative of πολύς, *larger*; *more*; *a considerable number of*, Ac. xxi 10, &c.; οἱ πλείονες, *the majority*, 1 Cor. xv 6: ἐπὶ πλεῖον, as adv., *more, to a greater extent.*

πλέκω, *I plait.*

πλεονάζω, (a) intr. *I abound, I increase*; (b) tr. *I make to abound, I cause to increase*, 1 Thess. iii 12.

πλεονεκτέω, *I take advantage of, I overreach, I defraud* (sometimes with reference to adultery and the injury thus done to the husband).

πλεονέκτης, *a greedy, covetous, rapacious, acquisitive, self-aggrandizing person*; *a defrauder, one who tramples on the rights of others.*

πλεονεξία, *covetousness, greediness, rapacity, entire dis-*

regard of the rights of others, a word active in meaning and wide in scope.

πλευρά, *a side* of a human being.

πλέω, *I travel by sea, I sail, voyage.*

πληγή, *a blow*, especially, caused by the lash, *a stripe, a stroke.*

πλῆθος, *a multitude, a crowd, a large number*

πληθύνω, (a) tr. *I multiply, I increase*; (b) intr. *I multiply, I go on increasing*, Ac. vi 1.

πλήθω, see πίμπλημι.

πλήκτης, *a striker; a pugnacious person.*

πλημμύρα, *a flooding, flood.*

πλήν, (a) conjunction, (1) *however, nevertheless*, Mt. xxvi 39 (Lk. xxii 42), Mt. xi 22, 24, xxvi 64, &c.; (2) *but*, Lk. xii 31, xxiii 28; (3) πλὴν ὅτι, *except that, save that*, Ac. xx 23; (4) *only, in any case*, ending the discussion and calling special attention to the essential, especially in Paul, e. g. 1 Cor. xi 11, Eph. v 33; (b) preposition, *except, apart from.*

πλήρης (sometimes, from about the beginning of our era, indeclinable, and used for any case singular or plural, a usage perhaps derived from commercial life: e. g. Mk. iv 28 (?), John i 14, where πλήρης agrees with δόξαν, and there should be no parenthesis, Ac. vi 5 (v.l.)), *full.*

πληροφορέω (lit. *I carry full*), (a) *I complete, carry out fully*, 2 Tim. iv 5, 17, Lk. i 1 (?); (b) *I fully convince*, Rom. iv 21, xiv 5; perhaps *I satisfy fully*, Col. iv 12; (c) *I fully believe*, Lk. i 1 (?).

πληροφορία, *full assurance, conviction (confidence).*

πληρόω, (a) *I fill, I fill up*, e. g. Lk. ii 40, iii 5, John xii 3; (b) much oftener, *I fill up to the full, I fulfil, I give fullness (completion) to, I accomplish, carry out*, of prophecies or other statements which are absolutely and completely confirmed by reality (actual occurrence), or of duties; *I preach fully*, Rom. xv 19, cf. Col. i 25; in Eph. i 23 the Messiah *is being fulfilled (completed)* by the Church.

πλήρωμα

πλήρωμα (indicates the result of the activity denoted by
πληρόω), (a) *a fill, fullness*; *full complement*; *supply,
supplement*, Mk. ii 21, Mt. ix 16; (b) *fullness, filling,
fulfilment, completion*.

πλησίον, adv. (*near*, John iv 5), used as adj. and (especially with article ὁ) noun, *neighbouring, neighbourly*;
a neighbour.

πλησμονή, *repletion, satiety*.

πλήσσω, *I strike*.

πλοιάριον, (*a little boat*, hence) *a boat*.

πλοῖον, *a boat*; hence *a ship* (the old word ναῦς having
become almost obsolete), Ac. xx 13, &c.

πλόος, *a voyage*.

πλούσιος, *rich, wealthy*: hence, met., of other than
material wealth.

πλουσίως, *richly*; *lavishly*.

πλουτέω, *I am rich* (*wealthy*): with εἰς and acc. the
person on whom the wealth is lavished is indicated:
with ἐν, *I abound in*, 1 Tim. vi 18.

πλουτίζω, *I enrich*.

πλοῦτος (masc. and neut.), *wealth*, material or spiritual.

πλύνω, *I wash*.

πνεῦμα (from πνέω, has as its earliest meanings *breath*
and *wind*, and it is from the former that the characteristic use is derived), (a) *wind*, John iii 8, Heb. i 7;
(b) *breath*, what distinguishes a living from a dead
body, (anima) the life principle, Mt. xxvii 50, Lk. viii
55, xxiii 46, John vi 63, xix 30, Ac. vii 59, 2 Thess. ii
8, James ii 26, Rev. xi 11, xiii 15; (c) the breath was
often in early times identified with the life or soul
itself. Hebrew employed three words for the breath-
soul, *nephesh, ruach, neshāmāh*, of which the first and
second are the more important, indicating respectively the personal soul and the invading spirit.
Nephesh, originally *breath*, (a) refers predominantly
to the emotional life; (b) is a strong personal or
reflexive pronoun; or (c) is equivalent to *person*.
Ruach, originally *wind*, indicates also especially,

(a) supernatural influences acting on man from without; (b) the normal breath-soul, the principle of life (like *nephesh*) or of its energies, directly derived from the wind at the bidding of God; (c) the resultant psychical life, like *nephesh*, 'heart', the inner life in general. It is distinguished from *nephesh* by its association with Yahweh. Normal human nature was regarded as animated by the same divine *ruach* to which its highest inspiration is due. In the Greek O.T. *nephesh* is represented by ψυχή (which see) and *ruach* by πνεῦμα (a purely Hebraistic usage of the word). In the N.T. πνεῦμα (spiritus) refers nearly always to supernatural influences. Sometimes it is employed of the *higher nature* in man, e.g. Rom. i 9, and is hardly to be distinguished from the result of the influence of the divine πνεῦμα. Sometimes, e.g. Rom. viii 16, 2 Cor. vii 1, it denotes a normal element in human nature. But the Christian is essentially the product of the divine πνεῦμα, which is mediated to us by the Messiah. Parallel to the divine πνεῦμα are the unclean, evil spirits, the spirits of demons, &c., which act in a corresponding way on the spirit of man. πνεῦμα ἅγιον, *holy breath, spirit of holiness*, adopted originally from Deutero-Isaiah lxiii 10 f., Ps. li 11, practically synonymous with πνεῦμα θεοῦ, &c., gradually tends to become personalised. The first step in the process is reached by affixing the definite article and making it τὸ Πνεῦμα τὸ Ἅγιον (τὸ Ἅγιον Πνεῦμα). Each operation of *the* Holy Spirit is most commonly represented as due to *a* holy spirit.

πνευματικός, *having the characteristics of* πνεῦμα, *spiritual*, with general reference to the higher nature of man as directly in touch with and influenced by the divine, but sometimes (like πνεῦμα) associated with the demonic world, τὰ πνευματικὰ τῆς πονηρίας, *the spiritual hosts of evil*, Eph. vi 12: *supernatural*, 1 Cor. x 3.

πνευματικῶς, *spiritually, in a spiritual way; from a spiritual point of view.*

πνέω, *I blow*: τῇ πνεούσῃ (sc. αὔρᾳ, *breeze*).

πνίγω, *I choke, throttle, strangle*; hence *I drown*, Mk. v 13.

πνικτός, *strangled* (i.e. killed without letting out the blood).

πνοή, (a) *breath*, Ac. xvii 25; (b) *gust, breeze, wind*, Ac. ii 2. (Cf. Augustine, *De Natura et Origine Animae* I 14 § 19).

ποδήρης (talaris) (properly an adjective in the expression χιτὼν ποδήρης), *a tunic* or *robe reaching the feet*.

πόθεν (unde), *whence? from what place?* also indirect interrogative: hence *how?* e.g. Mk. xii 37, John i 48.

ποία, *a green herb*: Moulton and Milligan, reading double γάρ in James iv 14 and dropping the interrogation point, would thus interpret the word (*Expositor* VII 10, p. 566).

ποιέω (facio), (a) *I make, manufacture, construct*; (b) *I do, act, cause*; μετά τινος (Hebraistic idiom), *on some one's behalf*, Lk. i 72, Ac. xiv 27, &c.; with an object indicating time, *I spend*, e.g. James iv 13: ὁδὸν ποιεῖν, Mk. ii 23 (v.l.), which ought to mean *to construct* (*pave*) *a road*, is incorrectly used for ὁδὸν ποιεῖσθαι (cf. μνείαν ποιεῖσθαι, Eph. i 16), *to journey* (cf. Lk. xiii 22): with καλῶς, see under **καλῶς**.

ποίημα (concrete), *creation, workmanship, handiwork*; plur. *pieces of work*.

ποίησις, *doing.*

ποιητής, (a) *a 'maker'*, *a poet*, Ac. xvii 28 (the reference is to Epimenides' *Minos*); (b) *a doer, a carrier out.*

ποικίλος (uarius), *manycoloured, particoloured*; hence *varied, various* (plurality as well as difference seems sometimes to be suggested).

ποιμαίνω, *I shepherd, I tend, I herd*: hence *I rule.*

ποιμήν, *a shepherd*: hence met., of the feeder, protector, and *ruler* of a flock of men.

ποίμνη, *a flock*; *herd* (of goats perhaps, in 1 Cor. ix 7).

ποίμνιον, *a little flock* : hence, of men.

ποῖος (qualis), properly direct interrogative, *of what sort ?*, then often weakened to *what ?* simply : also indir. interrog. : ποίας (local genitive, sc. ὁδοῦ), *by what way*.

πολεμέω, *I war, carry on war*.

πόλεμος, *a war* ; also, *a battle*, Lk. xiv 31, &c.

πόλις (ciuitas), strictly *a free city, city-state* of the Greek (particularly the Athenian) type, comprising not only the city in the modern sense, but territory (often considerable) around it. The word is used rather of the citizens than of the locality (cf. the examples below). Its constitution commonly consisted of an ἐκκλησία (assembly of free citizens) and a βουλή (an advisory and deliberative council, in N.T. times a mere honorary corporation). Examples are :—Mt. viii 34, xii 25, Mk. i 33 : ἡ ἁγία πόλις (cf. Ἱερο- in Ἱεροσόλυμα), *the holy city*, i. e. Jerusalem, as containing the temple of Yahweh.

πολιτάρχης, *a politarch*, *a city-magistrate* (a special, characteristically Macedonian, title of the chief magistrates (5 or 6 in number) of Thessalonica and a few other cities).

πολιτεία (ciuitas), (a) *commonwealth, polity* ; *citizen body*, Eph. ii 12 ; (b) (the Roman) *citizenship, citizen-rights, franchise*, Ac. xxii 28.

πολίτευμα (properly, *that which one does as citizen*), *the constitution* ; *citizenship, franchise* ; *the state, the community, the commonwealth*. The word sometimes means *a colony* of foreigners, whose organization is a miniature copy of the πολιτεία at home, and this gives excellent sense in Phil. iii 20.

πολιτεύομαι (a characteristic Greek idea), *I live the life of a citizen* ; *I live as a member of a* (citizen) *body* ; *I fulfil corporate duties* : in Phil. i 27 some take simply of *manner of life*.

πολίτης (ciuis), *a citizen* : *a fellow-citizen*, Lk. xix 14, Heb. viii 11.

πολλάκις, *often, frequently*.

πολλαπλασίων (multiplex), *manifold, many times over*.

πολυλογία, *much-speaking, loquaciousness, volubility*.

πολυμερῶς, *in many portions* (one at one time, another at another, and so on).

πολυποίκιλος, *much varied, very varied*.

πολύς (compar. πλείων and superl. πλεῖστος, which see), a word indicating quantity and number, not size, sing. *much*, plur. *many*: οἱ πολλοί (plerique), *the majority*: πολλῷ (multo), before a comparative, *much*: πολλά, as adv., *much* (often in Mk., an exact translation of Aramaic), like the more regular πολύ : πολλοῦ (magni), *for much, at a great price*, Mt. xxvi 9 : with sing. words indicating time, *long* is the most suitable English rendering : πολλάς (sc. πληγάς), Lk. xii 47. The καί following, Ac. xxv 7, is superfluous according to our idiom.

πολύσπλαγχνος, *full of tender feeling* (a Hebraistic idiom, the bowels [σπλάγχνα, which see] being regarded as the seat of compassion and pity, &c.).

πολυτελής, *expensive, costly* : hence *precious, valuable*, 1 Pet. iii 4.

πολύτιμος, *costly, expensive* : hence *valuable, precious*, 1 Pet. i 7.

πολυτρόπως, *in many ways, under many aspects* (with reference probably to different laws or injunctions).

πόμα, *drink*.

πονηρία (malignitas), the active exercise of vicious propensity, *malignity, wickedness* : plur. *iniquities*, Mk. vii 22, Ac. iii 26.

πονηρός (malignus), *evil, wicked, malicious*, particularly as active : especially, ὁ πονηρός (even Mt. vi 13, [Lk. xi 4], according to the almost unanimous opinion of the early Church), *the evil one*, i.e. Satan, the devil (a Hebraism) ; many passages like these, being in the oblique cases, are unfortunately ambiguous, but Mt. xiii 19, 1 John ii 13, 14, v 18 are absolutely certain examples of the masculine, and in many other passages there is a strong probability : τὸ πονηρόν, *the evil* in the world, *all that is wicked*, e. g. Rom. xii 9.

πόνος, *labour, toil ; trouble.*

Ποντικός, *belonging to Pontus* (which see).

Πόντιος, *Pontius*, the second or gentile name of Pilate.

Πόντος, *Pontus*, a Roman province in the north of Asia Minor, bordering on the Black Sea, governed along with Bithynia.

Πόπλιος, the Greek form of the Latin name *Publius* (originally the same in form as the Greek form); a governor of Malta.

πορεία, *a journey.*

πορεύομαι, *I travel, journey* : sometimes weakened to the sense, *I go* : *I depart* this life, *I die*, Lk. xiii 33 (?), xxii 22 : Hebraistically, of manner of life, 1 Pet. iv 3, &c.

πορθέω, *I devastate, lay waste* : hence, *I bring destruction upon, I destroy.*

πορισμός (quaestus), *a means of gain, a way of making a living, a livelihood, a living.*

Πόρκιος, *Porcius*, the middle (gentile) name of the procurator Festus.

πορνεία, *fornication*, the practice of consorting with πόρναι or πόρνοι, habitual *immorality.*

πορνεύω, *I practise fornication*, especially of men consorting with πόρναι.

πόρνη, *a prostitute.*

πόρνος, *a male prostitute* : the weaker sense, one who consorts with πόρναι, *a fornicator*, is generally adopted for N.T.

πόρρω (procul), *far, at a distance.*

πόρρωθεν, *from a long distance*, Heb. xi 13 : hence (cf. ἔξωθεν), *at a long distance, far away*, Lk. xvii 12.

πορφύρα, *a purple* robe, *purple* ; *a red-coloured cloak*, such as common soldiers wore, Mk. xv 17, 20.

πορφύρεος, *dyed with purple*, Rev. xvii 4, xviii 16 : *dyed scarlet*, John xix 2, 5 (see πορφύρα).

πορφυρόπωλις, *a* woman *dealer in purple-dyed* garments.

ποσάκις

ποσάκις, *how many times ?, how often ?*

πόσις, *drinking* : hence, concrete, *drink*, as perhaps in all N.T. passages (certainly in John vi 55).

πόσος (quantus), *how great ?, how large ?* : in plur. (quot, later quanti), *how many ?* : πόσῳ (quanto), before compar. (cf. Mt. xii 12), *by how much ?, how much ?*

ποταμός, *a river.*

ποταμοφόρητος, *river-borne, carried off by a river.*

ποταπός, (*from what country ?, in what country born ?,* and then) *of what sort ?, how fashioned ?* (hence, practically, *how great ?,* 1 John iii 1).

πότε, *at what time ?, when ?* : ἕως πότε, *till what time ?, till when ?, how long ?* Also in indirect interrog. clauses.

ποτέ, indefinite temporal particle, *at any time, ever, at some time* ; *at one time,* especially with past tenses : for μή ποτε, see **μήποτε.**

πότερον (utrum), *whether.*

ποτήριον (poculum), *a wine cup.*

ποτίζω (poto, potiono), *I cause to drink, I make to drink, I give drink to.*

Ποτίολοι, *Puteoli* (now Pozzuoli), the great harbour for traffic with Alexandria, &c., on the Bay of Naples.

πότος, *a drinking bout.*

ποῦ, *where ?* : also used (for the obsolete ποῖ) in the sense, *whither ?, to what place ?*

που, (a) *anywhere,* Ac. xxvii 29 ; *somewhere,* Heb. ii 6, &c. ; (b) *about,* Rom. iv 19 : for δή που and μή που, see also **δήπου, μήπου.**

Πούδης (Latin), *Pudens,* a Christian man in Rome.

πούς, *a* (human) *foot.*

πρᾶγμα, (a) *a deed, action* ; (b) used more vaguely, *a matter, an affair* ; πρᾶγμα ἔχειν πρός τινα, *to have something against one, to have ground for a lawsuit against one* (where πρᾶγμα = causa), 1 Cor. vi 1 : ἐν τῷ πράγματι, *in the matter in hand* (i. e. sins of the flesh), rather than generically, *in business,* 1 Thess. iv 6.

πραγματεία, *business, business transaction.*

πραγματεύομαι, *I do business, I trade.*

πραιτώριον (Latin praetorium, meaning originally, *the quarters (residence) of the general*), (a) *the official residence of the procurator*, which in Jerusalem was the palace of Herod on the west side of the city; (b) personally, *the imperial guard, the praetorian guard*, or perhaps, *the law officers of the Crown*, Phil. i 13.

πράκτωρ, (usually, *a collector of revenue*, but in Lk.) *an officer (usher) of the court*.

πρᾶξις, (a) abstr., *conduct*; *function*, Rom. xii 4; (b) concrete, in plur. *doings, deeds*.

πρασιά, *a vegetable* or *flower bed*: πρασιαὶ πρασιαί, colloquial type of phrase, *like vegetable* or *flower beds*, referring to the rectangular arrangement of the groups.

πράσσω (ago, referring rather to the purpose, motive of an action than to the actual doing), (a) tr. *I act, do*; (b) tr. *I exact, extort*, Lk. iii 13, xix 23; (c) intr. *I fare*: εὖ πράξετε, *you shall fare well*, Ac. xv 29, τί πράσσω, *how I fare*, Eph. vi 21.

πραϋπάθεια, *meekness (gentleness) of spirit*.

πραΰς, *meek, gentle*.

πραΰτης, *meekness, gentleness*.

πρέπω, *I suit*: generally impersonal, or with neuter pronoun as subject, πρέπει, πρέπον ἐστίν, *it is becoming, it is fitting*.

πρεσβεία, *an embassy, delegation*.

πρεσβεύω (especially, *I am on embassy to the Emperor*), *I am an ambassador*.

πρεσβυτέριον, (a) amongst the Jews, *a college of elders*, who supervised the worship, &c., of the synagogue; hence, *the Sanhedrin* at Jerusalem; (b) the Christian analogue, *a college of elders* of a particular church.

πρεσβύτερος, (a) of age simply, *the elder* of two, Lk. xv 25; *old, aged*, Ac. ii 17, 1 Tim. v 1; plur. our (their, &c.) *ancestors*, Mt. xv 2, Mk. vii 3, 5, Heb. xi 2; (b) a title of honour applied among the Jews to various classes of dignitary, because such offices were originally conferred on the old, e. g. *a member of*

πρεσβύτης

the *Sanhedrin*, Mt. xvi 21, &c., [τοῦ Ἰσραήλ], Ac. iv 8, τῶν Ἰουδαίων, Ac. xxv 15, τοῦ λαοῦ, Mt. xxi 23, &c.: *magistrates* of a particular city, Lk. vii 3; (c) among the Christians, *an elder* of a congregation or church, Ac. xi 30, &c., τῆς ἐκκλησίας, Ac. xx 17, James v 14, one of whom was commonly appointed ἐπίσκοπος; hence the two words are practically identical in meaning, the former indicating status, the latter function; (d) *an elder* of the twenty-four in the heavenly assembly, Rev. iv 4, &c. [The title was applied in Egypt (a) to holders of a communal office in civil life, who were responsible for the peace of the village, and received a small salary, (b) to priests of pagan temples.]

πρεσβύτης, *an old man.*

πρεσβῦτις, *an old woman.*

πρηνής (a medical term, denoting a disease, and corresponding to **πίμπρημι,** which see), *swollen up, inflamed.*

πρίζω, *I saw, I saw through.*

πρίν, used either with or without ἤ (*than*) and with the infin. following (once with ἄν and subjunctive, Lk. ii 26, once with the optative, Ac. xxv 16), *before.*

Πρίσκα, Πρίσκιλλα, *Prisca, Priscilla,* the former being the more correct and formal name, the latter a diminutive and more familiar; a Roman lady, probably of good birth, wife of the Jewish Christian Aquila.

πρό, (a) of place, *before, in front of*; (b) of time, *before, earlier than*; found even with article and the infinitive =πρίν: πρὸ ἓξ ἡμερῶν τοῦ πάσχα, *six days before*, &c., John xii 1, πρὸ ἐτῶν δεκατεσσάρων, *fourteen years before*, 2 Cor. xii 2.

προάγω, (a) tr. *I lead forth*, Ac. xvi 30; in the judicial sense, into court, Ac. xii 6, with ἐπί c. gen. of the person who is to try the case, Ac. xxv 26; (b) intr. and tr., *I precede, I go before*; so pres. pcpl. *preceding, previous*, Heb. vii 18; *I lead forwards* to a definite goal, 1 Tim. i 18; (c) intr., *I go too far*, 2 John 9.

214

προέρχομαι

προαιρέομαι, *I choose deliberately.*
προαιτιάομαι, *I make a prior accusation.*
προακούω, *I hear beforehand.*
προαμαρτάνω, *I sin previously.*
προαύλιον, *a forecourt,* a courtyard in the front part of
a building.
προβαίνω, *I go forward, move forward, advance*: met. *I
advance* (in years), Lk. i 7, 18, ii 36.
προβάλλω, (a) tr. *I put forward;* (b) *I put forth shoots,
I sprout, burst into leaf,* Lk. xxi 30.
προβατικός, *connected with sheep*: προβατική (sc. πύλη) *the
Sheep Gate* of Jerusalem: if κολυμβήθρᾳ be read,
προβατικῇ agrees with it.
προβάτιον, lit. *a little sheep;* the diminutive is here used
to express tender affection.
πρόβατον, *a sheep.*
προβιβάζω, *I instruct.*
προβλέπομαι, *I provide; I resolve on.*
προγίνομαι, *I happen (come about) previously.*
προγινώσκω (properly, *I get to know (I learn) beforehand),*
(a) *I know previously;* (b) *I designate before* (to
a position or function), 1 Pet. i 20.
πρόγνωσις, *foreknowledge.*
πρόγονος, *an ancestor.*
προγράφω, (a) *I write previously (aforetime),* Rom. xv 4,
Jude 4; *I write above (already),* Eph. iii 3: (b) *I
evidently pourtray* or *I placard, advertise,* Gal. iii 1.
πρόδηλος, *perfectly clear (evident).*
προδίδωμι, *I give previously.*
προδότης, (a) *a betrayer;* (b) *traitorous, treacherous,*
2 Tim. iii 4.
πρόδρομος, *a forerunner.*
προεῖδον, see προοράω.
προεῖπον, *I said beforehand (previously).*
προελπίζω, *I hope before* another, *I am the first to hope.*
προενάρχομαι, *I begin earlier (previously).*
προεπαγγέλλομαι, *I promise beforehand.*
προέρχομαι, (a) intr. *I go in front (before)*: sometimes
215

προερῶ

with acc. of distance covered, Ac. xii 10; (b) tr. *I precede*, Mk. vi 33, Lk. xxii 47.

προερῶ, only in perf. act. (and pass.), *I have previously said; I have said above.*

προετοιμάζω, *I prepare beforehand.*

προευαγγελίζομαι, *I proclaim the good news beforehand.*

προέχω, *I excel, surpass*; pass. in Rom. iii 9.

προηγέομαι, *I lead in front, I give a lead to.*

πρόθεσις, (a) οἱ ἄρτοι τῆς προθέσεως (Hebraistic), lit. *the loaves of the laying out* (*before* God), i. e. *the loaves laid out*, grecized in Heb. ix 2, ἡ πρόθεσις τῶν ἄρτων: (b) *deliberate purpose* (*plan, scheme*).

προθεσμία, *a term* (or *age, date*) *previously indicated* (*fixed, laid down*).

προθυμία, *eagerness, zeal, enthusiasm.*

πρόθυμος, *eager*: in Rom. i 15 τὸ κατ᾽ ἐμὲ πρόθυμον may be = ἡ ἐμὴ προθυμία, *my good will*, but perhaps it is better to read πρόθυμος (sc. εἰμί) with some authorities.

προθύμως, *eagerly.*

πρόϊμος (not πρώϊμος, but from πρό), *early* in the year (understand ὑετός or some other word meaning *rain*): reference is to that beginning in October: opposed to ὄψιμος.

προΐστημι: in intr. tenses, *I take up a position* (*stand*) *in front*: *I take the lead, I rule*; hence, c. gen. *I lead, supervise, manage*; also *I practise, exercise* a calling or profession.

προκαλέομαι, *I call out, challenge.*

προκαταγγέλλω, *I announce beforehand.*

προκαταρτίζω, *I prepare* (*arrange*) *beforehand.*

πρόκειμαι, *I am set* (*placed, put*) *before, I am already there.*

προκηρύσσω, *I proclaim previously.*

προκοπή, *progress, advance.*

προκόπτω (originally of the pioneer cutting his way through brushwood), *I advance, progress, make progress.*

πρόκριμα, *prejudgement* (favourable or unfavourable).

προκυρόω, *I make valid beforehand.*

προλαμβάνω, (a) *I take* *before* another (perhaps); *I am in a hurry to take, I take eagerly, I seize,* 1 Cor. xi 21 ; (b) προέλαβεν μυρίσαι, *has by anticipation anointed* (perhaps an Aramaism), Mk. xiv 8 ; (c) (deprehendo) *I catch, capture, overtake* (*before* he can escape).

προλέγω, *I tell* (*say*) *beforehand.*

προμαρτύρομαι, *I call* (God) *beforehand to witness.*

προμελετάω, *I practise beforehand, I prepare, I get up.*

προμεριμνάω, *I am anxious beforehand.*

προνοέω, act. and mid., *I take thought for beforehand, I provide for.*

πρόνοια, *forethought, foresight*; πρόνοιαν ποιοῦμαι = προνοέω.

προοράω, *I see beforehand, I foresee, I see previously,* Ac. xxi 29 : mid. *I pay regard to, set before me,* Ac. ii 25.

προορίζω, *I foreordain* (lit. *I bound* [*limit*] *beforehand*).

προπάσχω, *I suffer previously.*

προπάτωρ, *a forefather.*

προπέμπω, (a) *I send in front* (*forth, forward*), *set forward, start on their way* (in Tit. iii 13, of being provided with necessaries for the journey); (b) (prosequor), *I convoy, I escort on* (*his,* &c.) *way,* as a mark of affection and respect, Ac. xv 3, xx 38, xxi 5, Rom. xv 24, 3 John 6.

προπετής (of thoughtless haste), *impulsive, rash, reckless.*

προπορεύομαι, *I journey in front, I go before.*

πρός, (a) c. gen., *on the side of, in the interests of, for* (literary), Ac. xxvii 34 ; (b) c. dat., *close to, close by, near, at*; (c) c. acc. (of persons, places, things), (1) *to,* with verbs of coming, sending, bringing, saying ; (2) *near,* after the verb 'to be', &c. (instead of παρά τινι) ; (3) *near,* instead of παρά, Ac. v 10, *into the house of,* Ac. xi 3 ; (4) of time, *near,* Lk. xxiv 29 : *for* (a time), and no longer, Lk. viii 13, John v 35, Heb. xii 10, &c. ; (5) of hostile or friendly relations, *with,* μάχεσθαι, εἰρήνην ἔχειν, &c. ; τί πρὸς ἡμᾶς ; *what have we to do with it ?* Mt. xxvii 4, John xxi 22 ; *with reference to,* *of,* Mk. xii 12, cf. x 5, Mt. xix 8, Lk. xii 41, xviii 1, xx 19, John xiii 28, &c. ; (6) with ἀγαθός, ὠφέλιμος, δυνατός, &c., *for,* 2 Cor. x 4, Eph. iv 29, 1 Tim. iv 8, where it indicates also the destination, purpose, result, e. g. Lk. xiv 32, xix 42, John iv 35, xi 4 (cf. 1 John v 16, 17), Ac. iii 10 ; (7) *in conformity with, according to,* Lk. xii 47, 1 Cor. xii 7, 2 Cor. v 10 ; *with respect to,* Heb. i 7, 8 ; (8) *in comparison with,* Rom. viii 18.

προσάββατον, *the day before the Sabbath,* i. e. from 6 p.m. on Thursday to 6 p.m. on Friday.

προσαγορεύω, *I designate as* by addressing by a certain title ; *I recognize as.*

προσάγω, (a) (adduco), *I lead to, I bring to* ; characteristically, *I bring* a subject *into the presence of* a king), *I present to, I introduce,* 1 Pet. iii 18 ; (b) intr. *I approach,* Ac. xxvii 27 (v. l.).

προσαγωγή, *access, entrée,* or perhaps a metaphor from the concrete sense *landing-stage.*

προσαιτέω, *I beg, I am a beggar.*

προσαίτης, *a beggar.*

προσαναβαίνω, *I go up to, I come up to.*

προσαναλίσκω, *I spend in addition.*

προσαναπληρόω, *I fill up by adding, make up, supply.*

προσανατίθεμαι, *I turn* (*have recourse*) *to.*

προσαπειλέομαι, *I add a threat* (or *threats*) *to the* warning.

προσαχέω (Doric form for προσηχέω), *I sound near,* Ac. xxvii 27 (v. l.).

προσδαπανάω, *I spend in addition.*

προσδέομαι, *I need* (*have need of*) something *additional.*

προσδέχομαι, (a) *I await, expect* ; (b) *I receive, welcome* (originally *to* my house), e. g. Lk. xv 2, Rom. xvi 2, Phil. ii 29 ; (c) *I accept,* Ac. xxiv 15.

προσδοκάω, *I expect, wait for, await.*

προσδοκία, *expectation, waiting.*

προσεάω, *I permit* to go straight *onwards.*

προσεγγίζω, *I come near to, I approach.*

προσεργάζομαι, *I produce in addition, I gain.*

προσέρχομαι, *I come up to, I come to*; *I come near (to), I approach*; *I consent (to),* 1 Tim. vi 3.

προσευχή, (a) *prayer* (to God); τοῦ θεοῦ, *to God,* Lk. vi 12; (b) *a place for prayer,* Ac. xvi 13 (used by Jews, perhaps where there was no synagogue).

προσεύχομαι, *I pray*; c. acc., *I pray for*: sometimes with Hebraistic tautology, προσευχῇ or διὰ προσευχῆς is added.

προσέχω, (a) (τὸν νοῦν was originally added, *I direct the mind*), *I attend to, pay attention to,* c. dat., Ac. viii 6, xvi 14, &c. cf. (c); (b) with ἐμαυτῷ, or absolutely, *I attend to myself, I pay attention for myself,* Hebraistic for *I am cautious, I beware, I take care for (of) myself,* Lk. xvii 3, Ac. v 35, with ἀπό governing the thing *of* which one has to beware, Mt. vii 15, Lk. xii 1, &c.; so with μή, *lest*; (c) sc. ἐμαυτόν, *I attach myself to, I join,* Ac. viii 10, 1 Tim. iv 1; *I devote myself to* (by way of enjoyment or of work), 1 Tim. i 4, iii 8, iv 13, Tit. i 14, Heb. vii 13.

προσηλόω, *I nail to.*

προσήλυτος (lit. *that has come to*), *a proselyte,* that is a non-Jew, who has been circumcised and has adopted the Jews' religion.

πρόσκαιρος, *for an occasion, transitory.*

προσκαλέομαι, *I call to myself.*

προσκαρτερέω, (a) *I continue all the time, I continue stedfast, I persist,* either of remaining in a place, or of persisting in a certain course of action; (b) *I attach myself assiduously to,* Ac. viii 13, x 7; (c) with a lifeless subject, *I continue near (at hand),* Mk. iii 9.

προσκαρτέρησις, *constant attendance, persistence, perseverance, constancy.*

προσκεφάλαιον, *a pillow* or *a cushion.*

προσκληρόω, *I allot (assign) to* (as disciples), Ac. xvii 4, where, if the passive has a middle force, we may translate, *threw in their lot with.*

προσκλίνω, mid. *I attach myself to, follow.*

πρόσκλισις, *inclination*; possibly, *taking sides, party spirit*.

προσκολλάω (lit. *I glue* one thing *to* another), *I join (unite) closely*: fut. pass. probably as middle, *I cleave (to)*.

πρόσκομμα (lit. *striking against*, generally in the Hebraistic genitive, after λίθος, a stone or loose boulder in the way, *against* which the traveller may *strike* his foot), *an obstacle, a cause of stumbling*; *stumbling*: hence met. especially.

προσκοπή, *causing of stumbling* (met.).

προσκόπτω (offendo), *I strike against*; intr., Mt. vii 27, &c., also absol. *I stumble*, John xi 9, 10, Rom. xiv 21; *I stumble at*, 1 Pet. ii 8. Sometimes met. (cf. **πρόσκομμα**).

προσκυλίω, *I roll to (up to)*.

προσκυνέω, *I go down on my knees to*; *I do obeisance to*; *I worship*.

προσκυνητής, *a worshipper*.

προσλαλέω, *I speak to*.

προσλαμβάνομαι, (a) *I take to myself*; (b) *I take aside*, Mk. viii 32, Mt. xvi 22, Ac. xvii 5, xviii 26; (c) *I welcome*, Ac. xxviii 2, Rom. xiv 1, &c.

πρόσλημψις, *taking to one's self*; *assumption* into God's favour.

προσμένω, *I remain*: c. dat., *I abide in, I remain in, I persist in*.

προσορμίζομαι, *I anchor at* a place.

προσοφείλω, *I owe besides (in addition)*.

προσοχθίζω, *I entertain anger (disgust, abhorrence)*.

πρόσπεινος, either *inclined to hunger* or *very hungry*.

προσπήγνυμι, *I fix to* anything.

προσπίπτω, *I fall upon*; *I fall at (beside)*.

προσποιέομαι, *I pretend*.

προσπορεύομαι, *I come to*.

προσρήγνυμι, *I dash against*.

προστάσσω, (a) *I instruct, command*; (b) *I appoint*, Ac. xvii 26.

προστάτις (a development of the political sense of προστάτης [patronus], *a political sponsor* of resident aliens), *protectress, patroness.*

προστίθημι (addo), *I place* (*put*) *to, I add*: mid. c. infin. (perhaps a Hebraistic idiom), best translated by representing the verb in the infinitive by the indicative, and adding the word *besides*, &c., thus:—προσέθετο πέμψαι, *besides* (*in addition, further*) *he sent*, Lk. xx 11.

προστρεχω, *I run* (*run up*) *to* a person.

προσφάγιον, *a relish, delicacy,* or *tit-bit* eaten with bread (commonly it would be fish).

πρόσφατος (from πρός and the root of φόνος, therefore originally *newly slaughtered, fresh-killed*), *now for the first time made, new.*

προσφάτως, *freshly, recently.*

προσφέρω, (a) *I bring to*; (b) characteristically, *I offer* (of gifts, sacrifices, &c.).

προσφιλής, *lovable, amiable.*

προσφορά, *an offering* (especially to God).

προσφωνέω, c. acc. *I call, I summon*: c. dat. *I call* (*out*) *to*; *I address, I give a speech to*, Ac. xxii 2, cf. absol. Ac. xxi 40.

πρόσχυσις, *pouring upon* the altar (as was done in later times, not in that of Moses).

προσψαύω, *I touch, handle.*

προσωπολημπτέω (from προσωπολήμπτης, Hebraistic, later than LXX), *I favour specially.*

προσωπολήμπτης (from πρόσωπον and λαμβάνειν, Hebraistic, later than LXX; see under the latter), *a special favourer* of one more than of another, *a respecter of persons.*

προσωπολημψία (a Hebraistic expression, later than LXX), *favouritism, partiality.*

πρόσωπον, (a) *the* human *face*; often Hebraistically otiose, e. g. πρὸ προσώπου σου practically = πρὸ σοῦ, Mt. xi 10; πρόσωπον πρὸς πρόσωπον (Hebraistic), *face to face*; (b) hence applied to God, from His having

been originally conceived as in human form, *presence*
(cf. Ac. v 41); (c) *appearance, outward aspect* (Mt. xvi
3), Lk. xii 56, &c.; *surface*, Lk. xxi 35; (d) for the
practically synonymous Hebraistic expressions βλέπειν εἰς πρόσωπον, θαυμάζειν πρόσωπον, λαμβάνειν πρόσωπον, *to show special favour to*, see under λαμβάνω;
(e) by Hebraistic pleonasm (cf. (a) above), πρὸ προσώπου τῆς εἰσόδου αὐτοῦ, *before his entrance*, Ac. xiii 24;
(f) *person* in a rather loose sense as a possessor of
dignity or honour; *pride*, James i 11.

προτείνω, *I stretch forward, I put into a tense posture.*

πρότερος (becoming replaced by πρῶτος), *first of two,
former, previous, earlier*: acc. as adv. (τὸ) πρότερον,
on the former of two occasions, e. g. Gal. iv 13; *on
a previous occasion*; *at first, formerly, previously*,
sometimes used practically as an adj., as the latter
was dying out (see **πρῶτος**), 1 Tim. i 13.

προτίθεμαι, *I set before myself, I purpose openly*: but
perhaps, *I offer, I provide.*

προτρέπομαι, *I encourage.*

προτρέχω, *I run forward.*

προϋπάρχω, *I am (previously), I have been already.*

πρόφασις, *ostensible reason* for which a thing is done
(that is, commonly, the false reason), *pretence*; *excuse,
pretext*: προφάσει, *under colour, under pretence.*

προφέρω, *I bring forth (out), produce.*

προφητεία, the quality or action of a προφήτης, *declaration* of the will of God, whether with special reference
to the future, in which case it may be translated
prophecy, or not.

προφητεύω, I do the duty of a προφήτης, *I declare* the
will of God, sometimes with regard to what is to
happen in the future, in which case it may be rendered, *I prophesy.*

προφήτης, (a) a man specially endowed to *tell forth
(declare)* the will of God in speech, whether as touching
the present or as regards the future, *a prophet*: the
adoption of a literary form as seen in the prophetical

books of the O.T. is a later stage of a prophet's
activity; (b) Epimenides (in Tit. i 12) is so styled,
perhaps as related to the Cretans in the same way as
the prophets of Israel were to Israel.

προφητικός, belonging to a προφήτης or to προφῆται,
prophetic.

προφῆτις, *a prophetess.*

προφθάνω, *I anticipate, I forestall.*

προχειρίζομαι, *I appoint, elect* (for an important duty).

προχειροτονέω, *I appoint beforehand.*

Πρόχορος, *Prochorus,* one of the seven original 'deacons'
at Jerusalem.

πρύμνα, *the stern* of a ship.

πρωΐ, *early, in the morning* (in John xx 1, even of the
period before dawn).

πρωΐα, *early morning.*

πρώϊμος, see πρόϊμος.

πρωϊνός (from πρωΐ) (matutinus), *belonging to the morning, morning*: opposite ἑσπερινός.

πρῴρα, *the prow, the bow* of a ship.

πρωτεύω, *I hold the first (chief) place, I am the
head.*

πρωτοκαθεδρία, *the chief (most honourable) seat (chair,
stall).*

πρωτοκλισία, *the chief (most honourable) reclining-place*
on the dining couches at a dinner table.

πρῶτον (primum), *in the first place, first*: τὸ πρῶτον
(primo), *at first, at the beginning.*

πρῶτος, *first* (of time, then of status), strictly of more
than two, being a superlative, but also used where
there are two elements only, as πρότερος, the true
comparative, was dying out in N.T. times, Ac. i 1,
Heb. viii 7, 13, ix 1, 2, 6, 8, &c.: οἱ πρῶτοι, *the chief
men,* Mk. vi 21, Lk. xix 47, &c., cf. ὁ πρῶτος (primus),
an official title, equivalent to *the governor,* Ac. xxviii
7: πρῶτος μου, John i 15, 30, either = πρότερός μου,
earlier than I (cf. xv 18), or, with μου as possessive
genitive, *my chief, my lord.*

πρωτοστάτης, *one who stands in the front rank*, hence *a leader, ringleader*.

πρωτοτόκια (τά), *one's rights as first-born*.

πρωτότοκος, *first-born, earliest born, eldest*.

πρώτως, *for the first time* (v.l.).

πταίω, of incipient falling, *I trip, stumble*, lit. or met.

πτέρνα, *heel*.

πτερύγιον, *the gable, roof, projection of the temple roof, pinnacle*; or possibly (see ἱερόν), *the wall* surrounding the temple precinct.

πτέρυξ, *a wing*.

πτηνός, *winged*; hence as substantive, *a bird*.

πτοέω, *I scare, I strike with panic*.

πτόησις, *fear, terror* (or other violent excitement).

Πτολεμαΐς, *Ptolemaïs*, a coast city of Phoenicia, midway between Tyre and Caesarea.

πτύον, *a winnowing-fan*, a simple wooden pitchfork.

πτύρω, *I frighten, terrify*.

πτύσμα, *spittle*.

πτύσσω, *I roll up, close*.

πτύω, *I spit*.

πτῶμα, *a corpse*.

πτῶσις, *falling, fall*.

πτωχεία, (strictly *beggary*, but rather merely) *poverty*.

πτωχεύω, *I live the life of a poor man*.

πτωχός (strictly *a beggar*; weakened afterwards), *poor*; *a poor man*: met. (Mt. v 3, Lk. vi 20, Rev. iii 17), not of those who are poor in material things, but of the humble devout persons, who feel the need of God's help.

πυγμή, *the fist*: meaning of Mk. vii 3 (v.l.) still uncertain ('turning the closed fist of one hand about the hollow of the other', or 'as far as the elbow', or paraphrased by 'diligently', 'carefully'?).

πύθων, *a ventriloquist* (the utterance being supposed to be due to the presence of a familiar spirit [πύθων] within the body of the speaker).

πυκνός, (*spissus, thick*; hence) *frequent*: acc. plur. neut.

πυκνά as adv., *frequently, often* (cf. regular comparative of adverb, Ac. xxiv 26).

πυκτεύω, *I am a boxer, I box.*

πύλη, *a gate.*

πυλών (properly, *the passage which led from the street through the front part of the house to the inner court,* closed by a heavy πύλη at the streetward end), *entrance passage, gateway; gate.*

πυνθάνομαι, *I enquire.*

πῦρ, *fire; a fire,* both literally, and metaphorically, and eschatologically (as an instrument of punishment in the conception of later Judaism, *the fire* of the Divine wrath which burns in Gehenna).

πυρά, *a fire.*

πύργος, *a tower.*

πυρέσσω, *I have fever, I suffer from fever.*

πυρετός, *a fever:* medical writers use the plural (Ac. xxviii 8), where we should use the singular, because of recurring attacks of fever.

πύρινος, *as of fire,* that is, probably, *fire-coloured.*

πυρόω, (a) *I equip with fire,* Eph. vi 16 (of flaming darts), *I refine by fire,* Rev. i 15, iii 18, *I burn with fire, I fire,* 2 Pet. iii 12; (b) mid. or pass. met., of strong passion or feeling, *I burn with fleshly lust,* 1 Cor. vii 9; *I blaze with anger,* 2 Cor. xi 29.

πυρράζω, *I am red (ruddy).*

Πύρρος, *Pyrrhus,* father of the Christian Sopater of Beroea.

πυρρός, *red.*

πύρωσις, (a) *burning;* (b) met. *trial* as it were *by fire, fiery test,* 1 Pet. iv 12.

πωλέω (originally = uendito, *I advertise, put up for sale:* later = uendo), *I sell.*

πῶλος, (*the young* of various animals, hence, particularly) *the foal (colt)* of an ass.

πώποτε, *ever yet, yet at any time,* only used after a negative word.

πωρόω (from πῶρος, *a kind of marble,* then, *a bony forma-*

tion on the joints, and *a callus* or *ossification* uniting two portions of a fractured bone: thus πωρόω, *I petrify*, and *I cover with a callus*, and *I deaden, I dull*), *I make* (*render*) *obtuse* (*dull, dead*) ; *I blind* (intellectually or morally).

πώρωσις (originally *petrifaction, hardness* : then the result of this, as metaphorically applied to organs of feeling), *insensibility, numbness, obtuseness, dulling* of the faculty of perception, *deadness* ; intellectual (moral) *blindness*.

πῶς, (a) *how ?, in what manner ?*, also in indirect interrogations : πῶς γάρ ... *why, how* ... ; (b) = ὡς, ὅτι, *that* (variant readings sometimes occur), Mt. xii 4, Mk. xii 26, 41, Lk. vi 4, xiv 7, Ac. xi 13, 1 Thess. i 9.

πως, indefinite, enclitic, *in some way, in any way* : εἴ πως, *if in any way* ; see μήπως.

P

Ῥαάβ (Hebr.), *Rahab*, a Canaanitess, who rescued the Hebrew spies at Jericho, by tradition wife of Salmon (Mt. i 4, 5).

ῥαββεί (Aramaic), *my master*, a title given by pupils to their teacher.

ῥαββουνεί (Aramaic, a fuller form of ῥαββεί), *my master*.

ῥαβδίζω, *I flog* (*beat*) *with a rod* (*staff*), a Roman punishment.

ῥάβδος, *a staff, rod*.

ῥαβδοῦχος (lictor), (lit. *a rod holder, holder of rods*), *a lictor, an attendant* (*orderly*), of certain Roman magistrates, *a tipstaff*.

Ῥαγαύ (Hebr.), *Ragau*, an ancestor of Jesus.

ῥᾳδιούργημα, *a moral wrong, a crime*.

ῥᾳδιουργία, (*ease in working* ; so *unscrupulousness* : hence) *fraud, wickedness*.

ῥακά (or ῥαχά) (Aramaic), *empty foolish*.

ῥάκος, *a piece of cloth*.

Ῥαμά, *Rama*, a place in Ephraim, two hours north of Jerusalem.

ῥαντίζω, (a) *I sprinkle* and thus purify; (b) mid. *I sprinkle (purify) myself*, Mk. vii 4.

ῥαντισμός, *sprinkling*, as a symbolic purification (cf. Exod. xxiv 6–8).

ῥαπίζω, *I slap, strike*.

ῥάπισμα (colaphus), *a slap, a blow on the cheek with the open hand*.

ῥαφίς, *a sewing needle* (= classical βελόνη, used by Lk.).

ῥαχά, see ῥακά.

Ῥαχάβ (Hebr.), another spelling of Ῥαάβ.

Ῥαχήλ (Hebr.), *Rachel*, younger wife of the patriarch Jacob.

Ῥεβέκκα (Hebr.), *Rebecca*, wife of the patriarch Isaac.

ῥέδη (reda, a word of Keltic origin), *a carriage*.

Ῥεφάν, see Ῥομφά.

ῥέω, *I flow*.

Ῥήγιον, *Regium*, a city in the SW. corner of Italy opposite Sicily (modern Reggio).

ῥῆγμα, *a breaking up, collapse*.

ῥήγνυμι, ῥήσσω, (a) *I break*: *I rend, tear*: in Mk. ix 18, Lk. ix 42, it = either σπαράσσω, of convulsions, or *I throw on the ground*; (b) intr. *I break forth into joy*, Gal. iv 27.

ῥῆμα, (a) *a spoken word, an utterance*, the concrete expression of λόγος: hence, perhaps Hebraistically, (b) a subject as spoken about, a subject of speech, *a matter, a thing, a fact*, Mt. xviii 16, Lk. i 37, ii 15, &c.; (c) in a solemn sense, of a divine *word*, Lk. iii 2, Eph. vi 17, &c.; (d) the Christian *teaching, the gospel*, 1 Pet. i 25 *bis* (cf. Rom. x 8 ff.), (the first = the promise to deliver Israel); (e) the Christian confession, 'Jesus is Lord', which leads to salvation, and precedes baptism, Eph. v 26, cf. Rom. x 9, 1 Cor. xii 3, Phil. ii 11.

Ῥησά (Hebr.), *Resa*, an ancestor of Jesus.

ῥήσσω, see ῥήγνυμι.

ῥήτωρ

ῥήτωρ, *a rhetorician, a professional public speaker*;
hence, *a barrister*, acting as counsel for the
prosecution.

ῥητῶς, *in so many words, expressly, explicitly.*

ῥίζα, *a root*: hence met., *a source.*

ῥιζόω, *I root, I fix by the root.*

ῥιπή, *a glance* (indicating instantaneousness), *flash* of
an eye.

ῥιπίζω (from ῥιπίς, a fire-fan : hence, *I fan* either a fire
or a person), *I raise with the wind.*

ῥίπτω (iacio), ῥιπτέω (iacto), *I throw, cast; I shake,
toss*: ἐριμμένοι, *sunk powerless*, Mt. ix 36 : in Ac. xxii
23, *I toss about*, a sign of excitement and uncon-
trollable rage.

Ῥοβοάμ (Hebr.), *Rehoboam*, son of Solomon, and King
of Israel.

Ῥόδη (lit. *Rose*), *Rhoda*, a maidservant in the house of
John Mark's mother at Jerusalem.

Ῥόδος, *Rhodes*, an island in the Aegean sea, SW. of
Asia Minor.

ῥοιζηδόν (properly expressing the whizzing sound produced by rapid motion through the air), *with thunder-
ous crash (roar).*

Ῥομφά (vv. ll. Ῥομφάν, Ῥεφάν, &c.), *Rompha*, probably
a corruption of the Assyrian name for the planet
Saturn (= Chiun, Amos v 26).

ῥομφαία (properly a long Thracian sword), *a sword,
scimitar*: met. in Lk. ii 35 of acute suffering.

Ῥουβήν (Hebr.), *Reuben*, eldest son of the patriarch
Jacob and founder of a tribe.

Ῥούθ (Hebr.), *Ruth*, wife of Boes (Boaz) and mother of
Iobed (Obed).

Ῥοῦφος, *Rufus*, a Christian man in Rome (Rom. xvi
13), probably to be identified with the brother of
Alexander and son of Simon of Cyrene mentioned
in Mk. xv 21.

ῥύμη, *a street* or *lane* in a town or city.

ῥύομαι, *I rescue* (from danger or destruction).

228

ῥυπαίνω, *I make dirty, I stain* : mid. and pass., *I am filthy* (morally), *I am stained* (by sin) (v. l.).

ῥυπαρεύομαι, *I am filthy* ; hence (morally), *I am stained with sin.*

ῥυπαρία, *defilement.*

ῥυπαρός, *shabby, soiled* : hence morally, *filthy, corrupt, sinful,* Rev. xxii 11.

ῥύπος, *filth, dirt.*

ῥύσις, *flowing* ; ῥύσις αἵματος, *hemorrhage.*

ῥυτίς, *a wrinkle* of age.

Ῥωμαῖος, *Roman* ; *a Roman* : the plural, according to context, suggests either the imperial people (e. g. John xi 48) or citizens of the Roman Empire (e. g. Ac. xvi 21).

Ῥωμαϊστί, *in the Latin language.*

Ῥώμη, *Rome,* the famous city on the Tiber, the capital of the Roman Empire.

ῥώννυμι, *I make strong* : perf. mid. imperative, a formula of correspondence, at the end of a letter, ἔρρωσο, ἔρρωσθε (uale, ualete), *farewell.*

Σ

σαβαχθανεί (Aramaic), *thou hast forsaken.*

σαβαώθ (Hebrew), *hosts, armies.*

σαββατισμός, *a resting* as *on the sabbath.*

σάββατον (Semitic), sing. and plur., *the Sabbath,* a night and day which lasted from about 6 p.m. on Friday till about 6 p.m. on Saturday : πρώτη (μία) [τῶν] σαββάτων ([τοῦ] σαββάτου) (Hebraistic), *the first day after the Sabbath, the day following the Sabbath,* that is, from about 6 p.m. on Saturday till about 6 p.m. on Sunday, *Sunday.*

σαγήνη, *a fishing-net.*

Σαδδουκαῖος, *a Sadducee, a Zadokite priest,* a member of the aristocratic party among the Jews, from whom the high-priests were almost invariably chosen.

Σαδώκ (Hebr.), *Zadok,* an ancestor of Jesus.

σαίνω

σαίνω (properly of dogs, *I wag the tail, fawn* : then met. *I fawn upon, beguile*), *I draw aside, allure* from the right path : perhaps the v. l. σαίνεσθαι, *to be disturbed* (*troubled*), ought to be read.

σάκκος (a Semitic word), *sackcloth, sacking*, a rough mourning dress held together by string, and hanging on the bare body.

Σαλά (Hebr.), *Sala*, the name of two of the ancestors of Jesus (v. l. in Lk. iii 32).

Σαλαθιήλ (Hebr.), *Salathiel*, son of Jechonias and father (according to one tradition) of Zerubbabel.

Σαλαμίς, *Salamis*, a city at the eastern end of Cyprus.

Σαλείμ, *Salim*, a place eight Roman miles south of Scythopolis in the extreme north of Samaria.

σαλεύω, *I shake*, lit. and met. ; *I dislodge.*

Σαλήμ, *Salem*, doubtless identical with Jerusalem.

Σαλμών, *Salmon*, son of Naasson and father of Boes (Boaz) (v. l. in Lk. iii 32).

Σαλμώνη, *Salmone*, a promontory on the east of Crete.

σάλος, *a rough sea, surf.*

σάλπιγξ, *a bugle, a war trumpet*, used for signals and commands ; hence in eschatological passage as signal for Judgement or Resurrection.

σαλπίζω, *I sound the bugle, I give a blast of the bugle* : the subject is sometimes omitted, so that the word becomes practically impersonal.

σαλπιστής, *a bugler, trumpeter.*

Σαλώμη, *Salome*, wife of Zebedee and mother of James and John, the disciples.

Σαλωμών, see Σολομών.

Σαμάρεια, *Samaria*, a small district of Palestine, bounded by Galilee on the North, and by Judaea on the South, and taking its name from the city of Samaria, the ancient capital of the kingdom of (northern) Israel.

Σαμαρείτης, *a Samaritan, an inhabitant of Samaria.*

Σαμαρεῖτις, *a Samaritan woman.*

Σαμοθράκη, *Samothrace*, an island south of the province of Thrace.

Σάμος, *Samos*, an island in the Aegean sea off the coast of Asia Minor, near Ephesus and Miletus.

Σαμουήλ (Hebr.), *Samuhel, Samuel*, an Old Testament prophet.

Σαμψών (Hebr.), *Sampson, Samson*, one of the Judges of Israel.

σανδάλιον, *a sandal, an open-work shoe, a shoe*.

σανίς, *a plank, board*.

Σαούλ, (a) *Saul*, the first king of Israel, Ac. xiii 21; (b) *Saul*, the Hebrew name of the Apostle to the Gentiles (see **Σαῦλος**).

σαπρός (puter), *crumbling, decayed, decaying, rotten*; hence, *old and worn out, stale, worthless*: met. *corrupt*, Eph. iv 29.

Σάπφειρα (perhaps from an Aramaic word meaning *beautiful*), *Sapphira*, wife of Ananias, an early Christian.

σάπφειρος (Semitic), *a sapphire; lapis lazuli*.

σαργάνη, *a mat-basket*, a large basket of flexible material closed by sewing and usually employed to hold slices of salt fish (raisins and figs are also mentioned).

Σάρδεις, *Sardis*, an ancient city of Lydia in the province of Asia.

σάρδιον, *sardius, sard*, a quartz of a deep red colour.

σαρδόνυξ, *sardonyx*.

Σάρεπτα, *Sarepta*, a town in the district of Sidon in Phoenicia.

σαρκικός (carnalis), generally ethical, *belonging to* **σάρξ** (which see), belonging to the natural life of man as a creature of flesh, *with the characteristics of* **σάρξ**, *fleshly, unspiritual, carnal*.

σάρκινος (carneus), material, *made of flesh, consisting of flesh*.

σάρξ (in general used Hebraistically), (a) *flesh*, all the solid part of the body of man or beast except the

σαρόω

bones, plur. (Hebraistic), e. g. Lk. xxiv 39 (v.l.),
Rev. xvii 16; σὰρξ καὶ αἷμα, a Hebraistic periphrasis
for *human nature, a human being*; hence (b) the substance (material) of the body, *the body* : μία σάρξ, *one
body*, of husband and wife : it is contrasted sometimes with πνεῦμα, sometimes with ψυχή; (c) (Hebraistic) *mankind, humanity* as such, without any
necessary connotation of frailty, e. g. Rom. iii 20,
1 Cor. i 29, Gal. ii 16; (d) *the animal (sensuous) nature*
of man, the sphere of present existence, e. g. John
i 13, Rom. ix 3, 1 Cor. x 18, Heb. xii 9; (e) in reference to fleshly (physical) weakness, helplessness,
1 Cor. xv 50 (corruptible), 2 Cor. iv 11 (mortal), vii 5,
x 3, Eph. vi 12; intellectual weakness, Rom. vi 19,
Gal. i 16, Col. ii 18; cf. also 2 Cor. xi 18, Gal. vi 12,
13, Phil. iii 3, 4 *bis*; (f) in an ethical sense, characteristic of Paul, applied to part of human nature,
generally as ruling instead of being, as it ought to be,
in subjection; the two aspects are : (1) a general relation is implied between *the flesh* and sin, Rom. vii 5,
viii 3–9, 12, 13, 2 Cor. x 2, Gal. iv 29, Col. ii 11, 13;
(2) *the flesh* is in some sense active in the production
of evil, its desires (or lusts) are evil; in the physical
nature it is the immediate enemy of the higher life,
e. g. Rom. vii 7–25, viii 12, xiii 14, Gal. v 13, 16, 17,
19, 24, Eph. ii 3 *bis*, Col. ii 23.

σαρόω, *I sweep.*

Σάρρα (Hebr.), *Sarah*, wife of Abraham.

Σαρών, *Sharon*, the maritime plain between Carmel and
Joppa.

σατανᾶς (Aramaic, lit. *adversary*), both with and without
the article, a representation of the word which is
also translated ὁ διάβολος, *the enemy, Satan, the devil*,
the chief of the evil spirits.

σάτον (Aramaic), a large measure equivalent to 1½
modii, that is, nearly three English gallons.

Σαῦλος, the grecized form of the Hebrew name Σαούλ of
the Apostle to the Gentiles.

σβέννυμι, ζβέννυμι, *I extinguish, put out*: met. 1 Thess. v 19.

σεαυτοῦ, *of thyself (yourself)*.

σεβάζομαι, *I reverence, worship*.

σέβασμα, *an object of worship, a thing worshipped*.

Σεβαστός (official Greek equivalent of Augustus), *Augustus*, the name meaning 'worthy to be reverenced (worshipped)', given to Octavian by the Senate in Jan. 27 B.C., and retained by most of his successors, e. g. by Nero, to whom it refers in Ac. xxv 21, 25, where it is of course used by non-Christians: in Ac. xxvii 1 σπεῖρα Σεβαστή is the official equivalent of a *cohors Augusta* (a *cohors I Augusta* had its headquarters in Batanaea in NE. Palestine).

σέβομαι, *I reverence, worship*: generally in Ac. of godfearing, uncircumcised Gentiles who joined the Jewish synagogues (contrast Ac. xiii 43).

σειρός (properly *a pit, excavation* for the storage of grain), *a pit*: v. l. σειρά, *a chain, fetter*.

σεισμός (terrae motus), *an earthquake*.

σείω, *I shake*.

Σέκουνδος (Latin), *Secundus*, a Christian of Thessalonica.

Σελεύκεια, *Seleucia*, on the Syrian coast, the harbour of Syrian Antioch.

σελήνη, *the moon*.

σεληνιάζω, *I bring under the influence of the moon*: pass. *I am epileptic* (the state of an epileptic being attributed to the moon [σελήνη]).

Σεμεείν (Hebr.), *Semein*, an ancestor of Jesus.

σεμίδαλις, *the finest wheaten meal*.

σεμνός (grauis), *grave, worthy of respect*.

σεμνότης (grauitas), *gravity, dignified behaviour*.

Σέργιος, *Sergius*, the middle (gentile) name of the proconsul of Cyprus.

Σερούχ (Hebr.), *Seruch*, an ancestor of Jesus.

Σήθ (Hebr.), *Seth*, third son of Adam.

Σήμ (Hebr.), *Shem*, a son of Noah.

σημαίνω (a technical term for the speech of a communicator of an oracle), *I indicate by a word*; *I point out in a letter* (*by letter*), Ac. xxv 27.

σημεῖον (signum), *a sign, an outward* (*visible*) *indication* of secret power or truth; *a miracle* regarded from that point of view.

σημειόομαι, *I mark* (*notify*) *for myself*; hence, with an idea of disapprobation added.

σήμερον (hodie), adv. *to-day, this day*: ἡ σήμερον (sc. ἡμέρα, *cf.* hodiernus dies), noun, *to-day, this day*.

σήπω, tr. *I cause to rot*: 2 perf. σέσηπα, *I have rotted, I am rotten.*

σής, *a moth.*

σητόβρωτος, *moth-eaten.*

σθενόω, *I strengthen.*

σιαγών, *a cheek.*

σιγάω, *I am silent.*

σιγή, *silence.*

σιδήρεος, *made of iron.*

σίδηρος, *iron.*

Σιδών, *Sidon,* a great coast city of Phoenicia: in Mk. vii 31 perhaps an error for *Saidan* = Bethsaida.

Σιδώνιος, *belonging to Sidon, Sidonian*; hence, as subst., *a Sidonian*: ἡ Σιδωνία (sc. χώρα), *the region* or *territory of Sidon,* Lk. iv 26.

σικάριος (Latin, from *sica,* a stiletto), *an assassin, a murderer*; with reference to a fanatical Jewish political faction, accustomed to assassinate their opponents.

σίκερα (Aramaic), *an intoxicating drink, a strong fruit-wine.*

Σίλας (Western documents spell Σιλέας), *Silas,* a Jewish prophet and evangelist, a Roman citizen and a helper of St. Paul. The name is generally regarded as a pet-form (used in Ac. only) of Σιλουανός, and Silas is in consequence identified with him.

Σιλουανός (Latin, Siluanus) *Silvanus*: see Σίλας.

Σιλωάμ, *Siloam, Shiloah,* a spring (the only spring) within the walls, in the SE. corner of Jerusalem.

The name is Aramaic and really a substantive (= *discharge* or *gushing forth* of water).

σιμικίνθιον (Latin, semicinctium), *an* artisan's working-*apron*.

Σίμων (see also **Συμεών**), *Simon*, (a) the Apostle, son of Jonas (John) and brother of Andrew; (b) the Cananaean (former Zealot), one of the disciples; (c) a brother of Jesus; (d) a Pharisee, a former leper, at Bethany; (e) a native of Cyrene, Mk. xv 21, Mt. xxvii 32, Lk. xxiii 26; (f) father of Judas Iscariot; (g) Simon Magus, a sorcerer in Samaria; (h) a tanner at Joppa.

Σινά, *Sinai*, a mountain in Arabia: according to Hebrew allegorical methods of interpretation identified with Hagar, concubine of Abraham, Gal. iv 25 (Arabic *hadjar* = *rock, stone,* and thus comes the equation Hagar = Sinai).

σίναπι, *mustard*.

σινδών (Semitic), *a fine light dress* worn over the under-clothing, or *a nightgown*, or *a sheet* hastily seized, Mk. xiv 51 : of the grave-clothes of Jesus, probably *a piece of unused linen,* Mk. xv 46, &c.

σινιάζω, *I sift, winnow*.

σιρικός (an inexact spelling of *σηρικός*, adj. formed from **Σῆρες**, *the Chinese*, from whose country silk was obtained), *silken* ; *silk fabrics* (or *garments*).

σιρός, see **σειρός**.

σιτευτός (altilis), *fed up* (with grain), *fattened*.

σιτίον, *food made of corn, bread*.

σιτιστός, the same in meaning as the much commoner **σιτευτός**.

σιτομέτριον, *measure of corn, portion of corn, allowance of corn*.

σῖτος, *corn*.

Σιών, *Sion, Zion*, the mountain on which the Davidic citadel of Jerusalem was built, and thus the centre of the life of the people Israel.

σιωπάω, *I keep silence, I am silent*.

σκανδαλίζω (a Hebraistic, Biblical word), *I put a stum-*

σκάνδαλον

bling-block *in the way of, I cause to stumble, I set a trap for* (in the moral sphere).

σκάνδαλον (offendiculum) (a Hebraistic, biblical word), *stumbling, cause of stumbling* (in the moral sphere); πέτρα σκανδάλου (Isa. viii 14), *the native rock* rising up through the earth, *which trips up* the traveller, hence, of Jesus the Messiah, to the Jews who refused him: *some person* (Mt. xiii 41, xvi 23) or *thing which leads one to sin.*

σκάπτω, *I dig.*

σκάφη, *a small boat,* towed behind.

σκέλος, *a leg.*

σκέπασμα, strictly *roofing, shelter,* but with special reference to *clothing.*

Σκευᾶς, *Sceva,* an inhabitant of Ephesus.

σκευή (a collective noun), *tackle.*

σκεῦος, (a) (uas) *a vessel,* generally of earthenware, e. g. John xix 29; τὰ σκεύη, *utensils, goods and chattels, effects, property*; (b) (Hebraistic) met. of persons, e. g. of St. Paul as chosen *repository* of the power of Jesus, Ac. ix 15: either of one's own body as the case enclosing the soul, or of one's wife, 1 Thess. iv 4 (cf. 1 Pet. iii 7); (c) *tackle, furniture* of a ship, Ac. xxvii 17.

σκηνή, *a tent; a hut;* usually with reference to the temporary abode of Yahweh, which preceded the Temple; ἡ σκηνὴ τοῦ μαρτυρίου, *the tent as a witness to the covenant between God and His people*: in Heb. ix the two parts of the one σκηνή, separated from one another by the curtain, are each called σκηνή.

σκηνοπηγία, sometimes called ἑορτὴ [τῶν] σκηνῶν or ἑορτὴ [τῆς] σκηνοπηγίας, *the Feast of Tabernacles* (lit. *of booth-building*), the great festival of the Jews, held in October, originally the Feast of Ingathering.

σκηνοποιός, *a tentmaker.*

σκῆνος, *a tent*: so met. (used in Pythagorean philosophy) of the body as the temporary dwelling-place of the soul.

σκηνόω, *I dwell as in a tent, I encamp*.

σκήνωμα, *a tent*, really a humble word for the permanent building aimed at, Aç. vii 46 : of the body as the temporary abode of the soul.

σκιά, *a shadow, darkness, shade* : contrasted with the body casting the shadow, and used met. somewhat like *a pale reflexion*, Col. ii 17, Heb. viii 5, x 1.

σκιρτάω, *I leap, bound, jump*.

σκληροκαρδία (Hebraistic, from σκληρός and καρδία, as the seat of the will), *stiffness, stubbornness, unyielding-ness, obduracy*.

σκληρός (properly *hard*), (a) *strong*, James iii 4 ; (b) met. *harsh, rough* ; almost = *dangerous*, Ac. xxvi 14.

σκληρότης, *obstinacy*.

σκληροτράχηλος, *stiff-necked, stubborn*.

σκληρύνω, *I make unyielding*.

σκολιός, *crooked* : hence met. *perverse*, of turning off from the truth, *crooked* in nature.

σκόλοψ, originally *a stake* ; but commonly in N.T. times *a thorn* ; *a splinter* : met. referring to some physical trouble.

σκοπέω, *I look upon, I gaze upon, watch*.

σκοπός, *a mark* to be aimed at (e. g. by an archer).

σκορπίζω, *I scatter*.

σκορπίος, *a scorpion*.

σκοτεινός, *dark*.

σκοτία, *darkness* : hence met. of ignorance and sin.

σκοτίζω, *I darken*, especially of an eclipse of the sun, cf. Lk. xxiii 45 (v. l.) : met. of blindness, Rom. xi 10, ignorance, Rom. i 21.

σκότος, *darkness* : frequent in the conceptions of Jewish eschatology, Mt. viii 12, xxii 13, xxv 30 : met. of *the darkness* of ignorance and sin, Lk. i 79, John iii 19, &c.

σκοτόω, *I darken*, lit. or met.

σκύβαλον, *sweepings, refuse*, especially *dirt, dung* (popularly used of the human skeleton).

Σκύθης, *a Scythian,* an uncivilized inhabitant of NE. Europe.

σκυθρωπός, *with downcast countenance; sad-faced; gloomy.*

σκύλλω (originally, *I flay, skin*), (a) *I tire out by hunting; I distress,* Mt. ix 36; (b) (a slang usage in origin) *I worry, trouble.*

σκῦλον : plur. (spolia), *armour.*

σκωληκόβρωτος, *eaten by worms* (the word *scolex* is still used for the tape-worm at one stage of its growth).

σμαράγδινος (ζμαράγδινος), *of an emerald.*

σμάραγδος (ζμάραγδος), *an emerald.*

σμύρνα (= μύρρα), *myrrh,* a fragrant gum-resin from the Arabian Balsamodendron Myrrhae.

Σμύρνα (better spelling **Ζμύρνα**), *Smyrna,* a great port of the Roman province Asia.

σμυρνίζω, *I spice with myrrh.*

Σόδομα, *Sodom,* a city submerged by the Dead Sea.

Σολομών (oldest form Σαλωμών, next oldest Σαλομών), *Solomon,* son of David, King of Israel, and Bathsheba.

σορός, *a bier.*

σός, *thy, thine, your.*

σουδάριον (Latin, borrowed by Greek, and thence by Aramaic), *a handkerchief.*

Σουσάννα, *Susannah,* a woman of the retinue of Jesus.

σοφία, *wisdom,* the highest intellectual gift, of comprehensive insight into the ways and purposes of God; sometimes, e. g. Ac. vi 3, 1 Cor. vi 5, James i 5, (prudentia) *practical wisdom,* that endowment of heart and mind which is needed for the right conduct of life.

σοφίζω, *I make wise :* σεσοφισμένος, *fictitious,* 2 Pet. i 16.

σοφός, *wise :* (Hebraism) *skilled, an expert, a man of learning,* Mt. xi 25, 1 Cor. iii 10, &c.

Σπανία (Latin = Hispania), *Spain,* roughly co-extensive with the modern country of the name.

σπάομαι, *I draw my* (sword).

σπαράσσω, *I throw* on the ground.

σπαργανόω, *I swathe*.

σπαταλάω, *I am a voluptuary, I am wanton*.

σπάω, see σπάομαι.

σπεῖρα, *a cohort*, that is about 600 infantry, under the command of a tribune.

σπείρω, *I sow*, lit. or met.

σπεκουλάτωρ (Latin), *a scout; a courier:* also *an executioner*.

σπένδω, *I pour out* an offering of wine to a god : hence pass. met. of the *outpouring* of one's life blood in service and suffering.

σπέρμα (semen), (a) *seed*, commonly of cereals ; (b) *offspring, descendants*, in the animal kingdom (frequent in Hebrew).

σπερμολόγος (from σπέρμα and λέγω : a slang term in Ac.), used properly of a bird *picking up seeds* ; hence *a parasite, hanger on*: also of one who *picks up scraps* of information and retails them at secondhand, *an ignorant plagiarist*.

σπεύδω, *I hasten, hurry*.

σπήλαιον, *a cave* (especially as inhabited).

σπιλάς, adjectivally used with ἄνεμος understood, *a dirty, foul* (lit.), *miry wind*, perhaps of its effect on the water.

σπίλος, *a spot* of disfigurement.

σπιλόω, *I stain*, lit. or met.

σπλαγχνίζομαι (Hebraism), *I am filled with tenderness*.

σπλάγχνον (by-form σπλάγχνα [fem.] in Phil. ii 1, if text be genuine), usually plur. σπλάγχνα, *the nobler viscera*, heart, &c., and especially, Hebraistically, as the seat of certain feelings, or from the observed effect of emotion on them, *compassion* and *pity*.

σπόγγος, *a sponge*.

σποδός, *ashes*.

σπορά, quasi-collective, *seed*.

σπόριμος, *sown* : hence τὰ σπόριμα, *the crops*.

σπόρος, *seed*.

σπουδάζω, *I hasten ; I am eager (zealous)*.

σπουδαῖος, *eager, zealous; earnest.*

σπουδαίως, *eagerly, zealously; earnestly.*

σπουδή (characteristically in connexion with religion), *haste; eagerness, zeal; carefulness, care, anxiety; diligence, earnestness.*

σπυρίς, see σφυρίς.

στάδιος, στάδιον, *a stade,* a measurement of distance about twelve yards short of a furlong, or about 180–200 metres.

στάμνος, *an earthenware pot (jar).*

στασιαστής, *a revolutionary.*

στάσις, (a) *faction, sedition, discord; disturbance, upheaval, revolution, riot;* (b) in the more original but much rarer meaning, *standing, position, place,* Heb. ix 8.

στατήρ, *a stater,* that is four drachmae (which see), temple-tax for two persons.

σταυρός, *a cross* (crux), strictly the transverse beam (patibulum), which was placed at the top of the vertical part, thus forming a capital **T**. It was this transverse beam that was carried by the criminal: *the crucifixion* of Jesus.

σταυρόω, *I crucify*: hence met. Gal. vi 14.

σταφυλή, *a grape.*

στάχυς, *an ear (spike) of corn.*

Στάχυς, a Christian man at Rome.

στέγη (originally poetical), *a roof;* in Mk. ii 4 perhaps of thatch.

στέγω, (a) *I roof over, cover*: hence, *I conceal, hide,* but not in N.T.; (b) *I keep out* (weather): hence, *I keep close, put up with, endure patiently, bear up under.*

στεῖρα, *a barren (childless) woman.*

στέλλω (originally, *I set, place*: hence, *I bring together, make compact;* then, *I restrain, check*), mid. *I draw (shrink) back* from anything.

στέμμα (from στέφω, *I wreathe*), *a garland.*

στεναγμός, *a groan.*

στενάζω, *I groan.*

στενός, *narrow*.

στενοχωρέω (στενός and χῶρος, cf. English colloquial, *I keep some* one *in a tight place*), *I press upon, cramp, restrain*.

στενοχωρία (lit. *confinement in a narrow space*), *restriction, restraint; anguish, great trouble*.

στερεός, *solid; firm*, lit. or met.

στερεόω, *I make firm*, or *solid*: met., Ac. xvi 5.

στερέωμα (probably a military metaphor), *firm foundation, bulwark*.

Στεφανᾶς (a pet form of Στεφανηφόρος), *Stephanas*, a Corinthian Christian.

Στέφανος, *Stephen*, one of the seven original 'deacons' at Jerusalem, and the first martyr.

στέφανος, *a garland, wreath, chaplet, crown*, generally as the Greek victor's crown or chaplet, of perishable leaves (1 Cor. ix 25), won in athletic and other contests, and familiar to the Jews for generations: ὁ στέφανος τῆς ζωῆς (James i 12, Rev. ii 10), *the crown (reward), which is life*.

στεφανόω, *I wreathe, crown* as victor, 2 Tim. ii 5, hence met.

στῆθος, *the breast*.

στήκω (form arising from the need for an active form present in the intransitive sense, cf. ἵστημι) *I stand; I remain standing, stand firm*, lit. or met.

στηριγμός, *support*.

στηρίζω, (a) *I fix firmly*, Lk. xvi 26; τὸ πρόσωπον (Hebraism) *I direct myself* towards, *I have my face turned stedfastly*, Lk. ix 51; (b) generally met. *I buttress, prop, support; I strengthen, establish*.

στιβάς, *a wisp (bundle)* of brushwood, twigs or other light growth.

στίγμα, properly, *a brand* burned into, or *the mark* of a cut made in, the skin of a slave; in Gal. vi 17 τὰ στίγματα are the *marks* or *scars*, due to the lictor's rods at Pisidian Antioch and the stones at Lystra, *marking* Paul as the slave of Jesus.

241   R

στιγμή

στιγμή (lit. *a pricking*), *an instant, a moment*.

στίλβω, *I gleam, flash*.

στοά, *a portico, colonnade, porch* : that ' of Solomon ' was on the East side of the Temple.

Στοϊκός, see Στωϊκός.

στοιχεῖον (elementum), (a) plur. *the heavenly bodies*, 2 Pet. iii 10, 12 ; (b) *a rudiment, an element, a rudimentary principle, an elementary rule* ; but in Gal. iv 3 there is much to be said for taking the word in the sense of *spirit, demon* (possibly also in (a)).

στοιχέω, *I walk* (properly, in a straight line, in rank).

στολή, *a long robe*, worn by the upper classes in the East.

στόμα, *the mouth*, especially as an organ of speech in man and God : the sword has a mouth (*edge*), because it *drinks* blood, Lk. xxi 24, Heb. xi 34 : στόμα πρὸς στόμα (cf. πρόσωπον πρὸς πρόσωπον), *by word of mouth*, practically, *face to face*.

στόμαχος, *the stomach*.

στρατεία, *military service*, used met.

στράτευμα, *an army, a body of soldiers*.

στρατεύομαι, *I serve in the army, I am in the army, I am a soldier* (whether on active service or not) : hence met. *I make war, I take up war*, e. g. 1 Pet. ii 11.

στρατηγός (praetor), (a) in Jerusalem, ὁ στρατηγὸς τοῦ ἱεροῦ, *the commandant of the temple*, a priest, next in rank to the high-priest, and commander of the priests and Levites who guarded the temple, Ac. iv 1, v 24, 26 : under him were the στρατηγοί, *captains* of the temple-guards, Lk. xxii [4,] 52 ; (b) at Philippi, a Roman ' colonia ', *a praetor* or *a duumvir, a chief-magistrate* of the ' colonia ', Ac. xvi (there were probably two of them).

στρατιά, *an army*.

στρατιώτης, *a soldier* : hence (perhaps under the influence of the language of the Mysteries and that of philosophy), the worshipper as *the soldier* of his God, cf. 2 Tim. ii 3.

στρατολογέω, tr., *I enrol in the army.*

στρατοπεδάρχης (probably, princeps peregrinorum), *the chief of the camp, the commander of the corps* connected with the commissariat, custody of prisoners, &c., which was on detached duty.

στρατόπεδον, *a camp.*

στρεβλόω, (lit. *I twist, warp, stretch on the rack,* hence met.) *I twist, strain.*

στρέφω, tr. *I turn* ; hence, *I bring back* (?), Mt. xxvii 3 ; *I change,* Rev. xi 6 ; act. intr. Ac. vii 42 : mid. and pass. intr. *I turn,* also met. *I change.*

στρηνιάω, *I am wanton, I wanton.*

στρῆνος, *wantonness, luxury.*

στρουθίον, *a sparrow,* the cheapest of all birds for food.

στρώννυμι, στρωννύω (sterno), *I spread out, strew* ; in Mk. xiv 15, Lk. xxii 12 of the dining couches with the cushions ready for diners, cf. Ac. ix 34 of *making* one's *bed.*

στυγητός, *hated, hateful.*

στυγνάζω, (a) *I am sad,* Mk. x 22 ; (b) *I am dull* (*overcast*), Mt. xvi 3.

στύλος, *a pillar* for supporting an entablature or other structure ; hence metaph.

Στωϊκός (from στοιά, στοά, because of the original place of meeting), *a Stoic,* a member of one of the two leading schools of philosophy.

σύ, *thou, you*: τί ἡμῖν (ἐμοὶ) καὶ σοί; Mt. viii 29, &c., *what have we* (*I*) *to do with you?* but in John ii 4 it is probable that we ought to translate, *what have you and I to do with it? what concern is it of ours? never mind!* note the order ἡμῖν καὶ ὑμῖν (Mt. xxv 9), as in Latin : for καθ' ὑμᾶς, see **κατά**.

συγγένεια, collective, *all the* συγγενεῖς, *kindred, kin, relations.*

συγγενεύς, *a relation, relative* (v. l.).

συγγενής, *a relation, relative, kinsman* : in Rom. ix 3 the term is wide enough to include all Hebrews : in Rom. xvi 7, 11, 21 the reference may be narrower, to

συγγενίς

fellow-members of the same (Jewish) tribe (φυλή) in the city of Tarsus.

συγγενίς, *a kinswoman.*

συγγνώμη, see συνγνώμη.

συγκ., see συνκ. (a more correct spelling).

συγκυρία, *coincidence, chance.*

συγχ., see συνχ. (a more correct spelling).

σύγχυσις, *confusion, disturbance.*

συζ., see συνζ.

συκάμινος (a Semitic word), *the black mulberry tree.*

συκῆ, *a fig tree.*

συκομορέα, *a sycamore tree.*

σῦκον, *a fig.*

συκοφαντέω (calumnior), *I accuse falsely.*

συλαγωγέω, *I take away from as booty (plunder), I rob.*

συλάω, *I rob.*

συλλ., see συνλ.

συλλαμβάνω (συνλ-), (a) (conprehendo) act. and mid., *I arrest, catch, capture*: (b) *I conceive* (a child), cf. met. James i 15; (c) mid. *I lend a hand to, I help,* Lk. v 7, Phil. iv 3.

συλλέγω, *I collect, gather together.*

συλλογίζομαι, *I reason together* with others.

συμβ., see συνβ.

συμβαίνω, with neut. subject or impersonally, *I happen, occur: it happens.*

συμβουλεύω, .act. *I advise*: mid. συμβουλευόμεθα, *we counsel one another.*

συμβούλιον (consilium), (a) *a body of advisers (assessors)* in a court, *a council,* Ac. xxv 12; (b) abstr., *consultation, counsel, advice*; *resolution, decree*: διδόναι (Aramaism) Mk. iii 6.

σύμβουλος, *an adviser.*

Συμεών, *Symeon,* (a) the patriarch, son of Jacob and founder of a tribe, Rev. vii 7; (b) an ancestor of Jesus, Lk. iii 30; (c) an inhabitant of Jerusalem, who blessed the babe Jesus, Lk. ii 25, 34; (d) an Antiochian Christian, also called Niger, Ac. xiii 1;

(e) a form of the Hebrew name of Peter the Apostle, Ac. xv 14, 2 Pet. i 1 (v.l.).

συμμ., see **συνμ.**

συμμορφίζω (συνμ.), lit. *I cause to share the form* (see **μορφή**) *of another*, hence in Phil. iii 10 συνμορφιζόμενος = *being made to share the experience of.*

σύμμορφος, *sharing the form* of another.

συμπ., see **συνπ.**

συμπαθής, *sharing the experiences* of others.

συμπόσιον, properly *a drinking bout*, following dinner: συμπόσια συμπόσια (colloquial), *in companies of diners.*

συμφ., see **συνφ.**

συμφέρω, (a) tr. *I collect, bring together*, Ac. xix. 19; (b) intr. and generally impersonal, συμφέρει, *it is an advantage, it is expedient (beneficial)*; συμφέρον (sc. ἐστιν), 2 Cor. xii 1 = συμφέρει; τὸ συμφέρον, as substantive.

σύμφορος, *advantageous*: τὸ σύμφορον, as substantive.

συμφυλέτης, *a fellow tribesman, one of the same tribe*, doubtless with reference to Jews in Thessalonica, all enrolled in one city-tribe.

σύμφυτος, *grown along with, vitally one with, united with.*

συμφωνέω, (first of a harmony of voices, then) *I harmonize with, I agree with*; of more than one, *we agree together*: pass. impers. *it is agreed upon among* (possibly a Latinism, conuenit inter), Ac. v 9.

συμφώνησις, *harmony, agreement.*

συμφωνία, *bagpipes* (cf. Dan. iii 5), but perhaps *music, symphony.*

σύμφωνος, *agreeing*: ἐκ συμφώνου, *by agreement.*

συμψηφίζω, *I calculate together, I reckon up.*

σύμψυχος, see **σύνψυχος.**

σύν, *with* (Greek allows either the sense *plus* or the sense *including*).

συνάγω, *I gather together, collect, assemble*, persons or things: συναγαγὼν πάντα implies the converting of the goods into money, *having sold all off*, Lk. xv 13.

συναγωγή (in origin abstract, *a leading* [*bringing*] *together*, *convening* an assembly, then concrete, *a* [*religious*] *meeting*), *a meeting* (*assembly*), *a place of meeting* (*assembly*), particularly of Jews for the reading of scripture and for worship, *a synagogue*.   In certain passages it is doubtful whether the congregation (e.g. John vi 59, xviii 20) or the place of meeting (e.g. James ii 2) is particularly intended, but the sense is not seriously affected by the doubt.   In the O.T. *συναγωγή* and *ἐκκλησία* are practically synonymous, but in ordinary Christian writings the former is rarely used, and seemingly only of communities of Jews or Jewish Christians (e.g. James ii 2, where it is probably the building).

συναγωνίζομαι, *I struggle* (*contend*) *in company with*.

συναθλέω, *I compete together with* others, originally of athletic contests, and then met.

συναθροίζω, tr. *I gather together, assemble*.

συναίρω ; with *λόγον*, *I compare* (*settle*) *accounts, make a reckoning*.

συναιχμάλωτος, *a fellow-captive, a fellow-prisoner, a companion in chains*.

συνακολουθέω, *I accompany*.

συναλίζομαι (from *σύν* and *ἅλς*, 'salt'), *I have table fellowship with, I share a common meal with*. (Others take as *συναλίζομαι* (from *σύν* and *ἁλής*, 'crowded'), *I meet with*, from time to time.)

συναλλάσσω, *I attempt* (seek) *to reconcile*.

συναναβαίνω, *I go up with*.

συνανάκειμαι, *I recline at* (dinner-) *table with*.

συναναμίγνυμι, mid. *I associate intimately with*.

συναναπαύομαι, *I rest along with*.

συναντάω, *I meet, encounter*: in Ac. xx 22, with inanimate subject.

συναντιλαμβάνομαι, *I lend a hand along with, I take interest in* (a thing) *along with* (others), *I assist jointly* to perform some task, *I co-operate with, I take my share in*.

συναπάγω, *I lead away with, I carry along with* (in good or bad sense according to context) : mid. c. dat., *I condescend to,* Rom. xii 16.

συναποθνήσκω, *I die along with, I die together* (with others).

συναπόλλυμαι, *I perish along with.*

συναποστέλλω, *I send away in some one's company.*

συναρμολογέω (an architectural term, ἁρμός meaning 'the side of a stone', and -λογεῖν added by analogy with λιθολόγος without its proper force), *I fit together* (by means of all the elaborate preparatory processes necessary).

συναρπάζω, *I keep a firm grip of.*

συναυξάνω, *I make to increase (grow) together.*

συνβάλλω, (a) with λόγους expressed or understood, *I engage in discussion with,* Lk. xi 53 (v.l.), Ac. iv 15, xvii 18 ; (b) *I reflect, ponder,* Lk. ii 19 ; (c) *I meet with, I fall in with,* Ac. xx 14 ; in hostile sense, *I enter into conflict with, attack,* Lk. xiv 31 ; (d) mid. *I contribute to, benefit.*

συνβασιλεύω, *I reign along with (together with)* another, *I am a king with,* in met. sense.

συνβιβάζω, (a) *I bring together, join, unite,* Eph. iv 16, Col. ii 19 ; (b) *I put together, compare, examine closely,* hence *I consider, conclude,* Ac. xvi 10 ; *I deduce, prove,* Ac. ix 22 ; (c) (a Biblical sense, translation Greek) *I teach, instruct,* Ac. xix 33 (v.l.), 1 Cor. ii 16, Col. ii 2.

συγγνώμη, *indulgence, allowance* for circumstances.

σύνδεσμος, *a binding together, a means of holding together, a bond,* lit. and met. : in Ac. viii 23 the man is *in* (εἰς = ἐν) the grip of ἀδικία.

συνδέω, *I bind along with another* : συνδεδεμένοι, *fellow-captives.*

συνδοξάζω, *I glorify along with.*

σύνδουλος, *a fellow-slave,* either of an earthly master, or of the glorified Lord.

συνδρομή, *a running together, a tumultuous concourse.*

συνεγείρω

συνεγείρω, *I raise along with* the Messiah (from the dead, or from a dead spiritual state).

συνέδριον, *a council* of leading Jews, Mk. xiii 9, Mt. x 17, but elsewhere *the Jewish council at Jerusalem, the Sanhedrin* (Aramaic form of συνέδριον), *the High Court, the Senate,* composed of 71 members comprising members of high-priestly families, Pharisees learned in the law, and a lay element of Elders.

συνείδησις, (originally *consciousness,* e.g. 1 Pet. ii 19, where θεοῦ is objective genitive, but through the influence of the Stoic terminology) *conscience,* the innate power to discern what is good, an abiding consciousness bearing witness concerning a man's conduct.

συνεῖδον, *I perceived, I was aware of, I saw distinctly, I realized*: for the etymologically related σύνοιδα, see s.v.

σύνειμι, *I go with, I accompany,* Lk. viii 4.

σύνειμι, *I am with, I am in company with, I company with.*

συνεισέρχομαι, *I go in with, I enter with.*

συνέκδημος, *a travelling-companion.*

συνεκλεκτός, *fellow-chosen, fellow-elect,* understand ἐκκλησία.

συνεπιμαρτυρέω, *I add my testimony to that already given.*

συνεπιτίθεμαι (lit. *I join in attacking*), *I join in the charge.*

συνέπομαι, *I accompany.*

συνεργέω, *I work along with, I co-operate with.*

συνεργός, *a fellow-worker.*

συνέρχομαι, *I go along with, I accompany*; *I come (meet) together* with others, αὐτῷ in Mk. xiv 53 being = πρὸς αὐτόν: (conuenio) *I have sexual intercourse,* Mt. i 18.

συνεσθίω, *I eat in company with.*

σύνεσις, *practical discernment, intelligence, understanding.*

συνετός (lit. *one who can put things together,* from συνίημι), *intelligent*; in Mt. xi 25, Lk. x 21 it doubtless refers to Pharisees learned in the law.

248

συνευδοκέω, *I entirely approve of.*

συνευωχέομαι, *I feast along with.*

συνεφίστημι : 2 aor. intr. (*the multitude*) *rose up together, set upon together.*

συνέχω, (a) *I hold together*, hence *I restrain* ; *I close*, Ac. vii 57 ; *I press from every side*, Lk. viii 45, xix 43; (b) *I hold seized, I have in charge*, Lk. xxii 63, so pass. met. *I am pressed*, Ac. xviii 5 : esp. in pass. with datives, *I am seized* (*by*), *I am afflicted* (*by*), *I am suffering* (*from*), e. g. Mt. iv 24, Lk. viii 37 : *I urge, impel, compel*, Lk. xii 50, 2 Cor. v 14, Phil. i 23.

συνζάω, *I live along with* (*in company with*).

συνζεύγνυμι, *I yoke* (*harness*) *together, join.*

συνζητέω (lit. *I seek in company*), *I discuss, debate, dispute.*

συνζήτησις, *discussion, debate.*

συνζητητής, *a discusser, debater.*

σύνζυγος, *yoke-fellow, companion, colleague* (perhaps a proper name).

συνζωοποιέω, *I make living along with.*

συνήδομαι, *I delight in.*

συνήθεια, *custom, habit* : c. gen. *habituation to, intercourse with, familiarity with*, 1 Cor. viii 7.

συνηλικιώτης, *a contemporary.*

συνθάπτω, *I bury along with.*

συνθλάω, *I break in pieces, break completely.*

συνθλίβω, *I press closely upon, hustle.*

συνθρύπτω (lit. *I crush to pieces*), *I weaken thoroughly, unman.*

συνίημι, *I understand* ; *I have understanding.*

συνίστημι, συνιστάνω, (a) in transitive tenses, (1) *I recommend, commend, introduce*, Rom. xvi 1, 2 Cor. iii 1, iv 2, v 12, vi 4, x 12, 18, xii 11 ; (2) *I show, prove*, Rom. iii 5, v 8, 2 Cor. vii 11, Gal. ii 18 ; (b) in intransitive tenses, (1) *I stand with* (*by*), Lk. ix 32 ; (2) *I consist, I am held together*, Col. i 17, 2 Pet. iii 5.

συνκάθημαι, *I am sitting* (*seated*) *with* : in Ac. xxvi 30, perhaps to be compared with English *assessor.*

συνκαθίζω, (a) tr. *I cause to sit along with*; (b) intr. *I sit in company (together).*

συνκακοπαθέω, *I am ill treated along with, I take my share of suffering* (in 2 Tim. i 8 the dat. is not governed by συν, but = *for the benefit of*).

συνκακουχέω, *I treat evilly (with hardship) along with.*

συνκαλέω, *I call together, invite, summon*; mid. *I call together to myself.*

συνκαλύπτω, *I veil (cover) completely.*

συνκάμπτω, *I bend low, I cause to stoop low.*

συνκαταβαίνω, *I come down along with (together).*

συνκατάθεσις, *agreement, union.*

συνκατανεύω, *I join in agreeing.*

συνκατατίθεμαι, *I agree with.*

συνκαταψηφίζω, *I number (reckon) along with.*

συνκεράννυμι, (a) *I mix together, compound*, 1 Cor. xii 24 ; (b) pass. with dat. of instrument (πίστει), *I agree with*, Heb. iv 2 (reading acc. plur.).

συνκινέω, *I stir violently.*

συνκλείω, *I shut together*; *I enclose, I shut in on all sides,* e. g. Rom. xi 32.

συνκληρονόμος, *a joint heir, a fellow heir.*

συνκοινωνέω, *I have partnership in, I share in* (with others).

συνκοινωνός, *a fellow sharer* (in), *a joint partaker* (of).

συνκομίζω, *I carry (convey) together,* i. e. to burial; or *I take up* for burial; hence *I bury* (cf. effero) : perhaps, however, *I get back, recover* (the συν- expressing the collecting of the mangled remains).

συνκρίνω, *I compare.*

συνκύπτω, *I am bent double, bent in two, bowed down.*

συνλαλέω, *I speak together* (with).

συνλυπέομαι, *I am greatly pained (grieved).*

συνμαθητής, *a fellow disciple, a fellow scholar.*

συνμαρτυρέω, *I join in giving evidence (bearing witness)* with.

συνμερίζω, *I cause to share with* (in the sacrifices).

συνμέτοχος, *a fellow sharer, a partner.*

συνμιμητής, *a joint imitator, an imitator along* (*together*) *with* others.

συνοδεύω, *I journey* (*travel*) *along with.*

συνοδία, *a travelling company, caravan.*

σύνοιδα (conscius sum), *I share knowledge with* another, *I am privy to* anything. In fact the word especially implies consciousness of *guilt*, e.g. 1 Cor. iv 4.

συνοικέω, *I cohabit with, live in wedlock with.*

συνοικοδομέω, met. *I build together.*

συνομιλέω, *I talk with.*

συνομορέω, *I am contiguous with, I am next door to.*

συνοχή (lit. *compression*; then *narrowness*), met. *anxiety.*

συνπαθέω, *I suffer along with.*

συνπαραγίνομαι, *I arrive along with.*

συνπαρακαλέω, *I cheer* (*encourage*) *along with.*

συνπαραλαμβάνω, *I take along with me* (as helper).

συνπάρειμι, *I am present* (*here*) *along with.*

συνπάσχω, *I suffer together.*

συνπέμπω, *I send along with.*

συνπεριλαμβάνω, *I embrace closely.*

συνπίνω, *I drink* (wine) *along with.*

συνπίπτω, *I fall together, I fall in, I collapse.*

συνπληρόω, (a) *I fill up*, hence pass., by an idiom analogous to English, συνεπληροῦντο, Lk. viii 23, *they were filling up* (where it was really the ship that was filling up); (b) (Hebraistic) *I complete*, of the coming to an end of an interval of days before some event (in Ac. ii 1 the day of the event may be partly included).

συνπνίγω, met. *I choke utterly*: in Lk. viii 42 by exaggeration (possibly slang), of *pressing very hard upon, hustling*, in a crowd (cf. the more correct συνθλίβω).

συνπολίτης, *a fellow-citizen.*

συνπορεύομαι, *I journey with, I go with*; *I go together.*

συνπρεσβύτερος, *a fellow-elder.*

συνσ., see συσσ.

συνσταυρόω, *I crucify along with*, lit. or met.

συνστέλλω, (a) *I wrap round, swathe* in a sort of wind-

251

ing-sheet, or possibly, *I lay out*, Ac. v 6; (b) *I contract, compress*; hence *I shorten*, 1 Cor. vii 29.

συνστενάζω, *I groan together.*

συνστοιχέω (properly a military term, *I keep in line* or *file*), *I correspond exactly to.*

συνστρατιώτης, *a fellow-soldier, comrade in arms.*

συνσχηματίζω, mid. *I fashion myself in agreement with, I conform myself outwardly to.*

σύνσωμος, *sharing in a body*: it has been taken as *fellow-slave* (see σῶμα).

συντάσσω, *I direct, instruct, command.*

συντέλεια, with αἰῶνος, a characteristic expression of Jewish apocalyptic, *conclusion, consummation, end* of the present period of time.

συντελέω, *I bring to an end, complete, finish, exhaust*; *I accomplish, fulfil, bring to pass.*

συντέμνω, *I cut down*; hence *I contract, limit, restrict* the scope of.

συντηρέω, *I keep safe.*

συντίθημι, mid. and pass. *I make a compact (agreement) with (together), I covenant with, I agree.*

συντόμως, *briefly.*

συντρέχω, *I run (rush) together*, lit. or met.

συντρίβω, (a) *I break*; *I bruise*; (b) *I trample upon, crush*, Rom. xvi 20: *I maul*, Lk. ix 39; (c) met. pass. *I am stunned, crushed*, [Lk.] iv 18.

σύντριμμα, *destruction, ruin.*

σύντροφος, *foster-brother*: such is the lit. rendering, but it would appear to be a court title, and might therefore be translated *a courtier.*

συντυγχάνω, *I encounter, come up with, come close to.*

Συντύχη, *Syntyche*, a woman member of the church at Philippi.

συνυποκρίνομαι, pass. *I dissemble along with.*

συνυπουργέω, *I co-operate in a subordinate capacity.*

σύνφημι, *I express agreement with, I agree with.*

συνφύω, in 2 aor. pass. taking the place of a 2 aor. act., *I grow up together with* (another).

σφραγίζω

συνχαίρω, act. and pass. *I rejoice with*; perhaps *I con-gratulate*.

συνχέω (cf. συνχύννω), *I confound*.

συνχράομαι, *I have intercourse with, I associate with*.

συνχύννω, *I confound*.

σύνψυχος, *one in feeling with* others, *sharing the feelings of* others.

συνωδίνω, *I unite in suffering travail* (*birth pangs, severe pain*).

συνωμοσία, *a conspiracy, plot*.

Συράκουσαι (plur. because originally, as in many similar cases, both a citadel and a settlement in the valley), *Syracuse*, in E. Sicily.

Συρία, *Syria*, a great Roman imperial province, united with Cilicia.

Σύρος, *Syrian*, belonging to Syria.

Συροφοινίκισσα, *Syro-phoenician*, i. e. *Phoenician* (of Syria, in contrast to Carthage and its territory in N. Africa).

Σύρτις, *Syrtis*, a quicksand off the coast of N. Africa.

σύρω, *I drag, pull, draw*.

συσπαράσσω, *I throw violently* on the ground.

σύσσημον, *a signal agreed upon* between two parties.

συστατικός, *recommending, introducing*.

συστρέφω, (a) tr. *I gather together, collect*, Ac. xxviii 3 ; (b) mid. either, *I press together* (about one) or *I stroll*.

συστροφή, *a crowding together* ; hence, *a seditious meeting*, Ac. xix 40 ; *a conspiracy*, Ac. xxiii 12.

Συχάρ, *Sychar*, a ' city ' of Samaria.

Συχέμ, *Sychem, Shechem, Sicyma* (later *Neapolis*, from which modern *Nablus*), a city of Samaria.

σφαγή, *slaughter, sacrifice* (of an animal) ; πρόβατον σφαγῆς (Hebraism), *a sheep destined for sacrifice*.

σφάγιον, *a sacrifice* (of an animal).

σφάζω, *I slaughter* ; *I sacrifice*.

σφόδρα, *greatly, exceedingly, very much*.

σφοδρῶς, *exceedingly*.

σφραγίζω, (a) *I seal* and thus close, for guardianship or

253

σφραγίς

protection, Mt. xxvii 66, Rev. xx 3; (b) *I conceal*, Rev. x 4, xxii 10; (c) *I mark* with the impress of the signet ring, lit. or met.; (d) *I confirm, make undoubted*, John iii 33, vi 27; mid. Rom. xv 28 (cf. under (a)).

σφραγίς, *a seal*, a means not merely of attestation but also of closing, so that a cabinet, document, &c., could not be opened without breaking the seals.

σφυδρόν, *an ankle-bone*.

σφυρίς, σπυρίς (sporta, sportula), a flexible mat-*basket* made of rushes and such like, and used to carry either fish or eatables generally, *a fish-basket, a fisherman's basket*.

σχεδόν, *almost, nearly*.

σχῆμα, *the* outward (changeable) *fashion* (*form*).

σχίζω, *I cleave, split*; (of cloth) *I rend, tear*: of a crowd, *I divide* (sharply) *into two parties*.

σχίσμα, *a cleavage, cleft, split, rent*: so met. *a division* in a crowd, due to difference of opinion, *a party division*.

σχοινίον, *a rope*; *a cable, hawser*.

σχολάζω, (a) *I have leisure*, c. dat. *for*, 1 Cor. vii 5; (b) *I stand empty*, of a house, Mt. xii 44, [Lk.] xi 25.

σχολή, *a school*, or *lecture-hall*.

σώζω, (a) *I save, rescue* a life from death, e.g. Mt. viii 25, a person from grave illness (and thus restore to health), e.g. Mt. ix 21; (b) thus specially, of God and His Messiah, *I save, rescue, preserve*, from spiritual death (cf. Heb. v 7) or spiritual disease, that is, from sin and its effects: the process is regarded as complete on God's part by the sacrifice of Jesus (e.g. Eph. ii 5), but as progressive in our experience (1 Cor. i 18) or only to be realized in the future after acknowledgement of sin and expressed trust in Jesus.

σῶμα, (a) *the* human *body*, alive or dead (e.g. Mt. xxvii 58); *the physical nature*, and thus in Greek thought distinguished from πνεῦμα (e.g. 1 Cor. v 3) or ψυχή (e.g. 1 Thess. v 23); Hebraistic genitives (= adjec-

tives) ἁμαρτίας, σαρκός, sometimes follow; (b) figuratively, the Church is *the Body* of the Messiah who is
the Head (e. g. Eph. i 23); (c) *a slave*, as a mere
body and nothing more, Rev. xviii 13.

σωματικός, (a) *bodily*, hence almost = *visible, tangible*,
Lk. iii 22; (b) *bodily, physical*, contrasted with
'mental', 'spiritual', 1 Tim. iv 8.

σωματικῶς, *bodily, in a bodily way*, almost = *visibly*.

Σώπατρος (a pet-form of Σωσίπατρος), *Sopater*, son of
Pyrrhus, and a Christian of Beroea in Macedonia.

σωρεύω, *I heap*: c. acc. et dat., *I overwhelm* some one
with something, 2 Tim. iii 6.

Σωσθένης, *Sosthenes*, the ruler of the synagogue at
Corinth (Ac. xviii 17), probably to be identified with
the Christian of 1 Cor. i 1.

Σωσίπατρος, *Sosipater*, a Christian at Rome.

σωτήρ (a word familiar to the Graeco-Roman world as
a constant epithet of kings like the Ptolemies and of
the Roman emperors, especially in the phrase ὁ σωτὴρ
τοῦ κόσμου [cf. John iv 42, 1 John iv 14], connoting
probably *preserver* from the enemies of the nation or
the empire, and thus *a maintainer* of life and prosperity), *saviour, rescuer, preserver,* a term applied to
(the) God and to the Messiah with respect to the
human race and sin and its consequences.

σωτηρία (in extra-Biblical language [= salus] has
a reference generally to *bodily health, welfare* [so also
Ac. xxvii 34, Heb. xi 7], especially as recovered after
illness, but also to *deliverance* from every calamity,
victory over enemies), *the salvation* to be wrought by
the Messiah for the Jews, the release from the foreign
yoke in particular and the recovery of independence
(cf. John iv 22): in purely Christian terminology,
far fuller in content, including complete *recovery of
health* from the disease of sin, *release* from captivity
to it.

σωτήριον (neut. of adj. σωτήριος used as substantive,
properly that which produces σωτηρία, a sacrifice or

gift dedicated to bring salvation, or to give thanks for salvation), *the* Messianic *salvation* (cf. σωτηρία) in the wide sense.

σωτήριος, *bringing salvation, fraught with salvation.*

σωφρονέω, (a) *I am in my senses*, Mk. v 15 (Lk. viii 35); (b) *I am sober-minded, I am orderly* and *restrained* in all the relations of life.

σωφρονίζω, (lit. *I make* σώφρων, hence) *I admonish, warn.*

σωφρονισμός, *self-discipline.*

σωφρόνως, *sobermindedly.*

σωφροσύνη, *sound sense, sobermindedness.*

σώφρων (from σῶς, *safe, sound*, and φρήν, *the mind*), *soberminded, prudent.*

T

Ταβειθά, *Tabitha*, a Christian woman at Joppa.

Ταβέρναι, Τρεῖς Ταβέρναι (Latin) *Tres Tabernae, Three Shops*, the name of a village or town on the Appian Way, about thirty-three miles from Rome.

τάγμα (a military term), *rank; division.*

τακτός, *appointed, arranged.*

ταλαιπωρέω, *I am wretched (afflicted, in distress).*

ταλαιπωρία, *wretchedness, distress, misery.*

ταλαίπωρος, *wretched, miserable.*

ταλαντιαῖος, *a talent in weight* or *size.* (But ἀγῶνες ταλαντιαῖοι are games where the value of the prizes amounted to a talent.)

τάλαντον, *a talent*, that is a talent-weight (see **ταλαντιαῖος**) of silver, both the weight and the value being different in different countries and at different times. A common value was 6000 *denarii*, that is somewhat between £175 and £235, but with much greater purchasing power.

ταλειθά (Aramaic), *maiden.*

ταμεῖον (syncopated from ταμιεῖον, and first appearing in syncopated form in first cent. after Christ), *an office, a private room*: also *a store*, Lk. xii 24 (being derived from ταμίας, 'a steward').

τάξις, (a) *appointed order*, Lk. i 8 ; *regulation, rule*, perhaps *office*, Heb. v 6, &c. ; (b) *right order*, 1 Cor. xiv 40, *orderly attitude*, Col. ii 5.

ταπεινός, *of low estate, poor* (and thus despised by the mass of mankind) ; also *poor in spirit, meek*, a notion often combined by the Jews with the previous.

ταπεινοφροσύνη, *meekness* ; *lowliness, humility*.

ταπεινόφρων, *meek-minded* ; *humble-minded*.

ταπεινόω, lit. *I make low, I lower*, Lk. iii 5 : generally met. *I humble*.

ταπείνωσις, *a being brought low*, Ac. viii 33, James i 10 : *meekness* ; *humility* (ταπείνωσις et humilitas uirtutis dicitur et humilitas adflictionis, Ambrose, *expos. ps. cxviii* **20** 10 § 2).

ταράσσω, *I disturb, trouble*.

ταραχή, *disturbing, ruffling*.

τάραχος, *disturbance*.

Ταρσεύς, *belonging to Tarsus, a Tarsian*.

Ταρσός, *Tarsus*, the capital of the Roman province Cilicia.

ταρταρόω, *I send to Tartarus* (Tartarus being in the Greek view a place of punishment under the earth, to which, for example, the Titans were sent).

τάσσω, (a) *I put in its place, assign, fix*, Mt. viii 9 (v. l.), Lk. vii 8, Ac. xiii 48, xxii 10, Rom. xiii 1, 1 Cor. xvi 15 ; (b) *I order*, c. acc. et inf. Ac. xv 2 : mid. *I order by virtue of my power* (authority), Mt. xxviii 16 ; with plural subject, *we fix upon* among ourselves, Ac. xxviii 23.

ταῦρος, *a bull* ; *an ox*.

ταφή (sepultura), *burial*.

τάφος, *a tomb* ; sepulchral *monument*.

τάχα, *perhaps*.

τάχειον, see ταχέως.

ταχέως, *quickly, swiftly, speedily* : compar. form τάχειον (with superl. force in all places except John xx 4) : superl. ὡς τάχιστα, *as quickly as possible*.

ταχινός, *speedy*, possibly *sudden*.

1423

257

S

τάχιστα

τάχιστα, see *ταχέως*.

τάχος, *quickness*; *ἐν τάχει*, adverbially, *speedily, quickly*.

ταχύ (neut. of *ταχύς* as adv.), *quickly, speedily*.

ταχύς, *quick*.

τε, an enclitic connective particle, weaker in force than *καί*, to which it is related as *-que* to *et* (*ac, atque*), *and*: *τε ... τε, τε ... δέ, both ... and*.

τεῖχος, *a wall*, especially *the wall* of a city.

τεκμήριον, *an infallible proof*, a piece of certain (convincing) evidence.

τεκνίον (a diminutive form, suggesting affection, applied to grown up persons), *little child*.

τεκνογονεῖν, *to bear a child* (*children*), *to become a mother*.

τεκνογονία, *child-bearing*; *motherhood*.

τέκνον, (a) *a child*, used affectionately also of grown up persons; (b) met. (Hebraistic, cf. *υἱός*) c. gen., of those who show qualities like that expressed by the genitive; *σοφίας*, cf. Lk. vii 35, those who draw from wisdom the impulses which mould their lives, and are as it were its representatives to others in speech and acts, *those who show* wisdom, *φωτός* Eph. v 8, *ὑπακοῆς* 1 Pet. i 14, *τέκνα θεοῦ*, *of godlike nature, of godly nature*.

τεκνοτροφέω, *I bring up children*.

τέκτων, *a worker in wood, a carpenter*.

τέλειος (from *τέλος*, 'final end'), (a) *full-grown, mature, complete*, having reached its utmost development, e.g. Eph. iv 13, Heb. v 14; (b) *completely good* (simply), James i 4; *completely operative*, James i 17; *perfect*, as dealing with universal principles, James i 25; *perfect* in character, Mt. v 48, James iii 2, &c.

τελειότης, moral *completeness* (*perfection*).

τελειόω, *I bring to completion, I complete*: of persons, *I bring to ethical* or *spiritual maturity* (*completeness*): *I fulfil*, John xix 28.

τελείως, *perfectly, absolutely*, with *νήφοντες*, 1 Pet. i 13.

τελείωσις, *a bringing to completion* (*perfection, fulfilment*).

τελειωτής, *a completer, perfecter*.

258

τελεσφορέω, *I bring* (the fruit) *to maturity*.

τελευτάω (lit. *I end*), *I die*.

τελευτή (lit. *end*), *death*.

τελέω, (a) *I end, complete, accomplish, finish*: also *I fulfil*; in Gal. v 16, possibly *I perform*; (b) of taxes, dues, *I pay*, Mt. xvii 24, Rom. xiii 6.

τέλος, (a) sing. (τέλος dicitur Graece quod nos Latine et *finem* dicimus et *consummationem*; τέλος autem et *consummationis* ipsius *finis* est, Ambros. *expos. ps. cxviii* 12 45 § 1) *the end, the final end* of anything; εἰς τέλος, *continually*, Lk. xviii 5; *the result, the culmination*, e.g. 1 Pet. i 9; *fulfilment*, Lk. xxii 37; (b) especially plur. *revenues, dues*, Mt. xvii 25, also sing. Rom. xiii 7: of the spiritual *revenues* of the ages, 1 Cor. x 11.

τελώνης, *collector* (*receiver*) *of customs, tax-gatherer, revenue official*, of any rank, but especially of Jews of the lower rank, who collected revenue for the Roman overlord, detested by their fellow-countrymen and practically identified with ἁμαρτωλοί.

τελώνιον, *a revenue office*; *a custom-house*.

τέρας, *a prodigy, an extraordinary occurrence* (*appearance, act*), *a startling portent*.

Τέρτιος (Latin), *Tertius*, a Roman (?) Christian, who wrote the Epistle to the Romans at Paul's dictation.

Τέρτυλλος (Latin), *Tertullus*, a barrister acting as professional prosecutor of St. Paul at Caesarea.

τεσσαράκοντα (the spelling τεσσεράκοντα is late and illiterate), *forty*.

τεσσαρακονταετής, *of forty years, forty years long*.

τέσσαρες, *four*.

τεσσαρεσκαιδέκατος, *fourteenth*.

τεταρταῖος, *of the fourth day* (Greek idiom often personalises such adjectives), *four days since* he died.

τέταρτος, *fourth*.

τετρααρχέω, *I rule as tetrarch*.

τετραάρχης, *a tetrarch*, that is, the ruler of a fourth part of a territory divided into four parts for efficient government, a division sometimes found in the Roman East.

τετράγωνος, *with four corners, square*.

τετράδιον (quaternio), *a quaternion*, a group of four soldiers.

τετρακισχίλιοι, *four thousand*.

τετρακόσιοι, *four hundred*.

τετράμηνος, adj., *of four months* (understand χρόνος): hence, *four months*.

τετραπλόος (quadruplex, quadruplus), *fourfold, four times as much*.

τετράπους (quadrupes), *four-footed; a quadruped*.

τεφρόω, *I cover with*, or *I convert into, ashes*.

τέχνη, *art, handicraft, trade*.

τεχνίτης, *a craftsman, an artisan*: c. gen. *a designer*, Heb. xi 10.

τήκομαι, *I melt* (intr.).

τηλαυγῶς (so old MSS. [including W, the Washington (Freer) Gospels], *clearly from afar, clearly*: but others of equal age read δηλαυγῶς, which see).

τηλικοῦτος, *so large, so great*.

τηρέω, (a) lit. *I watch, observe*; (b) *I guard, preserve, keep, protect*; (c) of commandments and regulations, *I observe, keep, obey*.

τήρησις, (a) *a keeping, an observance*, 1 Cor. vii 19; (b) *a place of custody*.

Τιβεριάς, *Tiberias*, a town in Galilee on the western border of the sea called after it.

Τιβέριος, *Tiberius*, the second Roman emperor (died A.D. 37).

τίθημι, *I place, put, set forth*: sometimes with two accusatives, the second in the predicate, e. g. πατέρα πολλῶν ἐθνῶν τέθεικά σε, Rom. iv 17, *I have made you a father*, &c.: τίθημι γόνατα, *I kneel*: τίθεμαι εἰς ὦτα, ἐν καρδίᾳ, *I put into my ears, into my mind*, i.e. *I attend to*, e. g. Lk. i 66, ix 44: τίθημι (pono) ψυχήν, e.g. John x 11, &c., for the synoptic and usual δίδωμι, *I give up my life, I offer up my life*.

260

τίκτω (of a woman), *I bear, give birth to, bring forth*:
hence met., of the earth, Heb. vi 7, of evil desire,
James i 15.

τίλλω, *I pluck, pull, pick.*

Τιμαῖος, *Timaeus*, father of the blind beggar Bartimaeus.

τιμάω, *I honour, give honour to.*

τιμή, (a) *honour*, e.g. John iv 44; (b) *price*, e.g.
Mt. xxvii 6.

τίμιος, *precious, valuable*, in the literal sense (of money
value), e.g. Rev. xvii 4, and also, e.g. Ac. v 34, in
an extended sense.

τιμιότης, *preciousness.*

Τιμόθεος, *Timothy*, a Christian of Lystra, helper of
St. Paul.

Τίμων, *Timon*, one of the seven original 'deacons' at
Jerusalem.

τιμωρέω, *I punish.*

τιμωρία, (deserved) *punishment.*

τίνω, *I pay.*

τίς, masc. and fem., τί neut., interrogative pronoun and
(sometimes) adjective, *who? what? which?* (usually
of more than two, but sometimes = πότερος, of two
only, e.g. Mt. xxi 31): τί = *what reward?* Mt. xix
27: τί neut. as predicate to ταῦτα, e.g. Lk. xv 26,
Ac. xvii 20 (v.l.), John vi 9 (*what* use are they?),
also adverbially = *why?* Mt. vi 28, Lk. ii 48, Ac. xiv
15, like διὰ τί and ἵνα τί (sc. γένηται), as well as τί ὅ, τι
(ὅτι) = τί γέγονεν ὅτι (or δι' ὅ,τι) (cf. John xiv 22): τί
ἄρα ὁ Πέτρος ἐγένετο (cf. Fr. que devenir), *what then had
happened to Peter*, Ac. xii 18, τί ἄρα τὸ παιδίον τοῦτο
ἔσται; Lk. i 66, Ac. v 24 (τί in predicate), abbreviated,
οὗτος δὲ τί; *what will become of him?* John xxi 21:
(Hebraistic) *how*, Mt. vii 14 (v.l.), Lk. xii 49, 1 Cor. vii
16: τί πρὸς ἡμᾶς (sc. ἐστιν); *what have we to do with it?*
Mt. xxvii 4, cf. John xxi 22, 1 Cor. v 12 (see also
under σύ); τί γάρ; *what does it matter?* or *what
difference does it make?* Rom. iii 3, Phil. i 18; τί οὖν
(sc. ? ἐροῦμεν); Rom. vi 15, masc. ἐγὼ τίς ἤμην; Ac. xi 17:

double interrogative, τίς τί ἄρῃ, Mk. xv 24, τίς τί
(*what each*) διεπραγματεύσατο, Lk. xix 15 (v.l.). Sometimes τίς is confused with the relative ὅστις, ὅς, which
is rather a sign of illiteracy, Mt. x 19, Lk. xvii 8,
Ac. xiii 25 (according to one punctuation), James
iii 13 (if read as one sentence). In Lk. xi 5, 11,
τίς (= εἴ τις) (cf. Phil. ii 1) is non-Greek and Semitic.

τις (enclitic), masc. and fem., τι neut., indefinite pronoun and adjective, *some one, any one, something, anything*: *a* (*an*), *a certain, any, some*: special uses,
ἀπαρχήν τινα, softening the metaphor (quidam), *so to
speak, a sort of*, James i 18 : with numbers, making
indefinite, *about*, but τινας δύο, *a certain two*,
Ac. xxiii 23 (cf. Lk. xxii 50, John xi 49): with adjectives, strengthening (quidam), Heb. x 27, cf.
Ac. v 36, viii 9 : τι, *something special*, Gal. ii 6, vi 3.
Sometimes unexpressed, where it would be expected
(Hebraism?), John vii 40, xvi 17, Ac. xix 33,
xxi 16, &c.

Τίτιος, *Titius*, the second name (nomen) of a Christian
Roman citizen at Corinth, his first name (praenomen)
being unknown.

τίτλος (Latin) (titulus), *an inscription.*

Τίτος, *Titus*, a Greek Christian, helper of St. Paul,
perhaps also brother of Luke.

τοιγαροῦν, *accordingly, wherefore.*

τοίνυν, *so.*

τοιόσδε, *of such character, to the following effect.*

τοιοῦτος (talis), *of such a kind* (*character*), *such.*

τοῖχος, *a wall.*

τόκος (from τίκτω, cf. Shakespeare's '*breed* of barren
metal'), *interest.*

τολμάω, *I have courage, I dare, I have the hardihood;
I take courage*, Mk. xv 43 ; *I submit to*, Rom. v 7.

τολμηρῶς, *courageously.*

τολμητής, *a shameless and headstrong man.*

τομός, *cutting, with cutting power.*

τόξον, *a bow* (and arrows).

τρέφω

τοπάζιον, *a topaz.*

τόπος (locus), *a place*; κατὰ τόπους, *in various places,*
Mk. xiii 8, &c., διδόναι τόπον, *to make room for, give
place to,* Lk. xiv 9, &c.: met. *an opportunity,* Ac. xxv 16,
Rom. xv 23, Eph. iv 27, Heb. xii 17.

τοσοῦτος (tantus), *so great, so large*; of time, *so long,*
plur. (tot, later tanti) *so many*: τοσούτου, *at such and
such a price,* Ac. v 8.

τότε, *then, at that time*; ὁ τότε κόσμος, *the world of that
day,* 2 Pet. iii 6; ἀπὸ τότε, *from that time, thence-
forward,* Mt. iv 17, &c.: very often in Mt. representing Hebrew *wāw* consecutive, and thus simply
continuing the narrative.

τοὐναντίον (syncopated from τὸ ἐναντίον, *the opposite*), as
adv. *on the contrary.*

τοὔνομα (syncopated from τὸ ὄνομα), as adv., *by name.*

τράγος, *a goat.*

τράπεζα, *a table.*

τραπεζίτης (from τράπεζα, money-changer's *table*), *a
money-changer, a banker.*

τραῦμα, *a wound.*

τραυματίζω, *I wound.*

τραχηλίζω (from τράχηλος, 'neck', probably referring
originally to the bending back of the head in sacrifice
so as to expose the neck: but, whatever be the origin
of the expression, the met. sense is clear): τετραχηλισ-
μένα, *open, manifest.*

τράχηλος, *the neck*: τὸν ἑαυτῶν τράχηλον ὑποθεῖναι, *to lay
down their own necks,* i. e. *to risk their own lives.*

τραχύς, *rough.*

Τραχωνιτίς, *Trachonitic, belonging to Trachon,* adj.
applied to a hilly region (inhabited by a nomad
tribe), considerably to the south of Damascus, called
also Ituraean.

τρεῖς, *three*; μετὰ τρεῖς ἡμέρας = τῇ τρίτῃ ἡμέρᾳ.

τρέμω, *I tremble.*

τρέφω, *I nourish, feed*; *I bring up,* Lk. iv 16: met.,
James v 5.

τρέχω

τρέχω, *I run*; sometimes c. acc. of the course, Heb. xii 1 : also met., e. g. Gal. ii 2.

τρῆμα, *opening, hole*; *eye* of needle (perhaps a favourite term of medical writers).

τριάκοντα, *thirty*.

τριακόσιοι, *three hundred*.

τρίβολος, *a thistle*.

τρίβος, *a path, track*.

τριετία, *a period of three years, three years*.

τρίζω, *I grind, crunch*.

τρίμηνος, *lasting three months*: acc. neut. as adv. *three months*.

τρίς, *thrice, three times*.

τρίστεγος, *having three roofs, with three floors* (*stories*): hence neut. as noun, *the third floor*, but it is uncertain whether the ground floor was counted or not in this enumeration ; if so, we should have to translate, *the second floor*.

τρισχίλιοι, *three thousand*.

τρίτον, acc. neut. of adj., generally with definite article, as adv., *the third time*; *third, in the third place*, 1 Cor. xii 28.

τρίτος (see also **τρίτον**), *third*: ἐκ τρίτου, *a third time*: τῇ τρίτῃ ἡμέρᾳ (according to the ancient method of counting), *on the third day, two days after, on the next day but one, on the day after to-morrow*.

τρίχινος, *made of hair*.

τρόμος, *trembling*.

τροπή, any *change* undergone by any object; hence referring to night and day, or the waxing and waning of the moon, the solstice, &c.

τρόπος, *manner, way*: often acc. as adv. ὃν τρόπον, *in the way in which, as*, also with κατά, &c. ; *manner of life*, Heb. xiii 5.

τροποφορέω, *I bear* (*endure*) *the ways* (*disposition*) *of* (v. l.).

τροφή, *nourishment, food, sustenance*.

Τρόφιμος, *Trophimus*, a Christian of Ephesus in Asia.

τροφός, *a nurse* (and thus of a mother who suckles her own children).

τροφοφορέω, *I carry, dandle as a nurse* (v. l.).

τροχιά, (orbita [from orbis], *a track*; hence) *a road.*

τροχός, (*a wheel*; hence) *the chariot-wheel* of man as he advances on the way of life, following his appointed course.

τρύβλιον, *a dish.*

τρυγάω, *I gather* (always of *grapes*, τρύξ).

τρυγών, *a turtledove.*

τρυμαλιά, *an opening, hole*; *an eye* of needle.

τρύπημα, *a hole*; *an eye.*

Τρύφαινα, *Tryphaena,* a woman-Christian in Rome.

τρυφάω, *I live a luxurious life.*

τρυφή, *luxury.*

Τρυφῶσα, *Tryphosa,* a woman-Christian in Rome, perhaps a sister of Tryphaena.

Τρῳάς, *Troas,* a harbour city of Mysia.

Τρωγύλλιον, *Trogyllium,* a promontory somewhat to the south of Ephesus.

τρώγω (originally *I munch, I eat audibly*), *I eat.* (This word was displacing ἐσθίω in ordinary use.)

τυγχάνω, (a) c. gen. *I obtain*; (b) absol. *I chance, happen*: τυχών, *ordinary, everyday,* Ac. xix 11, xxviii 2; εἰ τύχοι (lit. *if it should happen*), *it may chance*; old acc. absolute, belonging to impersonal verbs, τυχόν, *perhaps.*

τυμπανίζω (from τύμπανον, 'drum' used in worship, then 'implement of torture'), *I break on the wheel.*

τυπικῶς, either *by way of example,* or *typically, prefiguratively.*

τύπος (originally, *the mark* of a blow, cf. John xx 25: then *a stamp* struck by a die), (a) *a figure*; *a copy, image*; (b) *a pattern, model*; (c) *a type,* prefiguring something or somebody.

τύπτω, *I strike.*

Τύραννος, *Tyrannus* an inhabitant of Ephesus, probably a rhetorician.

Τύριος, *a Tyrian, an inhabitant of Tyre.*
Τύρος, *Tyre,* an ancient city, the capital of Phoenicia.
τυφλός, *blind,* either lit. or met.
τυφλόω, *I blind, make blind,* lit. or met.
τύφομαι, intr. *I smoke.*
τυφόω : pass. *I am puffed up, I am haughty.*
τυφωνικός (from τυφώς, 'a vehement wind'); ἄνεμος, *a heavy eddying squall.*
Τυχικός (or Τύχικος), *Tychicus,* a Christian of the Roman province Asia.

Υ

ὑακίνθινος, *of the colour of the martagon lily,* that is, of a dusky red colour.
ὑάκινθος, *a sapphire* of dusky red colour like the martagon lily.
ὑάλινος, *glassy, transparent as glass.*
ὕαλος, *glass.*
ὑβρίζω, *I treat insolently (outrageously), I insult.*
ὕβρις, (a) *wanton insult, outrage,* 2 Cor. xii 10; (b) *injury, loss,* due to the sea.
ὑβριστής, noun as adj. *insolent, insulting, outrageous.*
ὑγιαίνω, *I am in* (good) *health, I am healthy* (well): hence met. in connexion with words and teaching, *I am right, reasonable.*
ὑγιής, *whole, in health, sound; restored to health :* met. *reasonable.*
ὑγρός, *moist, full of sap.*
ὑδρία, *a waterpot* (hence, of any pot).
ὑδροποτέω, *I drink water* (alone, not mixed with wine).
ὑδρωπικός, *dropsical, afflicted with dropsy.*
ὕδωρ, *water :* ὕδωρ ζῶν (aqua uiua), ζωῆς (Hebraistic genitive), *flowing water* (as opposed to stagnant), John iv 10, &c.
ὑετός (imber), *a shower of rain ; rain.*
υἱοθεσία, *adoption.*

υἱός, (a) *a son* in the ordinary sense, with this difference, that one must keep in mind the greater solidarity of the family in ancient times and the greater ease in identifying father and son thence arising; also *a male descendant*, Mt. i 1, &c.; (b) in special senses: with a genitive of the Deity, θεοῦ, ὑψίστου, εὐλογητοῦ ('sons of God' in Job i 6, &c., rendered by ἄγγελοι 'angels', are members of the heavenly court gathered round Yahweh, and all men could be called 'sons of God' as having been created by Him), rarely of a class of human beings, and in such cases only of those who perfectly perform God's will, those in and through whom His will is made known and who are thus like Him, e. g. Mt. v 9 ; generally of Jesus, who as *God's Son* in an unique sense, as specially united with Him, is the Messiah, God's representative on earth, by whom His will is perfectly performed, and thus at times as it were identified with Him, Mk. i 11, &c.: ὁ υἱὸς τοῦ ἀνθρώπου, (lit. *the Son of the Man,* an Aramaistic expression, originally equivalent to ὁ ἄνθρωπος, cf. Mk. iii 28, Rev. i 13, *the man, the human being,* simply, but) at some stage (cf. Dan. vii 13 and *Parables of Enoch* for the growth in the use of the expression) become a Messianic title, used by Jesus Himself, representing the whole human race in the one Man, *the Son of Man,* who has to suffer but will be glorified, Mk. viii 29, 31 f., Mt. xvi 13, 27 f., cf. Lk. ix 18, 22 f., &c.: a similar Hebraism with genitives indicating qualities, &c., ἀπειθείας, ἀπωλείας, γεέννης (cf. also διαβόλου), used of persons who so perfectly exemplify these qualities, &c., that they can be spoken of as having a family likeness to them (cf. τέκνον).

ὕλη, *wood, timber, brushwood.*

Ὑμέναιος, *Hymenaeus,* a backsliding Christian.

ὑμέτερος, *your.*

ὑμνέω, (a) intr. *I sing a hymn*; (b) tr. *I praise in a hymn.*

ὕμνος, *a hymn*, especially of praise to God.

ὑπάγω, *I go away, withdraw, depart*; *I depart this life*, Mt. xxvi 24.

ὑπακοή, *obedience*.

ὑπακούω, *I obey*: c. infin., Heb. xi 8.

ὕπανδρος, *under the authority of a husband*.

ὑπαντάω, *I meet*.

ὑπάντησις, *meeting, act of meeting*.

ὕπαρξις, *a possession*, generally of *personal property*.

ὑπάρχω, *I am*, denoting originally a state or condition still subsisting in contrast to what is temporary or accidental : τὰ ὑπάρχοντα, *one's belongings, possessions, personal property*.

ὑπείκω, *I yield, submit*.

ὑπεναντίος, *opposing, hostile* ; substantive, *adversary*, Heb. x 27.

ὑπέρ, (a) c. gen. (1) *for, on behalf of, for the sake of* (opposite to κατά, e.g. Mk. ix 40), *as agent of*, Philem. 13 ; perhaps, *in memory of*, 1 Cor. xv 29 ; (2) colourlessly, *concerning, about, as to*, John i 30, 2 Cor. viii 23, xii 8, Phil. i 7, iv 10, 2 Thess. ii 1, and perhaps elsewhere ; (3) of the goal one wants to reach, *with a view to*, 2 Cor. i 6, Phil. ii 13 ; (b) c. acc. *over, beyond*, indicating excess, so also with the comparative, *than*, Lk. xvi 8, John xii 43 (v. l.), Ac. xx 35 (v.l.), Heb. iv 12, and in compound expressions given below.

ὕπερ, as adverb, an ancient use, *more (than they)*.

ὑπεραίρω, lit. *I raise beyond*: pass. met. *I am exceedingly uplifted*.

ὑπέρακμος, of doubtful meaning ; probably *of excessive sexual vigour* (of the man), rather than *past the bloom of youth* (of the woman).

ὑπεράνω, *far above*.

ὑπεραυξάνω, intr. *I grow exceedingly*.

ὑπερβαίνω, intr. *I transgress*.

ὑπερβαλλόντως, *exceedingly*.

ὑπερβάλλω, intr. *I exceed, surpass*, c. gen. : pcpl. present, absolutely, *excessive, extraordinary*.

ὑπερβολή, *excess, abundance*; καθ᾽ ὑπερβολήν, *superlatively, exceedingly, beyond measure.*

ὑπερεῖδον, *I looked past, overlooked, pretended not to see.*

ὑπερέκεινος, lit. *beyond yonder* : τὰ ὑπερέκεινα, *the places beyond,* c. gen.

ὑπερεκπερισσοῦ, *most exceedingly.*

ὑπερεκπερισσῶς, *most exceedingly,* 1 Thess. v 13 (v. l.).

ὑπερεκτείνω, tr. *I stretch beyond the measure assigned to me.*

ὑπερεκχύννω, *I pour out so that it overflows.*

ὑπερεντυγχάνω, *I supplicate on behalf of.*

ὑπερέχω, absol. or c. gen. or c. acc. *I am superior, I am supreme* ; *I surpass.*

ὑπερηφανία, *haughtiness, arrogance.*

ὑπερήφανος, *haughty, disdainful, arrogant.*

ὑπερλίαν (lit. *more than very much*): in irony, οἱ ὑπερλίαν ἀπόστολοι, *the super-apostles.*

ὑπερνικάω, *I score a heavy victory* ; *I am more than a conqueror.*

ὑπέρογκος (lit. *of great* or *excessive bulk*), *arrogant.*

ὑπεροχή, *superiority,* 1 Cor. ii 1 ; *a position of superiority,* 1 Tim. ii 2.

ὑπερπερισσεύω, (a) intr. *I abound exceedingly* ; (b) mid. as act. *I overflow.*

ὑπερπερισσῶς, *most exceedingly.*

ὑπερπλεονάζω, *I abound exceedingly, I am exceedingly abundant.*

ὑπερυψόω, *I elevate greatly (exceedingly).*

ὑπερφρονέω, *I have high notions.*

ὑπερῷον, *an upper room, an upstairs room.*

ὑπέχω, *I undergo.*

ὑπήκοος, *obedient.*

ὑπηρετέω, *I serve, minister to.*

ὑπηρέτης, *a servant, an attendant.*

ὕπνος, *sleep.*

ὑπό, (a) c. gen., especially of a person as the original author (contrast διά), with a verb passive or quasi-passive (cf. Rev. vi 8), *by* ; (b) c. acc., (1) both lit.

and met., *under*, after a verb of motion, and so
answering the question 'whither?'; (2) both lit. and
met., after a verb of rest, and so answering the
question 'where?'; (3) of time (sub), *about*, Ac. v 21.

ὑποβάλλω, *I suborn*.

ὑπογραμμός, (properly a *piece of calligraphy, a copy*, for
children to imitate; hence) *a model, a type*, which has
to be followed.

ὑπόδειγμα, (a) *a sign, image* of something, Heb. viii 5,
ix 23; (b) *an example*, given for imitation.

ὑποδείκνυμι, *I point out, show*; hence *I advise, warn*,
Mt. iii 7, Lk. iii 7.

ὑποδέχομαι, *I receive under my roof, I welcome to my house,
I entertain hospitably.*

ὑποδέω (lit. *I bind under*), mid. *I put on* (my feet).

ὑπόδημα (cf. ὑποδέω), *a shoe*.

ὑπόδικος (a forensic word), *liable to* (*brought under*) *the
judgement of, answerable to.*

ὑποζύγιον, *a beast of burden*, either *an ass* or *a mule*.

ὑποζώννυμι, *I undergird, frap*, that is, I fasten cables
vertically round the hull of the ship to prevent the
timbers from straining or giving way.

ὑποκάτω, *underneath*.

ὑποκρίνομαι, *I act the part, pretend*.

ὑπόκρισις (*acting a part*, properly), *hypocrisy, pose*.

ὑποκριτής (properly *an actor*), *a hypocrite*, one who outwardly plays the part of a religious man to perfection,
but is inwardly alien to the spirit of true religion.

ὑπολαμβάνω, (a) (subueho) *I receive from beneath, I take
up*, Ac. i 9; (b) *I welcome, entertain*, 3 John 8; (c) *I
catch up* in speech, by answering or contradicting or
supplementing, Lk. x 30; (d) *I suppose, imagine*.

ὑπόλειμμα, *a remnant*.

ὑπολείπω, *I leave behind*.

ὑπολήνιον, *a wine-press*, probably the *lower* (ὑπο-) trough,
smaller but deeper than the ληνός proper, both being
cut out of the solid rock.

ὑπολιμπάνω (Ionic form) = ὑπολείπω.

ὑπομένω, (a) *I remain behind*, Lk. ii 43, Ac. xvii 14 ;
  (b) absolutely, *I stand my ground*, *I show endurance*,
  Mt. x 22, &c.; with τῇ θλίψει, Rom. xii 12, *in persecu-*
  tion, amid persecution, with εἰς = ἐν, Heb. xii 7 ; (c) tr.
  I endure, bear up against.

ὑπομιμνήσκω, *I remind* : pass. practically *I remember*,
  Lk. xxii 61.

ὑπόμνησις, *remembrance, recollection.*

ὑπομονή, *stedfast endurance*, the virtue shown by martyrs.

ὑπονοέω, *I suppose.*

ὑπόνοια, *a supposition, suspicion.*

ὑποπλέω, *I sail under the lee of (close to).*

ὑποπνέω, *I blow moderately (gently).*

ὑποπόδιον, *a footstool* (of the conquering king placing his
  foot on the neck of the conquered).

ὑπόστασις (lit. *an underlying*), (a) *confidence, assurance* ;
  (b) *a giving substance* (or *reality*) *to*, or *a guaranteeing*,
  Heb. xi 1 (where possibly *title-deed* is the sense) ;
  (c) *substance, reality*, Heb. i 3.

ὑποστέλλω, act. tr. *I withdraw*, Gal. ii 12 ; mid. tr. *I keep*
  back, Ac. xx 20; intr. *I withdraw*, Heb. x 38 ; *I shrink*
  from, *I shun* (c. infin. and answering negative), Ac.
  xx 27.

ὑποστολή, *withdrawal* ; *shrinking.*

ὑποστρέφω, intr. *I return* ; *I withdraw*, met., 2 Pet. ii 21.

ὑποστρωννύω, tr. *I spread underneath.*

ὑποταγή, *subordination, subjection, submission.*

ὑποτάσσω (lit. *I put in a lower rank, I rank under*,
  a military term), *I subject, I put into subjection* : mid.
  (and pass.) *I subordinate myself, I put myself into sub-*
  jection, I submit.

ὑποτίθημι, (a) *I place (put) under* some danger, *I expose* ;
  (b) mid. *I suggest, advise.*

ὑποτρέχω, *I run before* a wind *under* the lee of.

ὑποτύπωσις, *a figurative representation*, serving as *an*
  example.

ὑποφέρω, *I endure, suffer.*

ὑποχωρέω, *I withdraw.*

ὑπωπιάζω

ὑπωπιάζω (from ὑπώπιον, which is from ὑπό and ὄψ,
‘that part of the face under the eyes’), *I strike under
the eye, bruise*; hence, *I treat severely*, 1 Cor. ix 27,
I molest, annoy, harass, worry, exhaust, Lk. xviii 5.

ὗς, *a sow*.

ὕσσωπος, *hyssop*. In John xix 29 ὑσσώπῳ is a graphic
error for ὑσσῷ (pilum), *pike*.

ὑστερέω, (a) act. intr. *I come late, I am late*, Heb. iv 1 ;
I am left behind in the race for, I have no part in,
with ἀπό and the gen. of the end, Heb. xii 15 ; *I fall
short, I am inferior*, Mt. xix 20, 1 Cor. xii 24 (v. l.),
2 Cor. xi 5, xii 11 ; *I am wanting (to)*, Mk. x 21 (v. l.),
John ii 3 ; *I am without*, c. gen. Lk. xxii 35 ; (b) pass.
I suffer from want, absol., or c. gen., or c. ἐν and
dat. ; *I am worse off* (for honour), 1 Cor. viii 8.

ὑστέρημα, (a) *that which is lacking*, of things or persons ;
(b) *want, poverty*, Lk. xxi 4, 2 Cor. viii 14, ix 12, xi 9.

ὑστέρησις, *poverty, want*.

ὕστερον, *later, afterwards*.

ὕστερος, (a) comparative, *latter* ; (b) superlative, *last,
latest*.

ὑφαίνω, *I weave*.

ὑφαντός, *woven*.

ὑψηλός, (a) lit. *high, lofty* ; (b) met. μετὰ βραχίονος
ὑψηλοῦ (Hebraistic), of God ; with φρονεῖν, of
haughtiness, arrogance, boasting.

ὑψηλοφρονέω, *I am haughty (arrogant)*.

ὕψιστος, *highest*, always as epithet either of God, or of
the region where He lives.

ὕψος, (a) *height* ; (b) *heaven*, Lk. i 78, xxiv 49, Eph. iv 8 ;
(c) met. spiritual *height*.

ὑψόω, *I raise to a height, I lift up, I exalt*, usually met.

ὕψωμα, (a) *height*, Rom. viii 39 ; (b) *loftiness, haughtiness, (self-)exaltation*, 2 Cor. x 5 (but including concrete as well as abstract, *whatever is lofty*, &c.).

272

Φ

φάγος, *a glutton, gourmand.*

φαίνω, (a) act. *I shine, I shed light* ; (b) pass. (1) *I shine* ; (2) *I become visible, I appear;* cf. ἐφάνη, impersonally, Mt. ix 33 ; (3) *I become clear, appear, show myself* as, Mt. vi 5, 16, 18, xxiii 27, Rom. vii 13, 2 Cor. xiii 7, 1 Pet. iv 18 ; (4) of the mind and judgement (= δοκεῖ, uidetur), Mk. xiv 64, Lk. xxiv 11.

Φάλεκ (Hebr.), *Phalek,* son of Eber, and one of the ancestors of Jesus.

φανερός, *clear, visible* (as opposed to ' hidden ', ' secret ') ; εἰς φανερὸν ἐλθεῖν, *to come into the open, to appear before the public,* Mk. iv 22, Lk. viii 17, ἐν τῷ φανερῷ, *in public.*

φανερόω, *I make clear (visible, manifest).*

φανερῶς, *openly, overtly.*

φανέρωσις, *a showing forth,* with objective gen.

φανός, (*a light, a torch* ; then) *a lantern.*

Φανουήλ, *Fanuhel, Phanuel,* father of Anna the prophetess.

φαντάζω, *I make to appear* ; τὸ φανταζόμενον, *the appearance.*

φαντασία, *show, display.*

φάντασμα, *an appearance* : hence *a ghost, a spirit.*

φάραγξ, *a hollow place, a hollow, a valley.*

Φαραώ, properly a dynastic title (cf. Decebalus in Dacia, Candace in Ethiopia), but, though sometimes preceded by the definite article, probably everywhere understood as a proper name, *Pharaoh,* a king of Egypt.

Φαρές (Hebr.), *Phares,* son of Judah and one of the ancestors of Jesus.

Φαρισαῖος (lit. a Separatist, a Purist), *a Pharisee,* a member of the strict religious legalistic party in Judaism after the exile.

φαρμακεία, *the practice of drugging, drugging* ; hence, especially, from the use of mysterious liquids, *sorcery, witchcraft,* inextricably combined with idolatry.

φάρμακον

φάρμακον, *a drug*; hence plur., of those used in sorcery, and thus *sorcery*, Rev. ix 21 (v. l.).

φαρμακός (see **φαρμακεία**), *a sorcerer, magician.*

φάσις (from **φαίνω**), *information.*

φάσκω, *I say*, either *I say frequently*, or *I allege.*

φάτνη, *a manger, a feeding-trough.*

φαῦλος, *worthless, low, paltry*, implying not so much what is evil as the limitations and paltrinesses belonging to a low order of things.

φέγγος, *a light, ray, beam.*

φείδομαι, *I spare*, I exempt from punishment or injury (death).

φειδομένως, *sparingly.*

φελόνης (**φαιλόνης**), a metathesis from **φαινόλης** (Latin, paenula), *a mantle, cloak.*

φέρω (fero), *I carry, bear, bring*; *I conduct, lead*, both tr. and intr.; perhaps, *I make publicly known*, Heb. ix 16.

φεύγω, *I flee*; *I escape.*

Φῆλιξ (Latin), *Felix*, third name of (Marcus) Antonius Felix, procurator of the Roman province Judaea from an uncertain date (before A. D. 52 ?) till A. D. 59.

φήμη (fama), *a report, a rumour.*

φημί, *I say.*

φημίζω, *I bruit about (circulate) a report.*

Φῆστος (Latin), *Festus*, third name of (?) Porcius Festus, procurator of the Roman province Judaea from A.D. 59.

φθάνω, (a) *I anticipate, I precede*, 1 Thess. iv 15; (b) *I come, I arrive.*

φθαρτός, *perishable.*

φθέγγομαι, *I utter* (a word), *I open the mouth in speech.*

φθείρω, (a) lit. *I destroy, I waste*; *I damage, injure* (in being); (b) usually met. *I corrupt morally, I deprave, injure* (in character); *I seduce*, 2 Cor. xi 3.

φθινοπωρινός (derived from τὸ φθινόπωρον, which itself = φθίνουσα ὀπώρα, 'the concluding portion of the ὀπώρα'), *autumnal, in autumn*, when fruit is expected.

φθόγγος, *a* measured harmonious *sound,* of voice or instrument; *an utterance.*

φθονέω, *I envy.*

φθόνος, *envy, grudge*; plur. where related to various advantages.

φθορά, *rottenness, perishableness, corruption, decay, decomposition.*

φιάλη (poculum), strictly *a wine-cup,* much like a modern champagne-glass in shape; hence *a cup.*

φιλάγαθος, *loving what is good.*

Φιλαδελφία, *Philadelphia,* a city of the Roman province Asia.

φιλαδελφία, *love of brothers* for each other; hence, *love of the brethren, love of fellow-Christians,* all being sons of the same Father in a special sense.

φιλάδελφος, *loving one's brothers (fellow-Christians).*

φίλανδρος, *loving one's husband.*

φιλανθρωπία, (a) *love of (for) mankind*; (b) *humanity, kindness,* Ac. xxviii 2.

φιλανθρώπως, *kindly.*

φιλαργυρία, *love of money.*

φιλάργυρος, *loving money.*

φίλαυτος, *loving self.*

φιλέω, *I love,* of friendship (contrast ἔραμαι [of passion] and ἀγαπάω [of reverential love]): *I kiss,* Mk. xiv 44, Mt. xxvi 48, Lk. xxii 47.

φιλήδονος, *loving (sensuous) pleasure.*

φίλημα, *a kiss.*

Φιλήμων, *Philemon,* a Christian man of Colossae.

Φίλητος, *Philetus,* a backsliding Christian at Rome.

φιλία, *friendship.*

Φιλιππήσιος (Latin [Philippensis], for the pure-Greek Φιλιππεύς, Φιλιππηνός), *a Philippian, an inhabitant of Philippi.*

Φίλιπποι, *Philippi,* a great city of the Roman province Macedonia.

Φίλιππος (a Greek name), *Philip*: (a) one of the twelve disciples of Jesus; (b) tetrarch of the Ituraean and Trachonitic region, half-brother of Herod Antipas, tetrarch of Galilee; perhaps another half-brother is intended in Mk. vi 17 and parallels; (c) one of the seven original 'deacons' at Jerusalem and a missionary, Ac. vi 5, viii 5-40, xxi 8.

φιλόθεος, *loving God.*

Φιλόλογος, *Philologus*, a Roman Christian.

φιλονεικία (see φιλόνεικος), *emulation, rivalry.*

φιλόνεικος (φίλος and νείκη [νίκη] 'victory'), *contentious.*

φιλοξενία, *love to foreigners; entertainment of strangers.*

φιλόξενος, *friendly to foreigners; hospitable.*

φιλοπρωτεύω, *I love the first (chief) place.*

φίλος, *a friend.*

φιλοσοφία, *philosophy*, in a bad sense, and perhaps identified with ἀπάτη.

φιλόσοφος, *a philosopher.*

φιλόστοργος, *loving warmly (strongly).*

φιλότεκνος, *loving one's children.*

φιλοτιμέομαι, (earlier, *I am ambitious*; then, *I act with public spirit*; now,) *I am zealous, I strive eagerly.*

φιλοφρόνως, *with friendly thoughtfulness.*

φιμόω, *I muzzle*; hence, probably originally a slang use, *I silence*, φιμώθητι, *be quiet!* Mk. i 25, &c.

Φλέγων, *Phlegon*, a Roman Christian man.

φλογίζω, *I set on fire.*

φλόξ, *a flame*: πυρός (Hebraistic), *a fiery flame*: spiritualized, 2 Thess. i 8.

φλυαρέω, c. acc. *I chatter (gossip) against.*

φλύαρος, *chattering, gossiping.*

φοβέομαι, *I fear, dread, reverence*, absol. or c. acc. or c. infin.: also c. cognate acc. φόβον, πτόησιν, *I fear greatly*: c. ἀπό and genitive (Hebraism), *I am afraid of*, Mt. x 28 (Lk. xii 4): c. μή and conjunctive, *I fear lest, I fear that.*

φοβερός, *fearful, terrible.*

φόβητρον (φόβηθρον, probably more Lukan), *an instrument of terror, an object of fear, a bugbear.*

φόβος, *fear, terror*, often fear on the reverential side, in reference to God, and such as inspires cautious dealing towards men, cf. 1 Pet. i 17.

Φοίβη, *Phoebe,* a leading Christian woman in the church at Cenchreae.

Φοινίκη, *Phoenice, Phoenicia,* a northern coast strip of the Roman province Syria.

Φοινίκισσα (feminine), *Phoenician.*

Φοῖνιξ, *Phoenix* (perhaps modern Lutro), a bay on the south coast of Crete.

φοῖνιξ, *a palm tree,* John xii 13; *a branch of a palm tree, a palm,* Rev. vii 9.

φονεύς, *a murderer.*

φονεύω, c. acc. *I murder*; absol. *I commit murder.*

φόνος, *murder.*

φορέω, *I carry*; hence, very often, *I wear.*

Φόρον (Latin, Forum), *Forum, Market, Market-Town.*

φόρος (tributum), *tribute, war-tax.*

φορτίζω, *I load, burden.*

φορτίον, (a) *a burden*; (b) *a cargo,* Ac. xxvii 10.

Φορτουνᾶτος (Latin), *Fortunatus,* a Christian of Corinth.

φραγέλλιον (by dissimilation from Latin, flagellum), *a lash.*

φραγελλόω (Latin, flagello), *I lash, flog.*

φραγμός, *a hedge, a fence, a partition*; hence, *a path* bounded by hedges or fences, Lk. xiv 23.

φράζω, *I explain, I interpret.*

φράσσω, *I stop, close.*

φρέαρ, *a well*; hence, transferred, Rev. ix 1, 2.

φρεναπατάω (lit. *I deceive the mind*), *I deceive.*

φρεναπάτης (see **φρεναπατάω**), *a deceiver; deceiving.*

φρήν, *the mind.*

φρίσσω (used properly of the standing of the hair on end with fear), *I feel awe.*

φρονέω, c. acc. *I have in my mind, I think of, I set my mind upon,* suggesting my moral interest, thought, and study, and not a mere unreflecting opinion: intr. *I think, I cherish a habit of thought.*

φρόνημα, *an object of thought* (or *endeavour*).

φρόνησις, *understanding*, which leads to right action.

φρόνιμος, *sensible, prudent*.

φρονίμως, *wisely, sensibly, prudently*.

φροντίζω, *I am careful, I take care*.

φρουρέω, *I guard*, or rather *I garrison*, lit. and met.

φρυάσσω, (properly, of the snorting and neighing of a high-spirited horse; then) *I roar, rage*.

φρύγανον, *brushwood, copse*.

Φρυγία, *Phrygia*, an ethnic district in Asia Minor, the north-western part of which was in the Roman province Asia, and the south-eastern part in the Roman province Galatia: in Ac. xvi 6 Φρυγίαν is adj.

Φύγελος, *Phygelus*, a Christian of the Roman province Asia who deserted St. Paul.

φυγή, *flight*.

φυλακή, (a) (custodia) abstract, *guardianship, guard*, in cognate acc., Lk. ii 8, Ac. xii 6; (b) (custodia) *a guard*, Ac. xii 10; (c) much commoner, *a prison*; hence, *the place of confinement* of the spirits of the dead, 1 Pet. iii 19; (d) (uigilia), as a division of the night, (1) perhaps according to the old Jewish system by which there were three divisions, Lk. xii 38, (2) according to the Roman system, popularized in Judaea, by which there were four, Mk. vi 48 (cf. xiii 35), Mt. xiv 25, xxiv 43.

φυλακίζω, *I put in prison, I imprison*.

φυλακτήριον, *a phylactery, an amulet*, a parchment capsule containing little parchment rolls with the Hebrew texts, Exod. xiii 1–10, 11–16, Deut. vi 4–9, xi 13–21, affixed to the left upper arm or the forehead of men at morning prayer, and regarded as a protection (hence the name) against evil spirits.

φύλαξ, *a guard* (one person).

φυλάσσω, (a) *I guard, protect*, with personal or other concrete object, or (Lk. ii 8) cognate acc.; mid. *I am on my guard*, Lk. xii 15; (b) act. and mid., of customs or regulations, *I keep, I observe*.

φυλή, *a tribe*, especially one of the twelve tribes of

Israel, and perhaps (by analogy) of Christendom, James i 1.

φύλλον, *a leaf* of a tree.

φύραμα, *a mixture*; hence *a lump*, *a mass*, lit. or met.

φυσικός, *natural*; φυσικά, 2 Pet. ii 12, *creatures of instinct*.

φυσικῶς, *by instinct*.

φυσιόω (lit. *I inflate*), met. *I puff up*, with anger, conceit, &c.

φύσις, *nature*, *inherent nature*, in N.T. non-moral, neither good nor bad; φύσει, *by nature*, *in myself (itself, &c.)*.

φυσίωσις, *a puffing up* (due to conceit).

φυτεία (lit. *planting*), *a plant*.

φυτεύω, *I plant*.

φύω, *I grow*, *I grow up*.

φωλεός, *a hole* in the earth.

φωνέω, *I give forth a sound*, hence: (a) of a cock, *I crow*; (b) of men, *I shout*; (c) tr. *I call* (to myself), *I summon*; *I invite*, Lk. xiv 12; *I address*, John xiii 13.

φωνή, *a sound*; hence *a voice*.

φῶς, *a light*, particularly *the light* of the sun, but also *the heavenly bodies* specially, James i 17: as indispensable to life, it comes to be associated with life (cf. John i 4), and as universal beneficence, with God and the Messiah (cf. John i 8, viii 12), &c. (cf. John xii 36, Eph. v 8): τὸ φῶς, *the (bright) fire*, Mk. xiv 54, Lk. xxii 56.

φωστήρ, *a light*, perhaps *a sun*, Rev. xxi 11; *a star*, Phil. ii 15.

φωσφόρος (lit. *light-bringing*, lucifer), *the day-star* (the planet Venus, probably).

φωτεινός, *shining*, *brilliant*.

φωτίζω (of the public disclosure of what has been kept secret), *I shed light upon*, *I enlighten*; passive with acc. Eph. i 18: *I bring to light*, Eph. iii 9: in Heb.

φωτισμός

vi 4, x 32 φωτισθέντες, *having received enlightenment,*
having had experience of God's grace in conversion.
φωτισμός, (a) act. *enlightening,* 2 Cor. iv 4; (b) pass.
enlightenment, 2 Cor. iv 6.

X

χαίρω, (a) *I rejoice,* c. cognate acc. or c. dat., *I rejoice
exceedingly;* (b) in the imperative, χαῖρε, χαίρετε,
a greeting, *farewell,* Christianised in Phil. iii 1, iv 4
bis, by the addition ἐν κυρίῳ (and generally mis-
translated), cf. χαίρειν, imperatival infin., e.g. Ac.
xv 23 (cf. 2 John 10); also *hail!* Mk. xv 18, Mt.
xxvii 29.
χάλαζα, *hail.*
χαλάω, *I slacken.*
Χαλδαῖος, *a Chaldaean,* one living in southern Armenia.
χαλεπός, (a) *hard, difficult,* 2 Tim. iii 1; (b) *difficult to
restrain, dangerous,* Mt. viii 28.
χαλιναγωγέω, *I bridle,* met. *I keep in check, restrain.*
χαλινός, *a bridle.*
χάλκεος, *made of bronze, bronze.*
χαλκεύς, *a worker in bronze, a smith.*
χαλκηδών, *a chalcedony,* a small stone of various
colours.
χαλκίον, *a bronze vessel.*
χαλκολίβανος, a word of uncertain signification, translated 'aeramentum turinum' (incense bronze) in
certain Old Latin authorities, and 'orichalcum'
(= ὀρείχαλκος [mountain bronze]) in the Vulgate:
the latter was understood to be a mixture of gold and
copper.
χαλκός, *copper* or *bronze;* hence, *a copper coin; copper
money,* Mk. vi 8 (Mt. x 9), Mk. xii 41.
χαμαί (humi), *on the ground.*
Χαναάν, *Canaan,* the whole of Palestine (Ac. xiii 19) or
Palestine west of the river Jordan (Ac. vii 11).

Χαναναῖος, *Canaanitish, Canaanite,* a Biblical and archaic name for *Phoenician.*

χαρά, *joy;* *delight.*

χάραγμα, *an engraved work,* Ac. xvii 29; *an inscription engraved, a stamp.*

χαρακτήρ, *a representation.*

χάραξ, *a mound, rampart.*

χαρίζομαι, (a) *I graciously confer,* Lk. vii 21, &c.; (b) *I pardon, forgive,* 2 Cor. ii 7, 10, xii 13, Eph. iv 32, Col. ii 13, iii 13; (c) *I show kindness to,* Gal. iii 18.

χάριν, acc. sing. of *χάρις,* used as adv., *for the sake of, by reason of, on account of.*

χάρις (in early Greek literature, *gracefulness, graciousness; favour; a favour; gratitude; χάριν* as above: in LXX especially of the *favour* which an inferior finds in the eyes of his superior), (a) *grace,* as a gift or blessing brought to man by Jesus Christ, John i 14, 16, 17; (b) *favour,* as in LXX, e.g. Luke i 30, ii 40, 52, Ac. ii 47, &c.; (c) *gratitude,* Lk. vi 32 ff., xvii 9; *thanks,* e.g. in *χάρις τῷ θεῷ* and *ἔχειν χάριν* (*to thank*); (d) *a favour,* Ac. xxiv 27, xxv 3, 9; (e) a new Christian sense, often with a defining genitive, of the divine *favour, grace,* the freeness and universality of which are shown in the inclusion of the Gentiles within the scope of the love and care of the God of the Jews: St. Paul, as the apostle to the Gentiles, and the proclaimer of the universal Gospel, naturally makes most use of this term (but cf. also Ac. xiii 43, xiv 26, &c.), e.g. 1 Cor. iii 10, xv 10; 1 Cor. i 4, 2 Cor. vi 1; *grace* was given to him for his ministry to them, and to them through his ministry.

χάρισμα, *a free (gracious) gift, a gift, an endowment,* especially from God.

χαριτόω (properly, *I endow with χάρις*), *I endue with grace (the divine favour):* in Eph. i 6 followed by cognate acc. (genit.).

Χαρράν, *Haran,* identical with Carrae, in Mesopotamia.

χάρτης

χάρτης, *papyrus, paper.*

χάσμα (from χαίνω, *I yawn*), *an intervening space, a chasm.*

χεῖλος, *a lip*: hence *the edge*, Heb. xi 12.

χειμάζομαι, *I am in the grip of a storm.*

χείμαρρος, *a winter torrent.*

χειμών (hiemps), (a) *winter*; (b) *stormy weather*, Mt. xvi 3, Ac. xxvii 20.

χείρ, *a hand*: used also with reference to God, meaning, His power in action, Lk. i 66, 1 Pet. v 6, &c.; διὰ χειρός (χειρῶν), *by the instrumentality of*; and so also ἐν χειρὶ (Hebraistic), Ac. vii 35.

χειραγωγέω, *I lead by the hand.*

χειραγωγός, *one who leads* a helpless person *by the hand.*

χειρόγραφον, properly, *a signature*, hence, as a term of a court of justice, (a) *a bill, bond, certificate of debt*, or (b) any **written obligation** or **agreement**.

χειροποίητος, *made by hand, hand-made.*

χειροτονέω (lit. *I stretch out the hand*, thus expressing agreement with a motion, then, *I elect by show of hands* [of popular vote]), *I elect.*

χείρων, a comparative, *worse*: ἐπὶ τὸ χεῖρον, *to the (a) worse result (degree).*

χερουβείν (Aramaic, while -ειμ is Hebrew), *cherubin*, two golden figures of winged animals over the mercy-seat (and the ark) in the Jewish tabernacle.

χήρα, *a widow.*

χιλίαρχος (lit. *a ruler of a thousand*) (tribunus militum), *a tribune*, a Roman officer commanding a cohort, that is, about a thousand men), *a colonel.*

χιλιάς, *a thousand*, looked upon as a unit.

χίλιοι, *one thousand, a thousand.*

Χίος, *Chios* (modern Scio), an important island in the Aegean Sea, off the west central coast of Asia Minor.

χισ´ = ἑξακόσιοι.

χιτών (a Semitic word), *a tunic, an undergarment.*

χιών, *snow.*

χλαμύς, *a cloak.*

χλευάζω, *I scoff* by gesture and word.

χλιαρός, *lukewarm, tepid.*

Χλόη, *Chloe*, a woman, probably with business connexions either in Corinth or in Ephesus or in both.

χλωρός (from χλόη), *of the colour of grass, green* or *yellow*, as the case may be.

χοϊκός (from χοῦς), *made of earth* (*dust*) and with the quality attaching to this origin.

χοῖνιξ, a Greek dry *measure*, equivalent to 1·92 pints.

χοῖρος, *a pig.*

χολάω, *I am angry with.*

χολή (in LXX represents three Hebrew words meaning respectively, (a) *gall, bile*, (b) *wormwood*, (c) *poison*), (a) *gall, bile*, Mt. xxvii 34 ; (b) met. *bitterness*, that is, intense malignity.

χόος, see χοῦς.

Χοραζείν, *Chorazin*, probably the present Kerâze, ruins half-an-hour north-west of Tell-ḥum (Capernaum ?).

χορηγέω, *I supply* (with lavish hand).

χορός, *dancing.*

χορτάζω (sagino) (from χόρτος, in earlier Greek of feeding animals), *I feed to the full, I satisfy with food.*

χόρτασμα, *food, sustenance*, corn for man as well as beast.

χόρτος, *grass, hay*, such grass or herbage as makes fodder.

Χουζᾶς, *Chuza*, a steward of Herod Antipas.

χοῦς, *dust.*

χράομαι (from χρή 'necessity', properly, 'I make for myself what is necessary with something') (utor), *I use, employ* ; in 1 Cor. vii 21 perhaps understand τῇ ἐλευθερίᾳ : with persons, *I treat*, Ac. xxvii 3.

χράω, *I lend.*

χρεία, *need* ; any special *occasion* or *matter in hand*, Ac. vi 3, Eph. iv 29 (?).

χρεοφειλέτης, χρεωφειλέτης, *a debtor.*

χρή, *it is fitting*, it is congruous to a law or rather standard ; the word is somewhat vague.

χρῄζω

χρῄζω, *I need, have neea.*

χρῆμα, (a) plur. *property, possessions, riches*; (b) sing. *the money got, the proceeds,* Ac. iv 37.

χρηματίζω (originally, *I transact business*), (a) act., of God, *I warn,* Heb. xii 25; pass. *I am warned by God* (properly in response to an inquiry as to one's duty), Mt. ii 12, 22, Lk. ii 26, Ac. x 22, Heb. viii 5, xi 7; (b) (*I take a name from my public business,* hence) *I receive a name, I am publicly called . . .,* Ac. xi 26, Rom. vii 3.

χρηματισμός, *a response of God* (to an inquiry as to one's duty), *an oracle.*

χρήσιμος, *useful.*

χρῆσις, *usage, use.*

χρηστεύομαι, *I play the part of a kind person* (full of service to others).

χρηστολογία, *affectation of kind speech,* with insinuating tone.

χρηστός, *good*; hence *comfortable, kindly, not pressing,* Mt. xi 30 : often has the idea of *kind* (iuxta apostolum χρηστὸν 'bonum' intellegimus, quia dixit *Vide ergo bonitatem domini* [Rom. xi 22]; iuxta euangelium χρηστὸν 'suaue' accipimus; dixit enim *Tollite iugum meum quia leue est et onus meum quia suaue est* [Mt. xi 29, 30]; dixit enim τὸ φορτίον μου χρηστόν. unde merito bonitatem dei ab ipso quaerit doceri, &c. Ambros. *expos. in ps. cxviii* 9 9 §§ 1, 2).

χρηστότης, *kindness, kindliness* (see χρηστός).

χρίσμα, *anointing,* referring to the gift of holy spirit.

Χριστιανός (the formation is Latin, and indicates either *partisan of Christ* or more exactly *soldier of Christ,* cf. Fimbriani, Caesariani, Pompeiani), *Christian, a follower of Christ.* (See χριστός.)

χριστός (a rare verbal from χρίω, 'I anoint', and therefore *anointed,* ὁ χριστός being an epithet used at first practically in the sense of *the king,* anointing being the outward sign of his appointment to kingship, cf. 1 Sam. x 1, xii 3, xv 1 and often), (a) ὁ χριστός, *the anointed, the Messiah* (the Aramaic equivalent of ὁ χριστός, John i 41), *the* expected *king* of Israel, to be appointed by God as his vicegerent. In N.T. this epithet is, therefore, attached (either prefixed or affixed) to (ὁ) Ἰησοῦς, *Jesus*, recognized by his followers as the expected Messiah. The epithet with or without article is also found alone referring to Jesus; (b) gradually it tends to lose the meaning it originally had and to become merely a proper name, *Christ*. (By many the curious word was confused with χρηστός, 'good', which as a proper name was often a slave-name, and thus Χριστιανοί became Χρηστιανοί, confusion being due to the fact that the two words were pronounced alike).

χρίω, *I anoint*, to the kingly office, used generally with regard to dedication to Messiahship, &c.

χρονίζω, *I delay.*

χρόνος, *time*; *a time, period*: locative, πολλοῖς χρόνοις, *oftentimes*, Lk. viii 29, but instrumental, Lk. viii 27, Rom. xvi 25.

χρονοτριβέω, *I waste time.*

χρύσεος, *made of gold, golden.*

χρυσίον, *gold*: plur. *gold* (*golden*) *ornaments*, 1 Pet. iii 3.

χρυσοδακτύλιος, *with* (*wearing*) *a* (one or more) *gold ring*(*s*) on the finger(s).

χρυσόλιθος, a sparkling gem, of gold-yellow colour, possibly our *topaz*, almost certainly not our *chrysolite.*

χρυσόπρασος, a precious stone of leek-green colour, which sparkled golden-yellow, from India, perhaps *fluor-spar*, certainly not *chrysoprase.*

χρυσός, *gold.*

χρυσόω, *I adorn with gold, I overlay with gold.*

χρώς, *skin.*

χωλός, *lame*: generalizing neut., Heb. xii 13.

χώρα (regio, an official term), strictly used, *a region*, a great geographical (and sometimes administrative) division of a province, e.g. Ac. xvi 6, xviii 23, but often more loosely, *country, district*: hence met., e.g.

χωρέω

Mt. iv 16; sometimes almost *a field*, John iv 35, James v 4.

χωρέω, (a) intr. *I go away, I withdraw, I come,* lit. and met., Mt. xv 17, 2 Pet. iii 9; (b) intr. *I have room, find room,* John viii 37; (c) tr. *I contain, am capable of receiving, hold, grasp,* Mk. ii 2, Mt. xix 11, &c.; *I make room for* (*I give a place to*) some one in my heart, *I take into* my heart, 2 Cor. vii 2.

χωρίζω, (a) act. tr. *I separate, I put apart;* (b) mid. or pass. *I separate myself, I depart.*

χωρίον (diminutive of χώρα or χῶρος), *a place; a piece of land, a field,* enclosed.

χωρίς, *apart from, separately from; without.*

χῶρος (Latin, caurus, corus), *the north-west wind,* and so, the quarter of the sky from which it comes, *north-west.*

Ψ

ψάλλω, *I play on the harp* (or other stringed instrument).

ψαλμός, *a psalm,* that is a song of praise, &c., to God, with an accompaniment on the harp.

ψευδάδελφος, *a false brother,* i. e. an unreal (insincere) Christian.

ψευδαπόστολος, *a false apostle,* i. e. one who has received no commission from Jesus to preach the Gospel, though he pretends to have received it.

ψευδής, *false; untrue* in word, &c.

ψευδοδιδάσκαλος, *a teacher of false things.*

ψευδολόγος, *speaking false things, lying; a liar.*

ψεύδομαι, *I speak falsely:* c. acc. *I deceive by words,* Ac. v 3.

ψευδομαρτυρέω, *I give* (*bear*) *false witness.*

ψευδομαρτυρία, *giving of false evidence; false witness.*

ψευδομάρτυς, *a false witness,* one who gives untrue evidence.

ψευδοπροφήτης, *a false* (*untrue, unauthenticated*) *prophet.*

286

ψεῦδος, *that which is false, falsehood* ; *an untruth, a lie* ; *lying* : in Rom. i 25 abstract for concrete.

ψευδόχριστος, *a false Messiah, a pretended Messiah.*

ψευδώνυμος, *falsely named.*

ψεῦσμα, *a lie.*

ψεύστης, *a liar.*

ψηλαφάω, *I touch* : in Heb. xii 18 perhaps corrupt ; πεφεψαλωμένῳ has been suggested, *burnt to ashes, calcined, volcanic.*

ψηφίζω, *I count up* (lit. with pebbles).

ψῆφος, (a) *a pebble*, Rev. ii 17 : (b) hence, from their use in voting, *a vote.*

ψιθυρισμός, *whispering*, especially of secret attacks on a person's character.

ψιθυριστής, *a whisperer* (cf. **ψιθυρισμός**).

ψιχίον, *a crumb.*

ψυχή (consult also πνεῦμα) ; in the LXX there is, in general, a lack of sharp distinction between ψυχή (lit. *breath* [cf. anima], *breath of life* in the individual), πνεῦμα and καρδία, though ψυχή generally refers to appetite and desire : it is there as a rule a translation of the Hebrew *nephesh*, one of the words for the 'breath-soul', the personal soul: in Paul, soul (ψυχή) and spirit (πνεῦμα) are hardly to be distinguished (yet cf. 1 Cor. xv 45): (a) *life*, without any psychological content, Mt. ii 20, John x 11, 15, 17, Ac. xv 26, Rom. xi 3, xvi 4, 1 Cor. xv 45, 2 Cor. i 23, Phil. ii 30, 1 Thess. ii 8, &c.; (b) *an individual*, or as a strong personal pronoun (Hebraistic, cf. *nephesh*), cf. Mk. viii 36 (contrast Lk. ix 25), Ac. ii 41, 43, iii 23, Rom. ii 9, xiii 1, 2 Cor. xii 15; (c) psychical, *desire*, Eph. vi 6, Phil. i 27, Col. iii 23, cf. also 1 Thess. v 23, where the enumeration is not systematic. The general use of the word in the Bible is in the sense of whatever is felt to belong most essentially to man's life, when his bodily life has come to be regarded as a secondary thing. It comes near the modern conception, *self*. See also **ψυχικός**.

ψυχικός (from ψυχή, in the sense ' the principle of life

ψύχομαι

and the basis of its emotional aspect, animating the
present body of flesh, in contrast to the higher life '),
emotional or *sensuous*.

ψύχομαι, *I become cold*, met.

ψῦχος (frigus), *cold*.

ψυχρός, (a) lit. *cold*, neut. *cold water*, Mt. x 42 ; (b) met.
cold, frigid, indifferent, phlegmatic.

ψωμίζω, (a) *I confer a dole upon*, Rom. xii 20 ; (b) *I dole
out*.

ψωμίον, *a little bit, morsel*, or *crumb* of food.

ψώχω, *I rub*.

Ω

ὦ, the last letter of the Greek alphabet, *Omega* (at first
the long and short o sounds were represented by one
letter : when distinguished the short was called οὖ or
ὁ μικρόν, the long ὦ or ὦ μέγα).

ὦ, an interjection of address, *O*.

Ὠβήδ, see **Ἰωβήδ**.

ὧδε, *here*, both of rest and of motion to (*hither*): τὰ
ὧδε, *the things here, what is here, what is going on
here, the state of affairs here*.

ᾠδή, *a song*.

ὠδίν, *pangs of childbirth, birth-pangs*, 1 Thess. v 3 ;
in Ac. ii 24 Death is regarded as in *labour* and his
pains as relieved by the birth of the child ; hence, of
any *sharp sudden pain*.

ὠδίνω, *I suffer birth-pangs*: c. acc. of the children that
are being born, met., Gal. iv 19.

ὦμος, *shoulder*.

ὠνέομαι, *I buy*.

ᾠόν (ouom), *an egg*.

ὥρα, *an hour*, that is, a twelfth part of the period from
sunrise to sunset, and thus of constantly changing
length ; the shortest measurement of time among the
ancients ; sometimes generally of *time* ; ὥρα πολλή,

an advanced period of time, a considerable time,
Mk. vi 35 ; πρὸς ὥραν, *for a* (little) *time.*

ὡραῖος (lit. *in season*), *beautiful.*

ὠρύομαι, *I roar.*

ὡς, adverb and conjunction, (a) with superlative, ὡς
τάχιστα, *as quickly as possible,* Ac. xvii 15 ; with comparative, ambiguous, either *uncommonly* . . or *very* . .,
Ac. xvii 22 ; (b) before numbers, &c., *about* (vv. ll.) ;
(c) exclamatory, *how,* e. g. Rom. x 15 ; (d) often in
the predicate (nom. or acc.) *as,* e. g. Mt. xiv 5, xxii 30,
Lk. xv 19, 2 Cor. x 2 ; (e) with fut. pcpl., *as such who
have to* . . ., Heb. xiii 17 ; giving a reason, Lk. xvi 1,
xxiii 14, Ac. iii 12, &c. ; pcpl. sometimes has disappeared, e. g. Col. iii 23 ; (f) with absolute infin., ὡς
ἔπος εἰπεῖν, *one might almost say,* Heb. vii 9 ; (g) = ὥστε,
so as to, doubtful, Lk. ix 52 (v. l.), Ac. xx 24 (v. l.) ;
(h) οὐχ ὡς, *not as if,* e. g. Ac. xxviii 19 ; ὡς ὅτι = ὡς
c. gen. absolute, *as if,* 2 Cor. v 19, xi 21, 2 Thess. ii 2 ;
(i) ὡς correlative to οὕτως (with or without καί),
as . . . so ; ὡς introducing a clause can also have
something of a causal sense, Mt. vi 12 (= Lk. xi 4),
&c., so, ὡς with pcpl., and with prepositions (often in
Hellenistic), cf. Ac. xvii 14 (v.l.), Rom. ix 32 ; (k) (it is)
as (when), without connexion, either with what precedes or with what follows, Mk. xiii 34 ; (l) after verbs
of saying, thinking, &c., *how* ; (m) temporal, *when,
while, as long as,* Lk. i 23, Gal. vi 10, &c. ; ὡς ἄν, *when,*
Rom. xv 24 ; *as soon as,* 1 Cor. xi 34, Phil. ii 23
(but in 2 Cor. x 9, *as it were*).

ὡσαννά (Aramaic and Hebrew, originally a cry for help),
a cry of happiness, *hosanna* !

ὡσαύτως, *in the same way, likewise.*

ὡσεί, *as if, as it were, like* ; with numbers, *about.*

Ὡσηέ (Hebr.), *Hosea,* the Old Testament prophet.

ὥσπερ, *even as, as.*

ὡσπερεί (= ὥσπερ εἰ), *even as if, as if.*

ὥστε, (a) with an infinitive, expressing result, *so as to,*
Lk. iv 29 (v. l.), ix 52 (v. l.), xx 20 (v. l.), &c. ; (b) in-

ὠτάριον

troducing an independent clause, in indic., imper., subjunct. of exhortation, *so that*, John iii 16, Gal. ii 13 ; with result stated merely as a new fact, *consequently, and so, therefore*.

ὠτάριον (auricula, hence Fr. oreille), *an ear*.

ὠτίον (see ὠτάριον), *an ear*.

ὠφέλεια, *advantage*.

ὠφελέω, *I help, benefit, do good, am useful (to)*: absol. Rom. ii 25 ; with adv. acc. οὐδέν, *in no way*, τί, *in what way ?*; generally c. acc. of the person.

ὠφέλιμος, *beneficial, useful, serviceable*.

PRINTED IN GREAT BRITAIN AT THE UNIVERSITY PRESS, OXFORD
BY JOHN JOHNSON, PRINTER TO THE UNIVERSITY